YOUR FERTILE HOURS

by Emily Faugno

First Printing 1986
ISBN Number: 0-86690-295-3
Library of Congress Catalog Card Number: 85-71462

Cover Design: Lynda Kay Fullerton

Published by:
American Federation of Astrologers, Inc.
P.O. Box 22040, 6535 South Rural Road
Tempe, Arizona 85282

Printed in the United States of America

For my children —
Mary Lee, Thomas, Emily, and Gerard.
And for my husband, John,
who made them, and this book, possible.

Table of Contents

Part I
about Claire . . .

Part II
about famous women . . .

Prologue

In a speech to the United States Senate on February 18, 1835, Henry Clay, the outstanding statesman, lawyer and American political leader who lived in the era preceding the Civil War said, "Precedents deliberately established by wise men are entitled to great weight. They are evidence of truth, but only evidence. . . . But a solitary precedent . . . which has never been re-examined, cannot be conclusive."

We are not wise men, only students of the stars. And we have, it is true, only a solitary precedent to present. But, it is such a unique one, so pregnant with promise, that we hope you will think about it carefully and evaluate it thoroughly before you decide that it cannot be conclusive. Then we hope that you will re-examine this precedent yourselves, using your own research, until a body of knowledge and truth can be built up to give credibility to the conception account which we present in this book.

We intend to show you an intercourse chart of known date, place and hour which produced a child. The timing of such an event can be duplicated by those desiring a baby, in hopes that a conception can occur for them, too. Those couples not desiring conception would pointedly refrain from sexual relations at that particular time, thus producing a natural form of birth control.

The limiting of children is a greater problem today than it was in Clay's time. Born in 1777, the seventh of a family of nine children, he went on to raise eleven children of his own, of which only four sons outlived him. Today, thanks to medical science, most of our babies survive and are healthy, and childhood diseases are no longer the threat to life that they once were. A family of substantial size can now be obtained with a much smaller number of babies.

Clay, a naturally eloquent man, but with little formal schooling, became in turn a criminal lawyer, a senator, a member of the house of representatives, a leading statesman, a defender of the interests of the people of the United States. Today, however, it is not possible to succeed in a professional career without many years of formal, expensive education. Responsible couples must weigh such factors in determining the size of their families.

Henry Clay was called the "great compromiser." When our country was divided over the admission of Missouri into the union as a slave state, Clay was instrumental in instituting a compromise: Maine was to be admitted as a free state and Missouri as a slave state. Missouri also was to have a state constitution that excluded free Negroes and mulattoes from admission to the state.

Slavery was the outstanding moral as well as political issue which divided our citizens during Clay's years in public office. Today, another grave moral issue separates us as a people: those who favor abortion and those who are pro-life; those who support sterilization and artificial birth prevention and those — in the minority — who believe in natural birth control.

We cannot, as Henry Clay so ably did, propose a "compromise." Instead, we offer something new — astrological birth control in conjunction with natural family planning, or natural birth control — a method whereby we walk in step with our Creator, and step in perfect timing to His laws of nature to produce the family size that is right for each of us.

Whatever your position, whatever your opinions and beliefs, we hope this book will hold your interest, and maybe even bring you over to our side.

Welcome.

Emily Faugno
May, 1985

Introduction

In today's society, every option to succeed in all fields of endeavor is open to the modern woman. Yet, still she asks, and is searching for answers concerning her fundamental role as wife and mother — the role that biologically she finds difficult, if not impossible to ignore. For the most part, even the most Aquarian or unconventional eventually marries and then the following important questions must be answered:

1. Motherhood versus career?
2. Would I make a good mother? Do I have maternal instinct?
3. Am I physically able to have children? Am I fertile?
4. Could I have difficulties in pregnancy?
5. May I choose the sex of my future baby?
6. With so many second marriages and with more men acquiring custody of their children, how would I fare with step-children?
7. Should I adopt children if I could not have my own?
8. If sterilization mutilates our bodies; if we find abortion morally unacceptable or find that it causes future pregnancies to become impossible; if the Pill poisons and the I.U.D. infects; if mechanical contraceptives are unaesthetic; if ineffective spermicides damage sperm, which in turn cause defective fetuses; if on moral grounds no form of artificial birth prevention is permissible — to whom or to what can this woman turn?
9. Is there an alternate method of birth control that can pinpoint a woman's time of fertility each month, to be used if she desires to conceive and to be avoided if she does not?
10. If conception seems to elude a woman who desperately desires to become pregnant, are there any advances in the field of fertility, even experimental ones, that this woman may try?

Using the rules of astrology as our guide, and with initially one horoscope to give us a solid foundation to solve each individual problem, it is the purpose of this book to provide some of the answers to the aforementioned, significant questions.

And, the first question is. . . .

PART I

about Claire . . .

Chapter I
Astrological Aspects of Reproduction

"Do you have children?" she asked companionably and with a smile.

Claire nodded in a numb sort of way. "Four."

As the astrologer sifted through her papers, Claire's mind went back to how it all had started — how she had gotten there, in the astrologer's office, in the first place.

It was on a Sunday night television talk show — David Susskind's, to be exact — with a guest panel of astrologers, that Claire and her husband got their first glimpse of those strange (or so they thought) creatures. Claire was not impressed — "fortune telling is not for me" — and even though her husband purchased, the very next day, an astrology magazine, she rejected it completely.

A year passed, and then there was another astrology television talk show, another magazine. This time it " took." Claire decided that she should have lessons. She picked the name, "Doris Kaye," from a list obtained from the magazine, phoned this astrologer, and at her suggestion Claire agreed to a reading. With much trepidation.

So, here she was, trembling in body and uneasy in mind. Fleetingly she speculated, "Why did she ask me that question? Do I really look like a frumpy housewife with the harried expression that only four young children can bestow?" Not that Claire was so taken with the astrologer's appearance, either! For she wore a disquieting print dress of orange, yellow, black, and white wavy stripes that resembled a cross between a tiger and a zebra. Claire couldn't decide which. It was far-out alright, but Claire supposed she would have been disappointed with anything less startling. She only knew that it did nothing to add serenity to her already agitated mind.

However, aside from the attire, Claire found her fears to be groundless. Doris Kaye was intelligent, astute, and surprisingly accurate in her reading. So much so, that Claire was intrigued enough to sign up for six lessons which were to begin the following week.

The night-time New York subways 15 years ago were not as dangerous as they are today. Still, Claire had to take a bus and two subway trains to get from her Queens home to Manhattan where the lessons were to be held. Interested as she was in religious and metaphysical subjects, Claire believed that keeping the presence of God in her consciousness would ensure her safety throughout her nocturnal journey. So, she really felt protected as she repeated the mantra,

"God is," for the whole one and one quarter hours going and the one and one quarter hours coming home. Nevertheless, the prayer was fortified with a thick, five-inch-long nail which Claire held tightly in her right hand, hidden in the pocket of her fleecy, white coat. Just in case!

The trips were long, but thankfully uneventful, and Claire found it all worth the inconvenience, because there in a Manhattan apartment, on a starry March night, she was introduced, along with 12 to 13 other people, to the mystery of astrology. Claire couldn't remember any of the other students because as the lessons progressed, one by one each dropped out, and finally she alone was left. Doris agreed to give her private lessons.

Among other things, Claire found out what an astrologer was really like. A responsible person, Doris was taking care of an aging mother and she gave half of what she earned teaching astrology to charity. In the case of this particular class, it was zero. The robbers who were not on Claire's subway train were in a restaurant where Doris was eating after the lesson, and they absconded with all of her tuitions. She was far from being greedy. If Claire had not increased the price of those private lessons herself, Doris would have still charged her only the group rate — at a considerable loss to herself.

Doris was considerate, helpful, interesting and interested and she understood her subject thoroughly. From this one competent teacher, Claire concluded that, as a group, astrologers were just regular people, doing an extraordinary job with an out-of-the ordinary, unconventional subject.

For Claire, astrology had everything one could want — it is practical, exciting, immediate, spiritual, and helpful to others. It can be applied to any topic, anytime, anywhere. It is a subject that lends itself to home study — "Just immerse yourself in the signs, planets, and houses," Doris said. It is a study project that can go on forever. And, Claire wanted to study.

Now she would be able to set up her own natal chart. Now she would be able to find out for herself why the first question the astrologer asked her was, "Do you have children?" And then, Claire's interest extended out further than her own chart to include all mothers and their children and the subjects of:

1. fertility to have children,
2. limited fertility and how to overcome not having children, and
3. too much fertility and how to limit the number of children.

This is the birth data Claire gave Doris Kaye:
Date of birth — June 13, 1927
Place of birth — Brooklyn, New York.
Time of birth — 7 a.m. EDT.

This is the natal horoscope the astrologer erected: See Figure 1.
This is what the astrologer saw:
Planets divided by elements are:

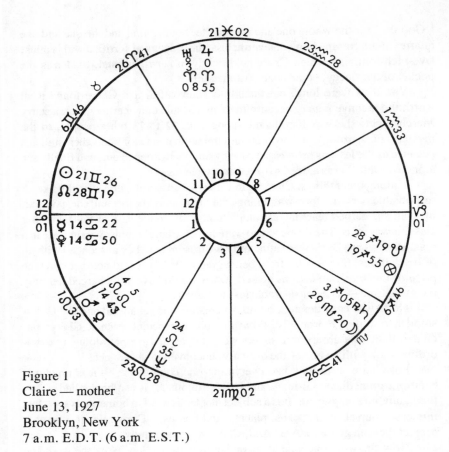

Figure 1
Claire — mother
June 13, 1927
Brooklyn, New York
7 a.m. E.D.T. (6 a.m. E.S.T.)

   1. in Fire signs — Venus, Mars, Jupiter, Saturn, Uranus, Neptune and South Node.
   2. in Earth signs — none.
   3. in Air signs — Sun and North Node.
   4. in Water signs — Moon, Mercury, Pluto, Ascendant, and Midheaven.
Planets divided by qualities are:
   1. in Cardinal signs — Mercury, Pluto, Jupiter, Uranus, and Ascendant.
   2. in Fixed signs — Moon, Venus, Mars, and Neptune.
   3. in Mutable signs — Sun, Saturn, North and South Nodes, and Midheaven.
Planets in dignities are:
   1. Pluto exalted in Cancer (in some reference books).
   2. North Node exalted in Gemini.
   3. Moon in fall in Scorpio.

4

Planets reciprocal:

Moon is in Scorpio, Pluto's home sign, while Pluto is in Cancer, Moon's home sign.

Planets in masculine signs — number 7.

Planets in feminine signs — number 3.

Planets above horizon — number 3.

Planets below horizon — number 7.

Planets in eastern half of chart — number 8.

Planets in western half of chart — number 2.

Planets divided by house placement are:

1. in angular houses — Mercury, Pluto, Jupiter and Uranus.
2. in succedent houses — Moon, Saturn, Venus, and Mars.
3. in cadent houses — Sun and Neptune.

Focal point of chart:

Moon, ruler of Ascendant, conjunct Saturn in fifth house of children — the only planets in the western half of the chart.

Major configuration of chart:

The grand trine — composed of Moon/Saturn conjunction in fifth house of children, trine the Venus/Mars conjunction in the second house of resources and values, trine the Jupiter/Uranus conjunction in the tenth house of career.

A picture is worth a thousand words. So they say. With this aphorism in mind, instead of listing a series of fertility rules that can readily be found in other astrology books, (some of which will be stated later on) we will focus our attention on this one chart, Claire's chart; thoroughly examine it; and then weave the results into one cohesive unit, to think about, study and remember. The results can then be applied usefully to other charts.

The Fifth House:

The fifth house of the natal horoscope denotes the ability of the native to bear children. The eleventh house, that is, the fifth from the seventh — the marriage partner — marks the fertility of the marriage partner. Therefore, if the astrologer wants to study fertility, he or she must start with those two houses. Of the two houses, the fifth, the native's own house of children, is the more important, so that is where we shall begin.

How important is the fifth house in this particular chart? Very important. It is the only tenanted house on the whole western or fated side of the chart. It is, therefore, strongly emphasized.

Is the sign on the fifth house cusp a fertile one? Yes, Libra is a fertile sign. Its ruler is Venus, a fruitful planet and significator of the female reproductive system. Venus makes the following favorable aspects: Venus conjunct Mars, Venus trine Jupiter, trine Uranus, trine Moon, and trine Saturn.

There is also an intercepted sign in this house, that is, one complete sign inbetween the cusps. Libra is on the fifth house cusp, Sagittarius is on the sixth, with Scorpio inbetween. Scorpio is a fertile water sign, tenanted here by the Moon — ruler of childbirth. The co-rulers of this intercepted sign, Scorpio, are Mars and Pluto.

Mars is conjunct Venus — primary ruler of the fifth house, and ruler of the female reproductive system, and therefore it makes the same trine aspects along with Venus to Saturn, Jupiter, and Uranus.

Pluto, co-ruler of Scorpio, is importantly placed on the Ascendant — ruler of personality. Pluto here is exalted in Cancer and in mutual reception with Moon — Moon being in Scorpio, Pluto's ruling sign, and Pluto being in Cancer — Moon's ruling sign. Also, this 29 degree Scorpio is in a Cancer decanate, while Pluto, at 14 Cancer, is in a Scorpio decanate. Therefore, there is a strong link here between motherhood and the personality of the native.

Fertility based upon fifth house rulerships is now firmly established.

Pluto is closely conjunct Mercury in Cancer on the Ascendant. Mercury thinks deeply (Pluto) in a motherly (Cancer) way. The close intertwining of Pluto — Mercury — Cancer on the Ascendant with Moon — Scorpio — fifth house shows the importance of fifth house matters to this native, Claire.

The principal fifth house interests in every natal horoscope are:

1. Creation — children. Also all literary, artistic, and technical creations.

2. Recreation — spectator sports, hobbies, theaters, all forms of entertainment, speculation, gambling, avocations, and love affairs.

3. Teaching and education which can be both creative and recreative.

The Scorpio Moon, which is in the fifth house of children, is ruler of the Ascendant, or first house which signifies the physical body and the personality. Moon rules childbirth and here it is heavily aspected. Its difficult aspects are its conjunction to Saturn and its square to Neptune. The Moon's favorable aspects are its trines to Venus — particularly helpful because Venus rules the female reproductive organs, and in Claire's chart, her fifth house of children, — and its trines to Jupiter, Uranus, and Mars. Remember, too, that the Moon is in mutual reception to Pluto, co-ruler of the fifth house.

While the aspects of the Moon are many and mostly fortunate and fertile, the Moon itself is in its fall and cannot function at its best. Therefore, since the Moon rules childbearing, trouble can be expected in this area at some time in the life. In addition, this Moon is at 29 degrees of Scorpio — that is — void of course; meaning that it forms no complete aspect before leaving its sign. A void of course Moon is said to be ineffectual and can deny many of the benefits otherwise promised in the natal chart. This Scorpio Moon is in an intercepted sign, again causing delays and disappointment. Claire just could not expect smooth sailing all of the time. All of her plans could not materialize; all of her wishes would not come true concerning the affairs of the house in which the Moon is placed, the fifth house, or of which it rules, the first house. Therefore, while the signs are fertile and the Moon makes many favorable aspects, the pathway to a large family, which was what Claire wanted, would have its detours. Still, Claire chose motherhood over career.

The tenth house — the career significator — is tenanted by Jupiter conjunct Uranus, a conjunction which is trine Mars and Venus, and trine Moon and Saturn. However, the tenth house ruler, Neptune, in the third house of the reasoning mind is square the Moon — motherhood — residing in the fifth house. Mentally, Claire could not combine a career outside of her home with motherhood. Also, the Gemini Sun, hidden in the twelfth house, plus seven planets below the horizon, and a Cancer Ascendant all help to produce a home-loving, introspective personality — not a socially, extroverted one. Besides Neptune, Pisces on the tenth house cusp is also ruled by Jupiter, placed *in* the tenth house. However, Jupiter is square to the Sun, causing tension between the will (the Sun) and career, ruled by Jupiter.

Yet, career cannot be ruled out with the four trines of Venus, Mars, Moon and Saturn to the tenth house Jupiter/Uranus conjunction. Claire might well have chosen a career that emanated from the security of a home base. And, indeed she did. As a pharmacist, for three years she lived in the back of her drug store, and later, for many years she ran a medical herb tea company from her home. Now, in the later years, with Virgo on the cusp of her fourth house — the end of life — and its ruler, Mercury, conjunct Pluto on the Ascendant, a Mercury/Pluto research type occupation could be in the offing, again from her home environment.

Moon Phases:

Not only does the Moon make aspects to the Sun and planets in each person's horoscope, it also goes through monthly phases. Because the Moon seems to be constantly changing in shape and size right before our eyes, and because women seem to be in rhythm with these changes, the position of the Moon in relation to the Sun at the time of a woman's birth seems to correlate with her reproductive system and monthly fertility period. All of the phases are equally fertile, but are timed differently and uniquely to each birth chart.

This Moon-phase, determined by the angle of the Moon to the Sun, or the number of degrees apart the Moon is from the Sun at the time of a woman's birth, is her own special fertility angle. Each month, throughout her reproductive life, she will be most fertile astrologically when her same Sun/Moon fertility angle is repeated by the transiting Sun and Moon.

When the night-time sky is in darkness and the Moon sheds no light, we call it a new Moon. The Sun and Moon are in the same degree of longitude, and are in the beginning position for the monthly phases. Every 45 degrees of longitude that the Moon progresses away from the Sun produces a new phase. As the Moon increases in light we have the crescent, first quarter, and gibbous Moon until finally the Moon is full and gloriously round — 180 degrees distant and opposite the Sun — the full Moon. This magical sight soon fades as the Moon starts its journey back around the other side of the zodiac to give us the disseminating, last quarter, balsamic, and finally a new, new Moon once more.

These different phases seem to present different behavioral and psychological meanings as far as our way of looking at life and acting out our destinies is concerned. According to the writings of the eminent astrologer, Dane Rudhyar, each phase appears to produce a different personality. A "catch" phrase to signify each phase is as follows:

1. New Moon, Moon 0 to 45 degrees ahead of Sun — one who is ready to begin new projects. Impulsive, subjective.

2. Crescent Moon, 45 to 90 degrees ahead of Sun — one who accepts challenges.

3. First quarter Moon, 90 to 135 degrees ahead of Sun — the manager, one who wants to get things in order.

4. Gibbous Moon, 135 to 180 degrees ahead of Sun — one who desires personal growth in order to contribute to society.

5. Full Moon, 180 to 135 degrees behind Sun — one who sees things clearly and is objective.

6. Disseminating Moon, 135 to 90 degrees behind Sun — one who wants to demonstrate to others what he has learned. The teacher.

7. Last quarter Moon, 90 to 45 degrees behind Sun — one who is a pioneer with principles to uphold.

8. Balsamic Moon, 45 to 0 degrees behind Sun — one who feels a social destiny and accepts sacrifice for the future.

In Claire's chart, with the Moon 158 degrees ahead of the Sun, we have a gibbous Moon, giving her the desire to grow. The gibbous Moon person has goals. He wants to contribute something useful, something valuable, something meaningful to society in his own particular field — be it as composer, banker, scientist, teacher, parent or mechanic. Everyone, even everyday, ordinary people with this placement feel the need to make a contribution; to leave something of value to posterity.

The Moon in the fifth house is said to be indicative of, and to produce a child who achieves fame and popularity if well aspected. For her children to be quietly useful members of society would be enough to fulfill Claire's hopes and dreams. At any rate, the Moon in the fifth is creative in some manner, and here, since it is gibbous as well, to create something beneficial is its goal.

The Seventh House of the Marriage Partner:
If our example chart is of the wife, Claire, then the seventh house becomes the significator of the husband and should be examined next. There are no planets within it. Since Capricorn is on the seventh house cusp, its ruler, Saturn, represents the husband.

In Claire's chart, the Scorpio Moon shares residence in the fifth house with Saturn at three degrees Sagittarius. Being only three degrees apart, these two planets are in conjunction, even if they are in different signs. Because Saturn, ruler of the seventh — the marriage partner — is in this close conjunction with the Moon, ruler of the first house and the native of this chart, this husband and wife are together closely involved in the affairs of the house they tenant — namely, this fifth house of children. Therefore, children are an important consideration in this marriage.

While the Moon is fortunate, fertile, and desirous of children in the fifth house, Saturn, in this same placement, denies, inhibits or is cautious concerning them. There is conflict here. The conflict is real but resolvable because of the helpful, harmonious grand trine which this Moon/Saturn conjunction makes with Venus, Mars, Jupiter and Uranus. Consequently, four children emerged from this union — two boys and two girls. Then stern, severe, lesson-teaching Saturn said, "No more. That's all you can have." In time, Claire suffered a miscarriage. After that, there were no more children.

Nevertheless, where Saturn limits, it may also give backbone. Saturn represents the skeletal structure of the body, and it gives to this soft, emotional, changeable, Sun-reflecting mass — the Moon — both uprightness and fixity of purpose. As it restricts, it narrows the focus to the affairs of its house, and here gives the Moon the determination to get what she wants. The Moon is the mother, the childbearer, who wanted children for herself in Claire's chart. Then, when her own childbearing years were over, the Moon wanted children for *all* women who were experiencing difficulty in conceiving.

In this manner and for these reasons came Claire's interest in research into Astrological Birth Control (for ease in expression, we often shall use only the initials, ABC). The gibbous Moon had found a new objective. Its contribution would be to try to correct infertility through astrological timing. This Astrological Birth Control, in conjunction with Natural Birth Control (again, we will often use only the initials, NBC), also called Natural Family Planning, are the two systems we shall investigate for use in limiting and spacing children in the natural way intended by our Creator.

The Challenging Square:

The Moon in Claire's chart at 29 degrees Scorpio is in a separating square aspect to Neptune at 24 Leo. While the grand trine is very protective of the Moon, a monkey wrench is thrown into the harmonious triangle in the form of this square. The Moon, of itself, because it is so vulnerable to outside stimuli, and because it controls emotions, tends to be fearful and anxious when squared or opposed. Neptune, of itself, when squared or opposed, causes worry and uncertainty; a cloud hangs over whichever house it inhabits; a fog surrounds the planets it touches by adverse aspect. Neptune here is in the house of the mind so the disturbance is mental. Since Neptune is square the Moon from the house of children, the couple, at times, were at odds in their thinking concerning children.

The Eleventh House:

If the seventh house of a woman's chart represents the husband, the eleventh house, or the fifth house from the seventh, signifies the husband's fertility, or ability to produce children. In Claire's chart the eleventh house contains no planets, so we look to its cusp, Aries, an infertile fire sign. Since there is an intercepted sign, Scorpio, in the fifth house, there must also be one in its opposite eleventh house. It is Taurus, a fertile earth sign.

The ruler of Aries is Mars, significator of male sex. The ruler of Taurus is Venus, denoting female sex. They are conjunct in Claire's chart in Leo, an infertile fire sign, in the second house of resources. Once again we have the grand trine hookup, with the emphasis this time on Venus/Mars from the second house, as co-rulers of the eleventh house of the husband's fertility. This Venus/Mars conjunction is semi-square the Sun from the twelfth house in mental Gemini. A semi-square can be an impediment, but the double grand trine can adequately handle the situation. Hence, there are no strong barriers to the husband's fertility, according to his significators in his wife's chart.

The husband's natal chart should be examined next. Now *his* fifth house shows *his* fertility, while his eleventh house signifies *her* fertility. In this particular case, however, we have no natal chart. Claire's husband is not absolutely certain of his birth date. Official birth records give one date, while family records state the day previous. The exact time of birth also is unknown. Without all of this very vital information, an exact horoscope cannot be erected. To try and rectify this chart is unnecessary. Claire's eleventh house can be the sole determinant of her husband's fertility. The approximate birth date of the husband is February 14 or 15, 1921.

Stepchildren:

Claire and her husband have been married for many years and only to each other. However, if she had been thinking of marrying a divorced man or a widower with children, we would again look at her eleventh house to determine if she could successfully handle the role of step-mother.

The eleventh house, as far as children are concerned, signifies three things:
1. the marriage partner's ability to produce children,
2. the marriage partner's children by a previous marriage, and
3. all other people's children.

We must examine the sign on the eleventh house cusp, aspects to the ruler of that house, and the planets therein and their aspects. The house is read in the same manner as for the husband's fertility. As the house in this instance shows fertility for the husband, it also shows adequate success for Claire as step-mother. However, she had nothing to consider in that area.

Personality:

While the fifth house shows fertility, it does not determine if Claire has a personality compatible with motherhood. The two major pointers of personality in the chart are the Moon and the Ascendant, or first house.

The Moon is maternal, the planet of fecundation, and the builder of the physical body. We have already considered it as tenant of the fifth house of children. In Claire's chart it does double duty, because, as ruler of the Ascendant:

1. Moon, as tenant of the fifth, desires children, and is capable of having them.

2. Moon, because it conjuncts Saturn, takes the job of motherhood seriously, and accepts willingly the responsibility for rearing a family. Saturn, because it denies, limited the number of children Claire could have and produced one miscarriage.

3. Moon, squaring Neptune placed in the third house of the mind, gave Claire mental problems concerning childbearing and childrearing. Yet, they were adequately solved because of the grand trine protection.

The Ascendant, as ruler of the native's outlook on life, his constitution, his vitality and his personality, is the most important house in the chart. The sign and degree on the first house cusp opens the door to the personality — a dominating factor in all of life's decisions. Whichever house or department of life we are studying — be it talent, work, the mind, marriage, money, schooling, or children — we must see it through the clearing house of the Ascendant. This house colors the entire horoscope.

In Claire's chart, the Ascendant is at 12 degrees Cancer, the sign ruling motherhood, the family, homebuilder and keeper, with a regenerative, sex-conscious, Scorpio decanate. Modifying this Ascendant, because it contains two planets close to its cusp, are Mercury at 14 degrees Cancer conjunct Pluto also at 14 Cancer. Mercury takes on added importance because it rules Gemini, the sign in which Claire's Sun is placed. Mercury is the thinker, and, here in Cancer, it thinks alot about the affairs of motherhood.

Pluto, as the planet making the closest aspect to Mercury in this chart, gives added depth to this thinking. In addition, because Pluto is the planet of universal welfare, the hope of this mother is for her children to contribute to the betterment of society, however small their capabilities. This line of reasoning paved the way for the secret commitment and the full-time obligation that Moon/Saturn accepted as each child was born.

The Moon molds personality through the feelings, emotions, and glands, while the Ascendant forms personality by being the focal gathering point for all of the other houses. The combination of the Moon plus the Ascendant gives us our distinctive, unique qualities. Here, in Claire's chart, the Cancer Ascendant equals motherhood while its ruler, the Moon, placed in the fifth house of children, also denotes motherhood. Is this what Doris Kaye, the astrologer, saw at first glance?

The Sun:

While all of the above is true, it is the Sun which signifies our individuality, and our separate, independent existence. Claire's Sun is in Gemini — *I think* — and here, in the twelfth house, the thinking turns to secret, occult subjects. The usually voluble Gemini Sun becomes more quiet and introspective. The probingly scientific, occult Scorpio Moon adds to this investigative inclination, while the Sun sextile Neptune aspect from the third house to the twelfth contributes a spiritual frame of mind.

Although Claire's Sun makes no major aspect to either the Moon or the Ascendant, its link to the motherhood sign, Cancer, comes through Mercury, ruler of the Sun's sign of the twins, Gemini. Posited in Cancer and importantly positioned on the first house cusp, Mercury has a dual role. In the early years, Claire concentrated almost exclusively on her children until they were grown. Then, as the Moon's labors lessened, the Sun's rays could more strongly shine, as Claire turned her attention from the raising of children to occult research (Mercury conjunct Pluto) in general and astrological birth control in particular.

How important then are the Ascendant, the Sun, and the Moon in our natal charts! Just as the combined harmony of Sun, Moon, and Ascendant produce the foundation for a successful life, so too do the Sun, Moon, and Ascendant, when in tune reproductively, create an astrological fertility that is the basis for a new *life*.

Keep this triad — this Sun, Moon, and Ascendant — which exercises such control and authority over our lives, in mind, to be brought forth in the following chapter, because it is the starting point for research into Astrological Birth Control.

Before continuing, however, we will digress for a page or two, to present the following astrological fertility rules that may not have been present or included in Claire's example chart. . . .

Chapter II
Astrological Rules Governing Fertility and Infertility

This is a partial listing of rules governing fertility and infertility culled from various astrology books, just to give you an idea of what to look for in a natal chart. Listed in detail in the bibliography, the following books pertaining to this chapter were used:

1. *An Encyclopaedia of Psychological Astrology* by C.E.O. Carter,
2. *Encyclopaedia of Medical Astrology* by H.L. Cornell, M.D., and
3. *Medical Astrology* by Omar V. Garrison.

At times this information may seem contradictory, but this is what has been handed down to us through the years. All of this material should be gathered together and thoroughly researched, and what is found to be false or no longer accountable should be eliminated.

While we absolutely and in no way whatsoever seek or intend to take the place of the gynecologist or obstetrician, for our own observations at least, we have guidelines for the possible sources and troubles of infertility.

Fertility Rules:

1. Maternal functioning is ruled by the Moon and Venus, their signs, houses and aspects, in the horoscope of the mother.
2. The fruitful signs are — Cancer, Scorpio, Pisces, Taurus, Capricorn and Libra.
3. The fruitful planets are — the Moon, Jupiter, Venus, and the North Node.
4. The fifth house is the principal house of children. It indicates whether children will be born or denied; whether they are a blessing or source of anxiety.
5. Indications of many children are as follows:

    a) The Moon in Cancer, Scorpio, Pisces, or in double bodied signs such as Gemini or Sagittarius.

    b) The Moon in the fifth house and well aspected by Jupiter or Venus.

    c) The Moon in the fifth house in a fruitful sign.

    d) The Moon in Taurus, her exalted sign, in the fifth house and well aspected.

    e) Jupiter, Venus, or the Moon in the fifth house and the Moon in good aspect to Jupiter or Venus increases the number of children.

f) Jupiter well aspected in Scorpio.

g) Venus in the fifth house in Cancer, Scorpio, or Pisces and well aspected.

h) Planets or the North Node in the fifth house and well aspected by the Moon or Venus.

i) Cancer on the Ascendant or on the fifth house cusp.

j) The ruler of the fifth house in a fruitful sign and on the Ascendant, if not afflicted.

k) Ruler of the seventh house placed in the fifth house.

Some of the above rules in Number 5 seem repetitive. Nevertheless, Claire had 7 of these rules in her chart to favor a large family.

6. When fruitful signs and fruitful planets are on the cusp and in the fifth or eleventh houses, and well aspected, they give children.

7. The uterus or womb is ruled by the Moon and Venus and the sign, Cancer.

8. The positions, signs, and aspects of the Moon and Venus are most important in a woman's chart because the Moon signifies motherhood and Venus signifies the female.

9. In a male chart: the fifth house signifies the first child; the seventh house signifies the second child; the ninth house signifies the third child; the eleventh house signifies the fourth child; and the first house signifies the fifth child.

10. In a female chart: the fourth house signifies the first child; the sixth house signifies the second child; the eighth house signifies the third child; the tenth house signifies the fourth child; and the twelfth house signifies the fifth child.

11. Maternal instinct is present when either the fifth house or the sign, Cancer, is well tenanted.

Amativeness, or the strong desire to propagate, is indicated by:

1. The signs Taurus and Leo prominent.

2. The fifth and seventh houses being strong influences in the natal chart.

3. A strong Leo characteristic, as Leo is the sign of children.

4. The Sun in Taurus, or Taurus on the Ascendant.

5. Mars in the fifth house makes one highly sexed, especially when in aspect to Venus.

6. Mars in the fifth house gives great desire for children.

7. Taurus, Leo, and Capricorn are strongly sex conscious.

Antipathy:

If a woman's chart shows antipathy toward the having and rearing of children, it would be best to find this out before the wedding ceremony.

According to an article written a few years ago by Donald Kotulak of the *Chicago Tribune*, a new risk factor that can kill fetuses has been uncovered by a team of California researchers: the pregnant woman's attitude. The article states:

"The death rate for new-borns of women who favored pregnancy was 11 for 1000 births, while the death rate for new-borns of women who resented their pregnancies was 27.7 per 1000. Also, infants of women with negative attitudes had one and one-half times more congenital abnormalities than infants born to women who were happy about being pregnant, according to the report." (Reprinted, courtesy of the *Chicago Tribune*.)

We must study the whole chart and then consider:

1. Saturn, Uranus, or Neptune in the fifth or eleventh house may show indifference or dislike, although, if the horoscope otherwise shows maternal tendencies, they may only denote troubles through them.

2. A preponderance of planets in positive or masculine signs — Aries, Gemini, Leo, Libra, Sagittarius, and Aquarius — often causes lack of maternal impulse.

Anxiety:

Anxiety, worry, and stress can cause infertility. Rules concerning these conditions are:

1. The nervous system in general is ruled by the third house, Mercury, and Gemini.

2. Uncommon nervous disorders are ruled by Uranus and Aquarius.

3. Nervous temperament is ruled by Mercury, Saturn, and Uranus.

4. Many of the endocrine glands are under the control of the nervous system via the hypothalamus of the brain and the pituitary gland which is suspended from it. The pituitary gland, ruled by Uranus and Saturn, controls sexual function.

5. Worry is produced by an ill-placed Neptune or by bad influences involving Pisces or the twelfth house.

6. Mutable signs feel and show worry most easily. Fixed signs show worry the least.

7. Water and air signs worry soonest.

8. The Moon tends greatly to fearfulness and anxiety.

When worry and anxiety are relieved, a woman often is finally able to ovulate normally and become pregnant.

Impotency:

Impotency is a Venusian disease, caused by afflictions to Venus. Astrological causes of impotency in a male chart are:

1. Venus heavily afflicted yields a low sperm count or other sperm deficiency.

2. Venus in an angle, especially the western angle (seventh house), and conjunct Saturn, or in mutual reception to or square or opposite Saturn.

3. Venus and Saturn in the seventh house.

4. Mars elevated above Venus.

5. Venus in feminine signs and alone.

6. Venus in Pisces — common in nativities of bachelors.

7. Mercury square Neptune gives mental and emotional difficulties and can cause impotency.

8. If Scorpio, Pluto and/or Mars are heavily afflicted by square or opposition, look for testicle abnormality.

9. 17 degrees of Gemini on the Ascendant is said to be a degree of impotency and loss of reproductive faculties.

10. Males nearly impotent — Sun and Moon configurated together in feminine signs, with Mars and Venus in feminine signs.

Husband Averse to Having Children:
1. Sun afflicted by Saturn in the woman's chart.
2. Saturn in the eleventh house in the woman's chart.
3. Venus afflicted by Moon and Saturn.
4. Venus in sign of Saturn.
5. Moon in sign of Venus.

Barrenness or Infertility:
1. Barren signs are Aries, Gemini, Virgo, Leo, Sagittarius, and Aquarius.

2. Barren planets are Sun, Uranus, Saturn, Mars, and the South Node.

3. The Sun and malefics in barren signs, dominating the fifth and eleventh houses.

4. The Sun in Capricorn and afflicted.

5. Rulers of the first house and the fifth house square or opposite each other, or with Saturn or Mars, yields barrenness.

6. The Sun square or opposite Venus by direction yields a barren time.

7. The Moon in the husband's horoscope and the Sun in the wife's, applying to Uranus, Saturn, or the South Node in the fifth house.

8. The Moon, Jupiter, or Venus weak, afflicted, and unfortunate at birth, and not in fruitful houses or signs tends to deny children.

9. Uranus afflicted in the fifth or eleventh house, or afflicting these houses.

10. Mars square or opposite the cusp of the fifth house with Saturn in the eleventh house.

11. The Sun afflicted by Saturn often shows sterility in a woman's chart.

12. When barren signs and planets are on the cusps or in the fifth or eleventh houses, they have a tendency to deny children.

13. Afflictions of Neptune in or to the fifth house often indicate denial of children.

14. In a horary chart:

a) Saturn in the eleventh house — if at the same time there are barren signs on the Ascendant or the cusp of the fifth house — has a tendency to deny children.

b) A barren sign on the cusp of the fourth house — the house denoting the end of all things — gives little hope of children.

If the astrologer judges the chart to be very unfortunate in the matter of childbearing and/or childrearing — that is, if there are many challenging aspects to the fifth house, many malefics in the fifth, or many signs of sterility in the chart — it might be best for the would-be parents to leave the matter alone. Nature has a way of making her wishes known, and maybe we should neither tinker with those requests nor force her hand. It might not be wise, either by the use of fertility drugs, artificial insemination, or test-tube intervention to do what is "not in the cards" for this particular couple.

Fertility drugs may cause multiple births and maybe, even defective children. The mother may suffer from ovarian enlargement, vasomotor flushes, nausea, abdominal discomfort, blurred vision, or nervous tension while taking them.

Adoption of children could be an alternative. This may be shown by Aquarius on the fifth house cusp, the natural sign of the eleventh house, which rules other people's children. Venus, Jupiter, or the Moon, either in the eleventh house or ruling it, in sextile or trine aspects to other planets, can indicate successful adoption of children or amicable relationships with stepchildren.

If neither of the above is the answer, one may wish to use his or her creativity in other fields.

On a more positive note, if the odds, either medical, emotional or astrological seem to be against giving birth to a child, one should not become unduly discouraged. No chart, either a very favorable or a very unfavorable one, can tell absolutely the final fertility story either for or against conception, childbirth, childrearing, the condition of the unborn fetus, or the health of the resulting baby.

Astrology is an ongoing research subject and since our knowledge concerning astrological fertility is still far from complete, our advice must always be tentative. As we continue, however, to delve into the mysteries of our solar system, we are mindful that man and woman are only pro-creators and junior partners with God. He alone is the Creator; He alone makes the final decisions concerning conception.

May we refresh your memory with a familiar Bible account in the Old Testament?

In the book of Genesis we read: Then God brought Abram (Abraham) outside beneath the nighttime Sky and told him, "Look up into the heavens and count the stars, if you can. Just so shall your descendants be." And Abram (Abraham) put his faith in the Lord.

At that time Abraham was 99 years old and his wife, Sarah, was 90. Sarah was long since past the time when she could have a baby. As told in Genesis: Sarah laughed silently. "A woman my age have a baby?" she scoffed to herself. "And with a husband as old as mine?" Then God said to Abraham, "Why did Sarah laugh? Why did she say, *Can an old woman like me have a baby?* Is anything too hard for God? Next year just as I told you, I will certainly see to it that Sarah has a son."

The impossible happened and Sarah had her child. We should try to cultivate a faith like Abraham's. For faith is more than believing. It is also trust in God; trying to discover His will, and then doing it; and if we want children, it is applying His natural laws to our lives via the new advancements in fertility, both physiological and astrological, that are now available to us.

We have determined that Claire's example chart showed fertility and the desire to have children. But, since the aspects were mixed, that is, both cooperative yet challenging, it also showed denial and limitation. When charts exhibit great fertility, the couple may now want to either:

1. limit the size of the family to a reasonable number of children, or
2. conceive at a specific time.

These two conditions might possibly be accomplished by means of — and so, we will now turn our attention to —

Chapter III
Astrological Birth Control

Enter an astrology book store, close your eyes, turn around three times if you want to, and point to a book — any book. Or, take an astrology book catalog, open it at random, and mark off a book — any book. If you are an astrology student, you should fine truly captivating whichever book you might have selected — even in such a silly, haphazard manner — because each volume would present something stimulating and exciting to add to your storehouse of knowledge concerning this irresistible subject of never ending dimensions.

One of the most fascinating of these literary works is one that first appeared on the book shelves about ten years ago, called *Astrological Birth Control,* by Sheila Ostrander and Lynn Schroeder. Not only are the ideas presented within its pages of new and invigorating proportions, they are also useful and full of new hope. Its concepts deal with, among others, two important subjects:

1. infertility, and
2. the controlling of birth by natural means.

The main thrust of the book propounds that, although the medical profession states that only *once* each month the female reproductive system releases one egg at a specified time, a certain gynecologist/psychiatrist — Dr. Eugen Jonas, Chief of the Psychiatric Out-Patient Clinic of the Nove Zamky District Institute of Public Health in Czechoslovakia at that time — had some success with a new theory. He believed that not only was an egg produced during the natural ovulation cycle, but that another egg burst forth one day each month, when the transiting Sun/Moon phase angle was the same number of degrees apart as it was at the moment of a woman's birth.

Doctor Jonas believed that the phase position of the Sun and the Moon when a girl baby is born determines the biorhythms of her reproductive system, including ovulation. This phase angle of the Moon to the Sun, which Dr. Jonas considers to be *the key to fertility,* is found by measuring the distance between the Sun and the Moon on the ecliptic in a counter-clockwise direction, starting with the new Moon, on the day of the woman's birth.

With this distance in mind, we must now calculate the one day each month of the current year on which this same distance of Moon to Sun occurs. In so doing, we find, that based on the Moon's cycle, there are approximately 12 or 13 days of maximum Moon phase fertility per year.

Example A: If at birth the Sun is at 10 degrees Cancer and the Moon is at 10 degrees Libra in a woman's chart, then the Moon is 90 degrees ahead of the Sun, with the Moon always traveling in a counter-clockwise direction. See Figure 2.

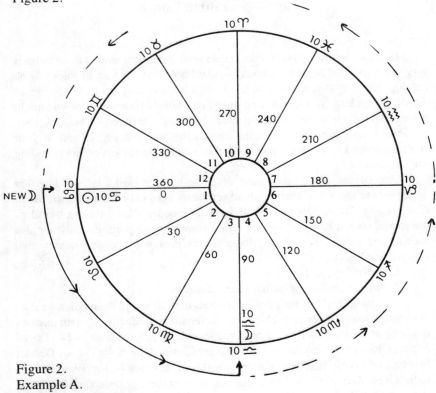

Figure 2.
Example A.
Sun/Moon Angle 90° apart

To determine a woman's astrological fertility date for any particular month in Example A, the Moon would have to be in that same phase angle, that is, 90 degrees forward, going counter-clockwise from the Sun.

If the current Sun was to be at 25 degrees Virgo, the Moon would have to be at 25 Sagittarius to get that same Sun/Moon angle of 90 degrees, and the day that this happened would be the woman's fertility date for that particular month.

When determining the Sun/Moon angle, *always put the Sun on the ascendant and start the Moon traveling from there.*

20

Example B: At a woman's birth the Sun is at 10 degrees Cancer and the Moon is at 10 degrees Aries, as in Figure 3.

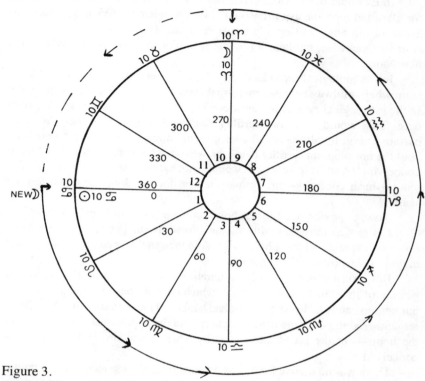

Figure 3.
Example B.
Sun/Moon Angle 270° apart.

Here, the Moon is 270 degrees away from the Sun because we count *counter-clockwise*. It is always the Moon in phase relation to the Sun.

To repeat: To count the number of degrees the Moon is from the Sun in a natal chart, the Sun always stands at the Ascendant while the Moon finds its place around the zodiac in a counter-clockwise position. To find this same number of degrees in any month, place the monthly Sun on the Ascendant, and find the monthly Moon's place which equals the distance of Moon to Sun in the natal chart.

In Example B, the Moon is 270 degrees ahead of the *last* new Moon. It is also 90 degrees in back of the *next* new Moon.

In Example A, the Moon phase day of astrological fertility of this woman for all of her reproductive life would always be when the Moon is 90 degrees going forward from the Sun, starting a first quarter phase.

In Example B, the Moon phase day of astrological fertility of this woman for all of her reproductive life would always be when the Moon is 270 degrees ahead of the Sun, starting a last quarter phase. The Moon is always moving counter-clockwise, but here it is actually moving *toward* the Sun for the next new Moon.

In the biological reproductive cycle, the natural ovulation day, which is somewhere midway between menstrual cycles, is the biological fertility date. In the astrological cycle, the Sun/Moon angle provides the astrological fertility date. That would mean *two* fertility dates and two eggs released. What an extraordinary, revolutionary idea! Seemingly impossible. But, if it were true, could it not pinpoint fertility dates for women who were having difficulty in conceiving? And, if it were true, would it not aid those who wanted to practice natural birth control — the primary reason for Dr. Jonas' original fertility search?

Now, to go one step further, how could one prove such an hypothesis?

Claire was intrigued with this new idea, as she put the astrology book down to let the novel thoughts sink in. And then she jumped up. "Maybe, just maybe, I can prove it," she mused.

But, no, it was really only an unrehearsed, impulsive, and spontaneous gesture of love, instigated by Claire, which couldn't have meaning to anyone but her husband and herself. And it had happened many years ago. Still, Claire remembered the day, the date, the place, and the approximate time — within the hour — of the act of intercourse by which their third child, Katie, was conceived.

There was no motive for recording the timing of these moments. Certainly it was not astrological, as Claire had no knowledge of astrology at that time. But, as she shyly, hesitantly points out, "It's just that — ask any woman and she will agree — there are some moments in a woman's life that she will always remember. . . ."

It is fortunate for us that she does remember, because she can now share with us the exact chart of that approximate moment of intercourse. We use no rectification, no deductive reasoning, no back-tracking of events to present this chart. The words, *apparent* and *theoretical*, do not apply. It's the real thing!

Remember, this is an intercourse chart, *not* a conception chart. The only way a valid, exact conception chart could be obtained would be to actually see, through a microscope, the sperm enter the egg placed in a Petri dish in a scientific laboratory.

In the following chapter on biological reproduction, you will learn that it takes several hours after intercourse before a sperm can prepare itself to penetrate an egg. Therefore, since we could never normally achieve such a feat — this exact timing of conception or fertilization — we must be grateful for the unusual data we are privileged to present to you now:

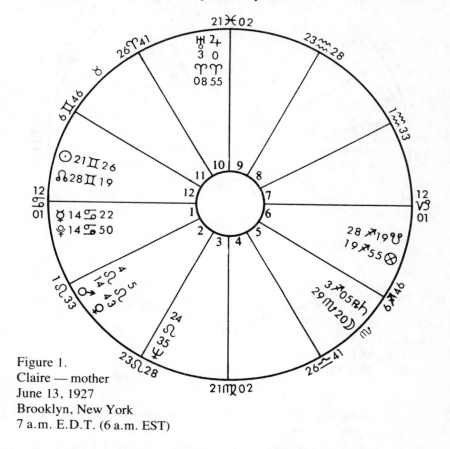

Figure 1.
Claire — mother
June 13, 1927
Brooklyn, New York
7 a.m. E.D.T. (6 a.m. EST)

Because this act occurred after 8 p.m. but before 9 p.m., this horoscope has been calculated for 8:30 p.m., EST.

Claire calculated her Sun/Moon angle in her natal chart. Then she set up the intercourse chart. She held her breath as she measured the intercourse Sun/Moon angle. They were almost the same, with approximately only 9 degrees difference.

Please study these three charts and experience this amazing story as it unfolds:

With the above three charts we now have all the information we need to study our method of Astrological Birth Control. To find astrologically a

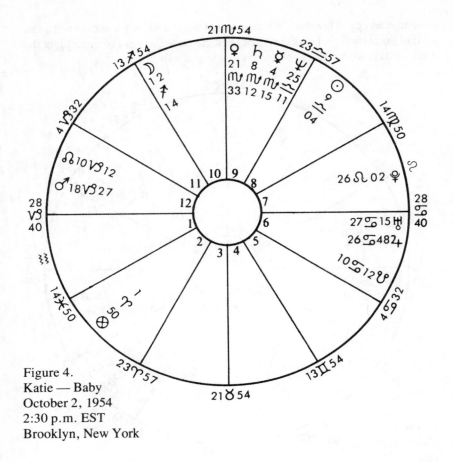

Figure 4.
Katie — Baby
October 2, 1954
2:30 p.m. EST
Brooklyn, New York

woman's fertility date and then the most fertile hours within that date, according to our experimental method, two basic factors must be known:

1. the number of degrees within the natal Sun/Moon phase angle, and

2. the *midpoint* number of degrees between the natal Sun and Moon, found on the left top of the aspect page, under MOON and to left of SUN.

It is always the number of degrees that the Moon has traveled away and around from the Sun since the last new Moon with which we will be working. It may not necessarily be the smallest number of degrees between Sun and Moon.

Using Claire's horoscope as an example, the procedure to calculate the natal Sun/Moon angle is as follows:

1. Find the number of degrees between the Sun and the Moon, with the Moon going in a counter-clockwise direction from the Sun, by first noting the number of degrees which each sign represents, as follows:

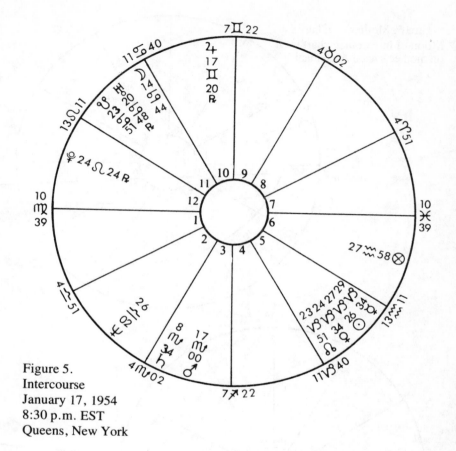

Figure 5.
Intercourse
January 17, 1954
8:30 p.m. EST
Queens, New York

Aries	=	0 degrees
Taurus	=	30 degrees
Gemini	=	60 degrees
Cancer	=	90 degrees
Leo	=	120 degrees
Virgo	=	150 degrees
Libra	=	180 degrees
Scorpio	=	210 degrees
Sagittarius	=	240 degrees
Capricorn	=	270 degrees
Aquarius	=	300 degrees
Pisces	=	330 degrees

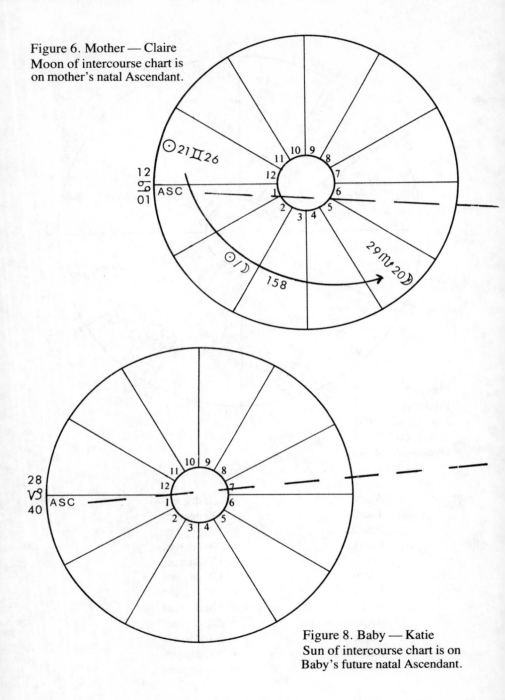

Figure 6. Mother — Claire
Moon of intercourse chart is
on mother's natal Ascendant.

⊙ 21 ♊ 26

12
♍
01

ASC

29 ♏ 20 ☽

⊙ / ☽
158

Figure 8. Baby — Katie
Sun of intercourse chart is on
Baby's future natal Ascendant.

28
♑
40

ASC

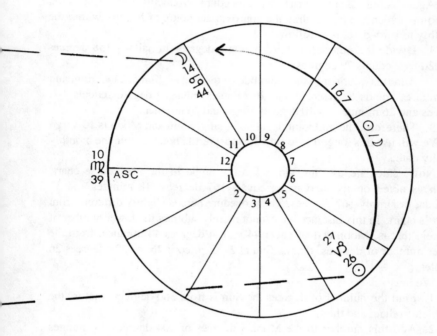

Figure 7. Intercourse
Ascendant of intercourse chart is the midpoint degree of mother's natal Sun/
Moon.

2. Find the number of degrees for the Sun and Moon:

Moon at 29 Scorpio 20 minutes equals 239 degrees and 20 minutes.

Sun at 21 Gemini 26 minutes equals 81 degrees and 26 minutes.

3. Subtracting the lower number of degrees from the higher gives us a difference of 157 degrees 54 minutes, or 158 degrees.

4. Therefore, Claire's Sun/Moon fertility angle for all of her reproductive life equals 158 degrees.

Again using Claire's chart, the procedure to calculate the Sun/Moon midpoint, which we use to time the approximate hours of fertility within the monthly fertility date, is as follows:

1. Divide the number of fertility angle degrees in half — 158 degrees divided by 2 equals 79 degrees.

2. Add this quotient to the longitude of the Sun — Sun at 21 Gemini and 26 minutes equals 81 degrees and 26 minutes, plus 79 degrees equals 160 degrees and 26 minutes, or 10 degrees Virgo and 26 minutes.

3. Therefore, the midpoint degree of Claire's Sun and Moon is 10 Virgo 26. We will use this longitude to find the most fertile hours within the monthly fertility date.

Now, calculate the Sun/Moon fertility angle in the intercourse chart, which as noted on its chart page, equals 167 degrees, 18 minutes and 37 seconds, or simply 167 degrees. The procedure here is slightly different from Claire's chart. In this instance we cannot merely subtract the lower number of degrees, that is, Moon at 14 Cancer 44 = 104 degrees 44 minutes, from the higher number of degrees, that is, Sun at 27 Capricorn 26, or 297 degrees 26 minutes.

We must:

1. Find the number of degrees the Sun is from 360 degrees, that is, the complete zodiac, and then,

2. Add this number to the Moon's degrees of 104 degrees 44 minutes because we must complete the zodiac before starting again in Aries.

Subtracting the Sun's number of degrees at 297 degrees 26 minutes from 360 degrees gives us a remainder of 62 degrees 34 minutes.

Adding this 62 degrees 34 minutes to the Moon's 104 degrees 44 minutes gives us a sum of 167 degrees 18 minutes, or 167 degrees. Therefore, the Sun/Moon fertility angle of the intercourse chart = 167 degrees.

Breaking down these three significant horoscopes — mother, Claire's, baby daughter, Katie's, and the chart of intercourse which produced Katie — we find the following important positions of Sun, Moon and Ascendant in all three charts, plus their *relevant transpositions* in Figures 6 through 11.

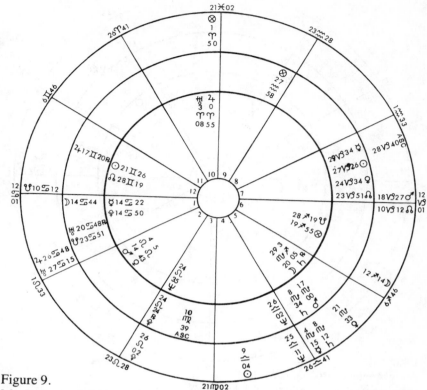

Figure 9.
Mother's natal chart — inner wheel
Intercourse chart — middle wheel
Baby's natal chart — outerwheel   Mother's house cusps

Notice the following:

1. In Figure 9, the mother's inner chart, the accent of the intercourse planets is on houses 1 and 7 which signify Claire and her husband, the father of Katie.

2. In Figure 10, baby daughter's inner chart, the accent of the intercourse planets is on the Ascendant point, plus the sixth house of the perfection of the self expression of the fifth house of children — the perfection being her own new life.

3. In Figure 11, the intercourse inner, chart the accent of its planets is in the fifth house of one's own children, and also the house which rules sexual intercourse, and in the eleventh house of other people's children.

4. In Figure 11, the intercourse chart, the mother's own Ascendant sign and degree is on the eleventh house of the partner's children, while the mother's seventh house sign and degree — signifying the husband — is on the fifth house

29

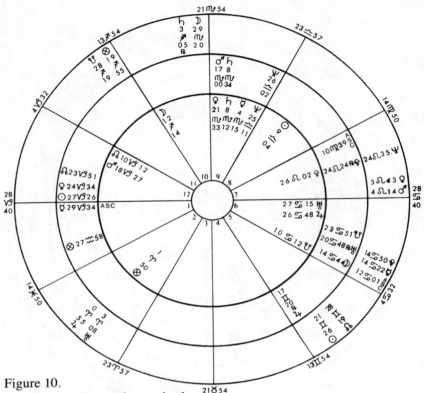

Figure 10.
Baby's natal chart — inner wheel
Intercourse chart — middle wheel
Mother's natal chart — outer wheel
Baby's house cusps

of the native's children. Each gave to the other to produce a new life. The baby daughter's North and South Nodes add importance to these cusps.

5. In Figure 11, the intercourse chart, the eighth house of sex force and sex energy is ruled by Mars, here in its rulership in Scorpio, and trine Moon, also in its rulership in Cancer, and ruler of the uterus, fertilization, and motherhood.

Since the Sun/Moon fertility angle of the intercourse chart is 167 degrees, and the Sun/Moon fertility angle of the mother's chart is 158 degrees, there is a difference of only 9 degrees. Therefore, the act occurred during the time of fertility as stated by Dr. Jonas — that is, the astrological fertility date.

On January 18, 1954, the Moon was at 20 Cancer 32 minutes, as taken from a noon ephemeris. On January 17, 1954, the Moon was at 7 Cancer 16 minutes. Therefore, the Moon moved 13 degrees and 16 minutes during that 24 hour period — slightly faster than 1 degree every 2 hours.

30

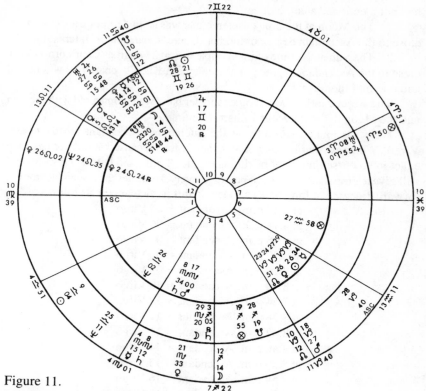

Figure 11.
Intercourse chart — inner wheel
Mother's natal chart — middle wheel
Baby's natal chart — outer wheel
Intercourse house cusps

Intercourse took place 9 degrees later than the mother's fertility angle degree and supposedly the release of an egg. If one degree of Moon travel equals 2 hours, then 9 degrees of Moon travel equals 18 hours. Therefore, approximately 18 hours before the act occurred, the egg was released and was waiting in the fallopian tube to be fertilized.

Books vary in their information concerning the life span of the released ovum during which it is capable of being fertilized. The variations are from 6 to 8 hours; to 24 hours; to 48 hours; with the 24 hour variation being the most popular. Add on the capacitation of sperm hours (to be discussed later) and our egg is still within the 24 hour capability limit. It was ready and waiting to be fertilized.

In addition, something startling was observed — something that Dr. Jonas had not mentioned at all. Notice:

1. The Moon at the time of intercourse was at 14 degrees Cancer — very close to the Ascendant degree of mother, Claire's, natal chart. Interesting.

2. The Sun at the time of intercourse was at 27 degrees Capricorn — very close to the Ascendant degree of baby daughter, Katie's, chart who was born 8 and one-half months later.

The Ascendants of both mother and her baby were connected with the Sun and the Moon in the intercourse chart. Exciting!

Now we looked carefully at the intercourse Ascendant at 10 degrees Virgo. We knew that it was not an exact degree because we did not have the exact intercourse time, but the timing of after 8 p.m. and before 9 p.m. would still give a Virgo Ascendant. To be exact, every 4 minutes the Ascendant moves forward 1 degree of longitude as shown in this particular case as follows:

at 8:10 p.m. Ascendant = 05 Virgo
at 8:14 p.m. Ascendant = 06 Virgo
at 8:18 p.m. Ascendant = 07 Virgo
at 8:22 p.m. Ascendant = 08 Virgo
at 8:26 p.m. Ascendant = 09 Virgo
at 8:30 p.m. Ascendant = 10 Virgo
at 8:34 p.m. Ascendant = 11 Virgo
at 8:38 p.m. Ascendant = 12 Virgo
at 8:42 p.m. Ascendant = 13 Virgo
at 8:46 p.m. Ascendant = 14 Virgo
at 8:50 p.m. Ascendant = 15 Virgo
at 8:54 p.m. Ascendant = 16 Virgo
at 8:58 p.m. Ascendant = 17 Virgo
at 9:02 p.m. Ascendant = 18 Virgo

Nevertheless, we were disappointed. Claire, the mother, had nothing of 10 degrees Virgo in her birth chart. In fact, she had nothing in Virgo at all except a 21 degree fourth house cusp in Virgo, which would have taken us to after 9 p.m.

And then, the brainstorm. Thinking along Sun/Moon lines, we calculated Claire's natal Sun/Moon *midpoint* — not the fertility angle which is 158 degrees — but the midpoint, which we showed you earlier. There it was: Sun/Moon midpoint equals 10 degrees Virgo. Unbelievable! So, we have:

3. Ascendant of chart at approximate time of intercourse was at 10 degrees Virgo — the same sign and degree as the midpoint of the Sun/Moon angle of the mother's birth chart.

Astounding, incredible timing because:

1. the Ascendants of all three charts,
2. the Sun and the Moon of the intercourse chart,

3. the midpoint of the Sun/Moon fertility angle of the mother's chart, together with,

4. the almost exact timing of the mother's natal fertility angle with the transiting Sun/Moon angle,

all combined and intertwined their energies into one cohesive unit which produced a new life. Once again we have that triad — the Sun, Moon and Ascendant — to which we owe so much.

Secondary Progression of Mother, Claire's Birth Chart:

Secondary progressions are zodiacal aspects formed by the orbital motions of the planets on successive days after birth, each day equalling one year of life. We will now progress the mother's birth chart to the day of intercourse — January 17, 1954. Claire was 26 and 1/2 years old. Shall we look to see if Claire's progressed Moon is involved in any way in our conception account?

Since Claire, the mother, was born at 7 a.m., EDT, (or 6 a.m., EST) on June 13, 1927, in Brooklyn, New York, her adjusted calculated date for secondary progressions is June 28. It is calculated in this manner:

Subtract one hour from the 7 a.m. EDT birth time to bring the time back to EST. It is now 6 a.m. Add a 5 hour adjustment for Greenwich Mean Time and we have a birth time of 11 a.m. GMT. Since Claire was born 1 hour before noon GMT, and 1 hour equals 15 days in secondary progression, add 15 days to the birth date to get an Adjusted Calculated Date of June 28.

When we secondary progress the birth date 26 years we have the following:

July 9, 1927 = June 28, 1953, and

July 10, 1927 = June 28, 1954.

The Moon on June 28, 1953 = 13 Scorpio 22.

The Moon on June 28, 1954 = 25 Scorpio 34.

The date of intercourse was January 17, 1954, inbetween the two above dates.

To find out how far the Moon traveled between June 28, 1953 and June 28, 1954, subtract 13 Scorpio 22 from 25 Scorpio 34. The moon traveled 12 degrees and 12 minutes during that year in secondary progression.

To find out how far the Moon traveled in one month, divide 12 degrees and 12 minutes by 12, because there are 12 months in a year. We find that the Moon traveled 1 degree and 1 minute each month between June 28, 1953 and June 28, 1954, in secondary progression. Then:

1953, Jun 28, Moon = 13 Scorpio 22'
1953, Jul 28, Moon = 14 Scorpio 23'
1953, Aug 28, Moon = 15 Scorpio 24'
1953, Sep 28, Moon = 16 Scorpio 25'
1953, Oct 28, Moon = 17 Scorpio 26'
1953, Nov 28, Moon = 18 Scorpio 27'

1953, Dec 28, Moon = 19 Scorpio 28'
1954, Jan 17, Moon = 20 Scorpio 08'
1954, Jan 28, Moon = 20 Scorpio 29'

When we divide the 31 days in December into the 61 minutes (1 degree and 1 minute = 61 minutes) that the Moon moved from December 28 to January 28, we find that the Moon moved 2 minutes each day. From December 28, 1953 to January 17, 1954 there are 20 days. 20 days times 2 minutes gives us 40 minutes which we add to the 19 Scorpio 28' of December 28, 1953 to give us a secondary progressed Moon on January 17, 1954 of 20 Scorpio 08 minutes. This is only 9 degrees away from the longitude of Claire's own natal Moon of 29 Scorpio 20 minutes.

Find now where the secondary progressed Moon is on the date of daughter, Katie's, birth, October 2, 1954, in Claire's natal chart. In secondary progression, July 11, 1927 equals June 28, 1955 when the Moon, as taken from a noon ephemeris, was at 8 Sagittarius 00 minutes. July 10, 1927 equals June 28, 1954, and here the Moon is at 25 Scorpio 34. There is a difference of 12 degrees and 26 minutes. Therefore, the secondary progressed Moon traveled 12 degrees and 26 minutes between 1954 and 1955 in Claire's progressed chart. Dividing this 12 degrees and 26 minutes by 12 months in a year, we find that the Moon moved forward 1 degree and 2 minutes every month between 1954 and 1955, as follows:

1954, Jun 28, Moon = 25 Scorpio 34'
1954, Jul 28, Moon = 26 Scorpio 36'
1954, Aug 28, Moon = 27 Scorpio 38'
1954, Sep 28, Moon = 28 Scorpio 40'
1954, Oct 02, Moon = 28 Scorpio 48'
1954, Oct 28, Moon = 29 Scorpio 42'

When we divide the 30 days in September into the 62 minutes (1 degree and 2 minutes = 62 minutes) that the Moon moved from September 28, 1954 to October 28, 1954, we find that the Moon moved forward 2 minutes each day. From September 28 to October 2, 1954, there are 4 days. Four days times 2 minutes gives us 8 minutes, which we add to the 28 Scorpio 40 minutes of September 28, 1954, to give us a secondary progressed Moon on October 2, 1954, of 28 Scorpio 48 minutes in Claire's progressed chart on her baby's birthday.

Let's review. The mother's progressed Moon at time of intercourse on January 17, 1954 is approximately 20 Scorpio 08. The mother's progressed Moon at the time of baby Katie's birth, 8 and 1/2 months later, on October 2, 1954, had traveled to 28 Scorpio 48. This is practically the same as Claire, the mother's, own *natal Moon* at *29 Scorpio 20*.

In other words, at time of Claire, the mother's birth, Moon was at 29 Scorpio 20 minutes, and 158 degrees away from the Sun. At the time of her baby, Katie's, birth, Claire's progressed Moon was at 28 Scorpio 48 — almost at 29 Scorpio — making the same angle to Claire's natal Sun at a distance of approximately 157 degrees and 22 minutes.

Of course, this phenomenon should only happen once — when a woman is 27-28 years of age — because it takes the Moon in the progressed chart that long to travel through all the signs of the zodiac and return to its original position. The next time this could possibly occur would be 27-28 years after the first progressed Moon return — at approximately 54 to 56 years of age — when the childbearing years should already have been completed.

Could this time — nine months before the progressed Moon returns to its original place in the chart, since it is once again in the exact same aspect to the natal Sun as it was at birth — be a time of *super fertility?*

The prospective mother, to take advantage of this super time of fertility, would be around 26 to 27 years of age. Do many young women today, by postponing pregnancy until after the age of 30, miss this very fertile time?

One must realize, of course, that the Moon at the time of intercourse, in its Sun/Moon fertility angle, can be on the mother's natal ascendant only *once* each year, because it takes the Sun one whole year to travel through all of the signs of the zodiac and the Moon must be in exact phase to it. Every month has its fertility Sun/Moon angle no matter which sign holds the Sun, but this *once-a-year-intercourse Moon* on the mother's natal Ascendant would be her very special fertility date for the year.

The Parallel:

There is one final item to consider — the Parallel — an aspect formed between two planets within 1 and 1/2 degrees of being in the same declination, either North or South (a declination being the number of degrees a planet is North or South of the Celestial Equator). The parallel functions the same as the conjunction, but the effects are internal rather than external.

The declination of the Sun at Claire, the mother's birth, was 23N10. The declination of the Moon at the time of intercourse was 23N28. The mother's natal Sun and the intercourse Moon are parallel, work as a conjunction, a new Moon, and a new beginning. The male and female symbols, Sun and Moon, joined forces in still another dimension to produce the creative atmosphere for a new life.

Finally, please note:

The only point of contact by conjunction between the parents' natal charts is the father's Mars, at approximately one degree Aries, with Claire's Jupiter, at approximately one degree Aries. Does this point of contact show up in their future baby's chart? Indeed it does! One degree of Aries is the longitude of Katie's Part of Fortune.

Once again the tie-up of Sun/Moon/Ascendant comes to the forefront because the Part of Fortune, supposedly the most fortunate degree in a natal chart, is calculated by adding the longitude of the Ascendant to the longitude of the Moon, and subtracting the longitude of the Sun from their sum.

Which sign and degree could more appropriately pioneer a brand new approach to fertility than this three-way conjunction being in the first degree of the first sign of the zodiac, Aries? When we consider that every four minutes the Part of Fortune increases by one degree its longitudinal placement in a natal horoscope, the mathematical precision surrounding the birth of this child, Katie, is astonishing.

To sum up:

1. the Sun/Moon angle at time of intercourse being the same as the mother's natal Sun/Moon angle,

2. the intercourse Moon on mother's natal Ascendant,

3. the intercourse Sun on future baby's natal Ascendant,

4. the midpoint of mother's natal Sun/Moon angle being the same as the Ascendant of the intercourse chart,

5. the sign and degree of the eleventh house of husband's children in the intercourse chart being approximately the same as the mother's natal Ascendant,

6. the mother's secondary progressed Moon at 20 Scorpio, conjunct future baby's Midheaven, timed so that at the baby's birth it would be at approximately the same position as at mother's birth — thereby creating a super Sun/Moon angle,

7. the parallel of the mother's natal Sun with the intercourse Moon, and

8. the one degree of Aries connecting the charts of mother, father, and future baby,

all coincided and came together at one special time in Claire's life. This particular time was neither plotted, nor planned, nor calculated in advance. Claire wanted a child and she asked Him, the Creator, for a baby. And, He said ''yes.'' Do you think it proves that if we live in harmony with the forces of Nature, Nature will yield its rewards?

It must further be tested to see if one can determine the optimum *time*, as well as *day*, for intercourse, by calculating the midpoint of the prospective mother's Sun/Moon angle, and making that sign and degree the Ascendant of the intercourse chart. It happened in Claire's chart as if by accident. Now we will show you how to experimentally calculate an —

Intercourse Time Chart for Women

1. Calculate your Sun/Moon fertility angle in your natal chart.
2. Ascertain its midpoint sign and degree.

3. This midpoint becomes the Ascendant sign and degree for your intercourse time chart.

4. In your tables of houses, find the intersection of the latitude where you are now residing and the ascending or first house sign and degree closest to the midpoint sign and degree of your Sun/Moon fertility angle.

5. Fill in the rest of the house cusps. This becomes your basic *Intercourse Time Chart*. It never varies, *unless you move to a different location*. It can be used each month for your entire reproductive lifetime. The cusps on the houses will always remain the same.

6. Determine your fertility date for the month in question. As previously discussed, it is the day on which the transiting Sun and Moon are the same distance apart as they were at your birth. Each month the Sun and Moon will be in different signs, but their number of degrees apart must always be the same.

7. Only the transiting Sun must be placed in the *Intercourse Time Chart*. Depending upon which house it is placed, according to sign, that is the approximate *time* during the Sun/Moon fertility angle day of that particular month that intercourse should take place — if you wish to conceive. It is the time you should especially avoid if you do *not* want to conceive, although remember, one must abstain for a number of days both before and after this calculated fertility time not only *hours,* for conception not to take place.

Standard Time must be used in all calculations.

When the transiting Sun is in the third house, intercourse should take place between midnight and 2 a.m.

When the transiting Sun is in the second house, intercourse should take place between 2 and 4 a.m.

When the transiting Sun is in the first house, intercourse should take place between 4 and 6 a.m.

When the transiting Sun is in the twelfth house, intercourse should take place between 6 and 8 a.m.

When the transiting Sun is in the eleventh house, intercourse should take place between 8 and 10 a.m.

When the transiting Sun is in the tenth house, intercourse should take place between 10 a.m. and 12 noon.

When the transiting Sun is in the ninth house, intercourse should take place between 12 noon and 2 p.m.

When the transiting Sun is in the eighth house, intercourse should take place between 2 and 4 p.m.

When the transiting Sun is in the seventh house, intercourse should take place between 4 and 6 p.m.

When the transiting Sun is in the sixth house, intercourse should take place between 6 and 8 p.m.

When the transiting Sun is in the fifth house, intercourse should take place between 8 and 10 p.m.

When the transiting Sun is in the fourth house, intercourse should take place between 10 p.m. and 12 midnight.

While some of these timings seem to be inappropriate, most couples with fertility problems would be willing to put up with these inconveniences in order to achieve pregnancy.

Example of how to set up an Intercourse Time Chart for a woman:

Birth date: May 30, 1963
Birth time: 8 a.m. EDT, or 7 a.m. EST. (Always use Standard Time only.)
Birth place: New York City, NY. Latitude 40N43.
The Sun is at 08 Gemini 22 and the Moon is at 11 Virgo 43.

1. Find the Sun/Moon fertility angle — that is, how many degrees of longitude has the Moon traveled away from the Sun, in a counter-clockwise direction, since the last new Moon position?

The Sun, at 08 Gemini 22, equals 68 degrees and 22 minutes. The Moon, at 11 Virgo 43, equals 161 degrees and 43 minutes. When we subtract the lower number from the higher we get a difference of 93 degrees and 21 minutes. Therefore, the Sun/Moon fertility angle = 93 degrees and 21 minutes, or simply, 93 degrees. Check with fertility tables of May 30, 1963, in back of book.

2. Find the Sun/Moon midpoint by dividing the fertility angle in half. 93 degrees divided by 2 = 46 and 1/2 degrees, or 47 degrees. Add this quotient to the longitude of the Sun, which, in this case is 68 degrees, and we get a sum of 115 degrees, or 25 degrees of Cancer.

3. Therefore, 25 Cancer becomes the Ascendant sign and degree for the Intercourse Time Chart of this particular woman.

4. Since this woman still resides in New York City, the place of her birth, the latitude which is used to find the house cusps in the tables of houses is still 40N43. With latitude 40N43 intersecting with Ascendant sign and degree of 25 Cancer, we have a midheaven of 9 Aries and the intermediate house cusps as shown in Figure 12.

5. Figure 12. Intercourse Time Chart for woman born on May 30, 1963.

6. What would be this young woman's fertility date for January, 1983?

It would have to be on a day when the Sun and Moon are approximately 93 degrees apart, the Moon going in a counter-clockwise direction from the Sun after the new Moon, when both were in the same degree of longitude for that month.

As we go down the days of the month in a noon ephemeris, stop at January 22, 1983. The Sun is approximately at 2 degrees Aquarius and the Moon is at 5

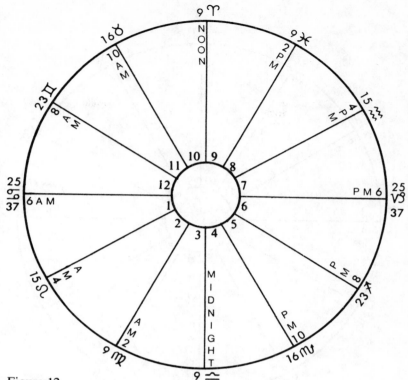

5. Figure 12.
Intercourse Time Chart for Woman born May 30, 1963
Latitude — 40N43
Ascendant — 25♋37

degrees Taurus, or 93 degrees apart. Therefore, January 22, 1983 is this woman's fertility day for the month of January, 1983, to be used if she wished to conceive a child, to be avoided if she did not. Again, see Tables for January 22nd, 1983, in back of book to verify these calculations.

Now, what would be her fertility *time* on this day of January 22?

7. Set up this woman's Intercourse Time Chart and place the Sun at 2 degrees Aquarius in its proper house according to sign as in Figure 13. The Sun, at 2 degrees Aquarius, is in the seventh house. Therefore, intercourse should take place between 4 and 6 p.m. on January 22, 1983, because, according to our experimental method, this is the most fertile day and time of day for this month for this woman *astrologically*. If she wishes to become pregnant she should have intercourse at this time on this day. If she wishes to avoid pregnancy, then she should abstain from sexual relations for a few days before and after this day of January 22, 1983.

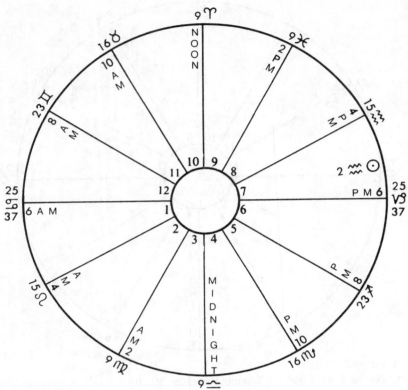

7. Figure 13.
Intercourse Time Chart with Sun
for January 22, 1983

Each month, the Sun of the Sun/Moon angle will be in a different sign and house. For our example woman above, when the Sun, during the month of June, is at 7 Gemini and the Moon is at 10 Virgo, the Sun will be in the eleventh house of her Intercourse Time Chart. For optimum fertility, according to our experimental system, intercourse should take place between 8 and 10 a.m.

Again, for our example woman, when the Sun, during the month of December, is at 7 Sagittarius and the Moon is at 10 Pisces, the Sun will be in the fifth house of her Intercourse Time Chart. For optimum fertility, intercourse should take place between 8 and 10 p.m. To avoid pregnancy — avoid these times.

Look back now to Figure 5, Claire's intercourse chart. The Sun is in the fifth house — the 8 to 10 p.m. house. Intercourse took place at approximately 8:30 p.m.

40

Remember, this is experimental research work based on only one chart — Claire's. It is not guaranteed to work. However, because all areas of Claire's chart dovetailed so conclusively, we feel we have a case worth studying and experimenting with.

We want to know:

Might this Intercourse Time Chart not give us an added edge in fertility planning? We invite you to test this theory.

Let us go back now and examine Claire's intercourse chart, Figure 5, in its wholeness. What was so potent about that moment in time for her?

The Moon, the mother principle, is at 14 Cancer, strongly placed in the sign of the mother and in its rulership, in the eleventh house of hopes and wishes, and in the house of the husband's children, being the fifth house from the seventh. Claire wished for a child. This Moon is trine — aspect for ease and harmony — to Mars, the male principle, here placed in Scorpio, also in the sign of its rulership, of sex and deep emotional involvement. Both are fertile water signs. With this same Moon confronting, conjuncting, and collaborating with Uranus, should we be surprised that a surprise was in the offing?

Mars, at 17 Scorpio, the male sex symbol, is sextile (opportunity) Venus at 24 Capricorn, the female sex symbol, placed in the fifth house of children. Venus in the fifth house begets children. Venus is also closely conjunct the Sun at 27 Capricorn, the Giver of Life. The aura of romance and charm indigenous to Venus, the Goddess of Love, is enhanced at this time — compliments of the close conjunctions to this planet from the North Node and Mercury. To express one's self emotionally becomes easy.

The logical Virgo Ascendant and the reasoning Gemini mid-heaven are both ruled by Mercury — the planet of the mind and ideas. The most powerful thought Claire had in mind at that time was to start a new life. The houses of personality and career wanted to find completion and satisfaction in procreating a child.

The Sun is supposedly not fertile in the fifth house, but here it is conjunct Venus, Mercury and the protective North Node, all in Capricorn, a fertile earth sign. The strong sense of purpose, which is the quality of Capricorn, helped in the accomplishment of Claire's deep desire. It is that grouping of three planets and the North Node in the fifth house of children that stands out in this intercourse chart because, as in Claire's natal chart, it is the only tenanted house on the western side of the chart. This grouping is square Neptune, here ruler of the seventh house of the marriage partner, and opposite the Moon/Uranus/ South Node conjunctions in the eleventh house, ruler of the husband's fertility. The husband was satisfied with his family of two children just as it was.

However, that seventh house cusp, Pisces, signifying the husband, is also ruled by Jupiter which is elevated and trine Neptune; and both Jupiter and Neptune are sextile Pluto, ruler here of the mental third house. He could be persuaded. Jupiter, as ruler of Sagittarius, also rules the fourth house, the end of the matter, and the trine to Neptune and sextile to Pluto bring the benefits of harmony, receptivity and integration.

It is important to realize, that as this intercourse chart represents the transiting planets as they appeared in the heavens at that particular time, they were there, as is, for everyone on our planet. However, they meant something different to each person. Some people used them, some didn't, and each for a different purpose according to how they aspected the planets in each birth chart. In Claire's chart of nativity, the emphasis was surely on herself and her husband in an attitude of awareness: Moon/Uranus/South Node, all in Cancer in Claire's first house, signifying herself, opposite the North Node/Venus/Sun/Mercury in Capricorn in the seventh house of the husband. And all the while, transiting Jupiter at 17 Gemini, stationed overhead, was radiating blessings upon Claire's own Gemini Sun and her husband's Sun, being trine both from the sign, Aquarius. You may find it interesting to apply these planets to Claire's husband's natal chart. His birth date is February 14 or 15, 1921, time unknown.

Katie, the result of that special moment in time, is, as are all of Claire's children, aside from the flaws common to all fallen human nature, the answer to any parent's prayer. Dubbed *Golden Girl* by her siblings because even as a child she was thoughtful, responsible, and caring (natal Ascendant in Capricorn), Katie is now a loving wife and mother, and a compassionate, dedicated Registered Nurse (natal Moon in her tenth house).

Before leaving our three inter-related charts, let us pause for a moment to absorb their comforting implications. Has Katie not shown us that each of our conceptions and birth times was not an accidental occurrence, but a precise moment decreed by a Master Planner? Are we not then, each and every one of us, special? We must be.

Sex Determination:

Another revolutionary theory of Dr. Jonas concerns sex determination of the fetus at the time of conception. He believed that the sign the Moon is in at the time of conception will determine the sex of the child. If the Moon is in a positive sign — Aries, Gemini, Leo, Libra, Sagittarius, or Aquarius — a male child will be born. If the Moon is in a negative sign — Taurus, Cancer, Virgo, Scorpio, Capricorn, or Pisces — a female child will be born. In Claire's intercourse chart, the Moon was at 14 degrees Cancer — a negative sign — and a girl baby was born.

Still, this was intercourse time — not conception time. As stated previously, it takes some hours for the sperm to penetrate and fertilize the egg. One must take into consideration not only the sign and degree of the Moon at the time of intercourse, but must add on sperm travel time and sperm capacitation time to make sure that the Moon is still in the desired masculine or feminine sign. Remember, the Moon travels forward approximately 1 degree every 2 hours. Those couples who would want to make extra sure that the Moon sign doesn't change, should choose a month when the Moon, in proper relationship to the Sun, is in an early degree of the desired sign.

Also, sperm, after intercourse, can lie in waiting for two or more days to fertilize an upcoming egg. The Moon, from intercourse time to fertility action, may have changed signs, because it does so approximately every 2 and 1/2 days; and when it changes signs, it always goes from positive (male) to negative (female), or from negative to positive. Unless a woman uses the fertility angle date, she will not know exactly when the egg is released and is waiting to be fertilized.

Much, much more research must be done in this area. Truthfully, the sex of the baby is relatively unimportant. All that most couples want is a healthy baby. There are astrological rules for fetus viability, but they go beyond the scope of this book. Ridiculous as the following may sound, we urge all astrologers to impress upon their clients that we are attempting to pinpoint fertility dates *only,* and cannot be held responsible for any imperfectly formed or diseased babies who might be born as a result of our calculations.

Couples must also realize that infertility which is caused by tubal blockage in either male or female, wherein egg and sperm cannot meet, cannot be helped by astrological timing until the blockage is corrected.

Now that we know how Katie's particular conception occurred astrologically, we should study how *every* conception occurrs biologically. . . .

Chapter IV
The Physical Aspects of Reproduction

By first studying reproduction and its ramifications from an astrological point of view, we have really placed the cart before the horse. Although we have seen how the modern woman can juggle career, marriage, and motherhood, have maternal instinct, be fertile, sidestep difficulties in pregnancy, produce the desired number of children of predetermined sex, and limit the size of her family by means of astrological knowledge in astrological birth control, or ABC, we must now come down from the heavens and look to our earthly, physical bodies. So, let's get back to Claire.

Some years ago, when she was awaiting the birth of her first child, a friend was expecting hers at the same time. June 19 was their approximate due date. June 19 came and went, as did June 20 and 21, and so on until the end of the month arrived. Still they waited. A neighbor, older and wiser than they, shook her head, and expressing an old-wives'-tale view, commented knowingly, "You must both now wait for the next full moon before your babies can be born." Why, that wouldn't be until July 10, Claire and her friend discovered as they hurriedly consulted a calendar!

Well, the neighbor was wrong. But another belief did hold true. One often hears that a child is born either 2 weeks before or 2 weeks after the due delivery date. The friend delivered her baby on July third, while Claire's child, who loves attention, firecrackers and parades, George M. Cohan songs, and James Cagney in *Yankee Doodle Dandy,* made her patriotic appearance on a hot, humid, 96 degree Fourth of July! (With the transiting Sun at 12 degrees Cancer exactly on Claire's Ascendant, the era of childbearing, which was to last until October 31, 1959, had begun.)

And yet, how could Claire have minded those two extra weeks of growing bigger, and fatter, and rounder, and clumsier when now, on her baby's special day, all of America joins in the celebration of her child's birth? At first, Baby, as spirited as a Roman candle herself, really did think that the festivities were all for her. And, in a way, she was right. But it wasn't until years later that Claire realized how important to each individual is his particular time, place, and date of birth, and how deserving he is of a big, brass band to announce his arrival!

And the woman's full Moon story — what was that all about? Could a woman know for herself, by studying her body, such things as ovulation dates, conception dates, and exact delivery dates? Were there tell-tale signs that could initiate each woman into the mystery that is her body? "The same God who gives us the rising and setting Sun, the new and full Moon, and the rebirth of springtime each year, must also have given order to the human body," thought Claire, with conviction. She realized that it would be up to her to discover this regularity. In order to fully understand this precision, Claire would first have to become acquainted with the basic physiology of human reproduction.

Knowing that fundamentals are very important, Claire searched for books that would be thorough, yet easy to understand. The books from which she studied, and which will be listed in their entirety in the *Bibliography* are as follows:

1. *The Ovulation Method — Natural Family Planning,* by John J. Billings, M.D.,

2. *The Art of Natural Family Planning,* by John and Sheila Kippley,

3. *It's Your Body,* by Niels Lauersen, M.D. and Steven Whitney,

4. *Anatomy and Physiology A SELF INSTRUCTIONAL COURSE,* by Ralph Richards and David F. Chapman, and

5. *How to Get Pregnant,* by Sherman J. Silber, M.D.

Adding an astrological slant, in the following pages and in a simplified manner, we will study what Claire has learned. As we discuss the male and female reproductive organs and the cycle of reproduction, we will attach to each its astrological rulership.

The rulerships given have been taken from, *The Rulership Book,* by Rex E. Bills. We are grateful for his thorough and competent work. Accordingly, we have assigned planets, signs, and houses to the different reproductive organs and functions. Mr. Bills, in some instances, has designated the rulerships in parentheses as being tentative. If each astrologer would research these rulerships more thoroughly, we should, in time, be able to dispense with the parentheses altogether.

The Gonads:

A gland is an organ in the body whose main function is to produce a biologically useful substance. The endocrine glands are the ductless glands in the male and female body which produce hormones for the different activities of the body. These hormones go to all the cells in the body by means of the blood stream. Endocrine glands, in general, are astrologically ruled by (the Sun, Mars, Scorpio, and Libra). The hormones, or chemical messengers, are under control of the anterior pituitary gland, are ruled by Uranus and Saturn, and are released upon demand.

The endocrine glands used in reproduction are the *gonads* which control sexual development and function. The gonads are as follows:

1. the *ovaries* in the female — ruled by Venus, Libra, the seventh house, (the Moon, Cancer, and Scorpio). The left ovary is ruled by (the Moon), and the right ovary is ruled by (the Sun).

2. the *testes* (testicles) in the male — ruled by Scorpio, Pluto, and Mars. The left testicle is ruled by (the Moon), and the right testicle is ruled by (the Sun).

In order to reproduce we need:

1. The male, to produce germ cells, or sperm. This virility is ruled in the male by the Sun and Mars.

2. The female, to produce eggs. This fertility is ruled in the female by the Moon and Venus.

3. The act to transfer the germ cells, or sperm, from the male to the female for fertilization of the egg — sexual intercourse — ruled by the fifth house, Pluto, Scorpio, Mars, and Venus.

4. The special place in the female for development of the embryo — the uterus or womb — ruled by the Moon, Cancer, the fourth house, (Scorpio and Venus).

Cycle of Reproduction:

1. Each month between the menstrual period — ruled by the Moon and Scorpio — an egg (ovum), ruled by Venus, is released from the ovary. This is called ovulation. Ovaries and ovulation are ruled by the seventh house, Venus, Libra, (Moon, Cancer, and Scorpio).

2. The egg is picked up by the fallopian tube — ruled by (Libra).

3. In the tube it may be fertilized — ruled by the Moon and (Venus) — by a sperm, the male germ cell, ruled by Venus, (Jupiter and Sun).

4. Spermatozoa (Sperm) are developed in the testes of the male — ruled by Scorpio, Pluto and Mars.

5. Several hundred million sperm are deposited in the female's upper vagina during sexual intercourse — ruled by the fifth house, Pluto, Scorpio, Mars and Venus.

6. The sperm swim through the neck of the womb (cervix) — ruled by Scorpio — then through the cavity of the womb and into the tubes.

7. If fertilization occurs, the fertilized egg passes into the cavity of the uterus — ruled by the Moon, Cancer, the fourth house, Venus and (Scorpio) — where it sinks into the thick lining prepared for it.

8. The embryo develops. In approximately 38 weeks the developed baby is expelled. This is childbirth and it is ruled by the Moon.

9. If fertilization does not occur, the lining of the uterus is shed approximately 14 days after ovulation. This shedding is the menstrual period — ruled by the Moon and Scorpio.

46

The Male Sex Organs:

1. Testes (testicles) — which produce sperm. The testes are ruled by Scorpio, Pluto and Mars. They lie in the scrotum.

2. Scrotum — the organ which contains the testes. The scrotum is ruled by Scorpio.

3. Penis — organ of intercourse — ruled by Scorpio, Pluto and Mars.

4. Sperm, the male sex cells, — ruled by Venus, (Jupiter and Sun). The sperm travel through tubes where they are added to secretions from glands and thus semen is formed.

5. Semen — the impregnating fluid that contains the sperm, the male source of life, — ruled by (Jupiter and Venus). Semen is ejaculated from the male sex organ, the penis, — ruled by Pluto, Scorpio and Mars.

During sexual intercourse, about 300 million sperm are ejaculated into the female genital tract. Sexual intercourse is ruled by the fifth house, Pluto, Scorpio, Mars and Venus. Reception of semen into the womb is ruled by (Moon).

The Female Sex Organs:

1. Ovaries — the primary sex organs which produce the eggs, — ruled by the seventh house, Venus, Libra, (Moon, Cancer, and Scorpio). The female sex hormones secreted by the ovaries are progesterone and estrogen which produce the female sex cell, the ova.

2. Ova — the eggs produced by the ovaries — ruled by Venus.

3. Fallopian tubes, the tubes attached to the uterus, — are ruled by (Libra). When an egg (ovum) is released by the ovary in which it is formed, it is picked up and then travels along in the fallopian tube. Here, if sperm are present, the egg may be fertilized.

4. Uterus (womb) — the organ in which the fertilized egg becomes embedded and develops. It is ruled by the Moon, Cancer, the fourth house and Venus. According to H.L. Cornell, M.D. in *Encyclopaedia of Medical Astrology* (and here we quote):

　a) chronic womb trouble is shown astrologically by Saturn afflicted in Cancer or Scorpio in the eighth house,

　b) defects of the womb are shown by afflictions in Scorpio,

　c) deformity of the womb is shown by Uranus afflicted in Scorpio, and

　d) disorders of the womb can be shown by: Venus afflicted in Aries or Scorpio; Venus afflicted by challenging aspects; Venus in Scorpio and afflicting the Moon or the Ascendant; the Sun or Moon afflicted in Scorpio; or the Sun afflicted in Pisces.''

5. Cervix — the neck or entrance to the womb (uterus) — ruled by Scorpio. Its position, its dilation, and its secretions give clues to monthly fertility.

6. Vagina — the tube which leads to the outside and through which the baby passes during the birth process. It is also the receptacle for the penis to deposit semen during intercourse. It is ruled by Pluto, Scorpio, and (Venus).

7. Breasts — the mammary glands which supply milk to the newborn baby — ruled by the Moon, Cancer, the fourth house and Venus.

The Menstrual Cycle — ruled by the Moon and Scorpio:
1. The wall of the uterus has a vascular lining called the endometrium.
2. Each month it undergoes changes to prepare itself in the eventuality that a fertilized egg should embed itself therein.
3. The cycle lasts approximately one month.
4. If a fertilized egg attaches itself to this lining, the lining becomes food for the embryo.
5. If there is no fertilized egg, the lining disintegrates and is shed in what is known as the monthly period, wherein there is a loss of blood from the uterus.
6. The ovarian hormones are in charge of this bleeding and are also in charge of building up the endometrium again for the following month and another fertilized egg.
7. Irregularity of menses is ruled by the Moon, Scorpio, and (Taurus). Excessive menses is ruled by (Mars).

Claire's menstrual periods, for many years, were irregular. Astrologically, this was probably due to the natal Moon at 29 Scorpio square Neptune at 24 Leo.

Ovulation, — ruled by Venus, Libra, the seventh house, (the Moon, Cancer, and Scorpio):
1. All females are born with their full supply of eggs already contained in the ovary. Each month one egg ripens.
2. Each egg is surrounded by cells forming a follicle.
3. Each month one follicle ripens, is now called a graafian follicle, and is a mass of cells which surrounds the ripened egg.
4. This graafian follicle produces hormones, enlarges, and then bursts to release the enclosed egg, which is then taken up into the fallopian tubes.
5. The graafian follicle then collapses, changes into a yellow substance called the corpus luteum, which secretes the hormones, progesterone and estrogen, for the next 7 to 10 days only.
6. If the egg is fertilized, it goes into the uterus and feeds on the endometrium.
7. If the egg is not fertilized, the follicle then disintegrates.
8. The hormones then stop being secreted, the endometrium breaks down, and menstruation begins.

Fertilization — ruled by the Moon and (Venus):

1. It takes 15 to 20 seconds for the egg, released from the ovary, to be grasped into the fallopian tube.

2. It takes approximately 5 minutes for the egg to be transported from the entrance of the tube to the region halfway toward the uterus. Here the egg sits and waits.

3. After the egg is released from the ovary (ovulation), it is only *fresh and capable of being fertilized* for 6 to 8 hours; *or* 24 hours; *or* 48 hours. *INFOR-MATION VARIES ON THIS VERY VITAL POINT.* The middle of the road — around 24 hours — is the time factor to which we shall adhere.

4. If the egg is not penetrated by sperm soon after ovulation — about 24 hours — it becomes over-ripe and dies.

5. During intercourse, about 300 million sperm cells are ejaculated by the male into the female genital tract. Sexual intercourse is ruled by the fifth house, Pluto, Scorpio, Mars and Venus. Sex force and sex energy are ruled by the eighth house, Pluto, Scorpio, Mars, and (the fifth house). Female sex organs are ruled by Pluto, Scorpio, the eighth house, and Venus. Male sex organs are ruled by Pluto, Scorpio, the eighth house, and Mars.

6. About one million sperm of the 300 million swim through the cervix, where mucus is thinned by hormonal activity during ovulation.

7. A few hours later, a few hundred sperm out of the one million sperm reach the upper fallopian tube.

8. Once sperm enter the canal of the cervix they are capable of fertilizing the egg for as long as 48 hours.

9. Sperm may live for up to 6 days, but they seem capable of fertilizing the egg for only *two days (48 hours)* after intercourse.

10. Since the egg is only fertilizable for 6 to 8 hours, *or* 24 hours, *or* 48 hours after ovulation, it is important to have a continuing flow of sperm across the fallopian tube, so that whenever the egg reaches the area, there will be sperm available.

The Importance of Cervical Mucus to Fertilization:

Study cervical mucus carefully. It may be as important an ingredient in Astrological Birth Control as it is in Natural Birth Control. Secretions of the body are ruled by the Moon and Saturn, while the *flow* of secretions is ruled by the Moon.

The cervix — the entrance to the uterus — produces a secretion called cervical musuc, a thick, clear, alkaline liquid which regulates the entrance of sperm into the uterus. There is only a very short, precise, biological interval during every month when a woman's cervical mucus is of the proper texture to permit sperm invasion. During the entire rest of the month, her cervical mucus presents a solid barrier to sperm penetration, according to books which Claire has researched. Therefore, let us take a very close look at cervical mucus because it is a key component to fertility. Its presence or absence, and its consistency, tells us when fertilization is a possibility or not.

The vagina is acid in nature and hostile to sperm. The semen which contains the sperm is alkaline, so the sperm must hurry through the acidy vagina to get to the safe, alkaline, cervical mucus in order to survive. Any sperm that have not gained access to cervical mucus within one-half hour of entrance into the vagina will not be able to do so later.

Facts to know about cervical mucus:

1. The amount is scanty just before and just after menstruation.

2. Within four days after the menstrual period has ceased, the cervical mucus gradually becomes more abundant until the time of ovulation.

3. At the time when ovulation is about to occur, the mucus is very, very abundant, and becomes optically clear, or transparent.

4. When fertilization becomes possible — that is, up to approximately 24 hours after ovulation — the cervical mucus is *very stretchy* and unbreakable.

Therefore, all of the changes in cervical mucus which occur around mid-cycle, or ovulation time, are designed to help sperm gain access to the womb. These are, once again — please review them carefully —

1. very liquidy mucus,

2. transparent mucus — admits the passage of light and can see objects through it,

3. very stretchable, unbreakable mucus, and

4. very abundant mucus.

All of the above symptoms tell us that an egg is available. All of these symptoms tell us that it is favorable for a sperm to swim to the egg, penetrate it, and fertilize it.

In natural birth control — to *prevent* sperm entrance up the uterus and into the tubes — we would need just the opposite condition of cervical mucus:

1. thick, sticky mucus,

2. translucent mucus — which admits the passage of light but one cannot see objects through it,

3. breakable mucus — not stretchy, and

4. scanty mucus.

Sperm swim through the cervical mucus at the speed of one-eighth of an inch per minute. Consequently, sperm can travel 4 inches and reach the fallopian tubes in approximately 32 minutes. Once sperm reach the opening to the tubes, they are detained and only slowly are allowed to enter in small numbers.

While travelling the above route, sperm undergo a process called *capacitation,* a period of time of several hours required by sperm to be outside the male reproductive tract before they are capable of fertilizing the egg. During this time they shed a surface coat of inhibiting factors which would otherwise prevent egg penetration.

The ovum (egg) is surrounded by cells and a thin membrane. Only one sperm cell is allowed to penetrate this membrane, fuse with the egg, and thereby fertilize it. The fertilized egg divides again and again, and travels through the fallopian tube to the uterus, where 5 to 7 days later it implants itself into the endometrium — the rich, nutritious, uterine lining. There it develops. Birth occurs about 38 weeks after fertilization of the ovum, that is, about 40 weeks after the last menstruation.

Remember — the time during which an egg in the female can be fertilized after it is ovulated is a brief 24 hours (varies up to 48 hours). Therefore, it must be fertilized promptly after its release from the ovary. Sperm, once deposited in the female tract, are capable of surviving 2 to 4 days (maybe even up to 6 days), but seem to be capable of impregnating the egg for only 2 days or 48 hours.

In a general way, we have tried to give you the highlights of physical reproduction. And yet, if you have read this chapter carefully, questions must be forming in your mind, as they were in Claire's. And, right off the bat, we seem to be in trouble! To repeat two key sentences:

1. There is only a very short, precise interval during every month when a woman's cervical mucus is of the proper texture to permit sperm invasion.

2. During the *entire rest of the month* her cervical mucus represents a solid barrier to sperm entrance.

We have a credibility problem here, and a contradiction. In a previous chapter we stated, that according to Dr. Jonas, one egg — in addition to, and independent of the natural periodic egg released each month — is also released each month during a woman's astrological Sun/Moon fertility phase angle. Are then two eggs released each month? And two buildups of the proper consistency of cervical mucus? Science says *no*.

Astrological rulings say that secretions of the body are under the dominion of Saturn and the Moon, and that the *flow* of secretions is ruled by the Moon. Then, could not the Moon, at the time of its fertility angle, independently of the natural order, start the proper flow of cervical mucus of the right consistency to provide sperm with its appropriate environment to live and travel up to a waiting egg? An egg which would also be released independently of the natural cycle because the ovaries are ruled, not only by Venus, but also by a Moon which is in fertility angle to the Sun?

In Claire's case, she neglected to record one valuable piece of information, that is, at what point she was in her natural monthly cycle, when this special intercourse took place, which resulted in the birth of Katie. We don't know if the egg which was released at that time of intercourse came from Claire's natural cycle or the fertility angle cycle. Maybe they occurred simultaneously. We do know that Claire's fertility angle coincided with the transiting Sun/Moon angle. Astrologically, an egg should have been released, and it was.

The precise and accurate synchronization of that mother — intercourse — baby trio of charts does prove that something special was going on; something that still fills us with wonder. Hopefully, we can combine the fertility lessons learned in astrological birth control via these 3 charts, with the natural biological fertility rhythm of natural family planning, the secrets of which we will unfold, if you will now follow along. . . .

Chapter V
Natural Birth Control

We all remember the amoeba from grammar or high school biology class — that one-celled animal which reproduces itself by merely dividing itself in half. Now we have two amoebas. Simple. But when it came to the higher animals and man, God to put it quite bluntly and disrespectfully, was rather diabolical. He made it complicated. We call this complication — *sex*. He decreed that there must be a union of two of the species, one male and one female, to reproduce the third new member. Problems.

Then, in order to insure the continuity of the species, in order to make certain that the male and the female would come together, He made it pleasurable. Very. More problems. Too much pleasure produces too many children, and so, humans needed to discover methods of lessening the number of children without decreasing the moments of pleasure. Enter birth prevention. Enter birth control.

Birth prevention physically denies life. It does it by abortion, by sterilization, by chemicals, and by mechanical devices.

Birth control, instead, regulates life. By intelligently following the natural laws of God and the astrological rulings of the universe, natural birth control — NBC — and astrological birth control — ABC — either limit the number of children to that which a couple can responsibly physically, emotionally, and materially care for, *or* aid in the conception of children by timing intercourse to the biologically and astrologically fertile periods in a woman's body.

Having already discussed ABC in the preceding chapter, it is time now to become familiar with the very positive and upbeat practice of natural birth control — NBC — also called natural family planning, or NFP. To be effective, ABC can never be used alone when a woman does not wish to conceive. It must always be used in conjunction with NBC or NFP.

In this book we can present only the highlights of natural family planning. The woman who really wants to practice it must first become acquainted with the rules of this system and then apply them to her own unique, physical body. She should also consult her obstetrician/gynecologist as well before using this means of family planning.

The following books are very thorough, are most helpful, and should be studied:

1. *The Art of Natural Family Planning,* by John and Sheila Kippley. It is published by: The Couple to Couple League International, Inc., P.O. Box

11084, Cincinnati, Ohio 45211. Please write to this address for information concerning this book and for a free copy of their newsletter.

2. *The Ovulation Method — Natural Family Planning,* by John J. Billings. It is published by: The Liturgical Press, Collegeville, Minnesota.

Natural family planning or natural birth control is based upon the fact that ovulation occurs approximately 2 weeks prior to the following menstruation. From this knowledge, the sympto-thermal method of NFP or NBC has been devised.

In other words, this method is based upon the fact that every woman has a periodic cycle, usually about one month long, within which she becomes naturally fertile and then becomes naturally infertile. There are certain bodily signs that occur just before, during and after the fertile phase of the cycle. The couple must learn what these signs are, recognize them, and interpret them correctly. It is very easy once you know exactly what to look for, but it takes commitment on the part of both parties. Hormones secreted by the pituitary gland and ovaries cause the changes in the menstrual and fertility cycles which signify to us when a woman can become pregnant.

A woman notes the following changes in her body:

1. In the cervical mucus — the most important change, and one already discussed in the preceding chapter.

2. In the cervix — the firm, cylindrical, one-inch long organ with a small opening which is the neck or entrance to the uterus from the vagina.

a) Before ovulation it is firm, closed, and easy to reach.

b) At ovulation it is soft, open, raised, and harder to reach.

c) After ovulation it firms up again, closes, and lowers. With practice and observation, the woman becomes adept at noting these changes.

3. In the temperature rise. After the ovarian follicle has ejected its ovum (ovulation), it releases the hormone, progesterone, which causes the woman's basal body temperature to rise slightly, or four-tenths of one degree. The woman takes her temperature each morning and notes its rise and fall according to the fertility temperature rules as stated in the above mentioned books.

Of all of these changes — mucus, cervix and temperature rise — the presence of healthy, cervical mucus is the most important factor in the determination of biological fertility.

To put it another way, natural birth control depends upon the fact that the female has a biological, monthly fertility cycle of:

1. preovulatory infertility (relative infertility),

2. the fertile time, and

3. post ovulation infertility (absolutely infertile from the biological standpoint). *Remember, however, that you can have astrological fertility at this time, just as you can have astrological fertility during the menstrual period.*

To describe the above three steps:

1. Preovulatory infertility begins with the first day of menstruation.
2. The fertile time begins approximately mid-way between the menstrual cycle when'
   a) cervical mucus is copious, transparent, and stretchy,
   b) the cervix is high, open, and soft, and
   c) just before the temperature goes up.
3. Post ovulatory infertility begins when:
   a) the cervical mucus is drying up and becomes tacky, breakable, and translucent,
   b) the cervix closes, lowers, and becomes firm, and
   c) the temperature is up.

While the egg after ovulation is capable of being fertilized for approximately only 24 hours, the sperm can live for up to 6 days in the genital tract, although supposedly capable of fertilizing an egg for only 2 of those days. Therefore, to safely prevent conception, intercourse must not take place for a few days *preceding* ovulation as well as for at least two to three days after ovulation.

By carefully monitoring her body and studying its signals, a woman will know when she is fertile and when she is not. When she uses this information correctly she will successfully be practicing natural birth control. Natural family planning or natural birth control is not a slap-dash affair. If one expects it to work effectively, its rules must be studied carefully, and applied properly. Teaching couples are available through the Couple to Couple League. They will competently answer all of your questions, put you in touch with other couples practicing natural family planning, tell you about their own experiences, and then encourage you to follow suit. (See above for address.)

This group of teaching couples has grown tremendously within the past few years. The organization sends out newsletters and periodicals to keep one abreast of current findings and new advances, and has an impressive book list of related subjects which it will send upon request. The Couple to Couple League is nonsectarian, and is really a very worthwhile group with which to keep in contact, for they seem to handle the job of naturally controlling births very well — even without astrological birth control — although, according to an article in the *Daily News* of February 12, 1984, the failure rate for NFP ranges from 2 to 25 percent. Therefore, we believe that by incorprating ABC into the NFP or NBC system, a safer and more effective method of natural birth control can be achieved.

The question remains: Why bother with all of this extra work when we have abortion, pills, sterilization, spermicides and mechanical devices that do a similar job of preventing and controlling birth — only, most people think — even more effectively? And, in another line of reasoning, aside from the possible unsureness of complete protection, there are the arguments against natural family planning from the perspective of romance. "Where's the spontaneity?", ask our adversaries. "Who wants to plot and plan!", they complain.

Think about it. When you were married, did you have even a small celebration? If so, didn't you make reception arrangements a year or more in advance, book the band, select the gown, choose your attendants, and decide on flower arrangements months ahead of time? Wasn't the honeymoon trip planned down to the last detail? Did such purposeful planning detract from your wedding night? Didn't the anticipation *add* to your fulfillment rather than diminish it?

A marriage using natural and astrological birth control may be kept busy constructing and figuring out charts, reading thermometers, and watching for changes in the female body; but it will never grow dull, never become stale, never lose its edge as it ebbs and flows, loses sex and then regains it. Such a marriage can remain young and vital forever. That's a pretty good side effect, wouldn't you say?

It is only the impatient and the immature who cannot see the logic and usefulness of this program. Inherent in the marriage vows is the obligation of each partner to help the other develop greater faith in God, greater faith in himself, increased self control, and a more mature sense of responsibility. Employing NBC and ABC will help the couple achieve objectives such as these as each member gives to the other the gifts of patience, consideration, and true friendship.

Complete success for such a way of life, however, rests, in the main, with the woman. It is she who is the everchanging Moon; she who keeps the timetable and regulates the tempo of the marriage; she who must unselfishly nurture the results of love. The struggle against selfishness within ourselves never ceases, just as wars among nations continue in never ending sequence. "The safest course," Mahatma Gandhi, pacifist leader of India's struggle for independence, told his followers, "is to believe in the moral government of the world and, therefore, in the *supremacy of the moral law (the natural law), the law of truth and love. . . .*"

Let's stop right here at the word *love* and try to define it. . . .

Chapter VI
Astrological Love Symbols

In our discussions on fertility we gave the stars first billing. Then we retraced our steps to examine human reproduction. Now, to retreat even further and start at the very beginning, we would like to presuppose that before we have sex, there is *love*.

Love means different things to different people, but basically there are three types:

1. Erotic or sexual love. It is unabashedly biological, glandular, and instinctive. It is an animal, bodily sensation and here what we really love is the pleasure the other person can give us. Becuase it is the pleasure and not the person which is most important, the partners can easily be, and often are, replaced. This passionate, bodily love is ruled by Mars.

2. Philia love. We find this love in the pure love of young lovers, in true friendship, in the love of parents for their children, and in marriage where the partner is not only lover, but *best friend*. The young lover, the sincere friend, the sacrificing and loving parent, and the devoted husband or wife are each irreplaceable. This type of love is based on service and interest in the other person's welfare. The pure love of the young lovers is ruled by Venus, Libra, and the seventh house. Conjugal or married love is also ruled by Venus, Libra and the seventh house. Brotherly love is ruled by Uranus.

3. Agape love. This is God-love. God's inexhaustible love and concern for us spills over into our daily lives. As it flows from God to you, from you to me, and then back again to God, it becomes a purified, unselfish, self-sacrificing love — another example of the harmony of the trine. Agape love is ruled by Neptune — higher sacrificial love, and by Pluto — universal welfare.

Once this agape love came into existence, it embraced and illuminated the eros and the philia. The sensual, erotic love became the sensible expression of Divine Love, while the friendly philia became sanctified by this Divine Love. Therefore, complete and all-encompassing married love should possess all three kinds of love:

1. erotic — the passionate, physically satisfying, and attracting Mars love,

2. philia — in which there is mutual respect, admiration, and desire to serve an irreplaceable partner, ruled by Venus, Libra, and the seventh house, and

3. agape — in which, at times, we unselfishly place the partner's needs ahead of our own, for love of God; and wherein the couple sacrifices uninhibited sex in order to live by the natural law designed by God for its own good. Neptune and Pluto rule this type of love in our charts.

Love is supreme. Nevertheless, besides love, for a marriage to endure and grow, there must be harmonious interaction between the charts of husband and wife. There must be:

1. a meeting of the minds — ruled by Mercury,

2. agreement on basic values — ruled by Venus,

3. unity in feelings, attitudes, and emotions — ruled by the Moon,

4. similarity of habits — ruled by the Moon, and

5. sexual attraction — ruled by Mars and Venus.

It is rare and almost impossible to find total accord in all of the above areas, but basically that is what we should strive for. Once the relationship is on solid ground, the young husband and wife seek to expand their union. They realize that to reproduce themselves is a sacred trust, a holy choice. They have the privilege:

1. to bear children,

2. to deny their coming,

3. to limit their number,

4. to use different methods of increasing fertility,

5. to restrain their animal passions when necessary, and then

6. to joyfully respond to human love — at which moment Divine Love intervenes, the sacred triad of the Creator, Mars and Venus is completed, and a new life begins.

God, the Creator, Who was here all the while, has finally entered the picture. For those discerning readers who are interested, let us look into, for just a few minutes, the spiritual side of making a baby.

Because we are thus mindful of God, we already know the answer to the following question. . . .

Chapter VII
The Spiritual Aspects of Reproduction

How can the reproductive act, which is so physical, also be considered spiritual?

Reproduction is a series of biological processes and physical actions, and yet, because it is God who breathes Spirit into the fertilized egg, it is also a spiritual happening. And, as we consent to bear His children, we become co-producers with Him.

Is the astrologer qualified to speak of the spiritual aspects of reproduction, or to give a spiritual interpretation to any problems at all? As we reflect upon astrology's spiritual heritage, and read some of our spiritually oriented astrology books, we can draw inspiration from Alan Leo, Alan Oken, Isabel Hickey, Marc Edmund Jones, John Jocelyn, Dane Rudhyar, and other writers who perceive astrology to be a sacred science.

While being neither a man or a woman of the cloth nor a licensed physician, in his own particular context, the astrologer can preach the good news by encouraging others to live in harmony with God's natural laws, particularly in the field of birth control. There is even the far-out possibility that, in time, he might "heal the sick" through his attempts to aid those with infertility problems, by teaching couples to engage in sexual intercourse at those times of the month deemed fertile both physically and astrologically.

If people look to astrology to answer such spiritual questions as:
1. Why was I born?
2. What is my purpose?
3. What is my real personality? and
4. What are my true values and talents?

might they not also seek, through astrology, solutions to population control and infertility which would be in compliance with the spiritual laws of their Creator? If astrology has uncovered a celestial law — that of the relationship between the Sun and the Moon at each woman's birth which affects her fertility — is it not our duty to uncover it, to stand behind it, and to present it to the public once it has successfully passed the test of reliability?

Our own deep convictions can be backed up by Inez Eudora Perry, who, in *Part Two* of the astrology book, *The Zodiac and the Salts of Salvation,* published by Samuel Weiser, Inc., states that there are 3 stages to man — the animal, the human, and the spiritual, which she explains as follows:

1. The animal man lives in a state of *de-generation*. He co-habits solely for the sake of pleasurable sensation. The prefix, de, means to take away from generation. When we use abortion, sterilization, pills and devices to retain the pleasures of sex without the responsibilities of it, we are acting in a way of

taking away from generation or new life. In other words, we are acting *degenerately.*

2. The human man *generates* new life as he accepts parenthood. He engages in the sexual act not only for pleasure, but also so that a child might be conceived. He lives in the state called "generation" by doing nothing against the natural law to inhibit a new life. He also lives responsibly — using natural and astrological birth control — by accepting the number of children he can materially, mentally, and physically provide for.

3. The spiritual man lives a *re-generated* life. He gives up sex willingly — the priest, nun, and single person such as a teacher, doctor, or nurse — and devotes his entire life to helping others. Every child becomes his child. He attains the highest degree of efficiency in body and the greatest creativity of mind because all of his energy and strength is directed out of the sexual area and into the spiritual, for love of God, through people. He is living out agape love.

Does not Mahatma Gandhi come to mind? At a still vigorous age he renounced sex and material possessions to take on voluntary celibacy and poverty. As self-interest decreased, concern for the welfare of others increased. As carnality left him, so did self-centeredness.

When self-centeredness leaves, self-control enters. Self-control takes us back to Saturn, the taskmaster, the one which denies, but also the planet that can be our best friend. It is the planet which brings us face to face with ourselves — to make us better human beings. Self-control engenders trust, devotion and obedience from others. The man who can control himself becomes the *Master.* When we follow the spiritual laws of natural and astrological birth control, we too are following the paths of self-control and self-mastery.

Another book, *Initiation,* by Elizabeth Haich, published by George Allen and Unwin Ltd., London, while not strictly an astrology book, also has an interesting message concerning continence — that the energy not used sexually, if properly harnessed, can be used as healing energy or creative energy on a higher level. Married people who do not abuse their life-giving privileges, can consciously attain a degree of healing or creative capacity other than children. The use of natural/astrological birth control permits the alternating practice of both sexual activity and continence to continue side by side within the framework of the wife's fertility periods, allowing the best advantages of both worlds!

Living the natural law is a small price to pay for what we receive in return — peace of mind, the sparkle of health and increased creativity. How exciting to think that astrology is doing its share toward contributing to this natural way of life!

Yet, for all of our good intentions we do not always think correctly. Sometimes, through ignorance we do the wrong thing, as Claire did some years ago. . . .

60

Chapter VIII
Induced Birth

Claire was growing impatient. Her fourth baby was already one week overdue. Today was her study, inquisitive, second child's fifth birthday and Claire was hoping for a double celebration. Instinctively she felt, even without knowledge of astrology, that a shared day of birth, five years apart notwithstanding, would impart a mutual coloration to their personalities. What mother wouldn't want another upright, clear-headed, industrious, sober-faced, yet so loving a little fellow as the one she already had at home? But, all was quiet within.

The next morning Claire visited the doctor. "You're ready," he said, "so if you want to come to the hospital this evening, we'll induce (bring on artificially by means of drugs) the birth."

It would really be convenient. Claire could give the three kids an early supper, and then her brother-in-law would drive her to the hospital (Claire's husband would still be working), and then take the children home to his wife who would care for them during Claire's hospital stay. No rush, no last minute upheavals, no pain-punctuated drive on icy streets through obstructing city traffic!

The doctor was waiting at the hospital, annoyed that Claire hadn't come earlier than her 7 p.m. arrival. A vein in her arm sipped a magic potion and at 10:35 p.m., on January 8, 1957, EST, the future M.D., Michael, came into her life. It was the easiest of all the births and the only baby borne to Claire during the night-time hours. It wasn't until years later that Claire realized her blunder. What price convenience! What effrontery!

Her child's first independent gesture, his statement to the world — *"Here I am"* — Claire had dismissed as unimportant. "How could I have taken this most precious possession — his birth time — so lightly, just for my own accommodation?" she asked herself with dismay. His own individual stamp, the true timing of his grand entrance — *forever lost!* Claire was inconsolable. Now, all she could do was set up Michael's horoscope with this artificial birth time and wonder if it would conform to her impressions of this young man she had come to know and love.

Gingerly, but with anticipation, Claire constructed the following chart for Michael, Figure 14, as follows:

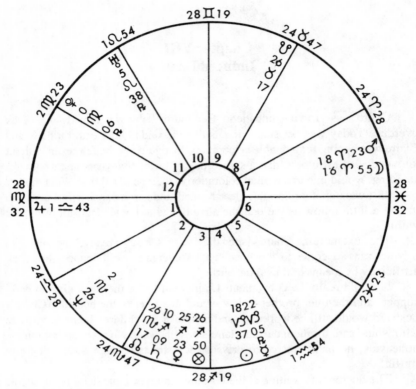

Figure 14. — Michael

Do the pieces fit?

Michael, according to his mother, Claire:

A quiet young man, unassuming in demeanor, refined in manner and speech, reserved. Handsome, with good, strong, facial bone structure, at age 28 he still retains a boyish attractiveness. Well proportioned, with wide shoulders and trim waist, he stands a slim 5 feet and 10 and 1/2 inches tall. Wavy, no curly brown hair — the kind women find attractive.

Curiously, this oft-times tousled head of curls, his "perma-pressed" shirts which (to a mother's eye) belie their manufacturer's description, his casual dress and easy manner — all do nothing to counteract the aura of neatness and orderliness, and the seriousness of purpose which Michael projects. In fact, this relaxed yet somehow tidy appearance, which seems to put others at ease, is part of his unconscious charm.

A low key fellow who likes his music loud. A good mimic with incisive sense of humor. Finicky eater. Peaceful quality that draws others to him. Reticent, minds his own business — appreciates it when others do the same. Not outwardly emotional. Socially popular, good company when the company is good. Lucky — things come his way.

In a high school test to determine vocational aptitude, he scored highest as an *adventurer* — at least in thought! His passive, unruffled exterior, his laconic attitude both conceal that fact. Undramatic, normally happy boyhood, he took school in stride, played baseball, ran on the track team, and thought he might become a history teacher. (With Gemini on the tenth house of career; the four angles in mutable signs; Saturn, signifying history, in Sagittarius, the teacher, in the mental third house of education, all indicate a natural aptitude for such a vocation.) If he possessed worldly ambition, a business sense, or competitive spirit — it did not show.

Teachers being overly plentiful at that time, at his father's suggestion Michael started pharmacy college and completed three years. When a medical school in the Caribbean opened its doors to qualified American students, once again it was his father who urged Michael to attend.

Reluctantly, on June 10, 1977, at 8:15 a.m. EDT, Michael boarded the plane for Santo Domingo, Dominican Republic, when the transiting Moon, which touches off proceedings, was at 11 degrees Aries. It would exactly touch his natal Moon/Mars action conjunction before the day was over. Three days later, on June 13, 1977, Michael started the Spanish language school in San Pedro de Macoris, in preparation for medical classes which were taught only in Spanish and which were to begin that coming September.

In August, 1977, with the language classes completed, Michael returned home, determined not to continue at the medical school. The climate had been too hot and energy depleting. Eager flies, hungry mosquitoes, and huge cockroaches overran the poor, humble town which resembled the set of an Old West movie. The food was abominable, especially for this fussy eater; the water, unsafe to drink; the water-pressure, at times nonexistent; and the electric power disappeared without notice almost every day for hours at a time. Michael still couldn't understand the language — much less study medicine using a foreign vocabulary. It was primitive living at its worst and he decided that he really didn't want to be a doctor, anyway!

Days slipped by. And then, at long last, the adventurer in Michael surfaced and a transformation took place. He went back to that sun-baked, sweaty, uncomfortable, backward town, and with English and Spanish medical books side by side, he learned the language, learned how to study, discovered that he possessed remarkable stamina, immense will power, high ambition, great intelligence and a strong determination to attain a Doctor of Medicine degree.

The stage had already been set by the following placements in his birth chart:

1. A Virgo Ascendant — which rules medical doctors, healing and health matters. Virgo also gives an "ear" for languages, which had not been tested until that particular time.

2. Sagittarius on the fourth house cusp. The fourth house is the home, while Sagittarius stands for foreign lands. Michael's home for four years was in a foreign land, the Dominican Republic.

3. Venus, ruler of Taurus, the sign on his ninth house of foreign lands, is at 25 Sagittarius, again the natural ruler of foreign soil, and is in the third house of education. This is another strong indication of study in a foreign land — the only one of Claire's children to do so. Venus is widely conjunct Saturn in Sagittarius — to supply staying power. Venus is also conjunct the Part of Fortune at 27 Sagittarius — to give inspiration and encouragement while absorbing knowledge.

The lackadaisical, casual, non-committed student became a thoroughly dedicated one once Michael realized that he was interested in medicine. Astrologically this was due to the Virgo Ascendant; Jupiter, the Doctor, in the first house of personality; and Pisces, signifying hospitals, on his sixth house of work.

All of the angles in the chart are in mutable signs, so outwardly he may appear passive and noncommital, but 5 planets in fire signs, 5 planets in cardinal signs, and 5 planets situated in angles gives a definite Aries tone to the chart. Aries gives the call to action, is impulsive and assertive, is pioneering and accomplishing, and these feelings eventually had to come to the forefront. Epitomizing all of the Aries qualities is the seventh house Moon/Mars conjunction in Aries, the *handle* to the *bucket* arrangement of planets in this chart, which is square Sun/Mercury, giving the challenge for hard work, and trine Saturn/Venus/Part of Fortune in the studious third house, paving the way for successful learning accomplishments.

The secondary progressed Moon in our charts often sets off important turning points in our lives. Does it do so in Michael's chart?

As we did for Claire's chart, to find the secondary progressed Moon we must first determine Michael's Adjusted Calculated Date. Michael was born on January 8, 1957, at 10:35 p.m. EST, in Brooklyn, NY. Adding a 5 hour GMT adjustment to the birth hour gives us 3:35 a.m. GMT of the following day. Subtracting 3:35 a.m. from the following noon gives us an interval of 8:25. Adding this interval to the sidereal time of Michael's birthdate, 19:11:05, gives us a new sidereal time of 3:36:05. The GMT is a.m. of the day *after* birth, so look *backward* in the noon ephemeris to an earlier date to find the nearest sidereal time to the new one above of 3:36:05. On May 16, 1956, the sidereal time equals 3:36:42. Therefore, Michael's Adjusted Calculated Date is May

16, meaning that for our calculating purposes, Michael's birthdate is May 16, 1956 instead of January 8, 1957.

The most important decision in Michael's young life up to that point was when he decided to take his father's advice and apply to medical school. The date Michael wrote on the application blank was December 8, 1976. We progress the birth chart to that date as we similarly did for Claire, as follows:

January 28, 1957 equals May 16, 1976.

January 29, 1957 equals May 16, 1977.

The progressed Moon for May 16, 1977 = 24 Capricorn 12 minutes.

The progressed Moon for May 16, 1976 = 12 Capricorn 15 minutes.

There is a difference of approximately 12 degrees. Therefore, the progressed Moon moved forward 12 degrees within the year, or 1 degree each month between 1976 and 1977.

If we add 1 degree to each month starting with May 16, 1976, when the progressed Moon was at 12 Capricorn 15 minutes, we find that the progressed Moon is at 18 Capricorn on November 16, 1976, and at 19 Capricorn on December 16, 1976. Therefore, on December 8, 1976, which is inbetween the two above dates, when Michael applied to medical school, the progressed Moon was at 18 Capricorn and some minutes, almost exactly conjuncting his natal Sun at 18 Capricorn 38 minutes, forming a new Moon conjunction — and, a new beginning for Michael. This same secondary progressed Moon, at 18 Capricorn, is square the natal Moon/Mars conjunction which gives impetus and incentive to act positively and purposely.

After completing medical school, yet still not certain about which specialty in which to major, Michael spent his first year of hospital work as an intern in Internal Medicine. Then, desiring to learn about the organs of the body and the causes of disease at first hand and from the inside out, he took a one-year Pathology residency before settling down to his final decision — Family Practice.

Although personal calls were discouraged in the Pathology lab, one day Claire had to relay an important message to Michael while he was working. "I'm sorry," said the secretary icily, "but the Doctor cannot come to the phone right now. He's cutting!"

Abruptly terminating their conversation, the secretary could not hear Claire's cry of joy, nor would she ever realize the beauty of those two ordinary words. To Claire, they epitomized that standout, bucket-handled, Moon/Mars conjunction, and how important that placement is in Michael's horoscope. If Michael's birth had not been induced, he would have been born hours, maybe even days, after the conjunction, minimizing the *cutting* affinity the Moon/Mars conjunction signifies.

The Moon, because it travels approximately 1 degree every 2 hours, would have left Mars behind, no longer have been in conjunction with it, and the *cutting* aspect would have passed. Even if Michael has not chosen to become a surgeon, we know he has operating ability, and this talent will be useful in his specialty of Family Practice.

That bucket handle, Moon/Mars, if truly in the seventh house, would focus on relationships and people. During his year in Pathology, Michael learned much about disease and its effects on the human body, but cadavers do not make engaging companions and he longed to get back to work where the action is — with patients in a family practice setting. The tenth house, the career significator, contains no planets and has Gemini on its cusp. Its ruler, Mercury, is placed in the fourth or family house, along with and conjunct the Sun — thus the leaning toward Family Practice. Cancer, the family sign and natural ruler of the fourth house, is intercepted in the tenth, again giving Family Practice added importance, while its ruler, the Moon, is once again center stage.

Doors do not open automatically to foreign medical graduates such as Michael. The number of hospital residencies in Family Practice were limited, and the applications he sent out were not being answered. Taking the advice of a friend who worked there, on the afternoon of December 14, 1982, with portfolio in hand, Michael sought a residency in a New Jersey hospital.

"All of our residency posts for July, 1983, are already filled," answered the young lady at the desk, to Michael's request for an application blank.

"He looked so young, so sad, so disappointed," she said later, "that I just couldn't let him leave."

"Fill out an application, anyway," this angel-girl told Michael.

She called in a doctor to talk to Michael — just friendly conversation. Soon another doctor sauntered in, then entered the friend, and finally the doctor in charge of accepting new residents arrived to complete the assembly.

The job was already non-existent, but the company was congenial, so Michael relaxed and regaled the group with tales of medical school in San Pedro, and his experiences in his first year residencies in Internal Medicine and Pathology — all in the Spanish, Indian, Chinese, Korean, and Filipino accents of fellow doctor friends he had collected along the way — courtesy of his Virgo Ascendant talent. What of all those adventures he related so entertainingly? Certainly a gift from his Saturn, Venus and Part of Fortune placements in Sagittarius from the third house of communication.

Something expansive and benevolent was smiling down upon Michael that day, because a contract was placed in front of him. He signed it. A present from Jupiter on his first house cusp? A Jupiter in Libra, Venus' ruling sign, which in Michael's chart reciprocates with the other benefic, Venus in Sagittarius, Jupiter's home sign?

How did Michael obtain the job when there was no job? Certainly, by grades and experience, he was very well qualified, but the transits for the afternoon of December 14, 1982 helped, too. Transiting Moon, which sets things off, was at approximately 16 degrees Sagittarius, and coming to a conjunction with transiting Sun at 22 Sagittarius — a new Moon, and a new beginning. This new Moon is coming to conjunct Michael's natal Venus at 25 Sagittarius — ruler of charm and sociability — and, in Michael's chart, ruler of the ninth house of higher learning and doctorate degrees. While transiting Michael's third house residency-study-setting, this new moon trines Michael's Moon/Mars conjunction in the seventh house of relationships. For added luck, transiting Jupiter at 27 Scorpio is conjunct natal North Node, and transiting Neptune at 26 Sagittarius, ruler of the sixth house of work and the seventh house of relationships, is conjunct natal Venus and natal Part of Fortune.

Transiting Mars, planet of action, at 3 degrees Aquarius is opposite natal Uranus in the eleventh house, contributing to the unexpected awareness of new friends. Mars is also trine natal Jupiter in the first house of personality, adding again "just a little bit o' luck!"

Starting a first year residency again, Family Practice this time, Michael's career seems to be taking shape more slowly than is usual. Can his horoscope show why?

The planet, Saturn, is the timekeeper. It takes approximately 28 to 30 years for Saturn to travel through all the houses in a natal chart. Saturn signifies our relationship with the world around us and the extent of our role in society. It lets us know where we stand. When transiting Saturn is in our houses:

a) 1,2, and 3, — it is time for relative obscurity. We find out about ourselves and our talents; we think, grow, and learn.

b) 4,5, and 6, — armed with this new information, we emerge from the growing process and attempt to find our niche in the world.

c) 7,8, and 9, — we're climbing in our chosen work.

d) 10, — we're at the top.

e) 11, — we're holding.

f) 12, — our light gradually dims, and then it comes up again in the

g) first house, where a new phase of awareness begins as Saturn goes beneath the horizon once more.

There is no use to get impatient with Saturn. He takes his time, and he has his reasons, and we have nothing to do but go along with him. In May of 1981, when Michael graduated from medical school, Saturn had passed into his first house. While a resident, first in Internal Medicine, then in Pathology, and finally in Family Practice (natal Sun in the fourth house of home and family, conjunct Mercury, ruler of tenth house of career, and also ruler of Virgo on the first house cusp of personality), Saturn goes through the obscure houses of 1,2, and 3. Michael finds out about himself and his talents; he grows and learns.

Saturn does not enter the third house of education until December of 1984, and will not reach his fourth house cusp until the fall of 1988 — so Michael has many years of studying and learning ahead. Not only that. In November of 1986, when transiting Saturn conjuncts his natal Saturn, he will grow to an even deeper level of awareness. This is good. A Capricorn Sun does things slowly and deliberately (with a push here from the Moon/Mars square), thoroughly and well. Finally, at the appointed time, Michael will emerge and begin to take his place in the world as:

Physician *** Healer

Hopefully, success at last. The reasons?

1. Moon conjunct Mars trine Saturn — staying power and acceptance of responsibility.

2. Moon conjunct Mars trine Venus — good sense of values.

3. Moon conjunct Mars square Sun/Mercury in the fourth house — this is his father. The Capricorn Sun — his steadfast father, who placed this tremendous work-square into the young man's path. This Capricorn Sun — his devoted father, the guiding, organizing, encouraging, ever-shining force!

Yes, the pieces seem to fit. Maybe Claire did it right, after all! What do you think?

There may be times when it becomes absolutely necessary to induce birth. When this is so, avoid it if possible at new and full Moon, when risk of hemorrhage is increased.

DO induce birth when there are good transiting aspects to the Moon and Venus — the signs of motherhood and the reproductive organs — in the woman's chart.

DO NOT induce birth for the sake of convenience. It is foolhardy to tamper with Nature. When She is ready, the womb will release its fruit, according to Divine Plan.

Caesarean Birth:

There are times when babies cannot be born normally and surgical intervention becomes necessary. Such surgery is called Caesarean section. According to astrological rulings, some times are safer and more beneficial than others to undergo the knife.

With the permission of American Federation of Astrologers, Inc., we will include portions of *Surgery Guidelines,* by Carolyn Sellers, MAFA, from *Today's Astrologer, Bulletin, Volume 42, Number 3, March, 1980,* as follows:

Avoid surgery when:

1. The transiting Moon is in Scorpio, Leo, or is void of course.

2. The transiting Moon is in the sign of the part of the body — the uterus — where the surgery is to be performed — Cancer and Scorpio.

3. The transiting Moon's Nodes are in any degree of the natal planets or of the Ascendant.

4. Transiting Mercury is retrograde.
5. Transiting Mars is retrograde.

Have surgery:

1. During the transiting *new* Moon phase. In transiting full Moon phase there is more chance of hemorrhaging.

Never have surgery on the very day of the *full Moon*. Never have surgery on the very day of the *new Moon*. There may be excessive bleeding at these times.

2. When transiting Moon is in Pisces. At this time there is more fluid in the body and better circulation of the white cells and antibodies to the wound, bringing faster healing.

3. With as many good natal and transiting aspects to transiting Mars — the surgeon.

4. With as many planets in direct motion as possible, particularly Venus, (the Moon is alwasy direct), and planets in Cancer, Scorpio, Libra and Taurus.

5. With as many good transiting aspects to the natal chart as possible.

Claire, by unnecessarily inducing birth, unwittingly violated the rights of her body and of her baby.

Soon it would be her body which would cause a turnabout. . . .

Chapter IX
Miscarriage

It was Halloween time, when witches and goblins are about, that it happened. And every year, with each black cat and orange jack-o-lantern decoration that Claire sees, the thought returns, "Who was he, the one I lost? Why did I lose him?"

It is only a silent, poignant, momentary, sorrowful thought — and then it flies away again on its broomstick into the deep recesses of her mind. Still, these are the moments in a woman's life that she will never forget. . . .

There it was, almost November, and Claire was late in taking down her summer window fan. Two and a half months pregnant with her fifth child, she was fine except for the now familiar, but this time only slight nausea of the early months.

The metal fan was heavy. Claire pulled and tugged and finally got it out of the window; lugged it down two long flights of stairs to the basement; placed it in its bed-box for winter hibernation, and trudged up the two flights of stairs again.

Suddenly she felt a wetness. It was red. And, in the red wetness was the beginning of the end of her baby. Saturn had had the last word. Saturn had won the final round.

Had she been astrologically aware, Claire would have noted the exact time of this happening. However, this is what she remembers:

The bleeding started on the morning of Friday, October 30, 1959.

The miscarriage was completed on the afternoon of Saturday, October 31, 1959.

Watch the drama unfold as we place the secondary progressed Moon in Claire's natal chart and note the positions of the transiting planets for October 30 and 31, 1959. Remember, the Moon and Venus are the female principles. The Moon stands for the mother, childbirth, the uterus or womb, the baby, and also touches off events. Venus represents the ovaries and the ova, or eggs, hormones and the internal reproductive system in general.

As stated in previous calculations, Claire's Adjusted Calculated Date for secondary progressions is June 28. In secondary progression, to progress Claire's chart:

70

July 15, 1927 equals June 28, 1959, and the progressed Moon is at 0 degrees Aquarius and 51 minutes.

July 16, 1927 equals June 28, 1960, and the progressed Moon is at 14 Aquarius and 49 minutes. There is a difference of 13 degrees and 58 minutes or 14 degrees. Therefore, the Moon moved 14 degrees in 24 hours or, in progression, the Moon moved 14 degrees between June 28, 1959, and June 28, 1960. We are interested in knowing where the progressed Moon is inbetween those two dates, that is, October 30 and 31, 1959.

When we multiply 14 degrees times 60 minutes we get a product of 840 minutes, which is the number of minutes the Moon moved between June 28, 1959, and June 28, 1960, in progression. Dividing 840 minutes by 12 months we find that the Moon moved forward 70 minutes or 1 degree and 10 minutes every month during that period by secondary progression. Therefore, adding on 1 degree and 10 minutes each month, we arrive at the following positions of the progressed Moon:

Jun 28, 1959, progressed Moon = 0 Aquarius 51 minutes.
Jul 28, 1959, progressed Moon = 2 Aquarius 01 minutes.
Aug 28, 1959, progressed Moon = 3 Aquarius 11 minutes.
Sep 28, 1959, progressed Moon = 4 Aquarius 21 minutes.
Oct 28, 1959, progressed Moon = 5 Aquarius 31 minutes.
Nov 28, 1959, progressed Moon = 6 Aquarius 41 minutes.

If the Moon moved 70 minutes each month, and there are 31 days in October, then, by dividing 31 days into 70 minutes, we find that the Moon moved approximately 2 minutes each day from October 28 to November 28, 1959. If the progressed Moon on October 28 was at 5 Aquarius 31 minutes, then on October 30 the Moon was at 5 Aquarius 35 minutes and on October 31 the progressed Moon was at 5 Aquarius 37 minutes.

Hence, we find that on Friday, October 30, 1959, when the miscarriage started, the progressed Moon, which starts events, was at 5 Aquarius 35 minutes in Claire's natal eighth house of death, in almost exact opposition to natal Venus at 5 Leo 43 minutes, ruler of the internal reproductive system. On the following day, October 31, 1959, when the miscarriage was completed, the progressed Moon moved forward two more minutes, even closer in opposition to natal Venus. See Figure 15.

Now, let's look at Figure 16 which portrays the *transits* of Friday, October 30, 1959, at 7 a.m. EST, the day the miscarriage started while Claire was at home in Queens, New York:

1. Transiting Venus, symbol of the female internal reproductive system, is at 20 degrees Virgo (Venus is in its fall in Virgo), within 1 degree of square to Claire's natal Sun.

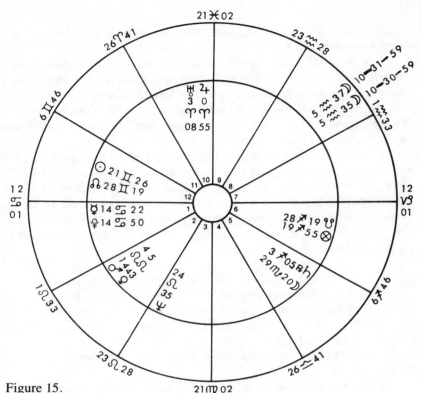

Figure 15.
Claire's natal chart — inner wheel
Secondary progressed Moon during miscarriage — outer wheel

2. Transiting Moon, at 16 Libra (one of the signs signifying the reproductive system), is in the fourth house which signifies the uterus, squaring Mercury and Pluto in Cancer, the motherhood sign, on the natal Ascendant.

3. Transiting Mercury at 29 Scorpio, the messenger, is conjunct the natal Moon at 29 Scorpio — the mother, the womb. The message is not a happy one.

4. Transiting Sun is at 6 degrees Scorpio 19 minutes.

5. Transiting Mars is at 6 degrees Scorpio 11 minutes.

6. Transiting Neptune is at 6 degrees Scorpio 41 minutes.

This powerful Sun/Mars/Neptune conjunction in Scorpio, sign of sex and death, is square Claire's natal Mars/Venus conjunction — the planets of sexual attraction, and the male and female symbols of reproduction — from the natal fifth house of children.

7. Transiting Jupiter, at 4 Sagittarius 54 is trine Venus, a protective influence for the mother.

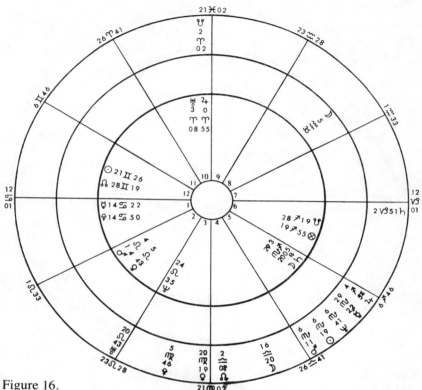

Figure 16.
Start of Miscarriage — Oct 30, 1959
Claire's natal chart — inner wheel
Secondary progressed Moon — middle wheel
Transits taken from noon ephemeris — outer wheel

8. Transiting Uranus, natal ruler of the eighth house of death, planet of upheaval and unexpected happenings, at 20 Leo, is sextile natal Sun in Claire's twelfth house of disappointments and trouble. It helped to cause this unforeseen event, but provided understanding at the same time for the unfortunate climax.

9. Transiting Saturn at 2 Capricorn, in the natal sixth house of health, is square natal Jupiter, ruler of this sixth house of health, and square natal Uranus, ruler of the eighth house of sex and death.

10. The transiting North Node at 2 Libra, which opposes the natal Jupiter/Uranus conjunction, and the transiting South Node which conjuncts it, give prominence and attention to these two natal significators of the houses of health and sex/death, but they are draining influences, not supportive ones.

11. Transiting Pluto at 5 Virgo, ruler of death, the sex force, and regeneration, squares the cusp of the natal sixth house of health.

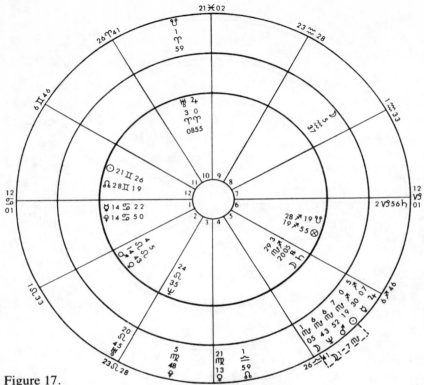

Figure 17.
End of miscarriage — Oct 31, 1959
Claire's natal chart — inner wheel
Secondary progressed Moon — middle wheel
Transits taken from noon ephemeris — outer wheel

On the following day, October 31, 1959, when the miscarriage was completed, the faster moving planets were significantly active, as depicted in Figure 17:

1. Mercury, having completed its task of carrying the Scorpio message of death to the Moon on October 30, has now entered Sagittarius.

2. Venus is now at 21 Virgo — exactly square Claire's natal Sun.

3. The transiting Moon has now entered Scorpio, the sign which rules miscarriage, and she is the one to watch:

On Oct 31, 1959, at 7 a.m. EST, the Moon = 01 Scorpio 5.5 minutes.
On Nov 01, 1959, at 7 a.m. EST, the Moon = 16 Scorpio 6.6 minutes.

There is a difference of 15 degrees and 1.1 minutes. Therefore, this very fast Moon moved forward 15 degrees within this 24 hour period.

15 degrees times 60 minutes equals 900 minutes that the Moon moved in this 24 hours. Dividing 900 minutes by 24 hours, we find that the Moon moved

37.5 minutes every hour. If on Oct 31, 1959, at 7 a.m. EST, the transiting Moon equalled 1 Scorpio 5.5 minutes, then adding on 37.5 minutes every hour we find that at:

08 a.m. the Moon = 1 Scorpio 43 minutes
09 a.m. the Moon = 2 Scorpio 20.5 minutes
10 a.m. the Moon = 2 Scorpio 58 minutes
11 a.m. the Moon = 3 Scorpio 35.5 minutes
12 noon the Moon = 4 Scorpio 13 minutes
1 p.m. the Moon = 4 Scorpio 50.5 minutes
2 p.m. the Moon = 5 Scorpio 28 minutes
3 p.m. the Moon = 6 Scorpio 05.5 minutes
4 p.m. the Moon = 6 Scorpio 42.5 minutes
5 p.m. the Moon = 7 Scorpio 20 minutes

The miscarriage was completed between 2 and 5 p.m. when the transiting Moon was between 5 and 7 degrees Scorpio. See Figure 16 for the important transits of October 30, 1959, when the miscarriage began, and Figure 17 for those of October 31, 1959 when the miscarriage was completed. At the time the miscarriage ended, the transiting Moon, between 5 and 7 degrees Scorpio, squares the secondary progressed Moon at 5 Aquarius, squares natal Venus at 5 Leo, and conjuncts the transiting Neptune/Mars/Sun stellium in Scorpio in the natal fifth house of children.

This transiting Sun/Moon conjunction is now the new Moon, whenbleeding and hemorrhaging are most likely to occur, and so the act of miscarriage is given added impetus, bleeding becomes profuse, the fetus is aborted, and pregnancy is terminated.

Had Claire been aware of these forbidding aspects, and had she taken better precautions with her health at this time, might she have averted this miscarriage? Since she had never had even the slightest problem previously, this miscarriage came as a complete surprise. Well, not really. Always very ill with morning sickness (that lasted all day) for the first three months with each of the other children, Claire had been happy, yet uneasy, that this time the nausea was not bad at all.

"Maybe my body is getting used to this," she reasoned, unscientifically. Maybe that should have been her signal, but she ignored it.

They say that women feel guilty; that somehow they believe that the miscarriage is their fault. Nonsense. The truth is: nothing disrupts a healthy fetus — not stress, not stars. Claire felt no pangs of conscience, only great sadness.

Miscarriage will commonly occur for two reasons:

1. The woman is healthy but the fetus is impaired.

2. The fetus is healthy but the woman's reproductive mechanism is faulty. Usually she will have a history of miscarriages.

Claire belonged to the first type. The fetus was probably genetically or anatomically abnormal and was unable to survive. The opposing vibrations from the progressed Moon to Claire's natal Venus; the transiting square vibrations of Sun, Mars, and Neptune to this same Venus; and then the final blow — the transiting Moon conjuncting transiting Sun to form a new Moon, and this also squaring natal Venus — proved to be too hostile and overpowering for this helpless, new, little life. It died. The planets decreed, and nature rectified its mistake by destroying what it had imperfectly begun. After sorrow comes gratitude as we realize that Mother Nature knows best, after all.

It is for the second type of miscarriage, however, where the woman's reproductive system is culpable, that astrology might be of some assistance. If this type of pregnant woman could be alerted to troublesome aspects and advised accordingly, she might better be able to safeguard the life of her unborn child, because the weakness is in her own self, not in the fetus.

An example of this could be actress Sophia Loren (we will study her chart in greater detail later), who suffered two miscarriages before successfully bearing two healthy sons in two succeeding pregnancies. But, she was willing to pay the price. Not waiting for astrological aspects, or taking any chances at all, Sophia spent the entire nine months in bed with the first baby, and eight months in bed with the second. Astrology, if called upon, might have been able to help her lead a more normal life.

If you are subject to miscarriages, take care when you are pregnant during the times aspects are unfriendly to your unborn baby, especially during the first two to four months of pregnancy when most miscarriages occur. The following astrological rules may be enlightening and helpful:

Astrological Rules Governing Miscarriage:

The following rules, which astrologically govern miscarriage (the premature expulsion of a fetus), are a summation of various astrology texts listed in the *Bibliography*. We should test and research them ourselves before blindly accepting them.

1. The signs Scorpio and Cancer, and the planets Venus and the Moon rule the uterus or womb.

2. Some women may be unable to carry a child to term if the sign Scorpio is heavily afflicted by malefics in her natal chart.

3. Mars in Scorpio at birth, when afflicted, may increase the risk of miscarriage.

4. Saturn in Scorpio, when afflicted, may hinder or retard the growth of a fetus.

5. If Uranus is in Scorpio at birth, and afflicted, it tends to cause a spasmodic action in the uterus and expulsion of the fetus when directions to Uranus are challenging during pregnancy.

6. Mars in Scorpio and afflicting the Moon or the Ascendant may cause miscarriage.

7. Mars in the sixth house of health and in Cancer or Scorpio, when afflicted, may cause miscarriage.

8. Saturn in the fifth house and square or opposite the ruler of the fifth may cause miscarriage.

9. Saturn, as ruler of the eighth house, and with a barren sign on the Ascendant or cusp of the fifth may cause miscarriage.

10. Miscarriage is more likely to occur at the time when the monthly menstrual period is normally due, when there are challenging aspects from transits and directions.

11. The South Node in the natal fifth house is indication of possible miscarriage.

12. An eclipse of the Sun or Moon in Scorpio, especially when the Sun, Moon, Mars, Saturn or Uranus were in Scorpio at birth, may cause miscarriage.

13. In horary questions, the South Node in the first house may be indication of miscarriage.

14. Again, in a horary chart, the Sun conjunct Uranus in Scorpio, the Moon conjunct Saturn in Scorpio, or Saturn conjunct Mars in Scorpio could indicate one who seeks an abortion.

Special note in Claire's chart concerning Venus, which represents the internal reproductive system in general and the ovaries in particular: At age 53, when secondary progressed Venus was at 21 degrees Virgo, in exact square to natal Sun, the menopause — the ovaries having exhausted their supply of eggs resulting in the end of childbearing — began in earnest for Claire.

The astrological rules handed down to us through the ages have been applied and have not been found wanting in this miscarriage account. For what society is thinking and doing in today's world with regard to reproduction, let us now turn to. . . .

Chapter X
Clippings Concerning Conception

In addition to the current news events of the day, one can learn many interesting facts from the daily newspapers. The tenor of the times and the gist of thoughts pervading the atmosphere are typed out in black and white for our perusal. When it comes to fertility and related subjects, for us at least, the words stand out in bold relief. That it is a popualr topic can be confirmed by the fact that, at least weekly, one can find an article concerning either conception or birth control, abortion or adoption somewhere within the columns of print. Since these articles, written in laymen's terms, are vital to our theme, we would like to pass along to you some of the prevalent, pertinent information which we have recently gathered.

From the *Daily News,* and from the columns, *Personal Notes,* by Judith Randal, we learned the following:

1. *Vitamin C can aid some male infertility.*

Among the many reasons that men can have difficulty in fathering children is that their sperm clump together instead of swimming singly. Stuck to each other in this fashion, individual sperm can't get enough momentum for any one of them to penetrate and fertilize a female egg.

The solution to this problem could be simply a few days of vitamin C therapy. In an experiment, 35 males with low fertility took a one-half gram vitamin C tablet every 12 hours for one week. With substantial increases in their vitamin C blood levels, the clumping of their sperm decreased dramatically, swimming powers increased, and the men were then able to impregnate their wives. (One should consult a physician before taking vitamins as therapy.)

2. *Blame the brain .*

"When a woman is infertile, it may be her brain, rather than her reproductive organs, that is to blame. That's because pregnancy cannot occur unless a part of the brain called the hypothalamus releases a hormone that acts on the pituitary gland which, in turn, releases another hormone that sends a signal to the ovaries to release an egg — the process known as ovulation.

One way to handle the problem is to inject the hormone ordinarily provided by the pituitary directly into the ovaries. However, this is expensive and besides, tends to result in multiple births. So at some medical centers the approach is to provide the would-be mother with a temporary substitute for her malfunctioning hypothalamus.

This is done by placing a catheter (tubing) into one of the patient's veins and attaching it to a small pump. The pump is filled with a synthetic version of the missing hormone and sends a small amount of it into the woman's bloodstream at 90-minute intervals. At the few medical centers where the therapy is available, it results in ovulation — though not always pregnancy — 80% to 90% of the time.

Among those trying the new method is Dr. Andrew Loucopoulos at New York's Presbyterian Hospital. One woman they treated there with the new method gave birth to a healthy boy, then became pregnant again after treatment a second time.''

3. *Miscarriage incidence and spermicides linked.*

Women who regularly use spermicidal contraceptives may be more likely to have girls than boys. And if they continue to use spermicidal contraceptives after they conceive, because they don't realize they are pregnant, they may be more likely than other women to miscarry. These findings are among those that turned up when Dr. Therese Scholl of the University of Medicine and Dentistry of New Jersey School of Osteopathic Medicine, and colleagues at Philadelphia's Temple University recently analyzed data from the 1976 National Survey of Family Growth. It seems that for women who continued to use the foams, creams or jellies for a month or more after becoming pregnant, the miscarriage rate of 27% was almost twice as high as would have been expected otherwise.

Furthermore, 60% of the babies born to women who used spermicides around the time of conception were girls, whereas only 49% of the babies born to the other women in the survey were girls. A possible explanation offered by Scholl and her colleagues is that spermicides are slightly acid and this may make them injurious to the y-chromosome-bearing sperm that dictate that a fetus will be male. These findings call for further research.

From the *Daily News,* in an article entitled, *New hope for impotence,* by Edward Edelson, we learn that the reasons for impotence are varied and can be caused by:

1. Hormonal problems — either too much testosterone, the male sex hormone, or too much prolactin — a hormone that affects sexual function, is produced. Injections or tablets can help to alleviate these problems.

2. Problems with the vascular system. Erection is obtained when the penis becomes engorged with blood. If the blood vessels become blocked because of arteriosclerosis, in which fatty deposits gradually choke off the flow of blood, sexual performance can suffer. A very small percentage of these problems can be corrected by surgery. Penile implants can be performed, but only on a small number of patients.

3. Medications taken for other ailments, particularly those given to control high blood pressure. In these cases, the prescription is changed.

4. Psychological problems — worry, anxiety, or poor self-image — which can be helped by psychotherapy.

Taking another aspect of our theme, newspaper articles will often highlight the emotions of anger, worthlessness, envy and despair entertained by couples who are infertile. Feeling incomplete, self-confidence is diminished and the marriage itself suffers.

There is help in several areas for these couples:

1. They can avail themselves of support groups where they will meet with others who are similarly afflicted, and wherein educational programs, medical information and telephone counseling are also provided. One such group, *Resolve, Inc.,* which has chapters throughout the country, can be contacted as follows:

Resolve, Inc., P.O. Box 474, Belmont, Mass 02178. Telephone: 1-617-484-2424.

2. Because white, American babies are scarce, they can consider adoption of children from other countries. From the *Daily News,* December 4, 1983, in an article entitled, *Going abroad to adopt,* by Ricki Fulman, we read that because it has become increasingly difficult to adopt healthy white babies, inter-country adoptions are becoming more popular. Families who already have children, but want to adopt additional children who are not necessarily babies, favor Korea, while infertile couples, because they want infants, turns to Columbia where more new-borns are available.

According to the most recent figures from the Statistics Division of the Immigration and Naturalization Service, in 1980, 2,683 children were adopted from Korea; 653 from Columbia. The average Columbian adoption costs between $5,000 and $6,000; the average Korean adoption, around $5,000.

For more information about Latin American adoptions, send a self-addressed, stamped envelope to: *Latin American Parents Association,* P.O. Box 72, Seaford, N.Y. 11783.

For more information about Korean adoptions, contact *Love the Children,* 221 West Borad St., Quakertown, Pa. 18951.

3. They can also consider adoption of older American minorities. For information concerning the adoption of black and other minority older children see the weekly column, *A Child is Waiting,* in the *Daily News.* Tracey Harden, in an article in the *Daily News* of September 16, 1984, writes: "Thanks to this (the above mentioned column) and other public awareness efforts, the total number of adoptions in New York City has gone up 19 per-cent since 1982. However, there are still close to 4000 children waiting. The average age is ten years old and, although these children sometimes require a little extra care and attention, the rewards for both parent and child can be enormous. For more

information about adoption, please call the Adoption Hotline at 1-(212) 732-0610.''

Test-tube babies are not such a rare occurrence any more, and as new techniques are developed and refined, an increased number of infertile couples are being helped. Still, according to Beverly Stephen, in her Options column entitled, *Test-tube pregnancy — a trying experience,* in the *Daily News,* of September 18, 1983, achieving pregnancy the ''test-tube way'' is an expensive, time-consuming, injection taking, hospital-staying, surgical procedure with only a 5% to 25% chance of success.

''It involves daily monitoring of the woman in the form of blood tests and ultrasonography of the ovaries; injections of a fertility drug for 12 to 15 days to stimulate the ovaries; and surgical removal of the eggs at the time of ovulation.''

The husband's sperm is placed in a Petri dish along with her eggs. When fertilization takes place the embryos that develop are then transferred to the wife's uterus, with progesterone injections to follow.

''If she does not become pregnant, the woman may repeat the process up to 3 times, resting a month between operations. The cost for each try is $3,500 and it is not covered by insurance.'' It has since come to our attention that the cost for each operation has now risen to $5,000.

According to the article, the grief of the couple is very intense when the procedure fails. The all-engrossing question we ask is this: Might *in vitro* fertilization have a greater rate of success, if the ripened ovum were to be extracted and made ready for fertilization, not only when the woman is biologically ready, but astrologically fertile and in tune as well?

Newsday, a fine Long Island newspaper, also ran a lengthy article on *in vitro* fertilization in its August 13, 1984 issue by Denise Grady, a free-lance science editor. Of necessity she drew the same conclusions as did Beverly Stephen — that is, that the emotional price for a small chance at pregnancy by this method is extremely high.

Then, why try? Why are more hospitals getting involved? Ms. Grady reports the following: ''In the New York area four hospitals have *in vitro* programs: North Shore University Hospital in Manhasset, Long Island; Glen Cove Community Hospital in Glen Cove, Long Island; and Mount Sinai and Columbia Presbyterian Medical Centers, both in Manhattan.''

They follow the Eastern Virginia Medical School in Norfolk, Virginia — the oldest and most successful *in vitro* fertilization clinic in the United States, established in 1980.

''The one encouraging note,'' continues Ms. Grady, ''is that success rates are climbing, gradually, at most clinics, as medical teams learn more about handling human eggs and sperm and using hormones to prime the body for pregnancy. In fact, Dr. Victor Reyniak, head of the team at Mount Sinai, says it may be reasonable for women under the age of 36 to postpone *in vitro* procedures for a year or two, to take advantage of the better odds that the future will bring.''

Will that future include astrological timing and astrological procedures in a scientific setting? It's up to us!

Because many young women, not only Catholic ones, may experience regret or pangs of conscience after having an abortion, we include this question, addressed to, and answered by, Ann Landers. syndicated advice columnist, which appeared on July 3, 1983, in the *New York Daily News*. The question concerned a young Catholic woman who had had an abortion, felt that she was automatically excommunicated from her church, but now wished to belong once more. Could she be reinstated?

Ann Landers replied:

''I asked Father Theodore Hesburgh, president of the University of Notre Dame, to answer this one. Here is his response:

It is true that there is an excommunication penalty attached to procuring an abortion. However, the person who has the abortion must be aware that this penalty exists and go ahead and have it anyway. The question of prime importance: Did the young woman know about this church law?

In the event that she did know and had the abortion anyway, she can be absolved of the sin by confessing it to any priest. I believe most bishops delegate to all their priests the power to absolve from this excommunication, even though it is technically known as a 'reserved sin.'

I would advise the woman to make a good confession, put this matter behind her and start anew. It certainly is not a question of the church not wanting her. The church exists to help everyone who needs it.''

Thank you, Ann Landers, for a compassionate answer to a problem that could arise as an aftermath of abortion.

Lastly, in a column concerning older women who have turned to motherhood after achieving success in outside the home pursuits, Beverly Stephen quotes one business woman who summed it up this way: ''With everything else I've done I've ended up saying, *'Is this all there is?'*. Having a baby is the one thing I've never felt that way about.''

While pregnancy at the proper time in life is the greatest of blessings, for the young teenager, to whom it never should have happened, it can be a devastating experience. *News America Syndicate* has made available a very timely and useful booklet, written by Ann Landers, called, *Sex and the Teenager*. Although some of her remarks are at variance with the author's own beliefs, this is an excellent booklet concerning sex and fertility which contains important information not only for teenagers, but for their parents as well.

Graphically citing the pitfalls of sexual activity at an early age, the booklet also explains the different methods for preventing conception. Abstinence, of course, heads the list. Fertility awareness, or the *"rhythm"* method is her least desirable choice because, in her opinion, it is too risky. On Page 35 she tells us why.

Here Ms. Landers discusses the same monthly biologically fertile days that we describe in our book, and which all of our readings confirm. But then, departing company as we do, she warns her readers that while the rest of the month is supposed to be *SAFE* it really is not — because an egg can be released, not only at the biologically fertile time, *but at any other time during the menstrual period.*

While she does not inform us that the reason for this occurrence could be astrological (and that it might be pin-pointed), she at least admits to the presence of this extra-monthly, out-of-biological-order-ovum. And although Ann Landers is not a physician, she is an honest and reputable reporter, and we can be certain that her statements have been validated by authoritative sources. This affirmative declaration — about which so little seems to be known — give public support to our hypothesis, and this is encouraging news for our cause.

To obtain this booklet, *Sex and the Teenager,* by Ann Landers, please send $2.00 to: Ann Landers, Field Newspaper Syndicate, Chicago Sun-Times Building, Chicago, Illinois 60611. Please enclose a long, self-addressed, stamped envelope (37 cents postage, as of this writing), and include your zip code.

We wish to thank the *New York Daily News* for permission to quote from their timely articles by Judith Randall, Edward Edelson, Ricki Fulman, Tracey Harden and especially, Beverly Stephen.

Copyright *New York News, Inc.* Reprinted by permission.

We thank *News America Syndicate* for permission to reprint the column by Ann Landers which appeared in the *New York Daily News* on July 3, 1983.

We also are grateful to Denise Grady and *Newsday* for their fascinating, in-depth article on *in-vitro* clinics and for permission to quote them here.

The following series of three letters, received by the author just weeks before this book went to press, have not been printed in any newspaper — although they are newsworthy enough, to us at least, to make the front page. With the permission of Crist Bursa who penned these letters, we record them here exactly as written.

The first letter, dated June 26, 1985, is as follows:
Dear Emily,

You were recommended to me by Sue Lovett in Toledo as an expert in fertility charts. My husband (6/24/50) and I (8/11/52) have been trying for 4 years to have children but to no avail. After assorted hormones, temperature charts and tests I finally had exploratory surgery last April. The surgery showed that I have a hard cyst (like an eye on a potato) on each ovary covering the opening to where the egg comes out. Even though I'm functioning otherwise normally, the eggs have been prevented from escaping the ovaries in order to get fertilized. I am now on medication that is supposed to force the egg from the ovary but has a 25% chance of working. Somewhere around the 23rd of August, if I'm not as yet pregnant, I will have to undergo surgery to scrape away the cysts. The problem is — is that the scar tissue can then be just as big a problem. The surgery increases my chances to about 50% chance of getting pregnant. I have explored all possibilities of adoption — but with abortion legal there are not as many babies available and waiting lists are 5 - 10 years.

I'm going to be 33. I'm very depressed about all this but try to remain as positive as possible. When in college an astrologist told me I'd have problems with pregnancy. She said I would either be an unwed mother or have to adopt. That forecast has always scared me to death. Sue Lovett and my mother's friend both told me I do not have a childless chart, and that there is a possibility of twins. I would love for them to be correct.

My question is this: Am I ever going to get pregnant? If I knew for sure I was, then I would relax and let nature take its course, but not knowing is driving me nuts. I'm not sure if a fertility chart of when to do it would do me any good as I'm on strict "sexual instructions" from a fertility specialist. However, if there is anything you can do, please let me know. Please let me know what charges are in advance.

I was born in Macon, Georgia, at pretty close to 12 noon. Steve was born in Tiffin, Ohio. If it helps, today is my 7th day of the cycle. I ovulate on the 18th day and it starts all over again on the 32nd day.

I look forward to hearing from you and appreciate your consideration.
Sincerely,
Crist Rowand Bursa

Going to work on Crist's natal chart, we found problems and obstacles, but harmonious and fruitful aspects as well. We sent Crist a packet containing her natal chart, her experimental Intercourse Time Chart determined by her natal Sun/Moon midpoint and current place of residence, and a year's supply of monthly fertility dates and times as determined by her natal Sun/Moon angle and Sun/Moon midpoint. To counteract any negative advice she had received from others, we assured Crist that there is neither a star in the heavens nor a creature on earth who could give her a child or hold one back, for God alone is the giver of Life. Since we are merely beholders of God's grace and only the instruments of His will, we encouraged Crist to ask God's assistance through prayer. Believing that Saint Gerard, the Mother's saint, could help Crist and intercede for her before God, we included 2 St. Gerard medals for Crist to wear and prayerful devotions to read. Assuring her of our prayers also, we looked forward to hearing from Crist again.

The tone of dejection and discouragement changes to one of hope as the second letter, dated July 8, 1985, arrives. It was a "thank you" note, the cover of which beautifully pictured a mother with her little girl, entitled *Maternal Kiss*, a pastel by Mary Stevenson Cassatt. Crist wrote:

Dear Emily,

Thank you so much for your fast reply. It came in a nick of time! Today I went to the doctor's for my ovulation shot. When I came home I found your package in the mail. Guess what? Your first recommended time is July 8, 4 - 6 p.m. My jusband and I are rushing home! Wish us luck.

Thank you also for the St. Gerard medals. That was very thoughtful and sweet of you. I shall wear them and pray as you suggest. I am Catholic so they were appropriate!

I will certainly keep you informed of my progress and you'll be one of the first to know of the outcome.

Thanks again and God bless you!

Sincerely,

Crist Rowand Bursa

True to her promise, on August 4, 1985, Crist happily and humorously wrote letter number three, and we joyously read the following:

Dear Emily,

I have good news — I'm pregnant! I'm not sure what did it, but here's the details. My doctor had me on 2 Clomids on day 5 - 9 and gave me shots on the ovulation day to soften the ovaries so hopefully the egg would get out around the cyst. Well, the day I got my shot to force ovulation I also got your package which said to do it that day (July 8, 4 - 6 p.m.). I called my husband at work and told him to get in the mood. Unfortunately, our car (2nd) had broken down and I had to pick him up from work. It was the hottest day of summer and he'd had a tough one — he was crankier than a hornet. The whole way home he yelled at me for driving too fast — not fast enough — not shifting in time . . . By the time we got home I wasn't speaking to him or him to me. Finally with tempers cooled we managed to try at 7:30. We also tried the next night as per doctor's orders. I also started wearing the St. Gerard medal that you sent me, and praying the same day as receiving your package. The rest is biological history. My husband suspected I was pregnant right away — he said I looked like it. I thought I was just getting fat and that I had a bad case of PMS. Anyway, last Tuesday we found out it was positive. Thank you for your package. I feel very grateful to be pregnant. I never thought I'd see the day. St. Gerard really helped as well as your timing and modern medicine.

Thanks again for everything, Emily. It was all very much appreciated.

Sincerely,

Crist Bursa and baby

While we can never really be sure if our astrological timing was instrumental in the achievement of this pregnancy, we do have good reason to believe so. Crist had been taking medication before our timing instructions were used, but still she had not become pregnant. Therefore, the equation upon which this book is based, stands: Biological fertility timing, plus astrological fertility timing, plus the grace of God, equals NEW LIFE.

On Easter Sunday, March 30, 1986, Crist gave birth to a beautiful baby girl — Stephanie Danielle. That truly says it all!

PART II
about famous women. . .

Source of birth data for the following natal charts is the book, *Profiles of Women,* by Lois M. Rodden. Her diligent efforts have helped to make our work possible and we are sincerely grateful.

The fifth and eleventh houses of fertility are not the only determining factors in the outcome of a woman's decision to have children. We must take into account her personality, values, talents, mentality, upbringing, health and husband — in short, *all* of the houses, planets and aspects must be evaluated with motherhood in mind.

In the following studies of famous women, according to their biographies and autobiographies, we have tried to give a short, but well-rounded picture of the whole person, so as to better understand the importance of motherhood in each life. Many thanks to the authors and their publishers for their insightful portrayals of these popular personalities, which have helped to make our research so interesting.

It is only the attempt of a third person removed, but please come along. . . .

Chapter XI
Katharine Hepburn

Katharine Hepburn is a unique person. As a natal chart is each person's one-of-a-kind personality report to the world — and this one fits Hepburn to her T-square — we are fortunate to have the opportunity of studying this horoscope, as shown in Figure 18, to try to discover why she was destined to become, on the one hand, an international star of stage and screen, while on the other, a wife of very short duration, and a mother not at all.

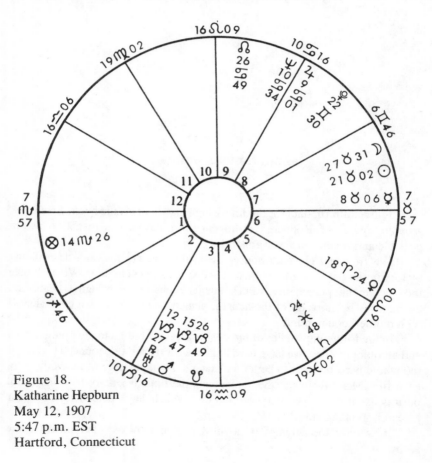

Figure 18.
Katharine Hepburn
May 12, 1907
5:47 p.m. EST
Hartford, Connecticut

If the fifth house represents both children — creation — *and* entertainment (film, stage, sporting events, gambling, love affairs) — recreation — how can we tell which vocation a woman will follow?

Since Claire represents the vocation of wife/mother, and Hepburn signifies the entertainer, we will study Hepburn's chart in relation to Claire's (review Figure 1 in Chapter 1, *The Astrological Aspects of Reproduction*) in an attempt to analyze the difference between them.

It wasn't because Hepburn was poor, or unnoticed, or didn't have social standing that caused her to need to make her mark as an actress, for she was wealthy, a socialite, and had had a happy home life. But, when she wanted something she got it! She has a strong personality as evinced by:

1. A Scorpio Ascendant — a determined, fertile, feminine, water sign of controlled emotion, co-ruled by Pluto in the eighth house of creative energy. Although Pluto is in square aspect to Saturn in the fifth house of children, an aspect which hinders childbearing, it is sextile Venus in the sixth house of labor, giving her the opportunity to do creative work.

The other co-ruler, Mars, exalted in the feminine, fertile, earth sign, Capricorn, giving the capacity for hard work and high, worldly ambition from the third house of communication is:

a) conjunct Uranus — inclination to do the unconventional (children are conventional),

b) opposite Jupiter and Neptune in Cancer, the motherhood sign, and both co-ruling the fifth house of children (the opposition is a hindrance to bearing children), and

c) square Venus, signifying the ovaries, the hormones, and the internal reproductive organs in the sixth house of work and sickness — causing obstructions to the bearing of children.

Claire's Ascendant is a water sign, too, but the sign is Cancer, the mother symbol, ruled by the childbearing Moon, and placed in the fifth house of children with many harmonious aspects. Cancer is the sign of religion (searching for the security of the Father-Mother God), and with Mercury/Pluto in Cancer on the Ascendant cusp, she was of a religious parenthood, and acknowledging also that birth prevention was, according to her religion, a forbidden practice. Hepburn's upbringing was totally different, influencing her to live a more radical life style.

2. The Moon, the mother principle, exalted in fertile, earthy Taurus in the seventh house, is:

a) conjunct the Sun in Taurus, a sign which indicates the *actress,*

b) sextile Saturn in the fifth house of entertainment — providing opportunities for all creative endeavors,

c) along with the Sun, very widely trine Uranus/Mars in the third house — giving a progressive mental attitude which allows one to defy convention and live a free, unhampered life, one not conducive to the constraints of motherhood, and

    d) widely square the cusp of the tenth house of career from her house of marriage. Hepburn did not think one could successfully combine career/marriage/motherhood — nor did she want to!

How does the horoscope show that marriage and motherhood were not the ideal way of life for Hepburn? Look to her seventh house of marriage:

    1. Mercury, strongly placed on its cusp, is ruler of the eleventh house of friends. It is —

    a) sextile Jupiter/Neptune on the ninth house, motherly Cancer cusp, and Miss Hepburn gives solicitous, loving care to her friends, even while on location in foreign lands.

    b) trine Uranus/Mars in the third house, creating easy communication and harmony of thought among friends at work (Mars, ruler of sixth house), brothers and sisters (Uranus/Mars in third house), and a happy home life (Uranus, ruler of fourth house).

    c) a planet which is neuter, neither male nor female. Hepburn, married for a brief three weeks, found that domesticity was not for her. Still, she kept her former husband as a life-long friend.

    2. The Sun and Moon in the seventh house are in a new Moon phase, only 6 degrees apart, in a very subjective *I am* placement that does not augur well for the attitudes of interdependence, cooperation, and sharing that marriage entails. (On the other hand, Claire's seventh house ruler, Saturn, is joined to her first house ruler, the Moon, in the fifth house of children and love affairs, suggesting that Claire needed and wanted one husband only with whom to live her life.) Maybe however, innately Hepburn chose wisely, for look now at the biggest stumbling block of all —

    3. The ruler of the seventh house of marriage, Venus in Aries, is in the sixth house of work and health. Venus is in its detriment in Aries, an infertile, masculine, fire sign; a singular, individualistic, another *I am* placement. It is the assertive, aggressive leader — just the opposite from the natural ruler of marriage, Libra, which denotes partnership and the need to care for and to be cared for by the opposite sex. Instead, Hepburn needed absolute freedom of action and thought and could not commit herself unselfishly to another person in the intimate bonds of matrimony. This Venus is —

    a) sextile Pluto, portraying a fundamental simplicity yet exuding a sexy charm,

    b) square Mars, generating impediments to sexual relationships,

    c) square Uranus, a divorce aspect, which defies convention and does not want the responsibility of belonging to just one person,

    d) square Jupiter, giving a certain arrogance; demanding in relationships, and

e) square Neptune, supplying great sensitivity and creative ability which she wanted to communicate *to the many* from the stage and screen — not to *one* man along.

Thus, Venus, squaring Mars, Uranus, Jupiter and Neptune, is the focal point of this T-square — a challenging aspect of great intensity, energy, and power.

Venus, signifying the ovaries, the eggs, the reproductive hormones, and the internal reproductive system in general, as tenant of the sixth house of health, and as focus of the T-square, faces a barrage of difficult vibrations. Physically, Venus square Jupiter/Neptune, as co-rulers of the fifth house of fertility because they rule Pisces on its cusp, hinders the bearing of children. A mental block to raising a family is the result of Venus square Mars/Uranus in the naturally mental third house, while the denial of children emotionally comes from Venus square the Jupiter/Neptune conjunction again in the sign of feeling, Cancer, on the naturally mental ninth house cusp.

The three fertile water signs, Cancer and Pisces in relation to the fifth house, and Scorpio, as ruler of the first house, all point to fertility. It is headstrong Venus in Aries that says, *no*. When we add the self-absorption of the Sun/Moon conjunction to the T-square, we reinforce the picture of negation to childbearing.

Venus, as tenant again of the sixth house of work, and once more the focal point of the T-square, directs its power now into the work dimension of the sixth house. An interesting approach to the seventh house ruler: it shows to what we are wedded; to what we want to join forces with; that to which we become attached. Here, the ruler of the seventh is Venus in the sixth house of work. Therefore, her work is what makes her happy.

The work that makes Hepburn happy is connected with an acting career. Venus is trine the cusp of the Leo 10th house of career, natural sign of entertainment, children, and creative efforts. The ruler of Leo is the Sun, here in the actor's sign, Taurus. It is sextile Saturn in the fifth house of entertainment, and conjunct her exalted Taurus Moon, signifying the masses. Katharine Hepburn is admired and loved by her public, her fans.

When the Moon is conjunct the Sun and is brand new, as in this chart, it sheds no light. While we cannot see her Moon in the night-time sky, her Sun continues to shine brightly on stage and screen for all to enjoy, and the motherly, caring, nurturing Moon side of her personality is reserved for her friends and loved ones. She was mother to the crew of whichever picture on which she worked, and with Virgo on the eleventh house, she nursed her friends through their illnesses.

In Claire's case, it is the Sun which is hidden in the twelfth cadent house, reinforcing the meditative, research, quiet nature of Claire — not a limelight position.

There is still another reason why Hepburn became a movie star instead of a mother. Look to her fifth house ruler, Pisces, fertile, feminine, romantic, sensitive, and the symbol of illusion, photography and films. Hepburn could portray the romantic, feminine leading lady of Pisces as well as the independent female signified by Venus in Aries.

Pisces is co-ruled by Neptune and Jupiter, and here they are conjunct in artistic Cancer on the cusp of the ninth house of foreign travel. Jupiter enhances and enlarges the aura of glamour and mystery indicative of Neptune, definitely not suggesting the stay-at-home wife and mother. Hepburn made a number of films in foreign lands — a seemingly fascinating way of life.

Claire's fifth house, on the other hand, has Libra, the marriage sign, on its cusp, ruled by Venus, which leads us to the double grand trine involving the second house of resources, the fifth house of children, and the tenth house of career. Claire's husband and children were her resources, her work and her career. She was a fulfilled woman.

Saturn in Pisces is the only planet in Hepburn's fifth house. Remembering Claire's chart, we know it denies, yet focuses attention upon the affairs of its house. Katharine Hepburn chose to deny birth to her natural children in order to focus on the creation of illusion, so as to provide for us moments of enchantment in the Neptunian world of fantasy and make believe. She succeeded.

We see her need for work; we understand why she chose acting as a career; but where did Hepburn's talent come from? Look to the second house, which rules both material and inner resources, or talent. Sagittarius is on the cusp, ruled by Jupiter, which is exalted in Cancer. Jupiter co-rules the fifth house of entertainment, is in itself the planet of the actor, and conjuncts Neptune, symbol of artistic creativity and inspiration. Jupiter and Neptune, rulers of talent and entertainment, are both on the cusp of the ninth house, which represents the results of the creative energy of the eighth house. With 3 Oscars and 11 Academy Award nominations, her talents are formidable; and they are totally accepted, admired, and appreciated by her vast audiences. Hepburn has also successfully bridged the gap between the glamourous, romantic, leading lady and character roles, because Neptune and Pisces hold dominion over character actors, and these are the rulers of her fifth house.

Claire has no exceptional faculty or skill, no extraordinary ability, even though Venus/Mars are in the second house with trines to the fifth house of children and to the tenth house of career. She and her husband are proud, however, that they have given to the world a lawyer, a Registered Nurse, a Medical Doctor, and a soon-to-be psychologist — through their children — the creative accomplishments of Claire's fifth house.

In conclusion, with 6 planets and the Lunar Nodes in fertile, feminine signs, a feminine, fertile Ascendant, the Sun and Moon both in "mother earth" Taurus, and thinking Mercury in the same domestic, conservative sign,

Katharine Hepburn could have overcome the self-centeredness of Venus in Aries *if* her family traditions had been more conventional. But, both of her parents were free thinkers; advocates of birth control; the mother having had been active in the suffragette movement. They encouraged in their children rebellion of the status quo for women — that is — marriage and motherhood.

Can we see this in Hepburn's chart? Yes. The instigator is progressive, non-conforming, independent and unconventional Uranus, ruler of Aquarius, the eccentric, reforming sign on the fourth house of the home, domestic environment, and family traditions. In trine to Mercury, this Uranus, from the mental third house, with ease and harmony, is able to alter Mercury's plodding, reserved, Taurean reasoning to its own radical way of thought.

Hepburn was intelligent enough, energetic enough and strong-willed enough to have combined successfully career/marriage/motherhood, but her early upbringing helped to decree otherwise. Now we see that the fifth house of childbearing is influenced, to some extent, by the house that precedes it — the fourth house of early conditioning and home environment. And yet, had Aquarius not ruled domestic environment — the fourth house — its opposite, Leo, the entertainment sign, would not have ruled career — the tenth house — and we would not have had

Katharine Hepburn *** Movie Star!

Chapter XII
Sophia Loren

A completely different type of horoscope awaits us as we leave the uppercrust New England society of Katherine Hepburn and travel to the small, poverty-stricken Italian town of Pazzuoli, near Naples, childhood home of another international motion picture star, Sophia Loren.

As we study the total picture of planetary placements in her natal chart, Figure 19, one conjunction stands out — just as this same conjunction is set apart in Claire's natal chart. Can you spot it? It is Moon conjunct Saturn.

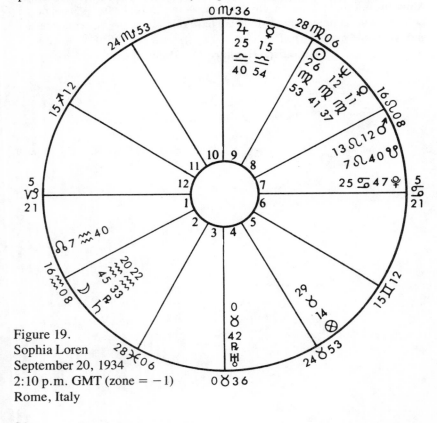

Figure 19.
Sophia Loren
September 20, 1934
2:10 p.m. GMT (zone = −1)
Rome, Italy

It is upon this Aquarian conjunction in the second house that the whole chart revolves because:

1. Moon and Saturn are the only tenants on the eastern or action-instigating side of the chart, and

2. Saturn is ruler of the ascending sign, Capricorn, which signifies Sophia, while the Moon rules Cancer, the sign on the seventh house cusp, which signifies her husband — film producer, Carlo Ponti. From this conjunction we realize that Sophia's husband is tremendously influential and important in her life, and that the purpose of their lives together stems from second house matters, since this is where the conjunction resides.

Sophia's symbol, Saturn, is very interesting. It rules Capricorn, but it is placed in the sign of its co-ruler, Aquarius. So here we have a personality ruled by two seemingly contradictory signs: one status quo, the other futuristic. The people who know Sophia intimately, her family, all describe her personality as a young girl in a similar vein: serious, dedicated to work, quiet, old and wise beyond her years, responsible, and mature. Do not these adjectives accurately depict her Capricorn Ascendant? Yet, as she grew older, while still maintaining her Saturnian qualities, the Aquarian attributes of intuitiveness, self-sufficiency, inventiveness and originality also manifested themselves.

Interestingly enough, Sophia is a combination of both the conservative and the unconventional; the person on whom one can rely, and the independent, unorthodox rebel; a free, liberated woman who still can take her responsibilities seriously. She, herself, describes her personality as shy, with controlled emotions off camera — her Capricorn reflection, and then liberated, uninhibited, and reckless on camera — her Aquarian counterpart.

Carlo Ponti's symbol, the Moon, is also a paradox because the Moon in astrology:

1. always is partial significator of the personality of the native,

2. always rules motherhood and childbearing in a woman's chart,

3. always represents the native's mother, and in this chart,

4. because it rules the sign, Cancer, on Sophia's seventh house cusp, it is symbolic of her husband.

The Moon, as a ruler of Sophia's personality:

It is placed in Aquarius, a friendly, fixed, progressive, infertile air sign, which reinforces the Aquarian sign in which Saturn, her Ascendant personality symbol is also placed. A devil-may-care attitude could be the result, but Saturn, which is conjunct the Moon, by its very nature is a controlling, inhibiting force which holds unbridled, free thinking in check. Yet, Saturn gives wisdom to those who care to learn its lessons. Sophia feels that she was born wise; also, that it was to her advantage to have been born in poverty. This was wise thinking in itself, for truly, she had no place to go but up!

With Moon/Saturn firmly ensconced in the second house, her life, together with her husband's, has developed along second house lines, and through this house she has acquired a famous name, money, property, jewelry and other material possessions, together with an intangible inner strength and the ability to develop her talents as an actress. Even the desire to have children, as an outgrowth of her marriage, stems from her second house, for this house in every natal chart rules:

1. self-acquired wealth, savings and finances,
2. material possessions,
3. inner resources, talents, moral growth, and
4. self-worth and self-preservation —

all accomplished in this particular chart in the emancipated, free-wheeling style of detached, tolerant Aquarius.

To understand Sophia's need for second house matters we must remember that she:

1. was born illegitimate,
2. was very, very poor, and
3. about age 6 lived under wartime conditions — bombs, air-raids, cold, hunger, thirst, lice, rats, and with death an imminent possibility in her war-torn home town.

Certainly she did not have a normal childhood, as Uranus, the unusual, on the fourth house cusp will attest! Sophia did not have the parental security of a father; the material security of food and clothing; or the emotional security of a home that would not be bombed to the ground. Is it any wonder, then, that the number one priority in her life was for:

1. the security that money supposedly can buy?
2. the home and material possessions she never had?
3. the development of her inner strength, her moral growth, and her talents so that no war, no famine, no lack of a father could ever again touch or destroy her?

Touchingly, the first item she ever bought for herself, the first tangible, visible, second house reward for her work, was a Venus-ruled mark of success — a tiny, diamond ring!

The Moon as ruler of motherhood and childbearing:

1. Its sign, Aquarius, is masculine and infertile.
/2. It is conjunct inhibiting Saturn (see Claire's chart) which is inimicable to childbearing.
3. It is square the fifth house cusp of Sophia's fertility and children, and also square the eleventh house cusp of her husband's fertility and children.
4. It is opposite destructive Mars.

None of the above aspects looks promising for ease in having children. On the positive side:

1. Mercury and Jupiter in Libra, from the ninth house of logic and judgment are trine Moon/Saturn. When Sophia finally and successfully became pregnant it was because she prudently followed the advice of a wise obstetrician.

2. Uranus on the fourth house cusp — the end of the matter — is sextile Moon/Saturn; the opportunity is there for ultimate success.

There is still another aspect to Moon/Saturn that we should particularly note: the unusual Finger of Yod or Finger of Fate which occurs when 2 planets which are sextile to each other are also in quincunx (150 degrees apart) to another planet or planets. In Sophia's chart, the Moon/Saturn conjunction is quincunx the Sun and quincunx Pluto, while the Sun and Pluto are sextile to each other. It supposedly points the way to some special task in life, which if handled wisely and well, can be very beneficial to one's character development. The quincunx is not an easy vibration because one should be motivated to serve rather than be served. It can cause confusion and stress, and as the Moon signifies the reproductive organs and childbearing, it can cause trouble in these areas. Sophia sacrificed for her unborn babies by remaining in bed throughout her two successful pregnancies.

The Moon as ruler of Sophia's mother:

As befits the value of this Moon/Saturn conjunction in Aquarius, her mother was extremely important to Sophia's development as a person and as an actress. Thwarted in her own plans for a movie career, this visionary, fiery, eccentric, stubborn, and uninhibited woman superimposed her own dreams onto a very willing daughter. It was really the mother's intense drive and ambition which paved the way for Sophia's stardom.

Yet now, Sophia's mother says, in their current relationship Sophia is the mother — the responsible Saturn, while the mother has become the more fickle Moon, and has taken the daugher's role. Sophia is the steadying, reassuring force — Saturn — in her mother's transient life — Moon. Mother/Moon lives in her daughter's image — Saturn. The faster traveling Moon is always strongly influenced by any slower moving planet which conjuncts it, and so Sophia/ Saturn, the slower moving planet, becomes the stronger motivating force to which the mother/Moon now clings.

The Moon, as symbol of husband:

The Moon, as ruler of the seventh house of marriage, gives to us in Carlo Ponti a sensitive man, gentle, creative, the protector and parent image, 22 years older than Sophia. Yet, he was aware of her inner strength and conscious of the fact that she took the Saturnine father's role in her early years. Starting in film work at age 15, it was she who was the provider on whom family members depended for support. In their marriage and working relationship, Sophia and Carlo are mutually dependent upon each other. He needed her youth and vitality; she required his mature, reflective mind and his stable and secure presence.

With both symbols in the second house, Sophia, as Saturn, worked as the actress. Ponti, as the Moon, helped her to perfect her talents; guided her in her choice of film roles; produced her pictures; insisted that she learn English; introduced her to the classics in literature; started her in American films; master-minded her career. In other words, he acted as her mother — Moon — for mutual second house rewards: money, fame, material possessions, and development, both before and behind the movie camera, of their respective talents.

We know that there is something unusual and radical about their alliance, both in the taking of marriage vows — Moon conjunct Saturn in Aquarius — and the married home life — Uranus, ruler of Aquarius, on the cusp of the fourth house of the home. Ponti had been a married man with two children. Since divorce was not recognized in Italy, a most unusual proxy divorce from his former wife, and an unconventional proxy marriage to Sophia was arranged and took place in Mexico. This marriage ceremony was not accepted in Italy, and until matters were straightened out, the couple lived for 8 years in an unorthodox, mixed-up marital relationship.

The Moon in the second house of talent:

Meanwhile, the partnership was producing successful films; fame and wealth came to the couple. While her mother had initially encouraged a film career, Sophia, even as a child, believed in her own talent, and had an inner knowing that she was indeed an "actress." Talent is a second house matter, and here, ruled by Aquarius:

1. It would be something original and unique.
2. It would figure importantly in her life because the Moon/Saturn within it is so prominent; it would also involve her husband/Moon.
3. It would be something special, accented by the Finger of Yod configuration.
4. It would involve the fifth-eleventh house axis because Moon/Saturn squares these houses, putting obstacles in the path of, but also giving energy for fifth house matters — fertility, her children, the entertainment world, and eleventh house matters — his children and fertility, and wishes to come true.

Another source of show business talent would come from the fifth house of entertainment, its planets and its ruler. This fifth house contains no planets, but does enjoy the presence of the Part of Fortune to give assistance and encouragement. With Taurus on the cusp, this house is ruled by Venus, symbol for the actress, the artist, and the beautiful, feminine things of life. Venus is conjunct

Neptune — planet of glamour, illusion, and romantic make-believe. Both are widely conjunct the Sun, Sophia's individuality, placed in the eighth house of money gained through partners — in this case, her husband. This triple Virgo placement of Venus/Neptune/Sun gives perception, analyzing ability, a natural knowingness of the rhythms of projection, an "ear" for phrasing, and a facility for picking up the cadences of foreign languages. (Remember Michael?) She speaks English fluently.

Venus/Neptune are trine the Ascendant, giving Sophia extraordinary beauty of face and form, an alluring charm, a fascinating personality, and the gift to be both photogenic and believable, whether it be in light comedy or serious drama.

Venus rules both Taurus and Libra. The Taurus rulership, concerned with monetary reward and second house matters, here on the fifth house cusp, spotlights primarily on financial considerations as Sophia's true motivation for a movie career. Even today, lending her name to a line of designer eyeglasses, promoting Coty cosmetics, and writing a successful beauty-care book, she combines the beauty and taste of Venus with the money-making practicality of the natural second house Taurus to create successful fifth house business ventures of creative usefulness.

The Libra rulership, concerned with artistic reward, stems from an intercepted ninth house placement of a reciprocal relationship between Venus at 11 Virgo in Mercury's sign, and Mercury at 15 Libra in Venus' sign. Many of her films have been recognized as artistic creations, particularly in the United States, a foreign land. These films have been commercial successes as well — Jupiter conjunct Mercury in Libra in the ninth house trine Moon/Saturn in Aquarius in the second.

Venus, as ruler of the fifth house of children and fertility:

Only one possession was missing, Sophia realized, as she approached her late 20's — *children*. She had always wanted them, but the upward climb to success and the mixed condition of her marriage had pushed the thought into the background. Now that she was firmly established, she decided that it was time. However, to her sorrow and chagrin, the aquisition of babies seemed to elude her. The fruits of a fifth house movie career were easier to attain than the fifth house fruit of her body.

In 1963, at age 29, Sophia suffered her first miscarriage. In 1967, at age 33, she had her second miscarriage. The astrological causes could be:

1. Saturn — Sophia — is in Aquarius, an infertile sign.
2. The Moon — her husband and her own motherhood — is also in infertile Aquarius.
3. Saturn conjunct the Moon is a deterrent to childbearing.

4. The Finger of Yod aspect to Moon/Saturn causes strain and/or unusual situations.

5. Moon/Saturn is square both the fifth house of Sophia's fertility, and the eleventh house of her husband's fertility.

6. Venus, as ruler of the fifth house, as ruler of the natural seventh house of marriage, as ruler of the internal reproductive system, the ovaries and the sex hormones they secrete — we have yet to consider:

a) Venus, weakly placed in its fall in Virgo, an infertile sign, cannot fully express its true nature and purpose as symbol of the ovaries which produce the eggs, and the hormones so necessary for the proper functioning of the reproductive cycle.

b) Venus, at 11 Virgo, is square the cusp of the sixth house of health at 15 Gemini. The medical reason, in Sophia's case, for losing two babies during the third months of pregnancy, was an imbalance of hormones. The ovaries, ruled by a weakened Venus in its fall, were not producing sufficient estrogen to hold the fetuses in the womb.

c) Venus is conjunct Neptune. Neptune, because it can be deceptive and make things seem that which they are not, when in aspect to a planet in a health situation, can demonstrate a condition which is difficult to diagnose. Here, Neptune casts its shadow over Venus and the parts of the body Venus rules — the ovaries and its hormones. Neptune, that misty disguiser, while beguilingly enhancing her screen image, obscured and undermined Sophia's reproductive functions.

Concerning the miscarriages:

In everyone's chart, when one reaches age 28 to 30, Saturn, after making one complete journey through the zodiac, returns to its own birth sign and house. One's life then should take on a deeper meaning, especially concerning the affairs of Saturn's house. For Sophia, then, second house Saturn caused matters of that house to loom large, and thus it was that her values took on a more serious coloration. Thoughts of career, money and fame recede, and now Sophia wishes to claim her birthright as a woman — to bear children.

She chose the wrong time. Twice. Knowing the years but not the dates of these miscarriages, we will study only the transiting outer planets as we try to examine their causes.

Throughout 1963, the year of the first miscarriage, Saturn made its return. It advanced to natal Saturn, rested on it, turned back, and then slowly started its way forward again. This phenomenon of retrogradation, when a planet seems to be moving backward in the sky, intensifies its vibrations to the planet being conjuncted. Here, Saturn reinforces its natal commitment to squelch the motherly Moon, and it thereby denied new life.

100

In 1967, time of the second miscarriage, transiting Uranus retrograded and then transited Sophia's natal Sun at 26 Virgo — the ruler of her eighth house of sex force. Always the planet of upheaval and the unexpected, Uranus now took its turn to disrupt Sophia's plans for motherhood. Nor was transiting Neptune of any assistance. Another retrograde planet, it exactly squared natal Moon/Saturn twice during the year.

Sophia's miscarriages were the worst experiences of her entire life. They left her nervous, defeated, and weak, with feelings of failure. But, she would not be denied. Finally, pregnant once more, and under a new doctor's care, estrogen injections were administered and Sophia was instructed to spend the entire nine months of pregnancy in bed. Willingly she did so, thinking of nothing but the new life developing within her. Triumphant at last, Sophia gave birth by Caesarean section to a healthy baby boy.

Four years later, again spending 8 months in bed, another baby boy was born to Sophia and Carlo. Her joy was now complete. With one-pointed concentration to the task at hand, Sophia used the stubbornness of Capricorn and the fixity of purpose of Aquarius to subdue and outwit Saturn, manipulating his stern, rigid qualities to her own advantage. Eventually, Saturn had to bestow its rewards, because Sophia was willing to pay the price. Now Sophia's second house could victoriously be stamped — *paid in full*.

What does the future hold for this famous couple? The gossip columns have them, at times, separated, each going his own way. This is not surprising since each of their astrological symbols is in freedom-loving Aquarius, and a certain Bohemian attitude goes along with Uranus, its ruling planet.

But, the symbols are Saturn and the Moon. A strong Saturn cannot easily shake responsibility and Moon is clinging and home loving. There is one more important element to consider — how progressions and transits affect natal planets. As time marches on, so do the planets, and as they travel, the aspects they make to each other change, bringing different people and conditions into the life.

The Moon and Saturn, however, when natally conjunct are peculiarly unique, because if they start life off together, they remain so throughout the life span. Saturn arranges it by transit; the Moon by secondary progression.

We have already noted that Saturn completes its zodiacal journey in 28 to 30 years by transit. The Moon, in secondary progression, uses the factor that one day in the ephemeris equals one year of life. Since it takes the daily Moon 27 to 28 days to complete its monthly journey, it is equal in secondary progression to 27 to 28 years. Therefore, wherever transiting Saturn is in the horoscope, the progressed Moon is somewhere in the vicinity.

Wherever Sophia/Saturn is, Ponti/Moon is in the vicinity. For as long as they both shall live.

In like manner it is so for Claire/Moon and her husband/Saturn.

Chapter XIII
Shirley Temple Black

Where else but in bright, warm, fun-loving California could such sunniness have been born. That light-hearted sunbeam, the child movie star, Shirley Temple, whose magical name brought a smile to one's lips at just the mention of it!

In her orphan-y, moppet movies, searching for love, she eventually always found it. In real life, family and friends, co-workers, the famous in all walks of life, in fact, people all over the world fell under this little girl's spell, showering her with spontaneous, overwhelming affection in return for that love which she so effortlessly and willingly extended to all who went to see her in the "pictures" during the 1930's.

As was the custom, the most popular and successful motion picture stars of the day left their imprint in the cement sidewalk in front of Grauman's Chinese Theater in Hollywood. In March, 1935, when it was Shirley's turn, she engraved her own unerasable message, *Love to you all*.

Certainly it should have been easy for her to love, for hadn't she been blessed with everything? An outgoing, positive personality, intelligence, talent, beauty, and the right people to guide her? The extraordinary attention and star treatment which she received at a very early age might have damaged a more fragile flower. Shirley, however, was at first unaware of her status, then enjoyed and even reveled in her phenomenon-ity, and then was able to grow beyond it.

Let's look at this golden horoscope, Figure 20, which offered to one little girl an overabundance of *everything* that most of us value, plus, and this is most important, the wisdom to cope with its use.

Shirley started in movies at the age of three. Obviously, she needed a mentor, and this she had in her mother, a woman who even before her child was born, tried to influence the growing fetus with love for music, art and things of natural beauty.

And so, we look to the Moon for clues concerning:

1. Shirley's mother,
2. Shirley's personality, along with the Ascendant,
3. Shirley's motherhood and fertility along with Cancer, the fifth house, and Venus, and
4. Shirley's breasts, along with Cancer and the fourth house. We note this because of a mastectomy of the left breast due to cancer.

102

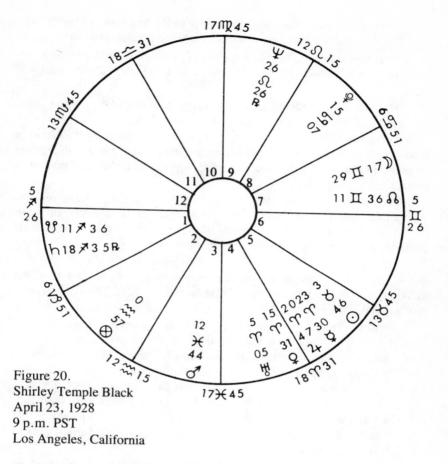

Figure 20.
Shirley Temple Black
April 23, 1928
9 p.m. PST
Los Angeles, California

The Moon at 29 Gemini, representing Shirley's mother:

Gertrude Temple, like Sophia's mother, her own show business dreams unfulfilled, directed Shirley's tiny rhythmic feet toward the motion picture studio. The Moon in Gemini, a mental teaching sign, is strongly placed on an angle — the seventh house of partnerships and relationships, and it is:

1. Sextile the Sun, Jupiter, and Mercury in the fifth house of entertainment, guiding her daughter toward a show business career.

2. Square Uranus in the fourth house, providing Shirley with an unusual upbringing and home life in the early years, although a protective one.

3. Sextile Neptune, ruling films, in Leo, sign of entertainment — again an emphasis on, and opportunity for movie work.

4. Opposite Saturn, an awareness aspect. There was an involvement, a close connection of responsibility on the mother's part — Moon — to develop

her daughter's talents, symbolized by Saturn in the first house of personality, which is the ruler of Capricorn on the second house of talent and resources.

5. A power pivot. This Moon has the dynamic job of setting off Shirley's most important configuration — the grand trine in fire situated in the houses of life.

This grand trine is the focus for her life and it envelopes all of her interests. By means of Saturn at 18 Sagittarius, it connects Shirley's first house — personality and attitudes — with Jupiter at 20 Aries and Mercury at 23 Aries in the fifth house of children, show business, and avocations, with the ninth house Neptune in Leo — the diplomatic service, aspiring thoughts, and interest in foreign lands and people.

The grand trine is an aspect of harmony and ease and promises rewards without too much effort. But, it does not have either the intensity, drive, or power of the square, or the awareness of the opposition aspect, and it needs something to give it a push and set it in motion.

This is where the Moon comes in. Being sextile Neptune and the fifth house planets, and opposite Saturn, it is the instigating force which sets off this active, goal-oriented, grand trine in fire in the houses of life. Therefore, it is the mother who is the provoking stimulus for Shirley's start in pictures.

Gertrude Temple was an outspoken partner (seventh house) and the mediator (Gemini) between her child and the moving picture industry. She was paid a salary to manage, chaperone, and dress Shirley; to keep her unspoiled and from growing up too fast. She was the coach, the teacher (Gemini). How Shirley should stand and walk; how she was to deliver her lines; her very expressions all originated with this careful, caring, supervising mother. But, she was not exploitative! When, in 1940, two pictures failed, the parents wisely bought up Shirley's contract, retired her from pictures, and Shirley went to regular classes for her high school years.

Having a patron to teach and guide one is not enough, however. There has to be something special about the child's personality itself. Just what was there about Shirley that was so enchanting, so entrancing? Let's look at that Moon again, this time as ruler of Shirley's personality:

1. Moon sextile Neptune gives Shirley creative talent in acting, art, music, and the dance. As an adult it gives her interest in the public welfare and the capability of relieving people's burdens.

2. Moon sextile Mercury gives Shirley an alert mind, good memory, and communication skills.

3. Moon sextile Venus (wide) gives popularity, charm, an attractive and loving personality, and the talent to work well with young people.

4. Moon sextile Jupiter supplies altruism, and the interest and ability to aid in the rehabilitation of handicapped persons.

5. Moon sextile Sun furnishes independence, self reliance, and the ability to relate easily to people.

6. Moon opposite Saturn obliges Shirley to take her responsibilities seriously. Saturn represents government service and with this planet in her first house, Shirley is drawn to this work in later years.

7. Moon square Uranus gives her the impulsiveness which led to her hasty first marriage. (Gemini on the seventh house cusp often indicates more than one marriage.) She also likes change and the feeling of being "on the move."

Place this powerful Moon in the seventh house and we have a "people who needs people" kind of Shirley. She needs to "do" for people and needs their attention and love in return. Consequently, even though this Moon is in infertile, masculine Gemini, its sextiles to the fifth house planets and her overall warm, responsive personality make her an excellent mother.

Cancer, the sign of motherhood, is on the eighth house cusp. The Moon, as its ruler and grand trine instigator:

1. Permits Shirley to gain through the public in both financial matters and personal acceptance.

2. Acts as an agent of —

a) rejuvenation — during the Depression of the 1930's, not only children, but even adults entered into her optimistic fantasy world through her make-believe movies, and found laughter, song, and good cheer along with new hope.

b) regeneration — as an adult, Shirley worked as a hospital volunteer for crippled children and became involved in many charity groups to help youngsters.

c) revitalization — Shirley has interests which are ecological in scope, including elimination of air pollution and the safeguarding of endangered species of animals. She encourages interest in world participation of an early warning system for natural disasters.

d) global healing — whereby she is committed to improving the quality of human existence, insuring human dignity, and urging all to work together for the rational management of our common resources. Shirley travels to many parts of the globe to accomplish these ends, always feeling a kinship with all human beings — ruler of the first house, Jupiter (Shirley), conjunct ruler of the seventh house, Mercury (other people).

e) personal healing — when in 1972, a cancerous lump in her breast necessitated a mastectomy, Shirley turned the painful experience into a source for good by informing the women of the world of her condition, thus alerting them to the necessity for self-examination and yearly medical checkups.

The Ascendant as indicator of personality:

The Moon is not the only indicator of personality; the first house is as well, and it contributes to how a woman looks at the role of motherhood. With Sagittarius as the rising sign, and its ruler, Jupiter, in the fifth house, we see why Shirley was drawn to early motherhood, as well as feeling perfectly at home on a movie sound stage at a very tender age. Jupiter gives the dimples that flash, a grin that widens, and an optimistic and expansive cheerfulness. Movie audiences were captivated by her infectitous good mood, her truly joyous vibrations, and a certain élan with which she enveloped the motion picture screen. Because Mercury is conjunct Jupiter, Shirley was able to communicate her exuberance to the people, who at that time were badly in need of uplifting, and it was her overflowing high spirits, more than her acting talent which endeared Shirley to her public.

Jupiter, a planet of radiance and faith, conjunct Venus, planet of personal magnetism, ruling the sixth house of work, make an unbeatable combination for success both in the movies and as a mother as they conjunct the fifth house cusp in Shirley's chart. With Uranus trine the Ascendant giving a one-of-a-kind incandescent quality, and Saturn responsibly keeping her two feet on the ground, at least figuratively, we have the reasons why this tiny child was a household name for many years and box office queen of the world during the years of 1935 through 1938. In 1938 her income was the seventh highest in America!

Why such phenomenal success during these particular years?

Saturn usually tells the story. In Shirley's chart, Saturn held a first house position at birth, and as it progressed down through the second and third houses an obscure, quiet learning process should have been taking place. But, in 1932, when Shirley was 4, transiting Saturn first conjuncted natal Part of Fortune and then squared the natal fifth house of entertainment, giving impetus to her baby career from the second house of self-earned money and talent. It conjuncted natal Mars, the action planet, and ruler of the fifth house in 1935. During the years of 1936-37-38, Saturn conjuncted the fourth house cusp, squared natal Saturn, and went on to conjunct natal Uranus (the picture industry) and Venus (the actress planet). These aspects, while strong, do not seem to carry enough weight for such huge success, so let's look to transiting Uranus.

Uranus starts life in Shirley's chart in the fourth house. In 1931, when Shirley was 3 and just starting in movies, Uranus, ruler of the motion picture industry, conjuncted her natal Venus — the entertainment planet and ruler of her sixth house of work. In 1932, Uranus conjuncted natal Jupiter, ruler of the Ascendant, then next conjuncting Mercury, ruler of the tenth house of career. During 1933 it remained in that area.

Finally, in 1935-36, the start of her two best years in movies, transiting Uranus conjuncted natal Sun — ruler of motion picture stars. It stayed in the fifth house for 1937-38, making a sextile to Mars, ruler of the fifth. Thus, the fifth house planets and ruler were activated. But, something more was needed, so let's look to natal Neptune, which rules movies, and study its transit through Shirley's chart.

Neptune, planet of illusion, films, and fantasy, is a very slow moving outer planet, taking 165 years to complete one journey through the zodiac. However, it was in just the right place and at just the right time for Shirley to become a super-star. It started at Shirley's birth in the ninth house at 26 Leo, and by 1935, transiting Neptune had traveled to 12 Virgo — just opposite natal Mars (ruler of fifth), and coming to a conjunction of the tenth house cusp of career while squaring Saturn in the first house.

In 1936-37-38 this Neptune crossed, retrogressed, came forward again and then went back, always at the very top of Shirley's chart, continuously squaring natal Saturn while Shirley was at the very peak of her career.

Saturn, planet of denial and restriction, allowing such tremendous success? Yes, because Saturn gives us what we deserve. In Shirley's chart, the Capricorn second house of talent and resources is ruled by Saturn, and here, placed in the first house, her talent is uniquely her own; a birthright; part of her very nature. Connect it to the Venus-Jupiter-Mercury-Sun conjunctions in the fifth house, and to Neptune in the ninth house by trines, and the charm, grace, earnestness of spirit, and yes, luck flow easily, instigated and prodded by this publicly placed, transiting Neptune which is originally part of the talented grand trine. Also note that natal Saturn makes its own T-square to the tenth/fourth axis, providing the impetus for success.

This resulted, for Shirley, in a seriousness about, and a sense of responsibility for her work, which while hidden beneath cuteness, froth, merriment and playfulness, made her the true trouper that she was.

Finally Neptune passed over, and with the square aspect to Saturn dissipated, Shirley's peak also waned. Neptune, in her lifetime, would never again come to this tenth house cusp and Shirley would never again attain this particular brand of success.

At age 17 Shirley determinedly left childhood behind, but was ill-prepared for her hasty marriage to John Agar — the Moon in the seventh house square Uranus. From this union came Linda Susan, born January 30, 1948, and Shirley was a devoted mother.

Rectifying her mistake, Shirley dissolved the marriage and wed Charles Black — business man, naval officer, environmentalist and conservationist — on December 16, 1950. It is a good, solid, happy marriage; successful because both share the interests of the other, each working alone but in parallel fields, the significators of each being in self asserting, solo-going Aries.

As in the charts of Claire and Sophia, the ruler of the first house (Jupiter-Shirley) is conjunct the ruler of the seventh house of the husband (Mercury-

Charles) so the relationship is a very close one. With one important difference: this conjunction is not alone, but is enclosed by Venus to the left and the Sun to the right in a stellium width of 18 degrees. Remember, too, that Mercury, ruler of the seventh, not only signifies the husband, but also expresses career, being ruler of Virgo, the tenth house sign. While being a wife is all-important to Shirley, work in movies (Venus is ruler of the sixth house) and diplomatic service as ruled by the Sun (ruler of the ninth house) were activities achieved independently of her husband.

Fertility and motherhood:

To Shirley, marriage and motherhood went hand in hand. But, was she fertile? Examaining her fifth house, the Moon and Venus we find:

1. Aries on the fifth house cusp in an infertile, masculine sign — unfavorable for childbearing.

2. A busy fifth house containing —
   a) Jupiter — favorable
   b) Mercury — neutral, but signifying husband, and conjunct Jupiter (Shirley), therefore favorable.

3. The ruler of the fifth house is Mars, which is square Saturn — unfavorable.

4. Mars in Pisces, a fertile water sign, is trine Pluto at 15 Cancer in the eighth house of sex — favorable.

5. Venus — signifying the ovaries, eggs and internal reproductive organs, is part of the grand trine, and therefore favorable, but it is in its detriment in Aries — unfavorable.

6. Moon in Gemini — masculine, infertile sign — unfavorable.

7. Moon opposite Saturn — unfavorable.

8. Moon square Uranus — unfavorable.

We have a mixture here of both favorable and unfavorable significators. Shirley had one child by her first marriage, Linda Susan Agar, born January 30, 1948, and then two more children by Black. She was a dedicated mother whose children were raised conventionally and who gave her no unusual problems. During their early years Shirley was a full time mother, but as the children gradually needed her less, she took her avocation (ruled by the fifth house) of volunteer work more and more seriously until it resulted in a recognized diplomatic career.

The second child, Charles Black, Jr. was born on April 28, 1952, by Caesarean section, with complications which briefly threatened Shirley's life. If you look up in your ephemeris this baby's birth planets, that is, those transiting the heavens on this day, you will notice the following:

1. The Moon, at 27 Gemini, is conjunct Shirley's Moon.

2. A cardinal T-square involving Mercury at 12 Aries/Venus at 22 Aries, opposite Saturn at 9 Libra/Neptune at 19 Libra, square Uranus at 10 Cancer. See how this configuration emphasizes the fifth-eleventh house axis of children in Shirley's chart.

The third child, Lori Black, was born on April 9, 1954, also by Caesarean section. Her birth planets involved a grand square composed of the Sun at 19 Aries, the Lunar Nodes at 19 Cancer-Capricorn, Neptune at 24 Libra, and Moon at 10 Cancer/Uranus at 19 Cancer. Again, notice the connection to Shirley's fifth and eleventh houses.

In September of 1972, Shirley discovered a lump in her left breast. The breasts are ruled by the Moon, the sign, Cancer, and the fourth house. Natally the Moon is opposite Saturn and square Uranus in the fourth house, denoting trouble; but its sextiles and trine (widely to Mars) are protective and hopeful. Look in a noon ephemeris at the transiting planets of November 2, 1972, the day the biopsy was performed, and which pronounced "cancer." Note the square and opposition of 4 planets to the natal Moon square Uranus which signified trouble to the breasts. Note, *for the third time* the connection with the fifth/eleventh house axis, the houses of fertility and reproduction of: Uranus at 20 Libra/Mars at 21 Libra, square Lunar Nodes at 20 Cancer-Capricorn. See how Mercury and Neptune, at 3-4 Sagittarius transited right to her Ascendant at that time to mentally inspire her with courage and optimism as they trined her third-house-ruled Uranus!

Shirley came through the ordeal with flying colors and within a month she resumed her active life and interests — her volunteer work. Charity and hospital work filled her days. When President Nixon was running for office she was a hardworking volunteer for him, which became a prelude to, and preparation for, a diplomatic career. Now, with political connections, in 1969 Nixon appointed Shirley as delegate to the United Nations.

On August 20, 1974, President Ford named Shirley Ambassadress to Ghana in Africa. Look these transits up and you will notice how the emphasis has changed from the fifth/eleventh axis of childbearing to the tenth/fourth axis of career (Lunar Nodes at 15 Sagittarius/Gemini, square Mars at 15 Virgo, opposite Jupiter at 14 Pisces). Notice transiting Sun at 27 Leo conjuncting Neptune in the ninth house of diplomatic service. Shirley was ready for the job!

And, take a look at transiting Neptune at 6 Sagittarius. Remember when it conjuncted her tenth house cusp during her hey-day movie years of 1935-1938? Well, here it is right on Shirley's Ascendant, her first house of personality, shedding its idealistic and creative vibrations for this new and challenging role.

On November 29, 1974 Ambassadress Shirley Temple Black left for sweltering Ghana where her job was to look after the interests of the United States in trade and diplomacy. Once again, study the transits. See how the focus of interest has changed to the first/seventh house axis of interpersonal relationships, and with it the objectivity of the full Moon (Neptune, Sun, Venus, and North Node conjunct the Ascendant, opposite the Moon at 5 Gemini and South Node at 10 Gemini, square Jupiter at 9 Pisces). For Shirley, it was a time of personal fulfillment, a goal realized, a dream come true.

Shirley believes that everything she has done in her life so far has directed her into international diplomacy. Her horoscope bears this out. Instead of directing her motherly, fifth house instincts and feelings toward only her immediate family, she has chosen to look at the larger picture and wishes to act as guardian to her whole country. Why? Because home and country are signified by the fourth house. Its cusp is Pisces, whose ruler, Neptune, is posited in the ninth house of international affairs. The Ascendant also has a ninth house emphasis, its sign being Sagittarius, the natural ninth house ruler. Shirley also has a talent or quintile aspect between the Sun and Pluto which rules organizations attempting to achieve better social conditions. One wonders why, however, especially with her ninth house (university) emphasis, Shirley did not go on to higher education to better prepare herself for government service. Did Jupiter make her over-confident, or over-optimistic about her capabilities?

At any rate, as the world needed Shirley's good cheer and positive outlook during the dark days of the Great Depression, so today we need her mature idealism and optimism, now tempered with wisdom.

What does the future hold for Shirley?

In December of 1982, Uranus, the planet of change, crossed her Ascendant and will remain in the first house through 1989, during which time it will conjunct her first house Saturn, setting off her grand trine. In 1986, Saturn in transit will conjunct her Ascendant and then make its second return to natal Saturn, always a time of introspection and change. The planets, which have always worked adventageously for Shirley in the past, should do so again and give her the opportunity of serving her country, which is her greatest wish; for maturity has not dampened either her first house spirit of adventure, her fifth house talent of creativity, or her ninth house love for diplomatic service.

Shirley Temple Black is an excellent choice to represent our country diplomatically, for she embodies the Christian ethics upon which our nation was founded. She has immense faith in God and her native land; boundless hope for peace among all peoples; and the message which she traced in concrete some 50 years ago still stands:

Love to you all

Chapter XIV
Beverly Sills

As opulent as grand opera itself, as plentiful and colorful as her golden-red hair, her full figure, her ornate operatic regalia, and her throaty laughter are the aspects in the horoscope of coloratura soprano, Beverly Sills.

Grand trine, opposition, square, sextile, conjunction — they're all here — mixing and meshing to produce a luxurious life style rich in material goods, interesting travel, rewarding work, international fame, and then, too, a measure of pathos and pain. The stuff from which operas are made.

Not that our heroine accentuates her troubles. In her autobiography, *Bubbles,* Miss Sills gives only a hint of the double blow that life has dealt her. An upbeat person who looks only on the bright side, even her bout with cancer is treated negligibly in her life story. She takes us mainly only on an upward journey into the stratosphere of her operatic career, making success seem, although it was not, effortlessly and quickly attained.

Certainly she was singularly blessed with an extraordinarily beautiful voice, the physical good health to maintain it, and the ambition to sustain it. The pursuit of excellence and the desire for growth, both onstage and off, which has been her aim from an early age, has resulted in the beloved and respected position Beverly Sills holds throughout the operatic world today.

Does her birth chart, as seen in Figure 21, really promise all of this?

The most noticeable planets in Beverly's chart are the Moon and Saturn, conjunct in Sagittarius and straddling the eleventh house cusp. They are prominent for two reasons:

1. They are the only planets in the southeast sector of the chart, emphasizing growth in social influence.

2. They are the handle for the bucket formation, a configuration made by the situation of all planets in one-half of the chart, save Moon/Saturn, which are trine to each end of the bucket.

While a new student can spot this conjunction at first glance, it takes the practiced eye of a trained astrologer to pick out one of the foremost reasons for Beverly's success in the operatic arena — where all the drive, all the personality, all the practice, and all the breaks must come to naught if the main ingredient is lacking — the talent of an operatic voice.

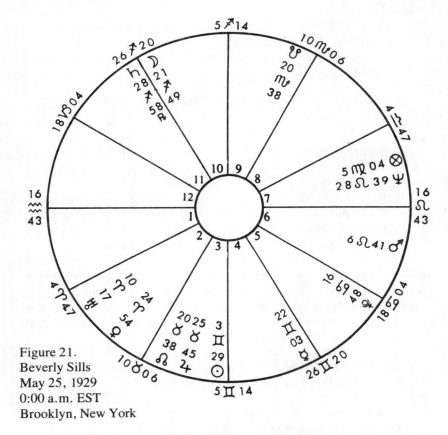

Figure 21.
Beverly Sills
May 25, 1929
0:00 a.m. EST
Brooklyn, New York

Such a profusion of quintile, biquintile and even a semi-semi-quintile studs this chart, as do the many jewels which bedeck the dazzling costumes of her regal characterizations — from Queen Shemakha in Rimsky-Korsakov's *Le Coq d'Or*, to Cleopatra in Handel's *Julius Caesar*, to her three Donizetti queens, Elizabeth I, Maria Stuarda and Anna Bolena — that there is no question that tremendous talent is present, and to spare.

Let's examine Beverly's horoscope, and before we tackle the major aspects of her natal chart, we will put the spotlight on these less-looked-for aspects, which because of their sheer number, we admiringly now stress as we count them off one by one.

First of all, what is a *quintile?*

A quintile is an aspect between two planets which are 72 degrees apart, with an allowable orb of 3 degrees. It is a beneficial aspect, and because 72 degrees is one-fifth of the complete circle of 360 degrees, it is related to fifth house affairs, which are — and by now you know them by heart — creativity, children, the entertainment world, speculation, avocations, and love affairs. It is an aspect which denotes artistic talent.

The biquintile is a larger offshoot of the quintile — 144 degrees between planets; two-fifths of the circle; double the quintile; also signifying artistic talent.

The semi-quintile, at 36 degrees, one-half of the quintile, is a creative aspect, while the semi-semi-quintile is one-fourth of the quintile — a mini aspect of 18 degrees between planets with an allowable orb of 1 degree — which supplies potential for innate knowledge of proper technique in artistic performance.

The quintiles are as follows:

1. Uranus at 10 Aries 17 quintile Mercury at 22 Gemini 03,
2. Jupiter at 25 Taurus 45 quintile Mars at 6 Leo 41,
3. Mercury at 22 Gemini 03 quintile the Part of Fortune at 5 Virgo 03, and
4. Midheaven at 5 Sagittarius 14 quintile the Ascendant at 16 Aquarius 43.

The biquintiles are as follows:

1. Saturn at 28 Sagittarius 58 Rx biquintile Jupiter at 25 Taurus 45,
2. Mars at 6 Leo 41 biquintile Saturn at 28 Sagittarius 58 Rx,
3. Saturn at 28 Sagittarius 58 Rx biquintile the North Node at 20 Taurus 39, and
4. Uranus at 10 Aries 17 biquintile the Part of Fortune at 5 Virgo 03.

The semi-semi-quintile is:

1. Sun at 3 Gemini 29 semi-semi-quintile Mercury at 22 Gemini 03.

These so-called minor aspects are important because they supply the fine-tuning for the creative talent furnished by Beverly's weighty, self-assuring grand trine in fire.

How could we possibly know that her talent would be singing?

Singing and opera are under the rulership of the sign, Taurus, and the planet, Venus. Therefore, this sign and this planet should figure prominently in Sills' chart. They do, because:

1. The ruler of the tenth house of career, having Sagittarius on its cusp, is Jupiter in Taurus (opera singing), in the third house of communication, conjunct the Sun in Gemini — the Sun ruling stars of the entertainment world. Jupiter is semi-sextile to Venus (opera singing), a productive aspect, which along with enlarging the Venus talent, gives her a personable quality, an inner sense of beauty, and an outer attractiveness as well.

2. Taurus on the cusp of the third house decides that Beverly communicates to her public primarily through singing. Its ruler, Venus, is placed in the second house of talent, widely conjunct Uranus, which is ruler of the first house

of personality and attitudes. Her talent is unusual and distinctive, and her personal magnetism is strong.

3. Pisces is intercepted in the first house and, therefore, it co-rules the Ascendant. Its ruler, Neptune (make-believe) in Leo (stage) is trine Venus (opera), so both co-rulers of the first house are connected importantly to Venus — Uranus by conjunction and Neptune by trine. Venus trine Neptune gives Beverly her love for music and art, and talent in those areas; it also imparts a sensitive, romantic nature.

4. Jupiter in Taurus not only rules the tenth house of career, but co-rules the first house as well (co-ruler of intercepted Pisces along with Neptune), giving further emphasis to a tenth-first house Taurus/Venus/opera singing influence.

5. The fifth house of entertainment is ruled by Gemini, with Mercury, its ruler, strong in its own sign, and sextile Venus, another link to the opera. Mercury is the melody; Venus is the harmony. Together they give artistic talent and musical ability.

6. Pluto at 16 Cancer, residing in the fifth house, is square Venus, challenging her commitment to bring the beauty of opera to as many people as possible. With Pluto ruling the ninth house of foreign lands and travel, Beverly has sung in opera houses all over the world and has been successfully acclaimed.

Venus square Pluto indicates a serious crisis in life which could transform preoccupation with self into a broader, more all-encompassing love for others. Pluto, being in the fifth house of children, centers the crisis there, resulting in two handicapped children. It did transform her.

7. Venus at 24 Aries in the second house is part of the fiery grand trine aspect of creativity — Venus trine Neptune trine Moon/Saturn. Its talent flows from the second house of inner resources to all of the people in the seventh house — Neptune at 28 Leo in the seventh. This talent is the basis for a tenth house career — the Moon at 21 Sagittarius in the tenth; a talent which results in an eleventh house fulfillment of hopes and wishes both professionally and monetarily — Saturn at 28 Sagittarius in the eleventh house.

Added individualistic talent stems from Uranus, ruler of the first house, trine Mars at 6 Leo (the entertainment sign) from the sixth house of work. (Rex E. Bills cites Uranus as possible ruler of singing.) This aspect gives Beverly the stamina for hard work, the ability to withstand difficulties, and the need for an exciting life occupation.

Following the now familiar pattern, it was Beverly's mother who was highly instrumental in providing a musical environment for her daughter. The weekly singing, dancing, and elocution lessons she insisted upon set the stage for a musical career. The lessons led to a local radio program, and at age 4 Beverly's voice was heard over the air — not singing, but talking! She was already displaying the precocious tongue and extensive vocabulary that only a

Sun in Gemini can produce. (Don't forget that Sun-Mercury semi-semi-quintile technique!)

Memorizing arias at a tender age — with Mercury quintile Uranus she was a quick study — was Beverly's own idea, however, as was the decision to become an opera singer. Her parents encouraged her efforts, and superior teachers took her the rest of the way.

The highly visible tenth house Moon, part of the grand trine, guarantees not only a public life for Beverly, but a mother who was always very much in evidence, and an important cog in her daughter's triangle of success. For many years she designed and sewed all of Beverly's opera costumes and was an appreciated traveling companion on many an operatic journey.

The pilgrimage to world acclaim as an opera star was slow, but steadily on the rise. If there were setbacks, Beverly scarcely mentions them in her book. We are privy mostly to the joys of the job, the grandeur of the music, and the re-creation of the roles she portrayed. The human voice, her gift from God which she so thrillingly projected across the footlights, was echoed back to her with love and appreciation from opera goers wherever she appeared.

Miss Sills chooses to emphasize the Sagittarian tone of her chart — 6 planets in fire signs, 4 mutable planets, and a tenth house cusp in Sagittarius, with its Jupiterian rulership accentuating optimism, good fortune, popularity and philosophical reasoning. The arrow of Sagittarius points upward, but never off course, because her Aquarian Ascendant, while ruled by non-conforming Uranus, is co-ruled by Saturn, a down-to-earth, sober, strait-laced, responsible influence.

Which brings us to Saturn conjunct the Moon.

Concentrate on Beverly's chart and you will see how pivotal this Moon/Saturn conjunction is. These two planets are:

1. being the most highly elevated, and the handle to the bucket configuration of the horoscope, the most importantly placed planets in the grand trine,

2. quincunx Jupiter, ruler of the tenth house and co-ruler of intercepted Pisces of the first house, — a decision-making aspect, wherein one benefits the most when he is motivated to serve rather than be served, and

3. opposite Mercury, ruler of the fifth house of children and entertainment. Emotions and reasoning clash concerning children.

Encompassing the eleventh house cusp, Moon/Saturn focuses its energy on:

1. her husband's children and his fertility,
2. her friends and followers,
3. her ability to overcome obstacles,
4. associations and organizations to which she belongs,
5. humanitarian causes, and
6. her hopes and wishes.

Saturn signifies restriction in all charts, but here in Beverly's chart, its discipline is doubly felt because:

1. It co-rules, along with Uranus, the ever-important Ascendant, giving a sober, realistic, responsibility-accepting personality. However, keep in mind the other Ascendant ruler, Uranus, which erases some of that restraint and puts friendliness and adventuresomeness in its place.

2. It also rules the twelfth house (Capricorn is on the cusp), the house which signifies life's hardest battles and most difficult tasks, troubles and handicaps, restrictions, and the hidden side of a person's life. Thinking about these things, we wonder how this could affect the Moon — motherhood — as Saturn holds this "light" in its grasp.

In Claire's chart, Saturn represented the husband, while in Sophia's chart, Saturn symbolized Sophia. In Beverly's chart, however, Saturn represents life's battles, handicaps, and troubles. The twelfth house is also supposedly the house of Karma, the house of self-undoing. For those who believe in Karma, it is here that one must make restitution for the transgressions of former lives.

And so, we realize that Saturn will restrict motherhood in some way as it conjuncts the Moon. It may deny children, cause trouble in having them, give trouble in raising them, or possibly produce afflicted children. In this case, with Saturn in the eleventh house of the husband's children, Beverly was given one mentally retarded step-daughter. With Saturn on the Moon of her own motherhood, Beverly gave birth to two handicapped children — one deaf and one mentally retarded.

This is where we must pause. While Beverly accentuated the glories of her career and rightly and proudly so, we must, because it is important to our study, explore the dark side of her troubles.

Marriage:

Beverly married wealthy newspaper man, Peter Greenough, on November 17, 1956. Leo, on the seventh house cusp of marriage in Beverly's chart, gives the Sun as its ruler and significator of the husband. Placed in the mental third house of communication, and in Gemini, sign of writing and everyday, concrete affairs (the "news" which papers provide), this Gemini Sun is also the sign of more than one marriage, and therefore, Peter, her husband, fits her horoscope exceedingly well. Having been previously married, Peter had custody of his three daughters, ages 9 and 6, and one still younger, mentally retarded, who was in a special school.

The new Mrs. Greenough adapted quickly and easily to this already established household, and continued with her career, traveling when necessary, while servants maintained the well-ordered home. The marriage is happy; the husband encourages her in her career, joining his wife on her tours whenever possible. Neptune in the seventh house of marriage, as part of the

116

talented grand trine, guarantees an harmonious relationship, with each partner supportive of the other. Life was busy and full, but soon Beverly wanted children of her own.

If the seventh house signifies the husband, then the eleventh house, or the fifth from the seventh denotes the children of the husband. Here we find this Moon/Saturn conjunction in Sagittarius opposite Mercury in Gemini, which is approaching the cusp of the fifth house, and rules the fifth — Beverly's fertility and childbearing house. Sagittarius is the upper, philosophical, mental sign; Gemini is the concrete, every-day mind. This opposition aspect on the fifth/ eleventh axis denotes the troubled mentality of one step-daughter and Beverly's own son.

Going one step backward — what does the husband's health show? It is signified by the twelfth house, or the sixth from the seventh; here ruled by Capricorn whose ruler is Saturn, the troublemaker, conjunct the Moon and opposite Mercury, ruler of the fifth house.

What about Beverly's health? Look to the sixth house. With Mars within, trine the Ascendant ruler, Uranus, Beverly is strong, healthy and energetic, but the ruler of the sixth, with Cancer on the cusp, is the Moon. Once again we are confronted with the Moon/Saturn conjunction opposite Mercury.

So, in Beverly's chart, the Moon and Saturn, as rulers of the houses of health of both husband and wife, are apparently the crux of the whole situation. This conjunction, settling on the eleventh house cusp of *his* children, and opposite the fifth house ruled Mercury of *her* children, gives us the astrological reasons for trouble in some form with children.

What form would the trouble take? The planets involved are: Moon, Saturn, and Mercury and their rulerships are as follows:

1. Saturn rules the organ of hearing — the ear; hearing ailments.
2. Mercury rules the sense of hearing.
3. Mercury rules the reasoning mind.
4. Mercury and Aries rule brain diseases.
5. Moon and Mercury rule functions and the substance of the brain.
6. Moon rules imagination, the creative aspect of mind.

Saturn, the taskmaster, ruler of the twelfth house of handicaps, touches the Moon and restricts sound; opposes Mercury and cuts off communication.

Beverly's fifth house of children and fertility:

1. The sign on the fifth house cusp is Gemini, a masculine, infertile, air sign — not conducive to bearing children.
2. Its ruler, Mercury, is a neutral, infertile planet, neither male nor female, opposite Moon/Saturn — not favorable.
3. Mercury is sextile Venus and Neptune and semi-sextile Jupiter — favorable opportunity aspects — giving Beverly two children. Venus, itself, is

placed in Aries, its detriment (see Hepburn and Shirley Temple), and not favorably fertile.

4. Pluto, the only planet in the fifth house, is square Uranus, ruler of the first house, producing upsetting circumstances. Pluto is also square Venus, the ovaries and the internal reproductive organs — an unfavorable aspect. Pluto, itself, is not favorably placed in the fifth house.

Beverly's first child, Meredith "Muffy" Greenough, was born on August 4, 1959. Studying her natal planets and finding the Sun, Moon, Mercury and Uranus all closely conjunct in Leo, we know that Muffy must be creative. She is. Enrolled in art school, she is developing her artistic talents and is interested in book jacket design. As far as her deafness is concerned, Saturn, organ of hearing, does not seem to be heavily afflicted. Mercury, ruling the sense of hearing, is conjunct Sun, Moon and Uranus and square Neptune and Jupiter in Scorpio, and exactly squaring their midpoint. Without knowing the time of birth, we cannot ascertain the sign or degree on any of the house cusps, especially needing the Ascendant and the sixth house of health for our study.

The second child, Peter Jr., nick-named "Bucky", was born on June 29, 1961. Check these natal planets. Born retarded, we try to find the astrological reasons for this affliction. Mercury, ruling the reasoning mind, is not heavily afflicted. The Moon, which a day earlier opposed Mercury, has now pushed too far ahead to be in an afflicting opposition aspect. The Moon, ruling the function and substance of the brain, is, in this chart, in its detriment in Capricorn and is conjunct Saturn, a restrictive influence. It is a conjunction similar to that which appears in his mother's natal chart. As with Muffy, we do not know where the planets are situated in Bucky's chart, or which houses they rule.

Now, we think and question. If Beverly had married someone else, would the outcome have been different? According to astrology, "no." The houses of health of both husband and wife are signified by the Moon/Saturn conjunction on the eleventh house of his children, opposite Mercury on the fifth house of her children, and also ruler of her fifth house. Her birth chart dictates the conditions as indicated by these planets. If we are to believe the chart, the results would have been the same no matter who she would have married.

How Beverly would handle the situation is another matter. That would be up to each individual who has a similar chart. It is the inner spirit and logical intelligence, that cannot be measured, which dictates the course of action and the outcome of each individual problem. Could Beverly have avoided this heartbreak and not have had children if she had been warned in advance? Possibly.

Would she have done so?

According to her chart, it is not in her nature to avoid battle. Her adventuresome, first house, Aquarian personality, her faith-giving fire signs, and her spiritual grand trine in fire would not have allowed this. Besides, the

118

wisdom of Saturn was there, as co-ruler of the first house and conjunct the Moon, to give her character the forebearance, the endurance, and the dutifulness to carry out her responsibilities with compassion.

Should an astrologer, if consulted, have warned Beverly of impending tragedy?

We think so. Because afflictions take many different forms, the astrologer, if he is certain that trouble is suggested in a chart, should mention same, but only in a general way, and in a positive a manner as possible. Also, he should always, always show a way out of the difficulty, especially if the chart provides it, and it usually does.

In Beverly's chart there are two ways out. This sorrowful mother discovered them for herself and then acted upon them. Muffy's deafness and Bucky's mental retardation were difficult situations to accept. Medically nothing could be done, but special schools handled the problems adequately.

As for Beverly, she kept her sanity and sense of proportion:

1. through *work* —

a) The ruler of the sixth house of work is the Moon, placed in the tenth house, part of the grand trine, giving her talent and the means of using it through an operatic career.

b) Mars at 6 Leo in the sixth house, trine Uranus at 10 Aries in the second house of inner resources and talent, and sextile the Sun which strengthens the will, encouraged Beverly to immerse herself in her operatic activities more energetically than ever, and she found solace there. Hard work became a refuge from personal problems. She continued with her singing lessons and operatic tours, meanwhile developing the inner fortitude she so critically needed.

And, out of her desperate need to sing, to give of herself, to lose herself in song, emerged a voice more electrifying and more beautiful than ever before.

2. through developing *inner resourses* —

Pluto at 15 Cancer in the fifth house is square Venus at 24 Aries in the second house of inner resources. This obstacle-producing square from the fifth house of children produced a crisis in Beverly's life. First, it devastated her, but as she struggled with these seemingly insurmountable problems, they started to transform her, then matured her, and in a strange way they brought this courageous woman an inner peace. Self pity, which came first, dissolved as she saw with what courage her children tried to overcome their difficulties. She learned from them how to be strong.

No longer worrying about being loved, she now wanted only to give love. To her children. To her husband. To her audiences. She found a new joy in giving of herself in song, and her listeners, feeling this love and joy, responded in kind.

Muffy may never hear her mother's beautiful voice raised in song. Bucky may never know how much he is truly loved by his parents. Beverly, accepting these difficulties, looked for a silver lining, and in it she found:

1. a more beautiful singing voice,
2. an unselfish maturity and growth as a human being,
3. an inner peace, and
4. a reason to earn money through her operatic career.

Since she has always been very splendidly supported financially by her husband, all of Beverly's operatic earnings go into a trust fund for Muffy and Bucky.

Aren't these reasons enough to argue against the abortion of fetuses found to be imperfect?

Now in her fifties, Beverly Sills has retired from the operatic stage as a performer, but her pivotal eleventh house of organizations gives her new fields of interest. She is:

1. National Chairman of the March of Dimes Mothers' March on Birth Defects in which she raises funds, makes speeches, and gives encouragement to mothers with problems similar to her own.

2. General Director of the New York City Opera where she:
   a) is spokesperson for the arts,
   b) spearheads fund-raising drives for the New York City Opera, and
   c) as administrator, she determines casts, auditions orchestra replacements, supervises advertising campaigns, and plans long range opera programs.

In 1984, as transiting Saturn travels through Beverly's ninth house, she acquires new experiences and new skills as an administrator. In December of 1985, transiting Saturn, the timekeeper, will conjunct her tenth house cusp and Beverly will be at the peak of her career as General Director of the New York City Opera. She will enjoy increased professional responsibility and public recognition for her achievements. Saturn will continue its journey through Beverly's tenth and eleventh houses through 1989, and Miss Sills should enjoy hugh success, popularity and career fulfillment during these years.

At this time, we are most fortunate to be able to see her on television where she is mistress of Ceremonies for the New York City Opera. Always beautifully gowned, she exudes a joy in, and love for the beauty of the opera program she is about to introduce. One can keenly sense that to find and develop new talent, and then to present it to the audience for its esthetic pleasure is indeed her pleasure, too.

We thank Beverly Sills for the beauty of her song.

More than that, we thank her for the beauty of her spirit.

Chapter XV
Joan Crawford

That this next topic is of interest to many people is easy to realize, because *Mommie Dearest,* the biography-autobiography by Christina Crawford about her mother, Joan Crawford, has sold millions of copies and was then made into a successful motion picture.

The book cover shows a photo of the beautiful, young movie star, Joan Crawford, with her small, fair-haired, adopted daughter, Christina, who are the leading characters in this cheerless life story — "the gospel according to Tina."

The title and photo impart the warmth, tenderness, and positive mother love such as was found in the relationship of our previous subject, Beverly Sills, with her mother, but the similarity stops at the cover, for the characters, story, and mood found within these pages are entirely different. Just as make-believe opera has its heroines and villains, so too do they exist in real life, and we're afraid that poor, dead Joan, who now has no way of defending herself, is the villain in this dreary account that keeps us quite permanently in the valley of shadows.

This is Christina's version of physical, mental, and emotional harassment and abuse meted out by a supposedly adoring mother to one of four adopted children — Christina, the oldest, Christopher, her adopted brother, and the twins, Cynthia and Cathy. Christopher shares Tina's plight, but not her penchant for broadcasting, while the twins have also chosen to remain silent.

Why did her adopted daughter, Tina, this chosen child, unveil to the whole world such a character-cutting chronicle of her famous mother? As a catharsis? To spit out the venom of a life that she thought had been unfair? After all, if your natural parents reject you, and your adoptive mother treats you cruelly and unjustly, you've got to tell somebody. Anybody. *Everybody!* As a writing experience with a built-in publicity gimmick to make a name for herself as an author? To make alot of money by feeding the voracious appetite of a scandal-hungry public?

Or, was it something else? Had her love for her mother been so great, so all-encompassing, so total that she had to write her experiences down to make them all seem real, before their memories washed away with the tides of time? On the other hand, if Tina would just put it all on paper, could she, maybe, be cleansed, purified, and freed once and for all?

For, even in death, the spirit of Joan Crawford seemed to hold sway over her daughter. Her last will and testament made no provision for Tina, "for reasons which are well known to her." Her parting, spiteful, humiliating blow? No nothing for Tina. . . .

Was that the final punishing thrust, which then compelled Tina to exhume the unsavory skeletons in the Crawford closet? At long last, Tina has the final say. But, how she wishes she could have said it all so differently. . . .

Before we can study the relationship between Joan and Tina, we should review just a little background. Joan's career and forceful personality are legendary, and we won't go into them here. It is enough to say that her beginnings were poor and of common stock.

In 1925, with an MGM contract and a movie-star dream to fortify her, Lucille Le Sueur, without benefit of a mother, became a reborn *"Joan Crawford"*, appeared in over 20 films within the next three years, and was on her way to becoming a superstar.

To obtain the culture, polish, respectability, and social standing which were not her birthright but which she so desperately wanted, Crawford first married Douglas Fairbanks, Jr., and then Franchot Tone, both actors. Her third marriage gave her companionship; her fourth, a new business career.

But none of these marriages gave her natural children.

Because she couldn't have them?

Because she didn't want them?

Let's look at her horoscope, Figure 22.

Immediately you should notice several similarities between Joan's chart and those of our preceding subjects. Can you spot what these charts have in common?

1. Joan's outer house cusps are in the same signs as those of Hepburn's chart, giving a Leo entertainment sign on the tenth house of career; a strong, determined, Scorpio first house personality; a Pisces-ruled (films) fifth house of entertainment and children. Distinctly her own, however, is a blazing, exalted, Aries Sun, dramatically occupying the fifth house and ruling the career tenth — a most fortunate placement for show business, if not for children.

2. Venus at 29 Aries 37 is in its detriment, as it is in the charts of Hepburn, Temple, and Sills. It is unfavorable for bearing children.

3. The Moon at 5 Aquarius is conjunct Saturn at 6 Aquarius. This conjunction, which inhibits childbearing, is now familiar to us, since it appears in the charts of Claire, Sills, and Sophia, here sharing Loren's sign, Aquarius.

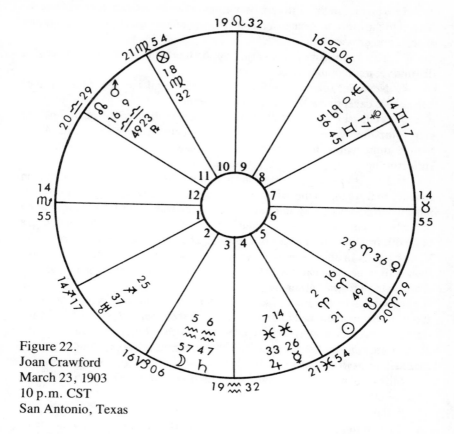

Figure 22.
Joan Crawford
March 23, 1903
10 p.m. CST
San Antonio, Texas

Therefore, we are not surprised if there were to be no children, or if there was trouble concerning them. It has been said that in 1932, Joan suffered a miscarriage during her marriage to Douglas Fairbanks, Jr. Years later it was bandied about that she'd really had an abortion. In those years it was not fashionable for movie stars to have children because it gave tell-tale proof of age, it supposedly ruined their figures, and it took time out from their careers. Consequently, some stars adopted children instead, gaining favorable publicity along with the little ones, and had abortions if they inconveniently became pregnant.

Looking at Joan's chart, it would be difficult to tell if she had had either a miscarriage or an abortion, but the following challenging natal aspects set the stage for either event:

1. The Sun in the fifth house of children, square Neptune, ruler of the fifth, in the eighth house of death. Unfavorable.

123

2. The Sun in the fifth, opposite Mars, ruler of the sixth house of health, placed in the eleventh house of the husband's, or adopted children — a cutting aspect, and unfavorable.

3. The Sun square Uranus, ruler of the fourth house of motherhood — a disruptive, unfavorable aspect.

4. Neptune, ruler of the fifth, square Mars, ruler of the sixth house of health — a deceptive aspect, and an unfavorable one.

5. Venus in Aries, in its detriment, in the sixth house of health, and signifying the ovaries and the internal reproductive organs, is square Moon/Saturn in the mental third house, indicating health problems. Unfavorable for childbearing.

In 1932, transiting Saturn — the inhibitor — traveled from 23 Capricorn in January to 0 Aquarius the following December, almost touching Joan's Moon/Saturn during April, May and June, when Saturn was at 3 to 4 Aquarius. During that whole year Saturn squared natal Venus — the ovaries — in the sixth house of health from the third house of the mind, activating the Moon/Saturn square Venus aspect in Joan's chart. Transiting Uranus, during 1932, hovered over Joan's sixth house cusp, indicating spasmodic action, tension, and disruption of the natural flow of affairs relating to health.

Nowhere in the book does Tina mention her mother being concerned about, or being interested in becoming a natural mother. She seemingly did not visit doctors or try in any over-extended way to become pregnant. Since fertility did not seem to be her problem and she preferred to adopt, draw your own conclusions as to what actually happened.

Still, we have many indications of both fertility and infertility, and mindful that the fifth house also signifies the world of motion pictures, we will review the aspects here as follows:

1. Sun in Aries, exalted, but in infertile fire sign, in the fifth house — unfavorable for childbearing but good for show business. Sun square Neptune and Uranus, and Sun opposite Mars only concretize this infertile placement. Sun sextile Moon/Saturn helps Joan achieve her show business goals.

2. South Node at 16 Aries in the fifth house — unfavorable for fertility.

3. The fifth house has Pisces on its cusp — a fertile water sign. Its ruler, Neptune, in Cancer, the fertile mother's sign, makes the following aspects:

    a) Neptune square Mars,

    b) Neptune square Sun,

    c) Neptune opposite Uranus, and

    d) Neptune quincunx Moon/Saturn — all of these are unfavorable for childbearing.

    e) Neptune sextile Venus and trine Jupiter bestow acting ability, beauty, glamour, success in motion pictures, and should aid in fertility.

124

4. Venus — the ovaries and eggs — in its detriment in Aries, is unfavorable for fertility. Its square to the Moon (motherhood) and Saturn (the inhibitor) is very unfavorable for childbearing, but the aspect is softened by Venus sextile Jupiter and Neptune, which again give Joan her glamour, acting ability, and success in films, plus aid in childbearing. Venus trine Uranus provides Crawford with her electrifying, exciting, magnetic screen personality and artistic talent. Since Uranus always does the unexpected, it might have given her children if she had wanted them.

5. The Ascendant contains no planets, but is ruled by Scorpio, a fertile water sign, whose co-ruler, Pluto, is square Mercury and Jupiter, opposite Uranus, and trine the North Node. Its other ruler, Mars, we have already discussed, with the conclusion being that the aspects of this house are mixed.

6. The Moon, motherhood, is in the infertile air sign, Aquarius, conjunct Saturn, which we now all know causes delays, denial, or trouble with children.

The eleventh house:

Since Joan wholeheartedly accepted responsiblity for four adopted children, the eleventh house of other people's children should figure prominently in her chart. It does, because:

1. The ruler of the eleventh house is Mercury, Virgo being on the cusp, and its aspects are:

a) Mercury trine the Ascendant — adopted children help Joan's self-image. This trine gives her talent as a dramatic actress and effective communicator.

b) Mercury at 14 Pisces conjunct Jupiter at 7 Pisces, both in the sign of films, with Jupiter ruling the second house of talent. Opportunity is here for Joan to develop her talent and use it effectively.

c) Mercury opposite the Part of Fortune on the cusp of the eleventh house — unfavorable for relationships with adopted children.

d) Mercury square Pluto, ruler of the Ascendant — insensitive to children; expresses herself harshly to them.

e) Mercury square Uranus, ruler of the fourth house — causes trouble in the home; outbursts of temper.

Mercury square Pluto, opposite the Part of Fortune, square Uranus forms a grand square in mutable signs, which results in trouble in communicating with her adopted children.

2. The North Node at 16 Libra in the eleventh house, trine Pluto and sextile Uranus, contributes happiness at times in this home for Joan's children.

3. Mars at 9 Libra in the eleventh house shows us where the action is. Here in its detriment, it is the fighter, the doer, the aggressive action planet which makes happen the affairs of the house it tenants — in this case the house of adopted children. Mars rules the sixth house of work, and here, placed in the

eleventh, the children are used as useful appendages to her work. The image of a painstaking, responsible, loving Mommie is a valuable asset for this working mother, which, according to Tina, was Joan's calculated plan.

4. Mars trine Pluto, the Moon, and Saturn are supportive aspects for harmonious thoughts with regard to these children, but Mars opposite Sun, the aspect which connects both houses of children, is competitive and warlike. Joan, who shows deep insecurity here, can assert herself and be in strict dictatorial command at her children's expense.

5. Mars square Neptune — produced mood swings which terrified Christina.

As we already know, the methods of studying a chart can be endless, and while the dissection of Joan's planets and aspects may seen repetitious, with each new circumstance we can judge the configurations from a different point of view. Take addiction, for example.

With the dimming of her moving picture star, Joan turned to alcohol, which along with drug addiction, is a Neptunian, Piscean, twelfth house matter. We see this problem astrologically as follows:

1. With Libra on the cusp of the twelfth house of drug addiction, its ruler is Venus, and once again we have the challenging square of Venus from the sixth house of health square Moon/Saturn in the third house of the mind. Certainly she was thinking poorly to so ruin her health by the excessive use of alcohol.

2. Neptune, ruler of both alcohol and addictive tendencies, ruler of the fifth house, and placed in the eighth house of death, is the focal point of a powerful T-square involving a square to Mars in the eleventh house of adopted children, and a square to the Sun, ruler of the career house and placed in the fifth house of entertainment. This alcoholic addiction played havoc with both Joan's adopted children and her movie career.

3. The co-rulers of the first house of personality are Mars, featured above, and Pluto, planet of compulsive behavior. Pluto is square Mercury, square the fifth-eleventh axis of children, and opposite Uranus.

Compulsive, obsessive drinking poisoned her body (first house ruler, Pluto), her mind (Mercury), her relationship to her children (fifth-eleventh house axis), and destroyed her second house acting talent and sense of values (Uranus in the second house).

The Moon/Saturn Conjunction:

Although the T-square involving Mars (action) in the eleventh house of adopted children, square Neptune (the deceiver, alcohol, addiction) in the eighth house of death, square the Sun (will power) in the fifth house of children and entertainment was the principal cause of trouble and friction in Joan's relationship with her children, let's go back to that Moon/Saturn conjunction in Aquarius in the third house to see how that contributed to Joan's tyranical attitude.

So far, we have been concentrating on the fifth-eleventh axis of children, the first house of personality, and the tenth house of career. However, maybe even more important in the scheme of things is the third-ninth axis, for, *as a man thinks in his heart, so is he,* may be the deciding factor in the way we live. We cannot separate the chart into neat little houses, judging one house to the exclusion of the others, because all are inter-related and each has a bearing, by commission or omission, on the subject in question.

Saturn inhibits the life-giving, motherly qualities of the Moon. Here, placed in Aquarius, an infertile air sign, it can be unemotional, without warmth, exploitative, exacting, undemonstrative and fanatical.

The Moon, signifying motherhood, imagination, and functions and substance of the brain, rules the mental ninth house (Cancer on the cusp) of aspirations, logic and judgment. Saturn, of impersonal, worldly concerns, the inhibitor, rules the third house of the every-day mind (Capricorn on the cusp) and co-rules the fourth house of home and motherhood, the womb, the soul, and the outcome of events of the life (Aquarius on the cusp). Not only do Moon/Saturn *rule* the two houses of mind, they are placed *in* the third house of the conscious mind, communication, nervous energy and correspondence.

In sum, this is a very, very mental Moon/Saturn, making a mental approach vital to the study of the problems of this chart.

This mental aspect helped Joan because Moon/Saturn is:

1. semi-sextile Jupiter — giving good luck and practicality,
2. sextile the Sun — integrates personality and the will, and lends harmony and strength,
3. trine Mars — supplying energy, courage and staying power, and
4. semi-quintile Mercury — a talent aspect.

With a passion, Joan thought about and wanted fame, stardom, power, and money. Action followed thought and she deliberately changed her inclinations, her ideas, and her image until she actually and calculatedly *became* what she conceived a film star should be. (Just to show us what a strong third-house-of-the-mind can do!) She even acquired children, according to Tina, to soften and enhance her image.

These favorable Moon/Saturn aspects figure prominently and importantly in another way, too. Helping to transform her into the epitome of a movie star were the members of the studio publicity department (third house of communication and news). It was they who helped launch her career by conspicuously and perpetually (in the early years) projecting her likeness before the public, and giving it much attention, for which Joan was forever grateful.

This mental aspect brought Joan grief because of:

1. Moon square Venus — With Taurus on its cusp, Venus rules the seventh house of marriage. With Libra on its cusp, Venus rules the twelfth house of sorrows. Joan found it difficult emotionally to give or to receive love and found disillusionment in love and marriage. Three of her marriages ended in divorce.

2. Saturn square Venus — a denial of love. Selfishness causes loneliness and limitation, especially as life advances because Saturn here co-rules the fourth house — the end of life.

The two significators of childbearing — Moon and Venus — are in stressful aspect, denying the fulfilling love that children can bring. This square also clouded her logic and judgment with regard to the upbringing of her four adopted children.

Joan and Tina:

The fact remains, that of all of the children that Joan could have adopted, Tina is the first one that she chose. Just what was it that brought these two people together, and kept them together, even when they were not physically together, or when they did not even want to be together? Can the planets uncover the mystery of this love-hate relationship, the hold of one person over another, so that even when one died the other felt obligated to perpetuate her mother's memory in an unflattering, although, according to Tina, factual way?

Chart comparison is a deeply involved and complex study, and not the purpose of our book, but even a cursory glance, as we place Tina's birth planets of June 11, 1939, around Joan's horoscope, should prove insightful as we study Figure 23. We shall see that Joan cannot be blamed for the deterioration of this relationship which started so beautifully, as Tina's Jupiter touched Joan's Sun in the fifth house of children. Yet, even these placements are in Aries, a Mars-ruled fighting sign, with patience and understanding *not* its keywords!

If Joan had sought to adopt children for ulterior motives, only then can we accuse her of wrongdoing. If not, then it is the unfortunate placement of planets, which neither mother nor daughter were strong enough to overcome, that is the culprit. As we compare the charts we find:

1. Tina has the same deceptive Sun square Neptune aspect as does her mother, with her Neptune on Joan's eleventh house cusp, bringing discord and abnormal behavior to their relationship. A conflict of egos. Tina's Neptune on Joan's Part of Fortune square Tina's Sun becomes part of the grand square in Joan's chart — a sacrificial placement stemming from the house of adoption.

2. Tina's Uranus at 10 Taurus is square Joan's tenth-fourth axis. Tina rebelled at her mother's perverted discipline at home (fourth house), and felt exploited and used for the advancement of Joan's career (tenth house). Uranus is trine the eleventh house, though, and sometimes they were good friends.

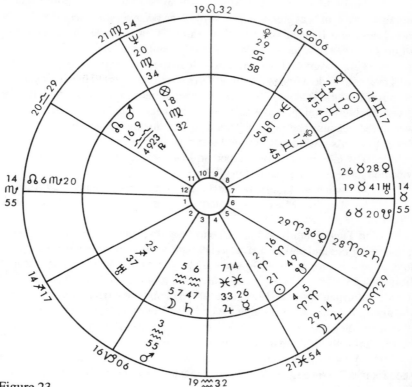

Figure 23.
Mother — Joan Crawford's natal planets — inner wheel, with natal house cusps
Daughter — Christina's natal planets, June 11, 1939,
(taken from a noon ephemeris) — outer wheel.

3. Tina's Sun at 19 Gemini is square Joan's fifth-eleventh axis of children — a battle of wills against her mother's despotism.

4. Tina's Moon is on Joan's Sun — and here Joan has the upper hand, being able to put her stamp on Tina's feelings and emotions.

5. Tina's Jupiter is on Joan's Sun — which should have been a lucky break for both of them. This aspect of mutual love, kindness, helpfulness, and growth surfaced from time to time, but submerged again and again as Joan's square from Neptune — alcohol — and her opposition from Mars — domination and violence — gave off negative vibrations.

6. Tina's Sun on Joan's Pluto — produces a clash of wills. Joan tries to change Tina into a carbon-copy of herself; Tina, instead, wants to dominate Joan.

7. Tina's Mars on Joan's Moon — Joan becomes emotionally irritated and upset by Tina's aggressiveness, while Tina becomes impatient with Joan's moodiness and hypersensitivity. Joan thinks Tina is crude and insensitive, while Tina sees Joan as weak, lazy, and self-indulgent.

8. Tina's Mars on Joan's Saturn — Joan tries to restrain the impulsiveness of Tina and endeavors to channel Tina's martial energy into disciplined, purposeful work. Meanwhile, Tina is angered because of what she feels are unreasonable restraints imposed by Joan. Joan feels that these restrictions are warranted because she regards Tina as overly impulsive, unwise, and also a threat to Joan's position, status, and security.

9. The most troublesome aspect in Joan's chart which denied children is repeated and even enlarged in Tina's chart —

a) Joan has Moon/Saturn at 5-6 Aquarius square Venus at 29 Aries.

b) Tina has Mars at 3 Aquarius, square Saturn at 28 Aries, square Pluto at 29 Cancer 58.

With Tina's Saturn on Joan's Venus, Saturn is the offender here, making Tina seem cold and unresponsive, as he, Saturn, squashes down the feelings of love Joan's Venus is trying to express. Maybe Saturn acts this way because Joan's Venus (movies) is trying to attain professional advancement and status at Tina's Saturnian expense. Here, too, Saturn (Tina) is the restraining, disciplining agent, the parent, squelching the beautiful Venusian movie star's desire for attention. Yet, this can be a stabilizing aspect and give durability to their relationship. Well, it did do that, right to the bitter end!

10. Tina's Moon opposite Joan's Mars — gives emotional conflict. Tina sees Joan as overly aggressive, domineering and insensitive. Joan thinks Tina is lazy, weak, moody, and too emotional.

11. Tina's Jupiter opposite Joan's Mars — pompous and sanctimonious is how Joan regards Tina; impulsive, rash, inconsiderate, and violent is how Tina thinks of Joan.

12. Tina's Neptune square Joan's Pluto — Tina sees Joan as oppressive, dominating, and power hungry. Joan sees Tina as indecisive, weak, and self-indulgent.

13. Tina's Mars square Joan's Venus — another obstacle in their relationship, it leads to lack of mutual consideration and erodes emotional compatibility. To Joan, Tina is brash, ill-mannered, and inconsiderate. To Tina, Joan seems self-indulgent, overly concerned with appearances, and unloving.

It is interesting to note, that according to the placement of planets and their aspects in these comparison charts, the mother, Joan, sees and loathes the same faults in the daughter that the daughter, Christina, despises in the mother, as each in turn tries to control and dominate the other.

With all of the pushing, pulling, touching, squaring, and interacting of so many planets, there was created a network of vibrations so strong, so cohesively bound together that the wills, thoughts, and emotions of this mother-daughter duo had to bump headlong into, and eventually hurt one another. But, there was no winner here.

One can learn much as he delves into the planets of these two individuals that fate had brought together by chance, or maybe, really by design. Chart comparison is a useful tool, and when used between parents and their children it can point the way to increased understanding, and the resulting closeness and caring that we all want within our families.

Through it all, Tina has survived, and we thank her for making this study possible. We'd like to think that only happy memories of Joan Crawford, who gave entertainment to so many through her films, will also survive.

Chapter XVI
Two Not-Plain Janes
Jane Russell *** Jayne Mansfield

While we have our minds still centered upon eleventh house matters and the adoption of children, let's look at another chart featuring adoption, but which has a much happier ending than our previous subject. In fact, we're going to show you the charts of two women — Jane Russell, who adopted three children, and Jayne Mansfield, who bore five natural children before her tragic and untimely death at age 33.

Actresses Jane, the brunette, and Jayne, the blonde, were both tall, statuesque, show-girl types, the "full-figured gals" Jane Russell proudly proclaims in her television ads. Both were successful sex symbols and pin-up girls, although neither possessed the mystique, nor attained quite the immense popularity of an earlier Jean Harlow or the later day Marilyn Monroe.

Could it have been partly because they share a common Ascendant — Cancer — a domestic, maternal sign, and deep down both were better suited for, and were more comfortable with marriage (three each) and motherhood than the glamorous life of a movie queen? Children, natural or adopted, did not stop either Jane from continuing with her public career, and each managed to do both well, but if a choice had had to be made, what would it have been — motherhood or show business?

Compare the chart of Jane Russell, Figure 24, with that of Jayne Mansfield, Figure 25, and see if you can tell which one depicts successful adoption and which demonstrates successful natural fertility.

We'll give you a hint. Study their Ascendants first. Jane Russell's is at 21 Cancer 55, while Jayne Mansfield's is at 2 Cancer 57. Both are in Cancer but in different degrees. Does that make a difference? Yes, in shades of meaning. When you want to determine the depth of a sign in greater detail, look to its decanate, that is, its sub-division by portions of 10 degrees each, creating a first, second, and third decanate, which incorporates the remaining two signs of its element.

132

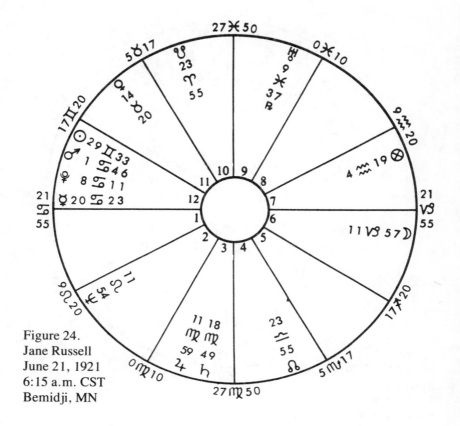

Figure 24.
Jane Russell
June 21, 1921
6:15 a.m. CST
Bemidji, MN

For example, the decanates of Cancer are the following:

1. degrees 1 through 10 equals the Cancer decanate, its own water sign,
2. degrees 11 through 20 equals the Scorpio decanate, the second water sign, and
3. degrees 21 through 30 equals the Pisces decanate, the third water sign.

Each decanate gives added flavor and expression to the original Cancer meaning.

Russell's decanate of 21 Cancer 55 is Pisces — the third water sign. Therefore, her Ascendant is Cancer-Pisces. Mansfield's decanate of 2 Cancer 57 is Cancer itself — the first water sign, giving her a Cancer-Cancer Ascendant.

Because Russell's Ascendant has a Piscean undertone, it gives her an empathetic quality, one of mentally understanding the feelings of others without having to actually undergo their experiences herself. Hence, her personality is maternal, caring, and service oriented.

133

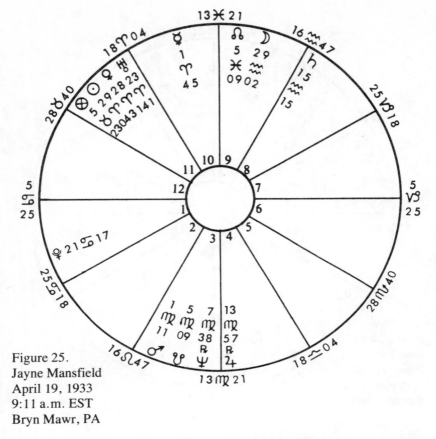

Figure 25.
Jayne Mansfield
April 19, 1933
9:11 a.m. EST
Bryn Mawr, PA

Mansfield's Cancer Ascendant is purely Cancerian, suggesting a feeling of compassion for others which is more sympathetic than empathetic. Her personality is geared to personal motherhood and personal family ties.

If you picked the 21 Cancer as Russell's Ascendant and the 2 Cancer Ascendant as Manfield's, you judged correctly. However, there is more to it than that, so now we'll study each chart individually.

Jane Russell:

This movie star and show business entertainer, not content with raising three adopted children in her own home, saw a need and tried to fill it. She helped to found, and is an active fundraiser for W.A.I.F., a national adoption organization situated at 67 Irving Place, New York, N.Y. 10003, which places homeless, parentless children, and children with special needs into the empty arms and vacant homes of loving, adoptive parents.

Why does she do this?

Let's look to her fifth house of natural children first, because if Jane could have had her own, she probably would never have become involved in the adoption of children, either for herself or for anyone else. Five degrees of Scorpio, a fertile water sign, occupies the cusp, with no planets within. It is squared by the Part of Fortune at 4 degrees Aquarius, not a conducive aspect for fertility. Its co-rulers, Mars and Pluto, are conjunct in maternal Cancer in the twelfth house of sorrows, limitations, loneliness, self-undoing, and denial — in this case the denial of children. Along with these negative nouns, however, the twelfth house also represents charity, charitable institutions, hospitals, welfare offices, and adoption agencies. This conjunction of Mars/Pluto makes the following favorable aspects:

1. Sextile Venus, which is in its rulership in Taurus, placed in, and also ruling the eleventh house of adopted children — advantageous for adopting children.

2. Sextile Jupiter, ruler of the sixth house of service and health. Jupiter is also co-ruler of the tenth house of career, increasing her desire to act on behalf of children.

3. Conjunct the Sun in the twelfth house, the ruler of the second house of money, talent, and inner resources. This conjunction is just one of the reasons that makes the twelfth house the most active one in the chart, as it connects the rulers of the fifth house of creativity and children, to the ruler of the second house of money, to the ruler of the twelfth house of adoption agencies, Mercury. This contributes greatly to Jane's go-getting, fund-raising abilities.

4. Trine Uranus in the ninth house, which gives its support by contributing lofty idealism.

5. Trine the fifth house of children, entertainment and creativity — encouraging a show business career, and sextile the eleventh house of adoptive children — helping her in that area as well.

The above aspects prove that her fifth house rulers, although denying natural children, had the opportunity to adopt children, the desire to help others do so also, plus the second house means to bring her plans to fruition.

Now, let's look to the Moon, ruler of Jane's Ascendant, and thereby representing her maternal personality, but which also rules the uterus and affects Jane's health by being in the sixth house. This Moon opposes the fifth house rulers, Mars/Pluto, as well as opposing the two planets surrounding that conjunction, the Sun to the left and Mercury to the right. These oppositions seem to be the main astrological reasons for infertility in this particular chart.

These oppositions and the houses in which they occur — the sixth/twelfth axis of service and health, so significant in the charts of doctors, nurses, policemen, the armed services, and all those who serve the needs of humanity — are the most insistently important focuses of the chart.

Now, the reason for this infertility? Could it be due to her crude abortion, the abortion Jane discloses to having had performed in 1942, in her autobiography, *Jane Russell: My Path and My Detours?* Are our twelfth house key-words — *self-undoing* — especially applicable here?

It is in this hidden house that Mars cut out and Pluto destroyed the new life that was being formed in the opposing Moon's womb. Ignorance, fear, and unethical medical practice butchered the reproductive organs, and the Moon, ruler in Jane's chart of the first house of SELF, is denied further opportunity for childbearing.

Costly, irreversible consequences, for sure. Yet, out of the ruins come Jane's renewal through W.A.I.F., our realization of accountability for the welfare of our own bodies and those of our offspring, and reverence for new life.

The Moon, in its detriment in Capricorn, the worldly business sign, which is too shrill and harsh for gentle, homeloving Moon, is tremendously noteworthy in Russell's chart, because not only does it rule the Ascendant, but it is connected by aspect with every other planet in the chart, as follows:

1. Moon opposite Sun, Mars, Pluto, and Mercury as stated above.

2. Moon quincunx Neptune, ruling the tenth, gives sympathy towards others, and a satisfaction in establishing social programs for public welfare. Neptune, being in the second house, supplies the talent and resources to make the dream become a reality.

3. Moon sextile Uranus in the ninth house gives Jane personal (Moon) humanitarian (Uranus) ideals (ninth house).

4. Moon trine Venus in the eleventh house imparts —

    a) maternal (Moon) feelings and love (Venus) for other people's children,

    b) interest in social organizations (eleventh house) and young people (Venus), and

    c) beauty, popularity, and acting talent (Venus).

Observe Venus, now, as ruler of the ovaries, the eggs and the whole internal reproductive system, in its rulership in earthy, fertile Taurus. It is active in this chart, being trine Moon in the sixth house of health, sextile Jupiter ruling the sixth house of health, trine Saturn, and sextile Uranus, Pluto, and Mercury. Then, where could there be trouble to the reproductive system? The only hostile aspect is a square to Neptune which causes negative, deceptive, and fearful feelings which could be a deterring factor concerning pregnancy.

5. Moon trine Jupiter in the third house grants altruistic thinking, a generous spirit, and interest in the training and rehabilitation of handicapped persons.

Moon trine Saturn in the third house bestows common sense, business sense (Moon in Capricorn also gives business acumen), devotion to duty, and organizational ability.

136

Therefore, the Moon, symbol of personality in its own right, and personality symbol as ruler of the Ascendant, is not only the focus for the opposition aspects of the twelfth house, but it is also part of the practical, realistic, earth grand trine from the sixth house of service.

Whichever way you look at it:

1. Jupiter/Saturn in third (thinks), trine Moon in sixth (to serve), trine Venus in eleventh (in the adoption of children). *Or,*

2. Jane founds an organization (pragmatic earth grand trine) to help (Piscean, twelfth house emphasis) children by providing homes for them (Cancer Ascendant).

How did Jane Russell's interests change from being principally an entertainer, to being an adoptive mother, to being the foundress of W.A.I.F. — a mother on a national scale? The answer is agape love, described in the chapter, *Astrological Love Symbols,* that unselfish love ruled by Neptune, higher sacrificial love, and Pluto, universal welfare.

To bring us back to our opening statements about Jane, this chart is very Neptune/Pisces oriented because:

1. It has a Cancer Ascendant with a Piscean decanate/Neptune rulership.

2. Pisces (ruler Neptune) rules the ninth house of abstract thought, religion, logic and judgment.

3. Pisces also rules the tenth house of career, signifying films, acting, child-caring institutions, and welfare work. Whenever one sign occupies two house cusps (instead of the usual one), it strengthens and emphasizes the importance of that sign.

4. Four planets inhabit the twelfth house — Sun, Mars, Pluto and Mercury — the natural house of Pisces, making it the most heavily tenanted house in the chart, again intensifying the meaning of Neptune and Pisces. This house is a spiritual one, a house of atonement; where one rid's one's self of superficiality and selfishness and then can be of service to others.

As for Pluto, it is the planet of social workers. It also symbolizes organizations which attempt to achieve better social conditions. Pluto, co-ruler of the fifth, did not give Jane natural children. But, activated by its co-ruler, Mars, it instigated, by opposition, Jane's maternal, service-oriented Moon, which then cooperated with the faith of Jupiter and the business experience of Saturn to culminate in the eleventh house Venus, planet of Love.

The Venusian love returns by sextile to Pluto/Mars, giving birth (fifth house) to W.A.I.F. — her contribution to the welfare of children everywhere.

For many, Russell's claim to fame may be her more than adequate physical, feminine proportions. We strongly disagree.

The biggest thing about this not-plain Jane is her *HEART!*

Jayne Mansfield:

Being 11 years older and a movie star of the 1940's, Jane Russell was no real competition to Jayne Mansfield's bid for stardom and public adulation in the 1950's. Although both women share a Pisces tenth house, signifying a film career, and a Cancer Ascendant, bestowing a caring, sympathetic personality, the fifth and eleventh houses, and other intermediate house cusps are all different, resulting in dissimilar experiences concerning what both wanted so very much — children.

Beautiful of face, striking of figure, and blithe of spirit, Jayne was a comely comedienne of stage and screen, and an entertaining television talk show guest. Inbetween publicity shots she married three times, having her first child at age 17 with her first husband; three more children with husband number two, and another with her third husband, before an automobile accident abruptly and tragically claimed her young life at age 33.

Jayne was happily pregnant with her fifth child when the following questions were put to her: "Won't having so many children spoil your '*love-goddess*' image, and destroy your sex appeal? After all, isn't that what your career is based upon?

Innocently, sweetly, and just a little primly, Jayne responded with a question of her own, "But really, isn't having babies what sex is all about?"

We probably would need another Cancerian Ascendant to agree with that remark, but that was Jayne's true motherly nature manifesting itself. Not that she didn't display her feminine charms and play up her sexiness to the hilt! She did, but children evidently gave her great delight and a feeling of accomplishment — no matter who the current husband!

And, no one had to ask, "Shouldn't you worry about keeping fit and in good shape?". To the contrary. Having babies did nothing to destroy either her good looks or her fabulous body, and she was an inspiration to any woman who might have qualms along those lines. Jayne was clearly ahead of her time as she watched her diet and exercised intelligently (with 4 planets in Aries she enjoyed physical exercise) with the expert assistance of muscle-man, Mickey Hargitay, her second husband. It is only recently that women have taken to the type of body building exercises that kept Jayne in perfect physical condition throughout her pregnancies, and afterwards as well.

Now to Jayne's chart, Figure 25. If you, at first glance, had picked this horoscope to be the one without natural children, we would not have been surprised because you probably would have noticed that:

1. Venus (the ovaries) is in Aries, in its detriment, as in the charts of:
    a) Hepburn, who had no children; didn't want any.
    b) Temple Black, who had two Caesarean births and a mastectomy.
    c) Sills, who had two handicapped children.

d) Crawford, who had no natural children and an unhappy relationship with at least one adopted child.

2. Moon is conjunct Saturn, as in the charts of:

a) Claire, who had one miscarriage.

b) Sills, who had two handicapped children.

c) Loren, who had great difficulty in carrying her two children, and also suffered miscarriages.

d) Crawford, who had no natural children.

Nevertheless, if you had stopped at the above conditions, you would have made a mistake because:

1. the whole chart should have been studied in its entirety,

2. you should have realized that each chart is an entity unto itself, and like no other, and

3. there are no absolutes. Free will, physical constitution, mental decisions, the husband's wishes, and upbringing can change the outcome of events.

Let's take a closer look at this Venus in Aries, significator of the ovaries, the eggs, the hormones, and the general internal reproductive system:

1. Venus claims sole responsibility for fifth house fertility because it is ruler of Libra, a fertile air sign which occupies the cusp, and there are no planets within. Saturn, ruler of the seventh house of the husband, however, is trine the fifth house cusp, aiding fertility.

2. Venus is placed in the eleventh house itself, and this is fortunate for the husband's fertility.

3. Venus conjunct Uranus projects a zest for living, an effervescent personality, and one willing to take chances.

4. Venus conjunct the Sun is conducive to a willingness to bear new life, gives an affectionate nature, and brings blessings into the life.

5. Venus conjunct the Part of Fortune brings good fortune to childbearing.

6. Venus trine Mars exudes sex appeal in abundance. Venus, ruler of the fifth — her fertility, is trine Mars, ruler of the eleventh — the husband's fertility, yielding a favorable, productive interaction and a strong indication for successful childbearing.

7. Venus square Pluto could cause malfunctioning of the generative organs, since Pluto is co-ruler of the sixth house of health, but co-ruler, Mars, by its trine to Venus offers protective vibrations.

8. Venus trine Neptune adds glamour, beauty, artistry and photogenicity.

9. Venus sextile Moon contributes another very strong indication for successful childbearing. Venus, ruler of the fifth, and the Moon, ruler of the first are in an opportunity aspect — in this case an exact, partile aspect — whereby the two main symbols of reproduction can work together in harmony.

10. Venus sextile the Ascendant results in an attractive and loving personality, and as ruler of the fifth, encourages and enjoys pregnancy and motherhood.

Jayne was able to overcome the detrimental significance of Venus in Aries because of all of its favorable and helpful aspects.

Now let's examine the Moon at 29 Aquarius 02 which has passed over and is 14 degrees ahead of Saturn at 15 Aquarius 15. Fourteen degrees apart may still be considered a conjunction because the Moon is involved, and aspects involving the Sun and Moon are given wider orbs than those involving other planets. However, this is a *separating* aspect, that is, the faster moving Moon had already passed, by 14 degrees, the fertility inhibiting Saturn at the moment of Jayne's birth. The aspect was spent, had lost its power, and the Moon is now free to enjoy, untrammeled, her triple power sextiles to Uranus, Venus, and the Sun.

Compare this separating, no-power conjunction with those of Claire, Sills, Sophia and Crawford. In each of these cases, the Moon is *applying,* that is, rapidly approaching by a close number of degrees, the forbidding, negative Saturn and its damaging effects. Applying aspects are much stronger than separating ones because their effects, whether positive or negative, are approaching fruition.

Once again we see, that as with Venus in Aries, the negative effects of Saturn, while strong in the above mentioned charts, do not apply in Jayne's chart because they never existed at all. Therefore, if any of you who might have Venus in Aries, or Moon conjunct Saturn in your own charts are unduly alarmed, you really have no cause to be. Your fears are groundless. One or two aspects or conditions do not determine the whole story.

WE have noted previously that while Russell's chart had a strong Piscean influence, Mansfield's is very positively Cancerian. This mother's sign carries a great deal of weight because:

1. The Cancer sign with Cancer decanate rules the first house of personality.

2. Cancer also rules the second house, supplying motherhood rulership over two houses of the chart. Here, feelings of inner worth stem from the bearing and caring of children.

3. Co-ruling the tenth house of career are Neptune and Jupiter, here straddling the fourth house cusp — the natural Cancer house. The fourth house signifies the home, domesticity, parenthood, the breasts, and the uterus or womb. Outwardly she enjoyed the glamorous public life, but her true love was home and family. She merely brought her glamour and attention-seeking proclivities into her home. A pink palace with pink, heart-shaped swimming pool could hearly escape attention!

4. The Cancer Ascendant ruler, the Moon, in an infertile, masculine, air sign, is a very active member of the chart, and also the most highly elevated. It makes the following aspects:

a) Moon sextile Uranus — alert mind; enjoys the unexpected; willingly accepts the idea of children.

b) Moon sextile Venus — already favorably discussed.

c) Moon sextile Sun — no conflict between Jayne's will (Sun), her reasoning (Sun, ruler of third house), and her feelings (Moon) to become a mother.

d) Moon trine Ascendant — motherhood as symbolized by the Moon, in harmonious, creative aspect to motherhood as symbolized by the Cancer Ascendant intensifies the desire for motherhood. It is, for Jayne, the only natural thing to do.

5. Moon opposite Mars — causes aggressiveness, impatience, proneness to accidents.

6. Moon opposite Neptune — talented, creative; tendency to escapism.

Since all of Jayne's planets, save Pluto, are in infertile signs, these many Cancerian persuasions provided by the Moon are necessary and useful.

Then it ended. Suddenly, violently, horribly. Due to an automobile accident on June 29, 1967.

This not-plain Jayne's life was short, but very full. She was not afraid to work hard, to play hard, to accept all that life had to offer, and she gave five new lives in return.

We should try to be as generous.

She also teaches us another valuable lesson. We learn from Jayne's chart, that interpretation is an intricate, detailed, many faceted task, and that only an experienced astrologer should attempt to analyze fertility and opportunities for pregnancy in any chart.

Chapter XVII
Ethel Kennedy

It was the early 1960's, the Kennedy Era, and one and all, from the Brothers Three — John, Robert, and Edward (Ted) — to their parents, wives, and children, their sisters and their friends, made fascinating media copy for the American people, Democrats and Republicans alike.

Claire, as avid a Kennedy watcher as the rest of the populace, had on this particular day, dejectedly put down her newspaper in disbelief and not a little envy. With one daughter in her early teens and the three other children just a few years behind, Claire's days were busy, tiring, full of endless responsibilities; and sometimes her strength, running out like ebb tide, failed to return as surely and quickly as the new, incoming waves are wont to do.

Yet, here was this slim, little Ethel Kennedy, wife of Robert, Attorney General of the United States, and brother of the President, just one year younger than Claire, pictured on the front page with her eighth bundle of new baby. She looked as chipper, bouncy, and ebullient as a teenager herself as she left the hospital to go home to her energy-charged brood, *with no sweat at all!* Saying she felt "Wonderful!" Meaning it. Looking it, too!

Consequently, but illogically, Claire, even from a distance, was all prepared not to like Ethel — one of those over-active, over-confident, over-zealous, pushy Aries people with her bunch of noisy kids. Nevertheless, for Claire, to whom having babies had been a weakening and energy-depleting experience, Ethel's positive attitude, her exuberance and her stamina, were qualities to be admired and imitated. If only one could!

Ethel was well-to-do, yes. With lots of household help, true. And a big, sprawling house with land, and animal pets, and room for children to play and grow. Still, having a family, which eventually would grow to number 11 children, is work and care, responsibility and accountability; an obligation not to be taken lightly. With several babies only one year apart, and no twins among them, Ethel was a fertile woman who seemingly enjoyed her pregnancies, which were taken as a matter of course, and she never let her condition interfere with either plans for travel, sports, or keeping up with her husband's busy career.

How did Ethel Kennedy make motherhood look so effortless and like so much fun? Let's scrutinize carefully this next horoscope of Ethel's, Figure 26, to see if she is truly representative, and deserving of the distinctive honor, bestowed by Claire, of being called a *Super Mom*.

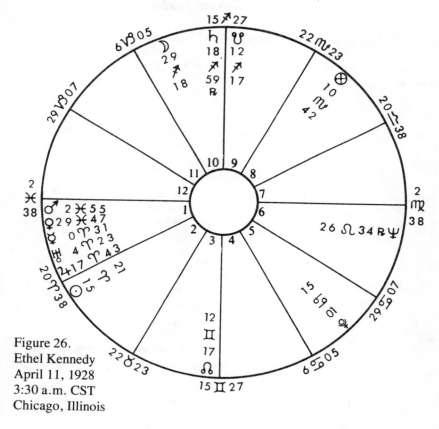

Figure 26.
Ethel Kennedy
April 11, 1928
3:30 a.m. CST
Chicago, Illinois

Hoping to give you a complete change of pace when we picked Ethel as our next subject, who is neither a movie star nor a career woman, we were surprised to find that she has much in common with our preceding *Two Not-Plain Janes* — not in looks or acting talent, maybe, but in a combination of their attitudes towards life, and we find fragments of each filtering through Ethel's strong first house personality. There are even shades of Shirley Temple here, born April 23, 1928, only 12 days after Ethel, yet seemingly of another generation because she was a newsmaker of an earlier decade. Inspect Table I and notice the similarities, which when combined, produce this positive, life-giving woman.

143

Table I

Astrological/Personality Similarities

Mansfield	Russell	Temple-Black	Ethel K.	Personality
Two Cancer-ruled cusps			Two Cancer-ruled cusps	Maternal emphasis
4 planets in Aries		4 planets in Aries	4 planets in Aries	confident, pioneering attitude
Separating Saturn/Moon conjunction			Separating Saturn/Moon conjunction	inhibiting child-bearing conjunction is no longer operable
		Mars in Pisces	Mars in Pisces	idealistic, worker for the handicapped and the under-privileged
		the four angles in mutable signs	the four angles in mutable signs	transference of energy to others
	Pisces rules Midheaven and Ascendant decanate		Pisces rules the Ascendant	Pisces — sign of service, empathy, and faith
	ruler of the Ascendant is part of grand trine	ruler of Ascendant is part of grand trine	ruler of Ascendant is part of grand trine	integrated personality

Within Ethel's personality then we find the following blend: Mansfield's sense of motherhood and her peppy, positive attitude; Russell's sense of service and religious belief; and Shirley's interest to better conditions in the world. Notice, that because Shirley is only 12 days younger than Ethel, the same grand trine in fire is operable in each chart, with only the Aries planets in different degrees. Both charts have Neptune at 26 Leo trine Saturn at 18 Sagittarius. To complete the grand trine, Ethel has the Sun and Jupiter in Aries, while Shirley has Venus, Jupiter, and Mercury in that first sign of the ram, giving both women faith, enthusiasm, spirit, and an harmonious, helpful outlook on life.

Such fertility as Ethel has displayed should show up in her chart, we reason, as we purposefully study:

1. the fifth house — Ethel' fertility,
2. the eleventh house — husband's fertility,
3. the Moon — motherhood, the uterus,
4. Venus — the ovaries and the internal organs of reproduction,
5. the Ascendant or first house of personality, and
6. the seventh house — marriage.

The Fifth House:

1. Cancer, the mother's sign, occupies the cusp, a fertile water sign, and a natural for wanting children. Its attitude and feelings toward children and childbearing are creative, old-fashioned, and romantic. To have children is taken for granted. Its ruler, the Moon is:

   a) square Venus (ovaries) — trouble with the internal reproductive system,

   b) square Mercury — conflict between mind and emotions,

   c) square Uranus — restless, accident prone; none of the above are favorable for fertility or childbearing,

   d) sextile Mars — good recuperative powers; opportunities for childbearing,

   e) trine Jupiter/Sun conjunction — very favorable,

   f) trine Neptune, completing the grand trine — very favorable, and

   g) separating from a conjunction to Saturn — no adverse effect.

Notice that the Moon (as with Mansfield) had already separated by 11 degrees from Saturn at the time of Ethel's birth. Once again Saturn cannot inhibit the Moon's motherly functions.

2. Pluto, in fertile Cancer, is the only planet in the fifth house. It is:

   a) square Jupiter/Sun — unfavorable for fertility and childbearing, and

   b) quincunx Saturn — unfavorable.

3. Mars, at 2 Pisces, is trine the fifth house cusp — favorable.

4. The Mercury/Uranus conjunction is square the fifth house cusp — unfavorable.

Besides its placement on the fifth house cusp, Cancer exhibits double influence by ruling also the sixth house of:

1. work — Ethel's primary work is her children, and

2. health — With the ruler, the Moon, exhibiting such mixed aspects, especially that square to Venus, we realize now that it was not always easy going for Ethel. When we learned that Ethel underwent 5 Caesarean operations, and that she was forced to remain in bed for the final two months of pregnancy with her eleventh child, we understand more fully the effects of adverse aspects.

The Eleventh House of Husband's Fertility:

Capricorn, a fertile earth sign, occupies the cusp, while its ruler, Saturn, importantly placed on the Midheaven, and the uppermost planet in the chart, indicates the great influence of the husband's symbol of fertility, which is:

1. trine the Jupiter/Sun conjunction, and trine Neptune, forming a grand trine which is very favorable for childbearing, and

2. widely square Venus (the reproductive system and the ovaries) — unfavorable.

Again the aspects are mixed. However, when we place the husband's birth planets in Ethel's chart, as shown here in Figure 27, we find the three benefics of childbearing — Venus, Jupiter, and the Moon beautifully placed in the eleventh house of her chart, that is, *his* house of children — the fifth from the seventh house of the husband. As we study further the relationship between the natal planets of Ethel and her husband, Robert (Bobby) Kennedy, with an emphasis on fertility, we notice the following:

1. To repeat, because this is important, his Venus, Jupiter, and Moon, the three most beneficial planets, fall into Ethel's eleventh house — his fertility house, and are sextile Ethel's Venus, representing the internal reproductive system.

2. Bobby's Part of Fortune at 6 Cancer is on Ethel's fifth house cusp — her fertility house — trine Ethel's Part of Fortune, trine Ethel's Ascendant, and trine Ethel's Mars at 2 Pisces conjunct the Ascendant.

3. Bobby's Mars at 4 Scorpio is conjunct Ethel's Part of Fortune, is trine the fifth house cusp, trine Ethel's Ascendant, and trine Ethel's Mars.

4. Bobby's Sun at 28 Scorpio, the male symbol, is trine Ethel's Venus at 29 Pisces, the female symbol.

By itself, Ethel's chart does not show exceptional fertility, but when united with Bobby's their sexual compatibility resulted in joyous and fruitful parenthood. They made a good team!

146

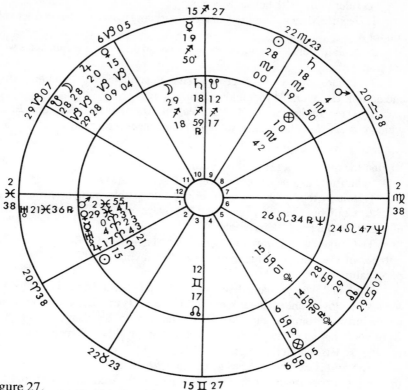

Figure 27.
Mr. and Mrs. Robert Kennedy — natal planets
Ethel — April 11, 1928 3:30 a.m. CST
Chicago, Illinois
inner wheel and house cusps
Robert — Nov. 20, 1925 3:11 p.m. EST
Brookline, Mass.   outer wheel

The Moon, symbol of Motherhood:

Ethel's Moon is in the infertile fire sign, Sagittarius, situated in the tenth house of career. Being a mother was her most important full time job, although by no means her only one. She was a very public figure (Moon in the worldly tenth house) in her roles of wife and mother, as she took her place along side of Bobby, either working with him or encouraging him from the wings. As the wife of a political figure (Moon in the natural house of Capricorn [politics]), Ethel can be a source for good because her influence with the public, especially women (Moon), is strong.

As ruler of the fifth house, Moon is:

1. Sextile Mars — she enjoyed the opportunity to be a mother and actively sought it.

2. Square Venus — underwent 5 Caesarean deliveries; pregnancies were not trouble free.

3. Square Mercury — over-impulsive; unpredictable in thought, speech and action. Unfavorable for childbearing.

4. Trine Jupiter/Sun and trine Neptune, forming favorable grand trine which protected her health and supplied strong inner resources.

Venus, the ovaries, organ of childbearing:

Beautifully exalted in fertile, watery Pisces, Venus is

1. Square the Moon — a very strong, unfavorable, partile aspect.

2. Conjunct Mercury, signifying Bobby, as ruler of Virgo on the seventh house of the husband — favorable.

3. Conjunct Uranus — giving an unusual number of children; an unusual number of Caesarean births; dynamic zest for living; sparkling, effervescent personality.

Thus far, we see that Ethel does not have either a fifth house, Moon or Venus unalloyed and without blemish. The aspects are mixed and one could never surmise from the above symbols of fertility, in this chart alone (without Bobby's), that so many children would be born to Ethel. Something more is needed, so lets search the chart.

The Sun is exalted in Aries and conjunct Jupiter — giving us the positive thinker, and because this conjunction is placed on the second house cusp, Ethel has deep inner resources, a strong belief in herself and in her ability to be a good mother. This belief is backed up by their trine to Saturn in Sagittarius, the sign of religion, and it is her shining faith in a Superior Being which lights up the Midheaven and illumines her path. Looking for still more reasons for such a large family, we look to our next determinant of fertility, the personality.

Personality:

An important reason for Ethel's large family must lie in her own personality. And it does. There is fertility and there is fertility. But after one is biologically fertile, other considerations must come into play, as follows:

1. The Ascendant or first house rules, among other things, one's character, physical constitution, disposition, attitudes, and temperament. Heavily tenanted with 5 planets, this is a busy, bustling, active, important area of the chart, mirroring, in a way, both Ethel's own childhood home and family life in Connecticut, as well as the much publicized Hickory Hill domicile in Virginia where the Robert Kennedys lived, cavorted, and raised their family.

148

The three Aries planets, Mercury, Uranus, and Jupiter, may more boisterously proclaim her active, sports-loving, devil-may-care inclinations, but Ethel's true nature, with Pisces on the first house cusp, containing a Pisces decanate and Mars and Venus in Pisces, is really quite different — empathetic, romantic, sensitive, and compassionate. She is a woman with tender feelings toward children (her formula for raising them: *just love them*), animals, and the underdog, in general.

Mars, the aggressive planet, is strongly placed on the Ascendant, but the edge and bite is lessened, and the action is tamed and toned down when situated, as it is here, in peace-loving, patient Pisces. There are definitely two sides to Ethel, and as Claire studied this complexity in greater detail, her view of Ethel changed. She realized that here was a woman who cared, who could take charge and help, who had a strong faith and an understanding of suffering — a friend, indeed.

2. With so many planets in the first house, and its ruler, Neptune, which is part of the grand trine, taking part in shaping her personality, Ethel is definitely not a loner. The ruler of the seventh house, Mercury, in the first house, brings to the fore the need of a husband and other people to help round out her own sense of beingness. Many children, too, their friends, activities and interests, would supply the full house and the abundant family life which she craved. Therefore, she joyously welcomed each new pregnancy.

3. If we break down the signs of Ethel's planets into their elements, something enlightening emerges. Seven planets and the Midheaven are in fire signs, and three planets and the Ascendant are in water signs, but there are no planets in the elements of earth or air. We are left with the realization that this is overwhelmingly a chart of *faith* and a chart of *belief*. The fire signs signify faith, spirituality, idealism and spirit. The Pisces placements betoken belief, love for what is mystical, the soul. The remaining planet, Pluto, is in Cancer, the mother's sign.

Because there are no earth signs, an air of practicality, a feeling of self-preservation may be missing. Without air signs there should be no unnecessary worrying, and deep, intellectual, troublesome thinking is supposedly lacking. Yet, with mutable signs on the angles, and Saturn in Sagittarius on the Midheaven, philosophical thinking and debating with others is important to Ethel.

During her childhood, priests and religious leaders met at her mother's home for informal discussion. Continuing in this same vein, the Kennedys held seminars in their home, with spirited discussions following lectures by philosophers and educators. Air signs may have been lacking, but Ethel's desire to grow and learn was not.

Brought up in a Roman Catholic home, and imbued with the Faith by a fervent mother, religious instruction was easily assimilated by Ethel as a child, grew with her, and became part of her as an adult. As any mother knows, however, even the best teaching and example are not sufficient to impart faith. It is a gift given by God to whomever He chooses. Evidently Ethel was chosen. Artificial contraception, being frowned upon by her Church, did not find favor in Ethel's life, either — a large family being the obvious result.

One can argue that the lack of earth and air signs might result in a lack of practicality and mature judgment in this matter of birth control. Not so. Faith, by its very nature, cannot be reasoned out. We can think of no more serviceable, productive tool for living than the possession of a workable faith such as Ethel's, and a belief in a God Who is always there to help her every step of the way; a God to Whom she can easily surrender her will, thereby opening her life to the fullness of His blessings.

Marriage:
A solid, secure marriage is the perfect backdrop for the raising of a large family. Mercury in Aries, ruler of the seventh house signifying the husband, is:

1. Conjunct Venus, ruler of the eighth house of sex, placed in the first house of personality, and signifying the woman who was truly beautiful in his eyes. Venus in Pisces is capable of idealistic, sacrificial love, and Ethel possessed such a love for her husband. This is a very close union; Ethel idolizes her Bobby; communication is good.

2. Conjunct Uranus. This marriage is exciting. Bobby had a stimulating career which included being Attorney General and Senator of the United States, and Ethel involved herself in her husband's work. Whether he travelled abroad or throughout the United States, Ethel, whenever possible, was at his side; while at home, both welcomed the unknown, uncharted atmosphere that each new baby brought into their lives.

Together, everything was an adventure. Therefore, we're not surprised that when questioned by a reporter as to what he thought was his most meaningful achievement, Robert Kennedy replied very simply, *marrying Ethel*. Not withstanding the temptations that much power and very much wealth can, and often do, bring — this should have been a happy marriage.

Let's go back again to Figure 27 — Ethel's chart with Bobby's natal planets in the outer circle, and see if their planets really do blend in mutual attraction and romance and if they show the compatibility that every good marriage must possess. We find:

1. His Sun at 28 Scorpio trine her Venus at 29 Pisces imparts romantic and sexual attraction. They enjoyed each other's company and found pleasure in raising their children together.

2. His Moon sextile her Venus yields romantic attraction, creates an harmonious domestic life, and grants emotional understanding of each other's moods and feelings.

3. His Mars trine her Ascendant again furnishes sexual attraction; they also worked well together.

4. His Mercury trine her Jupiter provided for the sharing of intellectual, spiritual, and philosophical interests.

5. His Mercury trine her Sun made for excellent communication between them.

6. His Mercury trine her Neptune bestowed a telepathic, psychic link between them.

7. His Mercury conjunct her Saturn, at the very top of Ethel's chart is *the point of contact* in their relationship, and it involves the grand trine in Ethel's chart. Ethel's upbringing was one of comfort and wealth, far removed from poverty and want. It was through Bobby that the world of the underprivileged came into her consciousness, and then his consciousness became hers also, and her responsibility as well.

Ethel and Bobby were well matched and well mated. Today, with all the female yearnings for vocational advancement and placement in male-oriented career categories, to be *first* in the heart of a *worthy* man and to bear his children is still what most women would trade anything for. Ethel, for a few brief years, possessed such a man and such a marriage.

Assassination:

When the shooting of Bobby Kennedy occurred, the transiting planets at that time seemed to affect Ethel's chart and planets in almost as dastardly and malevolently a manner as they did Bobby's. Examine the following three part chart wherein we use Ethel's house cusps, place Ethel's planets in the inner wheel, Bobby's birth planets in the middle section, and the assassination planets in the outer wheel, as shown in Figure 28.

Robert Kennedy was shot and fatally wounded on June 5, 1968, at 12:16 a.m. PST, in Los Angeles, California. Observing the transiting planets at that particular moment in time, which we have placed in the outermost wheel of Ethel's natal chart, we find the following aspects:

1. Transiting Mars, planet of violence, from the fourth house of endings is:
   a) opposite Ethel's Saturn,
   b) opposite Bobby's Mercury, and
   c) square Bobby's Uranus.
2. Transiting Pluto, planet of destruction, is:
   a) square Ethel's Saturn,
   b) square Bobby's Mercury, and
   c) opposite Bobby's Uranus.
3. Transiting Moon, which sets off events is:
   a) square Ethel's Moon in a partile aspect,
   b) opposite Ethel's Venus in another partile aspect, and

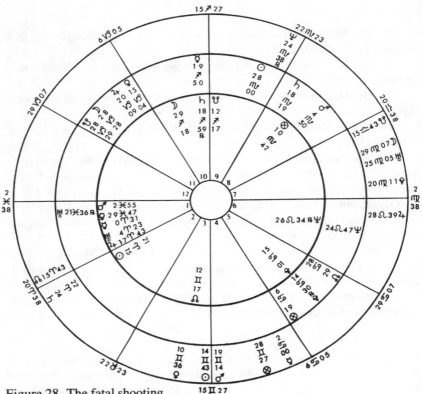

Figure 28. The fatal shooting.
Ethel house cusps and natal planets — inside
Bobby natal planes — middle
Bobby — shot — June 5, 1968, 12:16 a.m. P.S.T. Los Angeles, Calif. — outside

     c) strangely enough, sextile Bobby's Sun and trine Bobby's Moon.
  4. Transiting Saturn, planet of sorrow and distintegration is:
     a) conjunct Ethel's Sun, and
     b) square Bobby's Jupiter/Moon.

    It is very clear now, that when that assasin's bullet brutally ended Robert Kennedy's life, it drastically changed Ethel's, too. Not outwardly, however, for she maintained her home as before, surrounded herself with people, and busied herself with her children. Then, determined to keep alive the ideals of her dead husband, she set up the R.F.K. Memorial, a creation of "action fellowships" wherein young people are assigned to work in community projects identified with Robert Kennedy. They develop housing projects and health-service programs; develop experimental black studies curriculums, and educational programs for Indians on reservations; and provide free legal assistance to ghetto groups. They serve the poor, the uneducated, the minorities, and the underdog. Worthy projects, all.

It is inherent in Ethel's nature to be so involved because, besides being prodded by Bobby, Saturn, as ruler of her twelfth house of atonement and welfare, is in her 10th house of career, and exacts from her a life of service. Transiting Saturn is in her eighth house in 1984; in 1985, it will reside in her ninth house; it will reach her tenth house in 1987, bringing maximum power as it returns to its elevated position on the tenth house cusp.

This Saturn is on its way to completing its second journey through the zodiac, and is returning to its original place in the chart. For Ethel, it will be a time for wiping out the past; a time to go forward. A new lease on life will be in the offing, and therefore, a new direction will be needed.

The 1980's are not the 1960's. The blacks and other minorities have made great strides in the past 20 years. They can speak for themselves now. We have black mayors in our cities, Chinese anchor-women on national television, Koreans in our neighborhood stores, and a recent black Miss America representing our young womanhood.

Meanwhile, the drug problem in America has taken great giant steps forward, destroying the lives of our children at even the grade school level. What Ethel should ask herself, as she searches for a new direction, is this: "If Bobby were alive today, to which problem would he now be addressing his energies?"

The Kennedy family has for many years directed its resources and attention to alleviating the distress of mental retardation, and mental illness. No one is more mentally retarded than those trafficking in illegal drugs. No one suffers more than the addict, except those whom he rapes, robs, and kills. No one is more impoverished in mind and body, no one is less a human being than when under the spell of drugs. No one is in more need of legal restraint; more in need of education or health services than one hopelessly addicted to drugs. No one is more detrimental to society or more destructive to our children than the drug addict and the drug pusher.

Remember Bobby's, *"I dream things that never were and ask, Why not?"*? If we study it carefully, we will see that that slogan exemplifies Ethel's first house. The Pisces Ascendant is the dream, while Venus in Pisces represents idealism. Then, Mars in Pisces and four planets in Aries supply the action and energy to make the dream come true.

Pisces stands not only for dreams; it symbolizes drugs as well. If Ethel Kennedy uses her Saturn, soon to approach its zenith in her chart; if she chooses to accept this responsibility, she can be an effective leader, a teacher, a *Super Mom* in the fight to save our children from the horrors of drug abuse. She has the organizing ability, the pioneering spirit, the dutifulness, and the open door to high and low places to make a difference.

Most of all, she has the faith.

For in the final analysis, a faith like hers in God, our Father, is the only hope we have that Love will be waiting to welcome us into eternity — and hopefully to tell us, *"well done."*

The above, unchanged chapter was written months before the calamitous, drug-related death of Ethel's fourth child — her 28 year old son, David, on April 25, 1984. Born on June 15, 1955, it is said that a part of David, who had been especially close to his father, died on the day he saw his Dad struck down by an assassin's bullet.

While his loved ones had tried over the years to ease the hurt, and although he had completed a program to become clean of drugs and alcohol just a week before he died, it was all to no avail.

Once again the well-worn Kennedy family photo album was opened for our inspection; the happy and sad faces and circumstances now as recognizable and familiar as those of our own immediate families. We add still another image.

Striking is too harsh a word for the heart-rending portrait of Ethel, rosary beads in hand, praying at her husband's grave on the morning following their child's death. But, there it is in black and white: this glowing faith, this total trust in God visually represented through the bowed head but upright form of her silent, kneeling figure.

In memory, Claire returned to that aforementioned newspaper likeness of an earlier day, noting sadly the stark contrast between the two photographs. A new beginning then . . . a final ending now. A mother's confidence in God being the only constant.

Would that David could have partaken of even a fraction of his mother's life-giving, Piscean faith.

Chapter XVIII
Elizabeth Taylor

As sojourners of the fifth house in the charts of Claire and famous women, we have thus far concentrated on this house's significance primarily as it applies to conditions of fertility, the bearing of children, creativity, and the participation by these women in the field of entertainment — be it grand opera, films, the stage, or even politics in which showmanship is, these days, such an important ingredient.

Our predominant interest, naturally, is to study fertility, but when other fifth house matters take the forefront we should examine them also, so that in delineating charts, we will more clearly understand why sometimes other representatives of the fifth house take on greater meaning and importance, pushing fertility and children far into the background, as far as the native is concerned.

Not that Elizabeth Taylor did not want a family; not that she doesn't love her children. It is only because society seems far more interested in her extra-curricular activities — and we can learn from them, too — that we present this study, in which we *try* to combine all of Miss Taylor's interests.

Some of the other interpretations and conditions which we have not yet touched upon, but which also apply to the fifth house are:

1. speculation — the production of every film and theatre presentation is an expensive and time-consuming gamble, just as is the raising of a child,

2. the pleasures of social life,

3. indulgence and dissipation,

4. passion and love affairs — both legitimate and extramarital,

5. adornment and articles of adornment — jewels, cosmetics and so on, and

6. all material and physical pleasures, and sensuous enjoyments.

According to our reference book, *ELIZABETH TAYLOR The Last Star*, by Kitty Kelley, and the many newspaper and magazine articles written about her, Elziabeth has concentrated more fully upon the affairs of the above, latter paragraph than upon the concerns of our opening lines, although she has been working in movies for the past 40 years, and she has three natural children and one adopted daughter.

Important and incredible as her movie career has been — and she has achieved the enviable status of being a two-time Academy Award winner — it is her fifth-house-between-marriage-intra-marriage-private-life-made-public-love-affairs that still holds the most fascination for Taylor's adoring, or simply curious, followers.

Elizabeth Taylor has been honest enough to recognize that her popularity — or notoriety — has been enhanced and prolonged, in part, due to her unorthodox life style, and for many years she has obliged us by shedding one husband after another (7 in all), and just as promptly by acquiring a new lover to fill the gap between each (a fifth house emphasis). Once, when thousands of fans awaited the appearance of Liz and Richard Burton (husband number 5 and number 6) after a stage performance, Burton reveled in the presence of such an adoring public, not realizing, as did Elizabeth, that as she herself remarked, "they came to see sinners and freaks."

Part of her attraction, to be sure, must be that there is a certain vicarious satisfaction in knowing that no matter how often we ourselves may trespass, or falter in divorce, or act unwisely in affairs of the heart, Elizabeth is way ahead of us — trespassing even "better!" And what is more, regardless of her conduct, she is accepted with fanfare by both the powerful and the mighty as well as by the common man.

Do you wonder if her horoscope will illustrate her magnetic, forceful personality, her beauty and talent, explain her miscarriage and Caesarean births, and help us to understand her unbelievable media propensity — enough to sustain the interest of a usually fickle public for 40 years? Will it support her grandiose and bombastic manner, her gargantuan appetites and vulgarity in speech? If so, then it's time to begin our study of her natal chart, Figure 29, for if you are looking for the consummate fifth house person, one who has publicly savored almost every facet of this chamber of the zodiac — Elizabeth Taylor is that individual!

Elizabeth started off sweetly enough — a docile child who listened to her mother — a mother not unlike Loren's, Sills', Temple's and now Brooke Shields' — a woman enamoured of the motion picture business and the part her child might play in it. Astrologically, the importance to Elizabeth's career by this mother is shown by the Cancer (mother) ruled tenth house of career, whose ruler, the Moon (mother), is trine Pluto in Cancer in the tenth, providing ease and opportunity for achieving her ambitions. The reciprocity of the Moon in Scorpio with Pluto in Cancer (each being in the natural sign of the other) produced an increasingly smooth flow of beneficial energy which catapulted into view an extraordinarily beautiful child of spellbinding facial coloring, consisting of a porcelain, heart-shaped face, long, luxuriant, dark lashes framing exquisitely lovely, sapphire blue-violet eyes, and coal-black curls to complete the picture.

156

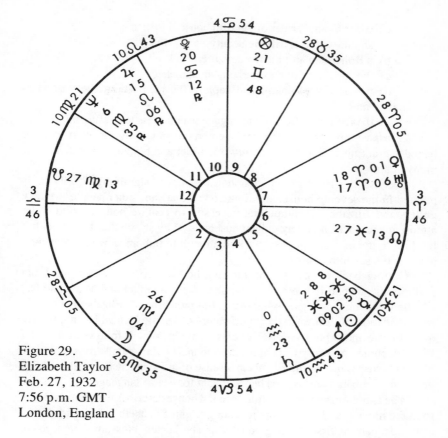

Figure 29.
Elizabeth Taylor
Feb. 27, 1932
7:56 p.m. GMT
London, England

To confirm such a breathtaking appearance, we must refer to that all-important Ascendant. What sign *should* be on its cusp if not Libra, the sign of beauty and adornment, the sign of love and romance, and the natural seventh house sign of spouses? The house contains no planets, so we look to its ruler, Venus in Aries, placed *in* the seventh house of husbands, and other people — in this case, her audience and her fans.

Let's stop for a moment at this Venus in Aries, in its detriment, which, we remember, is not usually conducive to easy childbearing or childrearing. It is not helpful for Elizabeth either, in this regard. But, there is something else of interest here, because out of our ten famous women subjects, 6 of them have this placement of Venus in Aries. That's 60%, signifying to us that the assertive, aggressive, pioneering, Mars-ruled Aries, when containing the female planet, Venus, produces women of initiative, courage, and resourcefulness in whichever field they choose to enter.

Venus is:

1. conjunct Uranus, ruler of the fifth house, imparting —

    a) an unusual, electrifying beauty,

    b) a Bohemian attitude towards life,

    c) the capability of mesmerizing an audience,

    d) the ability to charm and capture the men whom she wished to marry, and

    e) the feeling of freedom to engage in countless love affairs.

2. trine Jupiter in Leo, the sign of entertainment, in the eleventh house of friends, granting Elizabeth the faculty to attract and hold a vast audience for many years.

Because the ruler of the first house, Venus, signifying Elizabeth, is posited *in* the seventh house, signifying one's mate and other people, we now understand Elizabeth's compelling necessity to acquire both a world-wide, attentive audience and many gallant husbands. Why she couldn't, or wouldn't hold on to the men she married we will attempt to fathom as we subsequently analyze the seventh house.

Getting back to the sign on the first house cusp, we notice that Libra inhabits the second house cusp as well, and just as Ethel and Mansfield had double Cancer cusps intensifying interest in motherhood, Elizabeth enjoys an intensification of desire for the significators of female Venus, her impressive array of rare and expensive jewelry being a case in point. It follows then, that if Libra occupies two cusps, its opposite, the male, Mars-ruled Aries must also hold two cusps, increasing Elizabeth's sense of independence, but also adding egotism, combatativeness, and her penchant for coarse language.

The Libra-cusped, Venus-ruled second house describes Elizabeth's ability to make money, and to develop her acting talent. Elizabeth's dramatic ability, only adequate at first, grew gradually as she herself blossomed into young womanhood. Recognizing at an early age the power of sex and the spell she could cast over men and an audience, she quickly shed her little girl image and became a tantalizing woman of the world, although the child within never left as, bedecked and bejeweled, she sought constant admiration and attention. And, she received it.

But, why could she communicate sex so effectively in her films? Because:

1. The ruler of her tenth house of career is the Moon, her personality, in Scorpio, the sign of sex, square Mars, the male sex symbol, in Pisces (films), placed in the fifth house of entertainment.

2. The sign on the third house cusp of communication is Scorpio, the sex sign, whose ruler, Pluto, planet of sex, is placed in the public tenth house, is trine the Scorpio Moon, and reciprocal with it.

3. The ruler of the eighth house of sex is Mars, the male sex symbol, which is conjunct the Sun, planet of entertainment; with both planets in Pisces

(films) and placed in the fifth house of entertainment. This Sun and Mars are both conjunct Mercury, planet of communication, in the sign of films and in the house of movies, and all three planets are opposite Neptune, which is also their dispositor, and the planet of illusion and films.

Marriage:

Elizabeth was married 7 times (twice to Richard Burton) — the conjunction of Venus to Uranus in the seventh house accounting for the unusualness of this number. The Libra Ascendant imparts a "couple" personality, but once married, the Aries ruled seventh house may yield an independent nature not conducive to the togetherness that marriage entails.

The ruler of Elizabeth's seventh house is Mars in Pisces, placed in the fifth house of love affairs, children and the field of entertainment, and her marriages incorporated all three activities. Mars is:

1. trine the tenth house cusp. Every succeeding marriage engendered new publicity, renewed her popularity, and helped to rekindle interest in her career.

2. square the Moon, ruler of the tenth house. When the career was revitalized the marriages suffered, even though with each new marriage she vowed to become a housewife and mother, and to put husband and children before career.

3. conjunct the Sun. This is a very powerful aspect wherein the action of Mars combines with the will of the Sun to bring to fruition the affairs of its house. She worked with some husbands in movies, and had children with several; and while her love affairs with them were exciting, the marriages always fell short of her expectations.

4. opposite Neptune. This ruler of the sixth house of her glamorous, Neptunian work again produced incompability between marriage and career because work involved traveling and left little time for home and children. Sometimes, too, it was the absence of the husband, or too much professional competition between them, or excessive drinking which caused problems. But mainly it was the need for the stimulating and sensational vibrations of Neptune. When the love affair gave way to the commonplace reality of every day living, the spell was broken and the marriage dissolved.

Every marriage should be an ongoing love affair. If there are harmonious aspects between the fifth and seventh houses, chances are that it will be. In Elizabeth's case her love affairs often led to marriage, because not only is the ruler of her seventh house, Mars, placed in her fifth, but the ruler of the fifth house, Uranus, is placed in the seventh and is conjunct Venus (Elizabeth). However, both Uranus and Venus are square Pluto, and the emotional life brings more problems than satisfactions.

Claire's seventh house ruler is also in the fifth house, but the planet is serious, responsible Saturn and as it conjuncts the Moon (Claire), it encloses her within a white, picket fence where she is happy to remain. However, Saturn is in Sagittarius and the love within the fence would expand and grow for as long and as far as the Sagittarian arrow could carry it — out to infinity.

The fifth house of fertility and children:

The sign on the cusp is infertile Aquarius, representing the eleventh house sign of other people's children. During her marriage to Eddie Fisher, Elizabeth adopted a nine month old baby girl, Maria, born with a crippling hip deformity. Through a series of expensive operations the child was made whole, and is a beautiful, healthy young woman today, thanks to Elizabeth.

The planets within the house are Mars, the Sun and Mercury, none of which are fertile, although all are placed in the very fertile, water sign, Pisces. The major aspect of this very potent conjunction is its opposition to Neptune, ruler of the sixth house of health. Neptune is a hypersensitive planet and can cause deceptive health conditions which are hard to diagnose.

Elizabeth produced:

1. A miscarriage during her first marriage to Nicky Hilton. It is reported that one reason for the breakup of this marriage is that he wanted a child, but Elizabeth either could not, or would not give him one.

2. Two children during her second marriage to Michael Wilding, both by Caesarean section, as follows:

a) Michael Howard, born January 6, 1953. At this time transiting Venus at 1 Pisces conjunct transiting Mars at 5 Pisces set off Elizabeth's fifth house planets in Pisces.

b) Christopher, born February 27, 1955 (Elizabeth's birthday). Transiting Sun conjuncted her natal Sun and the other fifth house planets, and opposed Neptune.

3. One child, Liza, during her marriage to Mike Todd, born by Caesarean section. Transiting Saturn at 7 Sagittarius squared, and transiting Mercury at 10 Virgo opposed the fifth house planets, Mercury also conjuncting Elizabeth's natal Neptune. The baby did not breathe for 14 minutes after birth, and had to be placed in an incubator.

At this time doctors advised her husband that Elizabeth should not risk childbirth again and recommended a tubal ligation. Todd gave permission. Elizabeth, upon awakening to the news said, "It was the worst shock of my life — like being killed." We wonder at the wisdom of sterilizing a woman without her permission.

We note the following concerning Elizabeth's reproductive planets:

1. Venus, the ovaries is —
a) square Pluto, giving menstruating difficulties, and
b) trine Jupiter, allowing excessive gain weight during pregnancy.

2. Moon, the uterus is —

160

a) square Neptune, instigating difficult deliveries,

b) square Mars, causing the miscarriage and the Caesarean operations, and

c) in its fall in Scorpio and cannot function at its best.

3. Libra, the Ascendant sign, ruling the fallopian tubes, is ruled by Venus, which is square Pluto.

Elizabeth enjoyed having babies, but as they grew she became an indulgent mother, and did not give the children the discipline and secure life they needed. Sometimes they accompanied her on her travels, but for the most part they were brought up by servants and tutors, surrounded by every luxury except what they needed most — their own fathers and a full time mother. Her Moon, signifying motherhood, and homemaker, being the focal planet for the T-square involving the Neptune/Mars opposition, is probably the astrological reason for the manner in which she conducted her household.

In the final anslysis, it is Neptune, the planet of exaggeration and scandal, imagination and escapism which is the prime mover of this theatrical life, both on-stage and off. It sets off by opposition the three planets in the fifth house, giving Elizabeth husbands (Mars rules the seventh), an adopted child (the Sun rules the eleventh), and many illnesses (Neptune itself rules the sixth). As dispositor of those same three planets (they are all in Neptune's natural sign), it delivers children with difficulty, love affairs which don't last, and a film career spanning decades. It gave her the bright lights of the theatre marquee and the dim shadow of a beloved husband in death. It gave her excessive desires for the erotic, for food, for drink, and for adornment in exchange for excessive beauty.

Elizabeth, in return, gave us what we expected of her — scandal, escapism, and belief in the make-believe.

As time passes, we look to the fourth house to see what the heavens will bring in later years. Capricorn on the cusp promises a more structured existence, a seriousness, and a more purposeful life. Its ruler, Saturn, is placed within this house, in Aquarius, reinforcing a more staid, but altruistic philosophy. Saturn's trine to the Ascendant should also be a steadying, maturing influence.

Maybe it's time for Elizabeth to change her image, mentally as well as physically. Isn't she worthy of more inspiring news coverage than that of losing 20 pounds at a fat farm?

Recently, the wing of a children's hospital, to which Elizabeth contributed her efforts, was named in her honor, bringing into clear focus her Piscean/Neptune emphasis — this time signifying hospitals, empathy and compassion. That's the Elizabeth Taylor we would like to see more of in the future.

Chapter XIX
Saint Frances Xavier Cabrini

They're gone now — the circular driveway centered by the Sacred Heart statue and its surrounding rose bushes, the big mansion set back among stately, old trees, and the welcoming sign swaying slightly in the Westchester breeze which read, "SACRED HEART VILLA ACADEMY, Boarding School for Girls." But, in the 1930's, when Claire and I were students there, it was a small, thriving, private boarding school, grades one through eight, with only six or seven students in each class, a safe haven from the Great Depression which was affecting so disastrously the world outside its heavy, solid, securely locked doors.

Situated in Dobbs Ferry, New York, historic Revolutionary War territory, where our young nation had struggled for and won its independence so many years before, the school, isolated and insulated, was maintained by a strict order of Catholic nuns, the Missionary Sisters of the Sacred Heart of Jesus, whose foundress, Saint Frances Xavier Cabrini, is our final motherhood study.

She called herself simply, "Mother Cabrini." Her nuns, who in most orders at that time were called *Sister,* were also each called *Mother,* and they lived for their charges as well as any natural mother could — dedicating their lives to the scholastic achievement, character building, and obedience to the Faith of their girls.

Mother Cabrini died in 1917, before we were born, but this convent school which her nuns conducted reflected her teachings, followed her example and her rule, and we think it will give you a first-hand glimpse of her methods of caring for children. From the *Morning Offering* prayer recited even before arising at 6:20 a.m., to daily Mass, three nutritious, hot meals plus "lunch" at 3 p.m. (consisting of apronsful of apples, or cookies, or peanut butter sandwiches), classes, study periods, Italian, piano, embroidery, tennis, and dancing lessons, recreation periods at which we played a hot game of "rounders," library reading and evening chapel visits, until bedtime at 9 p.m. — the chiming of bells or the clapping of a Mother's hands led the students from one operation to the next — most of them being carried out in silence. At least they were supposed to be!

Decorum was the rule, and the students were expected to curtsy to each Mother they passed during the course of the daily activities. The navy blue uniforms, handmade by the sewing Mothers (somehow, whether we were fat or skinny all uniforms seemed to be cut to the same size — HUGE), were topped by a black sateen apron, while underneath we wore a handmade, cotton chemise, thick lisle stockings, black oxford shoes, and in the very early years — even black bloomers! The Sunday uniform, worn when parents were allowed their three hour weekly visit, had lace collar and cuffs; the stockings were silk; the shoes — black, patent-leather maryjanes.

The Mothers enjoyed candy as much as the kids, and every holiday, holyday and feast day we were treated to "sugars and gums" after the noonday meal. The sugars were prettily shaped and in pastel colors, but were pure sugar — too sweet to be anyone's favorite — so many transactions occurred as the trading of two sugars for one gum (a chewy gum-drop) went on throughout the recreation period that followed. The nuns loved to tell us that one of Mother Cabrini's last acts before she died was to fill boxes with Christmas candy for her girls.

Parents, however, were not to be trusted! Upon returning to school after any vacation, instead of the usual bountiful breakfast there stood by each child's place at table a solitary bottle of citrate of magnesia, or a one-half glass of thick, black, evil-smelling cascara sagrada — cleansing protection against the poisons of worldly germs and Mom's home cooking!

Claire's most eagerly awaited activity, and mine, too, came at the close of the day — the evening library period. Sitting sedately side by side at a long, majestic, mahogany table, we ostensibly read quietly, while all the time, beneath the table, our toes tapped surreptitiously to the soft, lilting rhythm of our behind-the-times collection of records (vintage circa the roaring 20's) which we played on an equally antique, wide-horned, hand-cranked victrola.

Choosing a book was an adventure in itself because one had to stoop low, and creep under unyielding rubber plants, lacey ferns, and other bushy foliage (each flourishing in its own hand-painted, fragile jardinière) before one could find one's treasure in the bookshelves hidden behind the greenery. Emerging flushed but victorious from this impenetrable jungle with desired tome in tow, this seeming inaccessibility only added a sense of accomplishment and excitement to the reading experience.

The library table was used for other purposes besides reading, however, because it was here that our *sewing works,* of which we each produced several, were placed on display for the parents to view at the end of each school year. With noisy curiosity the girls surrounded the table in search of their name-tagged handi-work. We gratefully suspected that these works would be hardly recognizable, for a minor miracle would take place between the time we handed in our embroidery and the time it appeared on the table.

Gone were the raggedy edges and the grimy-grey, limp material of our french-knotted pillow cases, our cross-stitched tea sets, and our lazy-dazied table scarves. Instead, blessedly cleansed, stiffly starched, meticulously pressed, and beautifully edged in lace, the Mothers had painstakingly rejuvenated our halting stitches and turned them into veritable works of art.

"Oh, to tame our charges' unruly little bodies as easily as pressing warm iron to wrinkled cloth," the Mothers must have sighed, as they deftly performed this second function, while endeavoring with supreme patience to accomplish the first!

Now, in our ancient wisdom, Claire and I finally appreciate the sagacity and dedication of such women, mothers all, who followed unswervingly the dictates of their leader and foundress, Mother Cabrini, the first American citizen to be declared *Saint* by the Roman Catholic Church.

What kind of woman was she, who exacted such confidence, loyalty and devotion; who eschewed the normal desires for marriage and motherhood to become instead Mother to the Italian immigrant, the poor, the homeless, the sick, the orphan, the prisoner, all for the love of God? Remember *agape love*? Is that the answer? Can we find it in her chart?

Are you eager now to make Mother Cabrini's acquaintance astrologically? Let's study her natal chart together, our final horoscope, Figure 30.

Agape love, wherein one unselfishly sacrifices for another out of love for God, was the basis for Mother Cabrini's whole life. Since it is ruled by Neptune — higher sacrificial love, and Pluto — universal welfare, these two planets should be important in her chart. They are. Because Neptune is in its rulership in Pisces, and Pluto is in its co-rulership in Aries, both planets can function to their highest potential, and were capable of instilling in this native the idealism, regenerative power, spirituality, and compassion needed to minister to others.

Born in Italy, the youngest of thirteen children, Mother Cabrini's desire had always been to become a Roman Catholic nun, devote her life to God, and, in a sense, become married to Him. With Aquarius on her seventh house cusp, and its ruler, Uranus, the highest placed planet, in the ninth house of religion, conjunct Pluto and sextile Neptune (the *agape* planets), her Bridgegroom and Spouse had to be Someone unusual and exceptional. She believed He chose her to do His work on earth and she willingly accepted. Her beautiful, sacrificial Neptune, ruler of the eighth house of dream consciousness, the mystical and the occult, placed in the seventh house of marriage, made it a gloriously spiritual union, and its trine to Mercury in Cancer helped her to envision the caring of children and the family unit as her prime responsibility.

Denied her wish to enter a convent because of delicate health (Saturn, ruler of the sixth house of health is square the Sun), Mother Cabrini eventually founded her own missionary congregation and was sent by the Pope to the United States to work among the Italian immigrants who had emigrated to the

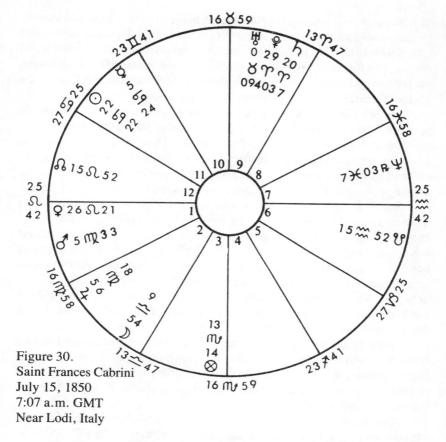

Figure 30.
Saint Frances Cabrini
July 15, 1850
7:07 a.m. GMT
Near Lodi, Italy

New World by the tens of thousands at the turn of the century. So many were uneducated, unemployed, uncertain, and lost in the big cities in which they congregated.

With her Sun in maternal Cancer in the civic-minded eleventh house, but close to the cusp of the spiritual twelfth — ruling hospitals, prisoners and welfare work — Mother Cabrini's objectives were to minister to the Italian speaking people, to renew the Catholic faith of the adults, and to care for and educate their children, so that as they grew they could eventually teach others. She opened schools, orphanages, hospitals and free clinics in many major cities of the United States, wherever she was needed, whenever she was called. Nicaragua, South America, Spain, France, England and her native Italy also were the recipients of her good works.

Pluto, ruler of her fourth house of the home and family, placed in the ninth house of foreign travel, with its conjunctions to Saturn, ruler of the sixth house

165

of work, and to Uranus, ruler of the seventh house of partnerships, and its trines to the Ascendant and Venus, helped her to criss-cross the ocean many times (often with helplessly seasick Daughtes) to establish in the above countries 67 houses, one for each year of her earthly life. Fifteen hundred Daughters taught, nursed and mothered those residing within their walls, with Mother Cabrini, the Mother General, the Grand Mother, overseeing them all.

Mother Cabrini's love for her spiritual daughters, for the children, the poor, the suffering and for those in prison was as unconditional as was her conviction that love is the reason for being. Such was her gift from Venus in Leo, dramatically placed so importantly on her Ascendant. From Venus, too, came charm, loveliness, charisma, a diminutive yet finely proportioned form, and large, beautiful, smiling blue eyes which radiated happiness.

Sun in Cancer can be shy and retiring, and while she really was so, her Mars in Virgo in the first house, supplying exceptional talent for organization, conjunct Venus, opposite Neptune, and sextile Mercury, colored warmly her whole personality to give her an eagerness, a daring, and the pioneering spirit needed to carry out all of her "think big" projects. From Jupiter in Virgo in the second house of resources came her aptitude for finance, and the many benefactors who miraculously seemed to appear just when she needed them, while the Moon in Libra, also in the second house, made her the social worker whose main concern was teaching the values of a Christian way of life.

As every mother really is, Cabrini was first and foremost a teacher and her horoscope bears this out: a Leo Ascendant; three planets in the ninth house of higher education and religious teaching; the fifth house of children in the teacher's sign, Sagittarius; and, the eleventh house of other people's children in the literary, mental Gemini.

A biological mother she chose not to be, and again her chart confirms this because there is no positive emphasis here: no planets in the fifth house; its ruler, Sagittarius, in an infertile, fire sign; Jupiter, ruler of Sagittarius, in infertile Virgo and square the cusps of the fifth and eleventh houses. While Jupiter does make a sextile to the Sun and a trine to the Midheaven, those aspects were used to help her career rather than for personal motherhood.

Claire and I smile sheepishly as we wonder what Mother would say about this feeble attempt to delineate her life astrologically. Was there room for the unusual, the unconventional, and the occult in her thinking? There should be, we reasoned, because her own career had been far from routine, far from the accustomed manner of living of the women of her day. Certainly it was unique and uncommon enough for *any* period in history. A whirlwind of activity, she had her prayerful, hidden, mystical side, too, and often in sleep she would be guided to new accomplishments by seeing in dreams the property she would later acquire for a new school, orphanage or hospital. On one occasion she was able to purchase, very inexpensively, a valuable piece of property of 450 acres

166

in West Park, New York, because, for among other reasons, the well of the Jesuit owners had run dry and no other water could be found on the land. Directed in a dream by the Blessed Mother, she went without hesitation to a wooded area, tapped with a stick a certain spot, and exactly there a mountain spring of crystal-clear water was uncovered. This was only one occult experience among many that occurred in her lifetime, while after her death many miracles were, and are even now being attributed to her intercession. People continue to pray to her . . . she is still Mother to us all.

As she traveled the length and breadth of this land, Mother Cabrini grew to love America, proudly became its citizen, and was instrumental in helping the Italian immigrant and his children become self-sufficient and educated so that they too could contribute to the building up of their new, adopted country. For this endeavor she was tangibly rewarded, for if you visit the Statue of Liberty in New York harbor you will find a plaque listing the names of those immigrants who enriched this country by their presence: Albert Einstein, Charles Steinmetz, and David Sarnoff, among others. Heading the list, and the only woman — *Mother Frances Cabrini.*

Why was she so successful? It had to be more than financial and organizational ability, shrewdness in buying real estate, or wisdom in understanding the American mentality. We cannot measure the fullness of the gifts God gave her: extraordinary faith, immense love for His Sacred Heart, an irrepressible spirit, vision, an indomitable will, intelligence, and most of all, obedience to His plan for her life.

Astrologically, we can only delineate Mother's chart in our small way, and say that she was helped to live in this inspired manner because her ninth house of faith and religion was the most heavily tenanted in the chart. It contains three conjunct planets as follows: Saturn, which rules the sixth house of work, Pluto, ruling the fourth house of the home, and Uranus, which rules the seventh house of partnerships. Therefore, her *work* was to establish *homes* in *partnership* with God for love of Him. Setbacks? Of course, and there were many, but invincible Mars, the motivating force as ruler of the ninth house, and positioned in the first house of personality, quickly disposed of them all.

To make her a leader, God gave her a Leo Ascendant, whose ruler, the Sun, the male principle, the giver of life, the *will,* He placed in the female sign, Cancer, builder of form, *the feelings and emotions,* and this is a ranking factor in Mother's chart. When she joined her will to God's will she believed that ''nothing is impossible'' and went on to prove it. She took that will and clothed, sculpted, shaded and softened it with the comeliness, receptivity and gentleness of her Cancer Sun sign ruler — the Moon. The world then saw that she was strong yet sensitive, vital although delicate, authoritative in addition to being courteous, ambitious even as she was tender, bold yet receptive, confident but flexible, and self-reliant besides being ever prayerful.

In a way, Mother Cabrini is the epitome of our Sun/Moon message — the theme of our book — and an example of what the practice of Astrological Birth Control and Natural Birth Control can do for you.

One of the arguments against the placement of women in positions of great responsibility is that they cannot be counted upon to act well under stress. That they are too emotional! N.B.C. and A.B.C. will give you exactly what you need — practice in putting *will* before *emotion*.

Mother Cabrini put the ruler of her Ascendant, the Sun, the will, *first* in her life, and her Sun-sign ruler's Moon, the emotions, *second*. As Moon is not always visible, and its reflected light is put on hold, so too must our feelings and emotions be held in check. We must put sex in perspective, abstain from it, let our heads rule our hearts, and let our wills rule our feelings for that period during the month when we are fertile but do not wish to conceive. Then, when we are physically and astrologically infertile, the feminine impulsiveness, fragile sensitivity, and romantic receptivity can assert itself and come to fruition, safe in the knowledge that our bodies will respond negatively to conception.

If we use intelligently Saturn's self-control inwardly, it will project its tenth house worldliness outwardly, and with it will come talent for leadership in areas outside the home.

It's your attitude that will get you there — your new-found air of command. Without exactly knowing why, people will put more trust in you, have greater faith in you, and respect you more fully than ever before. This concept may be new to you, but isn't it worth considering?

And yet, on a larger scale, just who was Saint Frances Xavier Cabrini? Essentially a mother. Just a mother. Doing what mothers do. And, if you wished to invoke her name in prayer, we're sure she'd prefer, that instead of *Saint*, you'd address her simply as *Mother*.

Come to think of it, in our book, the words "saint" and "mother" are practically synonymous.

Epilogue

We have reached a rest stop in our onward journey toward complete information concerning fertility. Our travels are not over yet, however, because astrologically, physically, and morally there are truths still to be discovered, revealed, discussed, and acted upon.

New books are continually being written, new clinics are springing up with experimental techniques to be tried, and new societies are being formed to help the infertile couple.

For names of these clinics, and for the names of individual specialists in a particular locality, you may write to: *American Fertility Society,* 2131 Magnolia Avenue, Suite 201, Birmingham, Alabama 35256.

Also available is a publication by Jane and Don Rosenberg, *Perspectives on Infertility* (P.O. Box 516, Yorktown Heights, New York 10598, at $25.00 per year), through which one can keep up with the latest developments and therapeutic techniques concerning infertility.

On the opposite side, the case for or against abortion is another problem in which we, as a nation, are still not united. With your permission, we would like to include the following thought-provoking statements which may help to clarify our own judgments concerning this issue.

Vox V.I. Populi:

What does the voice of the people — in this case, three well-known, Very Important People — have to say about the controlling of human fertility through birth planning, birth prevention, and abortion?

1. Ronald Reagan, President of the United States:

On January 30, 1984, President Reagan, addressing a convention of National Religious Broadcasters, said the following concerning abortion:

"We cannot pretend America is preserving her first and highest ideal — the belief that each life is sacred — when we have permitted the death of fifteen million helpless innocents. This nation cannot continue turning a blind eye and a deaf ear to the taking of some four thousand unborn children's lives every day — one every 21 seconds."

Reagan, quoting medical research, continued by saying, "that when the lives of the unborn are snuffed out, they often feel pain — pain that is long and agonizing."

These unborn babies were the future citizens of this country. They were denied the right to life, liberty and the pursuit of happiness. They were hostages, who were tortured and killed. No nation that murders its young can be blessed by God. No nation that is so short-sighted as to kill its new life can endure, grow and prosper, We wonder whose freedom we are celebrating on the Fourth of July, anyway. The baby is dead; its mother acting out the selfish barbarianism of these times.

2. Mother Cabrini, Saint:
"The enemy is not another person, or another country. The enemy is not the devil. The enemy is within . . . it is self-love."

Abortion is really just another name for self-love. The enemy is not only another foreign power, then, nor is it only nuclear weapons. Viewing the film, *The Day After,* a picture showing the horrors of nuclear war, and merely discussing its moral implications, will not solve our problems if our own house is not in order and ethically sound, because the question really is, "Have we acted responsibly the night before?".

3. Mother Teresa of Calcutta, foundress of an order of Roman Catholic nuns, in her own strong, candid manner:
"That is why abortion is such a terrible sin. You are not only killing life, but *putting self before God.* Yet people decide who has to live and who has to die. They want to make themselves almighty God. They want to take the power of God in their hands. They want to say, 'I can do without God. I can decide.' That is the most devilish thing that a human hand can do. That is why we are paying with such terrible things happening in the world. It is a punishment, it is the cry of those children continually coming before God. It is such a contradiction of even ordinary common sense and reason: we spend millions to prolong the life of an old person who is more or less dead, and yet, there is this young life for the future . . . I cannot understand."

Consider this woman. She is not a political figure, yet she is known throughout the world, and she commands the respect and possesses the influence of a person in very high office. With her tiny, energetic form wrapped in a blue bordered, white sari, this angel of mercy feeds the hungry, gives drink to the thirsty, clothes the naked, visits the sick, and buries the dead. And, she takes in homeless children — as many as she can find. She has patterned her life after that of Jesus Christ and she is dedicated to Life and Love. She is nurse *extraordinaire.*

No matter how much poverty she sees; no matter how many orphaned, undernourished children she gathers into her outstretched arms, she still sees birth prevention as evil and *not* the answer to the world wide problems of hunger, disease, and illiteracy. Natural birth control is what she stresses as the only morally acceptable solution.

Mother Teresa is the recipient of some of the highest awards that humanity can bestow. She is the winner of the Pope John XXIII Peace Prize, the Good Samaritan Award, the John Fitzgerald Kennedy Award, the Doctor of Humane Letters, and the Nobel Peace Prize, among others.

How is it then, that as we heap awards, present citations, and bestow highest praise upon this wise and loving Mother, we do not heed her admonitions? She chides us, but we do not listen!

Freedom and Progress:

If the problem of abortion is one of reasoning, how else can we see it? If at age eighty you are You, and at twenty-five you had been You, and at age three you were also You, then, at the moment of conception you had to be You, too, although physically each age altered your appearance. What else *could* that fertilized egg have been but You, in the process of becoming an older You?

If the crux of the matter is Beverly Stephen's grievance, then we have another problem. Beverly Stephen, syndicated columnist who concentrates on women's issues, in her column of January 22, 1984, discussed the eleventh anniversary of the United States Supreme Court's landmark ruling legalizing abortion. She grumbled that after more than a decade, the battle between the "pro-lifers," those who want to see abortion outlawed, and the "pro-choicers," those who believe that abortion should be a matter of conscience, still continues. Her complaint was that she might have to write about this struggle for the rest of her life, "unless some genius invents the perfect contraceptive and thus eliminates the primary reason for abortion."

No, we haven't come to that absolutely perfect contraceptive yet, and we know it. However, chapter by chapter and chart by chart we have tried to share with you, from the layperson's point of view, the many facets of human reproduction, its fertility and its control.

We hope you have found this material enlightening and are prepared now to look at sexuality in a new light.

In the light of progress and freedom.

Progress in the new dimensions astrology offers as we continue to uncover the secrets of our solar system. Freedom to explore these secrets until they are secrets no longer, but common knowledge accessible to all. Freedom to choose the size of our families through knowledge — not through the knife.

The modern woman does not need a throw-back to past times via the butchering by abortion and sterilization to solve her fertility problems. She does not need the stop-gap measures of devices and chemicals. How primitive are all of these practices in comparison to the truths that biology and astrology have recently brought to light.

That is why we need *YOU*. We need *you* to verify our findings. The paths of natural birth control and astrological birth control are not easy. It takes the will power of the Sun, the imagination of the Moon, the brains of Mercury, the rhythm of Venus, the courage of Mars, the generosity of Jupiter, the self-control of Saturn, the far-sightedness of Uranus, the spirituality of Neptune and the sexual power of Pluto to make them work successfully in our lives. The tools are available because we have all of these planets in our charts just waiting to be activated.

Now that you have read this book, enough confidence and enthusiasm should hopefully have been generated for couples to actively follow its precepts, and thereby help us to build up a body of concrete evidence to support our message. There is homework to be done!

In parting, since this is a book about mothers, with heartfelt gratitude I wish to pay special tribute to:

my Mother — who understood the value of education,

my sister, Julia — my 'little mother' away from home,

my sister-in-law, Lee — 'mother' to our children when I could not be there,

Mother Cabrini and all of her Mothers — who instilled within me the true values of life, and most of all,

mothers and would-be mothers — who hopefully may be helped by applying in their daily lives the principles set forth in this book.

Appendix

Tables of Sun-Moon Fertility Angles for Women
1940 - 2000

These Tables are computer calculated for
NOON, GREENWICH MEAN TIME.

The astrological Sun-Moon fertility angle is the number of degrees apart the Moon is from the Sun at the time of a woman's birth.

How to use the Tables:
Find your year, month, and day of birth in the Tables. The number coinciding with this information is your natal Sun-Moon fertility angle for all of your reproductive years.

To find your most astrologically fertile day for any particular month thereafter, look up, in the month and year in question, the one day during the month when the fertility angle or number coincides as closely as possible with that of your natal Sun-Moon fertility angle.

Example: If your birth date is January 21, 1950, your natal Sun-Moon fertility angle is 38. See Tables.

To find your most astrologically fertile day during July, 1980, check each day of that month until you come to the number closest to 38.

July 15 is the answer because its fertility angle is also 38.

Example: Again using 38 as the Sun-Moon angle, find the most astrologically fertile day during August, 1980.

Checking the August column, we find that the Sun-Moon angle on August 13 is 30, while on August 14 it is 41. Since the natal Sun-Moon angle of 38 is closer to 41 than it is to 30, then August 14 becomes the most astrologically fertile day for the month of August, 1980.

NOTE WELL:
Because the following Tables have been calculated for Noon, Greenwich Mean Time, they are most accurate for women born at noon in Greenwich, England. Since this is a rare occurrence, an adjustment must be made for each woman's particular place and time of birth. For more accurate and precise calculations it would be best to consult a professional astrologer.

DAY	1	2	3	4	5	6	7	8	9	10	11	12	13	14	15
JAN	260	273	286	299	311	323	335	347	359	10	21	32	43	54	65

DAY	16	17	18	19	20	21	22	23	24	25	26	27	28	29	30	31
JAN	76	87	98	109	121	133	146	159	173	187	201	215	229	242	255	268

DAY	1	2	3	4	5	6	7	8	9	10	11	12	13	14	15
FEB	281	293	305	316	328	339	350	1	12	23	34	45	56	67	78

DAY	16	17	18	19	20	21	22	23	24	25	26	27	28	29	30	31
FEB	89	101	113	126	139	153	167	181	195	209	223	236	249	263		

DAY	1	2	3	4	5	6	7	8	9	10	11	12	13	14	15
MAR	275	287	298	310	321	332	343	354	4	15	26	37	48	59	71

DAY	16	17	18	19	20	21	22	23	24	25	26	27	28	29	30	31
MAR	82	94	107	120	133	147	161	176	190	204	217	231	244	256	268	280

DAY	1	2	3	4	5	6	7	8	9	10	11	12	13	14	15
APR	291	302	313	324	335	345	356	7	18	29	41	53	64	77	89

DAY	16	17	18	19	20	21	22	23	24	25	26	27	28	29	30	31
APR	102	115	129	142	156	170	184	198	211	224	237	249	261	272	283	

DAY	1	2	3	4	5	6	7	8	9	10	11	12	13	14	15
MAY	294	305	316	327	338	349	360	11	23	35	47	60	72	85	98

DAY	16	17	18	19	20	21	22	23	24	25	26	27	28	29	30	31
MAY	112	125	139	152	166	179	192	205	218	230	242	253	264	275	286	297

DAY	1	2	3	4	5	6	7	8	9	10	11	12	13	14	15
JUN	308	319	330	342	353	6	18	31	43	56	69	82	96	109	122

DAY	16	17	18	19	20	21	22	23	24	25	26	27	28	29	30	31
JUN	135	148	161	174	187	199	211	223	234	245	256	267	278	289	300	

DAY	1	2	3	4	5	6	7	8	9	10	11	12	13	14	15
JUL	312	323	335	348	0	13	27	40	53	67	80	93	106	119	132

DAY	16	17	18	19	20	21	22	23	24	25	26	27	28	29	30	31
JUL	144	157	169	181	193	204	216	227	238	248	259	270	281	293	305	317

DAY	1	2	3	4	5	6	7	8	9	10	11	12	13	14	15
AUG	329	342	355	9	23	37	50	64	77	90	103	115	128	140	152

DAY	16	17	18	19	20	21	22	23	24	25	26	27	28	29	30	31
AUG	163	175	186	197	208	219	230	241	252	263	274	286	298	310	323	337

DAY	1	2	3	4	5	6	7	8	9	10	11	12	13	14	15
SEP	351	5	19	33	47	60	73	86	99	111	123	134	146	157	168

DAY	16	17	18	19	20	21	22	23	24	25	26	27	28	29	30	31
SEP	179	190	200	211	222	233	244	256	267	279	292	304	318	331	345	

DAY	1	2	3	4	5	6	7	8	9	10	11	12	13	14	15
OCT	360	14	28	42	55	68	81	93	105	116	127	138	149	160	171

DAY	16	17	18	19	20	21	22	23	24	25	26	27	28	29	30	31
OCT	182	193	204	215	226	237	249	261	273	286	299	312	326	340	354	8

DAY	1	2	3	4	5	6	7	8	9	10	11	12	13	14	15
NOV	22	36	49	62	74	86	97	108	119	130	141	152	162	173	185

DAY	16	17	18	19	20	21	22	23	24	25	26	27	28	29	30	31
NOV	196	207	219	231	243	255	268	280	294	307	321	334	348	2	15	

DAY	1	2	3	4	5	6	7	8	9	10	11	12	13	14	15
DEC	29	41	54	66	77	88	99	110	121	132	142	154	165	176	188

DAY	16	17	18	19	20	21	22	23	24	25	26	27	28	29	30	31
DEC	200	212	225	237	250	263	276	289	302	315	329	342	355	8	21	33

SUN*MOON ANGLES FOR 1941

DAY	1	2	3	4	5	6	7	8	9	10	11	12	13	14	15	
JAN	44	56	67	78	89	100	110	121	132	144	156	168	180	193	205	

DAY	16	17	18	19	20	21	22	23	24	25	26	27	28	29	30	31
JAN	218	231	244	257	271	284	297	310	322	335	348	0	12	24	35	46

DAY	1	2	3	4	5	6	7	8	9	10	11	12	13	14	15	
FEB	57	68	79	90	101	112	123	135	147	160	173	186	199	213	226	

DAY	16	17	18	19	20	21	22	23	24	25	26	27	28	29	30	31
FEB	240	253	266	279	292	304	317	329	341	352	4	15	26			

DAY	1	2	3	4	5	6	7	8	9	10	11	12	13	14	15	
MAR	37	48	59	69	80	92	103	115	127	139	153	166	180	194	208	

DAY	16	17	18	19	20	21	22	23	24	25	26	27	28	29	30	31
MAR	221	235	248	262	274	287	299	311	322	334	345	356	7	18	28	39

DAY	1	2	3	4	5	6	7	8	9	10	11	12	13	14	15	
APR	50	61	72	84	95	107	120	133	146	160	174	188	202	217	230	

DAY	16	17	18	19	20	21	22	23	24	25	26	27	28	29	30	31
APR	244	257	269	281	293	304	315	326	337	348	359	10	21	32	43	

DAY	1	2	3	4	5	6	7	8	9	10	11	12	13	14	15	
MAY	54	65	77	89	101	114	127	141	155	169	184	198	212	225	238	

DAY	16	17	18	19	20	21	22	23	24	25	26	27	28	29	30	31
MAY	251	263	275	286	297	308	319	330	341	352	3	14	25	36	48	60

DAY	1	2	3	4	5	6	7	8	9	10	11	12	13	14	15	
JUN	72	84	97	110	123	137	151	165	179	193	207	220	232	245	256	

DAY	16	17	18	19	20	21	22	23	24	25	26	27	28	29	30	31
JUN	268	279	290	301	312	322	333	345	356	7	19	31	43	55	68	

DAY	1	2	3	4	5	6	7	8	9	10	11	12	13	14	15	
JUL	81	94	107	120	134	148	161	175	188	201	214	226	238	249	260	

DAY	16	17	18	19	20	21	22	23	24	25	26	27	28	29	30	31
JUL	271	282	293	304	315	326	338	350	2	14	26	39	52	63	78	91

DAY	1	2	3	4	5	6	7	8	9	10	11	12	13	14	15	
AUG	104	118	131	144	157	170	183	195	207	219	230	241	252	263	274	

DAY	16	17	18	19	20	21	22	23	24	25	26	27	28	29	30	31
AUG	285	296	308	319	331	343	356	9	22	35	48	62	75	88	102	115

DAY	1	2	3	4	5	6	7	8	9	10	11	12	13	14	15	
SEP	127	140	153	165	177	188	200	211	222	233	244	255	266	277	288	

DAY	16	17	18	19	20	21	22	23	24	25	26	27	28	29	30	31
SEP	300	312	324	337	350	4	17	31	45	58	72	85	98	111	123	

DAY	1	2	3	4	5	6	7	8	9	10	11	12	13	14	15	
OCT	135	147	158	170	181	192	203	214	225	236	247	258	269	281	292	

DAY	16	17	18	19	20	21	22	23	24	25	26	27	28	29	30	31
OCT	305	317	331	344	358	12	26	40	54	68	81	93	105	117	129	140

DAY	1	2	3	4	5	6	7	8	9	10	11	12	13	14	15	
NOV	151	162	173	184	195	206	217	228	239	250	261	273	285	298	311	

DAY	16	17	18	19	20	21	22	23	24	25	26	27	28	29	30	31
NOV	324	338	352	7	21	35	49	62	74	87	98	110	121	132	143	

DAY	1	2	3	4	5	6	7	8	9	10	11	12	13	14	15	
DEC	154	165	175	186	197	208	220	231	242	254	266	278	291	304	318	

DAY	16	17	18	19	20	21	22	23	24	25	26	27	28	29	30	31
DEC	332	346	0	15	28	42	54	67	79	90	101	112	123	134	145	156

DAY	1	2	3	4	5	6	7	8	9	10	11	12	13	14	15
JAN	167	178	189	200	212	224	235	248	260	273	286	299	313	326	340

DAY	16	17	18	19	20	21	22	23	24	25	26	27	28	29	30	31
JAN	354	8	21	34	46	58	70	81	92	103	114	125	136	147	158	169

DAY	1	2	3	4	5	6	7	8	9	10	11	12	13	14	15
FEB	181	193	205	217	229	242	255	268	281	294	308	321	334	348	1

DAY	16	17	18	19	20	21	22	23	24	25	26	27	28	29	30	31
FEB	13	25	37	49	60	71	82	93	104	115	126	138	149			

DAY	1	2	3	4	5	6	7	8	9	10	11	12	13	14	15
MAR	161	173	186	198	211	224	237	251	264	277	290	303	316	329	341

DAY	16	17	18	19	20	21	22	23	24	25	26	27	28	29	30	31
MAR	354	6	17	29	40	51	62	73	84	95	106	117	129	141	153	166

DAY	1	2	3	4	5	6	7	8	9	10	11	12	13	14	15
APR	179	193	206	220	234	247	260	273	286	299	311	323	335	347	358

DAY	16	17	18	19	20	21	22	23	24	25	26	27	28	29	30	31
APR	10	21	32	43	54	65	76	87	98	109	121	134	147	160	174	

DAY	1	2	3	4	5	6	7	8	9	10	11	12	13	14	15
MAY	188	202	216	230	243	257	269	282	294	306	317	329	340	351	2

DAY	16	17	18	19	20	21	22	23	24	25	26	27	28	29	30	31
MAY	13	24	35	46	57	68	79	91	103	115	128	141	155	169	183	198

DAY	1	2	3	4	5	6	7	8	9	10	11	12	13	14	15
JUN	212	226	239	252	265	277	289	300	311	322	334	344	355	6	17

DAY	16	17	18	19	20	21	22	23	24	25	26	27	28	29	30	31
JUN	28	39	50	62	73	85	97	110	123	137	151	165	179	194	208	

DAY	1	2	3	4	5	6	7	8	9	10	11	12	13	14	15
JUL	221	234	247	259	271	282	294	305	316	327	338	348	359	11	22

DAY	16	17	18	19	20	21	22	23	24	25	26	27	28	29	30	31
JUL	33	45	56	68	80	93	106	120	133	147	161	175	189	203	216	229

DAY	1	2	3	4	5	6	7	8	9	10	11	12	13	14	15
AUG	241	253	264	276	287	298	308	319	330	341	353	4	16	27	39

DAY	16	17	18	19	20	21	22	23	24	25	26	27	28	29	30	31
AUG	52	64	77	90	103	116	130	144	157	171	184	197	210	222	234	245

DAY	1	2	3	4	5	6	7	8	9	10	11	12	13	14	15
SEP	257	268	279	290	301	312	323	334	346	358	10	22	35	48	60

DAY	16	17	18	19	20	21	22	23	24	25	26	27	28	29	30	31
SEP	74	87	100	113	126	140	153	166	178	191	203	214	226	237	248	

DAY	1	2	3	4	5	6	7	8	9	10	11	12	13	14	15
OCT	259	270	281	292	303	315	326	339	351	4	17	30	43	57	70

DAY	16	17	18	19	20	21	22	23	24	25	26	27	28	29	30	31
OCT	84	97	110	122	135	147	159	172	183	195	206	218	229	239	250	261

DAY	1	2	3	4	5	6	7	8	9	10	11	12	13	14	15
NOV	272	283	295	306	319	331	344	358	11	25	39	53	66	79	92

DAY	16	17	18	19	20	21	22	23	24	25	26	27	28	29	30	31
NOV	105	117	129	141	153	164	176	187	198	209	220	230	241	252	263	

DAY	1	2	3	4	5	6	7	8	9	10	11	12	13	14	15
DEC	274	286	298	311	324	337	351	5	20	34	47	61	74	87	99

DAY	16	17	18	19	20	21	22	23	24	25	26	27	28	29	30	31
DEC	111	122	134	145	156	167	178	189	200	211	221	232	243	255	266	278

176

SUN*MOON ANGLES FOR 1943

```
DAY    1    2    3    4    5    6    7    8    9   10   11   12   13   14   15
JAN  291  304  317  331  345  359   13   27   41   54   67   80   92  103  115

DAY   16   17   18   19   20   21   22   23   24   25   26   27   28   29   30   31
JAN  126  137  148  158  169  180  191  202  213  224  235  247  259  271  284  297

DAY    1    2    3    4    5    6    7    8    9   10   11   12   13   14   15
FEB  311  325  339  353    7   21   34   47   60   72   83   95  106  117  128

DAY   16   17   18   19   20   21   22   23   24   25   26   27   28   29   30   31
FEB  139  149  160  171  182  194  205  217  229  241  253  266  279

DAY    1    2    3    4    5    6    7    8    9   10   11   12   13   14   15
MAR  292  306  319  333  347    0   14   27   39   52   63   75   86   97  108

DAY   16   17   18   19   20   21   22   23   24   25   26   27   28   29   30   31
MAR  119  130  141  152  163  175  186  198  211  223  236  249  262  275  288  301

DAY    1    2    3    4    5    6    7    8    9   10   11   12   13   14   15
APR  315  328  341  354    7   19   32   43   55   66   77   88   99  110  121

DAY   16   17   18   19   20   21   22   23   24   25   26   27   28   29   30   31
APR  132  144  155  167  180  193  206  219  232  245  259  272  285  298  311

DAY    1    2    3    4    5    6    7    8    9   10   11   12   13   14   15
MAY  323  336  348    1   13   24   36   47   58   69   80   90  101  113  124

DAY   16   17   18   19   20   21   22   23   24   25   26   27   28   29   30   31
MAY  136  149  161  174  188  201  215  229  242  256  269  281  294  307  319  331

DAY    1    2    3    4    5    6    7    8    9   10   11   12   13   14   15
JUN  343  354    6   17   28   39   50   61   72   83   94  105  117  130  143

DAY   16   17   18   19   20   21   22   23   24   25   26   27   28   29   30   31
JUN  156  170  183  197  211  225  239  252  265  278  290  302  314  326  337

DAY    1    2    3    4    5    6    7    8    9   10   11   12   13   14   15
JUL  348  359   10   21   32   43   54   65   76   87   99  111  124  137  151

DAY   16   17   18   19   20   21   22   23   24   25   26   27   28   29   30   31
JUL  165  179  193  208  222  235  248  261  273  285  297  308  319  330  341  352

DAY    1    2    3    4    5    6    7    8    9   10   11   12   13   14   15
AUG    3   14   25   36   47   58   70   82   94  106  119  133  147  161  175

DAY   16   17   18   19   20   21   22   23   24   25   26   27   28   29   30   31
AUG  189  203  217  230  243  256  267  279  290  302  312  323  334  345  356    7

DAY    1    2    3    4    5    6    7    8    9   10   11   12   13   14   15
SEP   18   29   41   53   64   77   89  102  115  129  142  156  170  184  198

DAY   16   17   18   19   20   21   22   23   24   25   26   27   28   29   30   31
SEP  211  224  237  249  260  272  283  294  305  315  326  337  348    0   11

DAY    1    2    3    4    5    6    7    8    9   10   11   12   13   14   15
OCT   23   35   47   60   72   85   98  111  125  138  152  165  179  192  205

DAY   16   17   18   19   20   21   22   23   24   25   26   27   28   29   30   31
OCT  217  229  241  252  263  274  285  296  307  318  329  341  352    5   17   30

DAY    1    2    3    4    5    6    7    8    9   10   11   12   13   14   15
NOV   42   55   68   81   94  107  120  134  147  160  172  185  197  209  221

DAY   16   17   18   19   20   21   22   23   24   25   26   27   28   29   30   31
NOV  232  243  254  265  275  286  297  309  321  333  345  358   11   24   37

DAY    1    2    3    4    5    6    7    8    9   10   11   12   13   14   15
DEC   50   64   77   90  103  116  128  141  153  165  177  189  200  212  223

DAY   16   17   18   19   20   21   22   23   24   25   26   27   28   29   30   31
DEC  233  244  255  266  277  288  300  312  324  337  351    4   18   32   45   59
```

177

SUN*MOON ANGLES FOR 1944

DAY	1	2	3	4	5	6	7	8	9	10	11	12	13	14	15	16	17	18	19	20	21	22	23	24	25	26	27	28	29	30	31
JAN	72	85	98	110	123	135	146	158	169	180	191	202	213	224	235	246	257	268	279	291	304	317	330	344	358	12	26	40	53	67	80
FEB	92	104	116	127	139	150	161	172	182	193	204	215	226	237	248	260	272	284	297	310	323	337	351	5	20	34	47	60	74		
MAR	86	98	109	120	131	142	153	164	174	185	196	207	219	230	242	254	266	278	291	305	318	332	346	0	14	28	41	54	66	78	90
APR	101	112	123	134	144	155	166	178	189	200	212	224	236	248	261	274	287	300	314	328	341	355	9	22	35	47	59	70	82	93	
MAY	104	114	125	136	147	159	170	182	194	207	219	232	244	257	270	284	297	310	324	337	350	3	16	28	40	51	63	74	85	95	106
JUN	117	129	140	152	164	176	189	202	215	228	241	255	268	281	294	307	320	333	345	358	9	21	33	44	55	66	77	88	99	110	
JUL	121	133	145	158	171	184	198	211	225	239	252	265	278	291	304	316	328	340	352	3	14	25	36	47	58	69	80	91	103	115	127
AUG	139	152	166	180	194	208	222	235	249	262	275	287	299	311	323	334	345	356	7	18	29	40	51	62	73	84	96	108	121	134	147
SEP	161	175	189	204	218	231	245	258	270	282	294	305	316	327	338	349	360	11	22	33	44	55	66	78	90	102	115	128	142	156	
OCT	170	185	199	213	226	239	252	264	275	287	298	308	319	330	341	352	3	14	25	37	48	60	72	84	97	110	123	137	151	165	179
NOV	193	206	219	232	244	256	267	278	289	300	311	322	333	344	355	7	18	30	42	54	67	79	92	105	119	132	146	159	173	186	
DEC	199	211	224	235	247	258	269	280	290	301	312	324	335	347	359	11	23	36	49	62	75	88	101	114	127	141	153	166	179	191	203

178

DAY	1	2	3	4	5	6	7	8	9	10	11	12	13	14	15	
JAN	214	225	236	247	258	269	280	291	302	314	326	338	350	3	16	

DAY	16	17	18	19	20	21	22	23	24	25	26	27	28	29	30	31
JAN	30	43	56	70	83	96	109	122	134	146	159	170	182	193	205	216

DAY	1	2	3	4	5	6	7	8	9	10	11	12	13	14	15	
FEB	227	238	249	259	270	282	293	305	317	330	343	356	10	24	38	

DAY	16	17	18	19	20	21	22	23	24	25	26	27	28	29	30	31
FEB	52	65	78	91	104	116	128	140	151	163	174	185	196			

DAY	1	2	3	4	5	6	7	8	9	10	11	12	13	14	15	
MAR	207	218	229	240	251	262	273	285	297	310	323	336	350	4	19	

DAY	16	17	18	19	20	21	22	23	24	25	26	27	28	29	30	31
MAR	33	47	60	73	86	98	110	121	133	144	155	166	177	188	199	210

DAY	1	2	3	4	5	6	7	8	9	10	11	12	13	14	15	
APR	221	232	243	254	266	278	290	303	317	331	345	359	14	28	41	

DAY	16	17	18	19	20	21	22	23	24	25	26	27	28	29	30	31
APR	55	67	80	92	103	114	126	136	147	158	169	180	191	202	213	

DAY	1	2	3	4	5	6	7	8	9	10	11	12	13	14	15	
MAY	225	236	248	260	273	285	299	312	326	340	355	9	22	36	49	

DAY	16	17	18	19	20	21	22	23	24	25	26	27	28	29	30	31
MAY	61	73	85	96	107	118	129	140	151	162	173	184	196	207	219	231

DAY	1	2	3	4	5	6	7	8	9	10	11	12	13	14	15	
JUN	243	256	269	282	295	309	323	337	350	4	17	30	42	54	66	

DAY	16	17	18	19	20	21	22	23	24	25	26	27	28	29	30	31
JUN	77	89	100	110	121	132	143	155	166	178	190	202	214	227	240	

DAY	1	2	3	4	5	6	7	8	9	10	11	12	13	14	15	
JUL	253	266	279	293	306	319	333	346	359	11	24	36	47	59	70	

DAY	16	17	18	19	20	21	22	23	24	25	26	27	28	29	30	31
JUL	81	92	103	114	125	136	148	160	172	185	197	210	224	237	250	264

DAY	1	2	3	4	5	6	7	8	9	10	11	12	13	14	15	
AUG	277	290	303	316	329	341	353	5	17	29	40	51	62	73	84	

DAY	16	17	18	19	20	21	22	23	24	25	26	27	28	29	30	31
AUG	95	106	117	129	141	153	166	179	193	207	220	234	248	261	274	287

DAY	1	2	3	4	5	6	7	8	9	10	11	12	13	14	15	
SEP	299	312	324	335	347	359	10	21	32	43	54	65	76	87	98	

DAY	16	17	18	19	20	21	22	23	24	25	26	27	28	29	30	31
SEP	110	122	134	147	161	174	188	203	217	230	244	257	270	282	294	

DAY	1	2	3	4	5	6	7	8	9	10	11	12	13	14	15	
OCT	306	318	329	340	352	3	13	24	35	46	57	68	79	91	103	

DAY	16	17	18	19	20	21	22	23	24	25	26	27	28	29	30	31
OCT	115	128	141	155	169	183	198	212	225	239	252	264	276	288	299	311

DAY	1	2	3	4	5	6	7	8	9	10	11	12	13	14	15	
NOV	322	333	344	354	5	16	27	38	49	60	72	84	96	109	122	

DAY	16	17	18	19	20	21	22	23	24	25	26	27	28	29	30	31
NOV	135	149	163	178	192	206	219	232	245	257	269	280	291	302	313	

DAY	1	2	3	4	5	6	7	8	9	10	11	12	13	14	15	
DEC	324	335	346	357	8	19	30	42	53	65	77	90	103	116	130	

DAY	16	17	18	19	20	21	22	23	24	25	26	27	28	29	30	31
DEC	143	157	171	185	199	212	224	237	249	260	271	282	293	304	315	326

SUN*MOON ANGLES FOR 1946

```
DAY   1    2    3    4    5    6    7    8    9   10   11   12   13   14   15
JAN 337  348  359   11   23   35   47   59   72   85   98  111  125  138  151

DAY  16   17   18   19   20   21   22   23   24   25   26   27   28   29   30   31
JAN 165  178  191  204  216  228  239  251  262  273  283  294  305  316  328  339

DAY   1    2    3    4    5    6    7    8    9   10   11   12   13   14   15
FEB 351    3   16   28   41   54   67   80   94  107  120  133  146  158  171

DAY  16   17   18   19   20   21   22   23   24   25   26   27   28   29   30   31
FEB 183  195  207  219  230  241  252  263  274  285  296  307  319

DAY   1    2    3    4    5    6    7    8    9   10   11   12   13   14   15
MAR 331  343  356    9   23   36   50   63   76   89  102  115  128  140  152

DAY  16   17   18   19   20   21   22   23   24   25   26   27   28   29   30   31
MAR 164  176  188  199  210  221  232  243  254  265  276  287  299  311  324  337

DAY   1    2    3    4    5    6    7    8    9   10   11   12   13   14   15
APR 350    4   18   32   45   59   72   85   98  110  122  134  146  158  169

DAY  16   17   18   19   20   21   22   23   24   25   26   27   28   29   30   31
APR 180  191  202  213  224  235  245  257  268  280  292  304  317  331  345

DAY   1    2    3    4    5    6    7    8    9   10   11   12   13   14   15
MAY 359   13   27   41   55   68   81   93  105  117  128  140  151  162  173

DAY  16   17   18   19   20   21   22   23   24   25   26   27   28   29   30   31
MAY 184  194  205  216  227  238  250  261  274  286  299  312  326  340  354    8

DAY   1    2    3    4    5    6    7    8    9   10   11   12   13   14   15
JUN  23   36   50   63   75   87   99  111  122  133  144  155  166  176  187

DAY  16   17   18   19   20   21   22   23   24   25   26   27   28   29   30   31
JUN 198  210  221  233  244  256  269  282  295  308  322  336  350    4   18

DAY   1    2    3    4    5    6    7    8    9   10   11   12   13   14   15
JUL  31   44   57   69   81   93  104  115  126  137  147  158  169  181  192

DAY  16   17   18   19   20   21   22   23   24   25   26   27   28   29   30   31
JUL 204  216  228  240  252  265  278  292  305  319  332  346    0   13   26   39

DAY   1    2    3    4    5    6    7    8    9   10   11   12   13   14   15
AUG  51   63   74   85   96  107  118  129  140  151  163  174  186  198  211

DAY  16   17   18   19   20   21   22   23   24   25   26   27   28   29   30   31
AUG 224  236  249  262  275  289  302  315  328  342  355    7   20   32   44   55

DAY   1    2    3    4    5    6    7    8    9   10   11   12   13   14   15
SEP  66   77   88   99  110  121  132  144  156  168  181  193  206  220  233

DAY  16   17   18   19   20   21   22   23   24   25   26   27   28   29   30   31
SEP 246  259  272  285  298  311  324  337  349    1   13   25   36   47   58

DAY   1    2    3    4    5    6    7    8    9   10   11   12   13   14   15
OCT  69   80   90  101  113  124  136  149  162  175  188  202  215  229  242

DAY  16   17   18   19   20   21   22   23   24   25   26   27   28   29   30   31
OCT 256  269  282  294  307  319  331  342  354    5   17   27   38   49   60   71

DAY   1    2    3    4    5    6    7    8    9   10   11   12   13   14   15
NOV  82   93  104  116  129  142  155  168  182  196  210  224  238  251  264

DAY  16   17   18   19   20   21   22   23   24   25   26   27   28   29   30   31
NOV 276  289  301  312  324  335  346  357    8   19   29   40   51   62   73

DAY   1    2    3    4    5    6    7    8    9   10   11   12   13   14   15
DEC  85   96  109  121  134  148  162  176  190  204  218  232  245  258  270

DAY  16   17   18   19   20   21   22   23   24   25   26   27   28   29   30   31
DEC 282  293  305  316  327  337  348  359   10   21   32   43   54   65   77   89
```

SUN*MOON ANGLES FOR 1947

```
DAY    1    2    3    4    5    6    7    8    9   10   11   12   13   14   15
JAN  102  115  128  141  155  170  184  198  212  225  238  250  262  274  285

DAY   16   17   18   19   20   21   22   23   24   25   26   27   28   29   30   31
JAN  296  307  318  328  339  350    1   12   24   35   47   59   71   83   96  109

DAY    1    2    3    4    5    6    7    8    9   10   11   12   13   14   15
FEB  122  136  149  163  177  191  204  217  230  242  254  265  276  287  298

DAY   16   17   18   19   20   21   22   23   24   25   26   27   28   29   30   31
FEB  308  319  330  341  353    4   16   28   40   53   65   78   91

DAY    1    2    3    4    5    6    7    8    9   10   11   12   13   14   15
MAR  104  117  131  144  158  171  184  197  210  222  233  245  256  267  277

DAY   16   17   18   19   20   21   22   23   24   25   26   27   28   29   30   31
MAR  288  299  310  322  333  345  357   10   22   35   48   61   74   87  100  113

DAY    1    2    3    4    5    6    7    8    9   10   11   12   13   14   15
APR  127  140  153  165  178  190  202  213  225  236  247  258  268  279  291

DAY   16   17   18   19   20   21   22   23   24   25   26   27   28   29   30   31
APR  302  314  326  338  351    4   17   30   44   57   71   84   97  110  123

DAY    1    2    3    4    5    6    7    8    9   10   11   12   13   14   15
MAY  135  147  159  171  183  194  205  217  227  238  249  260  271  283  294

DAY   16   17   18   19   20   21   22   23   24   25   26   27   28   29   30   31
MAY  306  319  332  345  359   12   26   40   54   67   81   93  106  118  130  142

DAY    1    2    3    4    5    6    7    8    9   10   11   12   13   14   15
JUN  154  165  176  187  198  209  220  231  242  253  264  276  288  300  313

DAY   16   17   18   19   20   21   22   23   24   25   26   27   28   29   30   31
JUN  326  340  354    8   22   36   50   64   77   89  101  113  125  136  147

DAY    1    2    3    4    5    6    7    8    9   10   11   12   13   14   15
JUL  158  169  180  191  202  213  224  235  247  258  270  282  295  308  322

DAY   16   17   18   19   20   21   22   23   24   25   26   27   28   29   30   31
JUL  336  350    4   18   32   46   59   72   84   96  107  119  130  140  151  162

DAY    1    2    3    4    5    6    7    8    9   10   11   12   13   14   15
AUG  173  184  195  206  218  229  241  253  265  278  291  304  318  332  346

DAY   16   17   18   19   20   21   22   23   24   25   26   27   28   29   30   31
AUG    0   14   28   41   54   66   78   89  100  111  122  133  144  155  166  177

DAY    1    2    3    4    5    6    7    8    9   10   11   12   13   14   15
SEP  189  200  212  224  236  248  261  274  287  300  314  328  342  355    9

DAY   16   17   18   19   20   21   22   23   24   25   26   27   28   29   30   31
SEP   22   35   47   59   70   81   92  103  114  125  136  147  159  170  182

DAY    1    2    3    4    5    6    7    8    9   10   11   12   13   14   15
OCT  194  206  219  232  244  257  270  284  297  310  324  337  350    3   15

DAY   16   17   18   19   20   21   22   23   24   25   26   27   28   29   30   31
OCT   27   39   50   62   73   83   94  105  116  128  139  151  163  175  188  201

DAY    1    2    3    4    5    6    7    8    9   10   11   12   13   14   15
NOV  214  227  240  253  267  280  293  306  319  331  343  356    7   19   30

DAY   16   17   18   19   20   21   22   23   24   25   26   27   28   29   30   31
NOV   41   52   63   74   85   96  107  119  130  143  155  168  181  195  208

DAY    1    2    3    4    5    6    7    8    9   10   11   12   13   14   15
DEC  222  236  249  262  275  288  301  313  325  336  348  359   10   21   32

DAY   16   17   18   19   20   21   22   23   24   25   26   27   28   29   30   31
DEC   43   54   65   76   87   98  110  122  134  147  161  175  189  203  217  231
```

181

SUN*MOON ANGLES FOR 1948

DAY	1	2	3	4	5	6	7	8	9	10	11	12	13	14	15
JAN	245	258	270	283	295	306	318	329	340	351	2	13	24	35	45

DAY	16	17	18	19	20	21	22	23	24	25	26	27	28	29	30	31
JAN	56	67	79	90	102	115	127	141	154	169	183	197	211	225	239	251

DAY	1	2	3	4	5	6	7	8	9	10	11	12	13	14	15
FEB	264	276	287	299	310	321	332	342	353	4	15	26	37	48	60

DAY	16	17	18	19	20	21	22	23	24	25	26	27	28	29	30	31
FEB	71	83	95	108	121	135	148	163	177	191	205	219	232	244		

DAY	1	2	3	4	5	6	7	8	9	10	11	12	13	14	15
MAR	256	268	279	290	301	312	323	334	345	356	7	18	30	41	53

DAY	16	17	18	19	20	21	22	23	24	25	26	27	28	29	30	31
MAR	65	77	90	103	116	130	144	157	171	185	199	212	224	236	248	260

DAY	1	2	3	4	5	6	7	8	9	10	11	12	13	14	15
APR	271	282	293	304	314	325	337	348	359	11	23	35	48	60	73

DAY	16	17	18	19	20	21	22	23	24	25	26	27	28	29	30	31
APR	86	99	112	126	139	153	166	179	192	205	217	229	240	251	262	

DAY	1	2	3	4	5	6	7	8	9	10	11	12	13	14	15
MAY	273	284	295	306	317	329	341	353	5	17	30	43	56	70	83

DAY	16	17	18	19	20	21	22	23	24	25	26	27	28	29	30	31
MAY	96	109	123	136	148	161	174	186	198	209	221	232	243	254	265	276

DAY	1	2	3	4	5	6	7	8	9	10	11	12	13	14	15
JUN	287	298	310	322	334	347	360	13	26	40	53	67	80	94	106

DAY	16	17	18	19	20	21	22	23	24	25	26	27	28	29	30	31
JUN	119	132	144	156	168	180	191	202	214	225	236	247	257	268	280	

DAY	1	2	3	4	5	6	7	8	9	10	11	12	13	14	15
JUL	291	303	315	328	341	355	9	23	37	51	64	77	90	103	115

DAY	16	17	18	19	20	21	22	23	24	25	26	27	28	29	30	31
JUL	127	139	151	162	173	184	195	206	217	228	239	250	261	273	285	297

DAY	1	2	3	4	5	6	7	8	9	10	11	12	13	14	15
AUG	310	323	336	350	5	19	33	47	60	74	86	98	110	122	133

DAY	16	17	18	19	20	21	22	23	24	25	26	27	28	29	30	31
AUG	144	156	167	178	188	199	210	221	232	243	255	267	279	291	304	318

DAY	1	2	3	4	5	6	7	8	9	10	11	12	13	14	15
SEP	332	346	0	15	29	42	56	68	81	92	104	115	126	137	148

DAY	16	17	18	19	20	21	22	23	24	25	26	27	28	29	30	31
SEP	159	170	181	192	203	214	226	237	249	261	274	287	300	313	327	

DAY	1	2	3	4	5	6	7	8	9	10	11	12	13	14	15
OCT	341	356	9	23	36	49	62	74	85	97	108	119	129	140	151

DAY	16	17	18	19	20	21	22	23	24	25	26	27	28	29	30	31
OCT	162	173	185	196	208	219	231	244	256	269	282	296	309	323	336	350

DAY	1	2	3	4	5	6	7	8	9	10	11	12	13	14	15
NOV	3	16	29	42	54	65	77	88	99	110	120	131	142	154	165

DAY	16	17	18	19	20	21	22	23	24	25	26	27	28	29	30	31
NOV	177	189	201	213	226	239	252	265	278	291	304	318	331	344	356	

DAY	1	2	3	4	5	6	7	8	9	10	11	12	13	14	15
DEC	9	21	33	45	56	67	78	89	100	111	122	133	145	157	169

DAY	16	17	18	19	20	21	22	23	24	25	26	27	28	29	30	31
DEC	182	194	208	221	234	247	261	274	287	299	312	325	337	349	1	13

SUN*MOON ANGLES FOR 1949

DAY	1	2	3	4	5	6	7	8	9	10	11	12	13	14	15
JAN	24	35	46	57	68	79	90	101	112	123	135	148	161	174	187

DAY	16	17	18	19	20	21	22	23	24	25	26	27	28	29	30	31
JAN	201	215	229	242	255	268	281	293	306	318	329	341	353	4	15	26

DAY	1	2	3	4	5	6	7	8	9	10	11	12	13	14	15
FEB	37	48	58	69	80	91	103	115	127	140	153	167	181	195	209

DAY	16	17	18	19	20	21	22	23	24	25	26	27	28	29	30	31
FEB	223	237	250	263	275	287	299	311	322	333	344	355	6			

DAY	1	2	3	4	5	6	7	8	9	10	11	12	13	14	15
MAR	17	28	39	50	61	72	83	95	107	120	133	147	161	175	190

DAY	16	17	18	19	20	21	22	23	24	25	26	27	28	29	30	31
MAR	204	218	231	244	257	269	281	292	304	315	326	336	347	358	9	20

DAY	1	2	3	4	5	6	7	8	9	10	11	12	13	14	15
APR	31	42	53	65	77	89	102	115	128	142	156	170	184	198	212

DAY	16	17	18	19	20	21	22	23	24	25	26	27	28	29	30	31
APR	225	238	250	262	274	285	296	307	318	328	339	350	1	13	24	

DAY	1	2	3	4	5	6	7	8	9	10	11	12	13	14	15
MAY	36	47	59	72	84	97	111	124	138	151	165	179	193	206	219

DAY	16	17	18	19	20	21	22	23	24	25	26	27	28	29	30	31
MAY	231	243	255	266	277	288	299	310	321	332	343	354	6	18	30	43

DAY	1	2	3	4	5	6	7	8	9	10	11	12	13	14	15
JUN	55	68	81	94	107	121	134	148	161	174	187	200	212	224	236

DAY	16	17	18	19	20	21	22	23	24	25	26	27	28	29	30	31
JUN	247	258	269	280	291	302	313	325	336	348	0	13	26	39	52	

DAY	1	2	3	4	5	6	7	8	9	10	11	12	13	14	15
JUL	65	78	92	105	118	131	144	157	169	182	194	206	217	228	240

DAY	16	17	18	19	20	21	22	23	24	25	26	27	28	29	30	31
JUL	250	261	272	283	294	306	318	330	342	355	9	22	36	49	63	76

DAY	1	2	3	4	5	6	7	8	9	10	11	12	13	14	15
AUG	89	102	115	127	140	152	164	176	187	199	210	221	232	243	253

DAY	16	17	18	19	20	21	22	23	24	25	26	27	28	29	30	31
AUG	264	276	287	299	311	324	337	350	4	18	32	46	59	73	86	98

DAY	1	2	3	4	5	6	7	8	9	10	11	12	13	14	15
SEP	111	123	135	147	158	169	180	191	202	213	224	235	246	257	268

DAY	16	17	18	19	20	21	22	23	24	25	26	27	28	29	30	31
SEP	280	292	305	318	331	345	359	13	28	41	55	68	81	93	105	

DAY	1	2	3	4	5	6	7	8	9	10	11	12	13	14	15
OCT	117	129	140	151	162	173	184	194	205	216	227	238	250	261	273

DAY	16	17	18	19	20	21	22	23	24	25	26	27	28	29	30	31
OCT	286	299	312	326	340	354	8	22	36	49	62	75	87	99	110	121

DAY	1	2	3	4	5	6	7	8	9	10	11	12	13	14	15
NOV	132	143	154	165	175	186	197	208	220	231	243	255	268	280	293

DAY	16	17	18	19	20	21	22	23	24	25	26	27	28	29	30	31
NOV	307	320	334	348	2	16	29	43	55	67	79	90	101	112	123	

DAY	1	2	3	4	5	6	7	8	9	10	11	12	13	14	15
DEC	134	145	156	167	178	189	201	213	225	237	250	262	275	288	301

DAY	16	17	18	19	20	21	22	23	24	25	26	27	28	29	30	31
DEC	315	328	342	356	9	22	35	47	59	70	81	92	103	114	124	135

SUN*MOON ANGLES FOR 1950

```
DAY    1    2    3    4    5    6    7    8    9   10   11   12   13   14   15
JAN  147  158  170  182  194  206  219  232  244  257  270  283  297  310  323

DAY   16   17   18   19   20   21   22   23   24   25   26   27   28   29   30   31
JAN  336  349    2   14   26   38   49   60   71   82   93  104  115  126  137  149

DAY    1    2    3    4    5    6    7    8    9   10   11   12   13   14   15
FEB  162  174  187  200  213  226  240  253  266  279  292  305  317  330  342

DAY   16   17   18   19   20   21   22   23   24   25   26   27   28   29   30   31
FEB  354    6   17   29   40   51   62   72   83   94  105  117  129

DAY    1    2    3    4    5    6    7    8    9   10   11   12   13   14   15
MAR  141  154  167  180  194  208  221  235  248  262  274  287  300  312  324

DAY   16   17   18   19   20   21   22   23   24   25   26   27   28   29   30   31
MAR  335  347  358    9   20   31   42   53   63   74   86   97  109  121  134  147

DAY    1    2    3    4    5    6    7    8    9   10   11   12   13   14   15
APR  161  174  188  203  217  230  244  257  270  282  294  306  317  328  339

DAY   16   17   18   19   20   21   22   23   24   25   26   27   28   29   30   31
APR  350    1   12   23   34   45   56   67   78   90  102  115  128  141  155

DAY    1    2    3    4    5    6    7    8    9   10   11   12   13   14   15
MAY  169  183  198  212  226  239  252  264  276  288  299  310  321  332  343

DAY   16   17   18   19   20   21   22   23   24   25   26   27   28   29   30   31
MAY  354    5   15   27   38   49   61   73   85   97  110  123  137  151  165  179

DAY    1    2    3    4    5    6    7    8    9   10   11   12   13   14   15
JUN  193  207  221  234  246  258  270  281  292  303  314  325  336  347  358

DAY   16   17   18   19   20   21   22   23   24   25   26   27   28   29   30   31
JUN    9   20   32   44   56   68   80   93  106  120  133  147  161  175  189

DAY    1    2    3    4    5    6    7    8    9   10   11   12   13   14   15
JUL  202  215  227  240  251  263  274  285  295  306  317  328  340  351    3

DAY   16   17   18   19   20   21   22   23   24   25   26   27   28   29   30   31
JUL   15   27   39   52   64   77   90  103  117  130  144  157  171  184  196  209

DAY    1    2    3    4    5    6    7    8    9   10   11   12   13   14   15
AUG  221  232  244  255  266  277  288  299  310  321  333  345  357    9   22

DAY   16   17   18   19   20   21   22   23   24   25   26   27   28   29   30   31
AUG   35   48   61   74   88  101  114  127  140  153  166  178  190  202  213  225

DAY    1    2    3    4    5    6    7    8    9   10   11   12   13   14   15
SEP  236  247  258  269  280  291  302  314  326  338  351    4   17   31   44

DAY   16   17   18   19   20   21   22   23   24   25   26   27   28   29   30   31
SEP   58   71   85   98  111  123  136  148  160  172  183  194  206  217  228

DAY    1    2    3    4    5    6    7    8    9   10   11   12   13   14   15
OCT  238  249  260  271  283  294  306  319  332  345  359   12   26   40   54

DAY   16   17   18   19   20   21   22   23   24   25   26   27   28   29   30   31
OCT   68   81   94  106  118  130  142  153  164  175  186  197  208  219  230  241

DAY    1    2    3    4    5    6    7    8    9   10   11   12   13   14   15
NOV  252  263  275  287  299  312  325  339  353    7   21   35   49   63   75

DAY   16   17   18   19   20   21   22   23   24   25   26   27   28   29   30   31
NOV   88  100  112  123  134  145  156  167  178  189  200  211  222  233  244

DAY    1    2    3    4    5    6    7    8    9   10   11   12   13   14   15
DEC  256  267  279  292  305  319  332  347    1   15   29   43   56   69   81

DAY   16   17   18   19   20   21   22   23   24   25   26   27   28   29   30   31
DEC   92  104  115  126  137  148  158  169  180  191  202  214  225  237  249  261
```

184

DAY	1	2	3	4	5	6	7	8	9	10	11	12	13	14	15	
JAN	273	286	299	313	327	341	355	9	22	35	48	60	72	84	95	

DAY	16	17	18	19	20	21	22	23	24	25	26	27	28	29	30	31
JAN	106	117	128	138	149	160	172	183	194	206	218	230	242	255	268	281

DAY	1	2	3	4	5	6	7	8	9	10	11	12	13	14	15	
FEB	294	308	321	335	348	2	15	27	40	52	63	74	85	96	107	

DAY	16	17	18	19	20	21	22	23	24	25	26	27	28	29	30	31
FEB	118	129	140	152	163	175	187	199	212	224	237	250	263			

DAY	1	2	3	4	5	6	7	8	9	10	11	12	13	14	15	
MAR	277	290	303	316	329	342	355	7	19	31	43	54	65	76	87	

DAY	16	17	18	19	20	21	22	23	24	25	26	27	28	29	30	31
MAR	98	109	120	131	143	155	167	180	193	206	220	233	246	260	273	286

DAY	1	2	3	4	5	6	7	8	9	10	11	12	13	14	15	
APR	299	311	324	336	348	0	12	23	34	45	56	67	78	89	100	

DAY	16	17	18	19	20	21	22	23	24	25	26	27	28	29	30	31
APR	112	123	135	148	161	174	188	202	215	229	243	256	269	282	294	

DAY	1	2	3	4	5	6	7	8	9	10	11	12	13	14	15	
MAY	307	318	330	342	353	4	15	26	37	48	59	70	81	93	104	

DAY	16	17	18	19	20	21	22	23	24	25	26	27	28	29	30	31
MAY	116	129	142	155	169	183	197	212	226	239	252	265	278	290	301	313

DAY	1	2	3	4	5	6	7	8	9	10	11	12	13	14	15	
JUN	324	335	346	357	8	19	30	41	52	63	75	86	98	111	123	

DAY	16	17	18	19	20	21	22	23	24	25	26	27	28	29	30	31
JUN	137	151	165	179	193	208	221	235	248	260	272	284	295	307	318	

DAY	1	2	3	4	5	6	7	8	9	10	11	12	13	14	15	
JUL	329	340	350	1	12	23	34	46	57	69	81	93	106	119	133	

DAY	16	17	18	19	20	21	22	23	24	25	26	27	28	29	30	31
JUL	147	161	175	189	203	217	230	242	254	266	278	289	300	311	322	333

DAY	1	2	3	4	5	6	7	8	9	10	11	12	13	14	15	
AUG	344	355	6	17	28	40	52	64	77	89	102	116	129	143	157	

DAY	16	17	18	19	20	21	22	23	24	25	26	27	28	29	30	31
AUG	171	185	198	211	224	236	248	259	270	281	292	303	314	325	336	348

DAY	1	2	3	4	5	6	7	8	9	10	11	12	13	14	15	
SEP	359	11	23	35	48	60	73	86	99	113	126	139	153	166	179	

DAY	16	17	18	19	20	21	22	23	24	25	26	27	28	29	30	31
SEP	192	204	217	228	240	251	262	273	284	295	306	317	329	340	352	

DAY	1	2	3	4	5	6	7	8	9	10	11	12	13	14	15	
OCT	5	17	30	43	56	70	83	96	109	122	135	148	161	173	185	

DAY	16	17	18	19	20	21	22	23	24	25	26	27	28	29	30	31
OCT	197	209	220	231	242	253	264	275	286	297	309	321	333	345	358	12

DAY	1	2	3	4	5	6	7	8	9	10	11	12	13	14	15	
NOV	25	39	52	66	79	92	105	118	130	142	154	166	179	199	200	

DAY	16	17	18	19	20	21	22	23	24	25	26	27	28	29	30	31
NOV	211	222	233	244	255	266	277	288	300	312	325	338	352	6	20	

DAY	1	2	3	4	5	6	7	8	9	10	11	12	13	14	15	
DEC	34	48	61	74	87	100	112	124	135	147	158	170	181	192	202	

DAY	16	17	18	19	20	21	22	23	24	25	26	27	28	29	30	31
DEC	213	224	235	246	257	268	280	292	305	318	331	345	0	14	28	42

SUN*MOON ANGLES FOR 1952

DAY	1	2	3	4	5	6	7	8	9	10	11	12	13	14	15	
JAN	55	68	81	93	105	117	128	139	150	161	172	183	193	204	215	

DAY	16	17	18	19	20	21	22	23	24	25	26	27	28	29	30	31
JAN	226	237	249	260	272	285	298	311	325	339	353	8	22	35	48	61

DAY	1	2	3	4	5	6	7	8	9	10	11	12	13	14	15	
FEB	74	86	97	108	120	131	141	152	163	174	185	196	207	218	230	

DAY	16	17	18	19	20	21	22	23	24	25	26	27	28	29	30	31
FEB	242	254	266	279	292	306	319	333	347	1	15	28	41	54		

DAY	1	2	3	4	5	6	7	8	9	10	11	12	13	14	15	
MAR	66	78	89	100	111	122	133	144	155	166	177	189	200	212	224	

DAY	16	17	18	19	20	21	22	23	24	25	26	27	28	29	30	31
MAR	237	249	262	275	288	302	315	329	342	356	9	22	34	46	58	69

DAY	1	2	3	4	5	6	7	8	9	10	11	12	13	14	15	
APR	81	91	102	113	124	135	146	158	170	182	194	207	219	232	245	

DAY	16	17	18	19	20	21	22	23	24	25	26	27	28	29	30	31
APR	258	272	285	298	311	324	337	350	2	15	27	38	50	61	72	

DAY	1	2	3	4	5	6	7	8	9	10	11	12	13	14	15	
MAY	83	94	105	116	127	139	151	163	176	189	202	215	229	242	255	

DAY	16	17	18	19	20	21	22	23	24	25	26	27	28	29	30	31
MAY	269	282	294	307	320	332	344	356	8	20	31	42	53	64	75	86

DAY	1	2	3	4	5	6	7	8	9	10	11	12	13	14	15	
JUN	97	108	120	132	144	157	170	184	198	212	225	239	252	265	278	

DAY	16	17	18	19	20	21	22	23	24	25	26	27	28	29	30	31
JUN	291	303	315	327	339	350	2	13	24	35	45	56	67	78	89	

DAY	1	2	3	4	5	6	7	8	9	10	11	12	13	14	15	
JUL	101	113	126	139	152	166	180	194	208	222	236	249	262	274	287	

DAY	16	17	18	19	20	21	22	23	24	25	26	27	28	29	30	31
JUL	298	310	322	333	344	355	6	17	27	38	49	60	72	83	95	108

DAY	1	2	3	4	5	6	7	8	9	10	11	12	13	14	15	
AUG	120	134	147	161	175	190	204	218	231	244	257	269	281	293	304	

DAY	16	17	18	19	20	21	22	23	24	25	26	27	28	29	30	31
AUG	315	326	337	348	359	9	20	31	43	54	66	78	90	103	116	129

DAY	1	2	3	4	5	6	7	8	9	10	11	12	13	14	15	
SEP	143	157	171	185	199	213	226	239	251	263	275	286	297	308	318	

DAY	16	17	18	19	20	21	22	23	24	25	26	27	28	29	30	31
SEP	329	340	351	2	13	25	37	48	61	73	86	98	112	125	139	

DAY	1	2	3	4	5	6	7	8	9	10	11	12	13	14	15	
OCT	152	166	180	193	207	219	232	244	255	267	278	288	299	310	321	

DAY	16	17	18	19	20	21	22	23	24	25	26	27	28	29	30	31
OCT	332	343	355	7	19	31	43	56	68	81	94	107	121	134	147	161

DAY	1	2	3	4	5	6	7	8	9	10	11	12	13	14	15	
NOV	174	187	200	212	224	235	247	258	268	279	290	301	312	323	335	

DAY	16	17	18	19	20	21	22	23	24	25	26	27	28	29	30	31
NOV	347	360	12	25	38	51	64	77	90	103	116	129	142	155	167	

DAY	1	2	3	4	5	6	7	8	9	10	11	12	13	14	15	
DEC	180	192	203	215	226	237	248	259	269	280	291	303	315	327	339	

DAY	16	17	18	19	20	21	22	23	24	25	26	27	28	29	30	31
DEC	352	6	19	32	46	59	73	86	99	111	124	136	148	160	172	183

186

```
DAY   1    2    3    4    5    6    7    8    9   10   11   12   13   14   15
JAN 194  205  216  227  238  248  259  270  282  293  306  318  331  345  358

DAY  16   17   18   19   20   21   22   23   24   25   26   27   28   29   30   31
JAN  12   26   40   54   67   80   93  105  117  129  141  152  163  174  185  196

DAY   1    2    3    4    5    6    7    8    9   10   11   12   13   14   15
FEB 207  217  228  239  250  262  273  285  298  311  324  338  352    6   20

DAY  16   17   18   19   20   21   22   23   24   25   26   27   28   29   30   31
FEB  34   48   61   74   97   99  110  122  133  144  155  166  176

DAY   1    2    3    4    5    6    7    8    9   10   11   12   13   14   15
MAR 187  198  209  220  231  243  254  266  278  291  304  318  332  346    0

DAY  16   17   18   19   20   21   22   23   24   25   26   27   28   29   30   31
MAR  14   28   42   55   67   80   91  103  114  125  136  146  157  168  179  190

DAY   1    2    3    4    5    6    7    8    9   10   11   12   13   14   15
APR 201  213  224  236  248  261  273  286  299  313  327  341  355    9   22

DAY  16   17   18   19   20   21   22   23   24   25   26   27   28   29   30   31
APR  35   48   60   72   84   95  106  117  127  138  149  160  172  183  195

DAY   1    2    3    4    5    6    7    8    9   10   11   12   13   14   15
MAY 207  219  231  244  256  269  282  296  309  323  336  350    3   16   29

DAY  16   17   18   19   20   21   22   23   24   25   26   27   28   29   30   31
MAY  41   53   64   76   87   98  108  119  130  142  153  165  177  189  202  214

DAY   1    2    3    4    5    6    7    8    9   10   11   12   13   14   15
JUN 227  240  253  266  280  293  306  319  332  345  358   10   22   34   45

DAY  16   17   18   19   20   21   22   23   24   25   26   27   28   29   30   31
JUN  57   68   79   89  100  112  123  134  146  159  171  184  197  210  224

DAY   1    2    3    4    5    6    7    8    9   10   11   12   13   14   15
JUL 237  251  264  277  290  303  316  328  340  352    4   16   27   38   49

DAY  16   17   18   19   20   21   22   23   24   25   26   27   28   29   30   31
JUL  60   71   82   93  104  116  128  140  153  166  179  193  207  221  234  248

DAY   1    2    3    4    5    6    7    8    9   10   11   12   13   14   15
AUG 261  274  287  299  311  323  335  346  358    9   20   31   41   52   63

DAY  16   17   18   19   20   21   22   23   24   25   26   27   28   29   30   31
AUG  74   86   97  109  121  134  147  161  175  189  203  217  231  244  257  270

DAY   1    2    3    4    5    6    7    8    9   10   11   12   13   14   15
SEP 282  294  306  317  329  340  351    1   12   23   34   45   56   67   79

DAY  16   17   18   19   20   21   22   23   24   25   26   27   28   29   30   31
SEP  91  103  115  128  142  156  170  184  198  212  226  240  252  265  276

DAY   1    2    3    4    5    6    7    8    9   10   11   12   13   14   15
OCT 288  299  310  321  332  343  354    5   16   27   38   49   61   72   85

DAY  16   17   18   19   20   21   22   23   24   25   26   27   28   29   30   31
OCT  97  110  123  137  151  165  179  193  207  220  233  245  257  269  280  291

DAY   1    2    3    4    5    6    7    8    9   10   11   12   13   14   15
NOV 302  313  324  335  346  357    8   19   31   43   55   67   79   92  105

DAY  16   17   18   19   20   21   22   23   24   25   26   27   28   29   30   31
NOV 118  132  145  159  173  187  200  213  225  237  249  260  271  282  293

DAY   1    2    3    4    5    6    7    8    9   10   11   12   13   14   15
DEC 304  315  326  337  348    0   12   24   36   49   61   74   87  100  113

DAY  16   17   18   19   20   21   22   23   24   25   26   27   28   29   30   31
DEC 127  140  154  167  180  192  205  217  228  239  251  261  272  283  294  305
```

187

DAY	1	2	3	4	5	6	7	8	9	10	11	12	13	14	15
JAN	317	328	340	352	5	17	30	43	56	70	83	96	109	122	135

DAY	16	17	18	19	20	21	22	23	24	25	26	27	28	29	30	31
JAN	147	160	172	184	196	207	219	230	241	252	262	273	284	296	307	319

DAY	1	2	3	4	5	6	7	8	9	10	11	12	13	14	15
FEB	332	344	357	11	24	38	52	65	78	91	104	117	129	141	153

DAY	16	17	18	19	20	21	22	23	24	25	26	27	28	29	30	31
FEB	165	176	187	199	210	220	231	242	253	264	275	287	299			

DAY	1	2	3	4	5	6	7	8	9	10	11	12	13	14	15
MAR	311	324	337	351	5	19	33	47	60	74	86	99	111	123	134

DAY	16	17	18	19	20	21	22	23	24	25	26	27	28	29	30	31
MAR	146	157	168	179	190	201	212	223	234	245	256	267	279	291	304	317

DAY	1	2	3	4	5	6	7	8	9	10	11	12	13	14	15
APR	331	345	359	14	28	42	55	68	81	93	105	116	127	139	150

DAY	16	17	18	19	20	21	22	23	24	25	26	27	28	29	30	31
APR	160	171	182	193	204	215	226	238	249	261	273	286	299	312	326	

DAY	1	2	3	4	5	6	7	8	9	10	11	12	13	14	15
MAY	340	355	9	23	36	50	62	75	86	98	109	120	131	142	153

DAY	16	17	18	19	20	21	22	23	24	25	26	27	28	29	30	31
MAY	164	175	186	197	209	220	232	244	256	269	281	295	308	322	336	350

DAY	1	2	3	4	5	6	7	8	9	10	11	12	13	14	15
JUN	4	18	31	44	56	68	79	91	102	113	124	135	146	157	168

DAY	16	17	18	19	20	21	22	23	24	25	26	27	28	29	30	31
JUN	179	191	203	215	227	240	252	265	278	292	305	319	333	346	359	

DAY	1	2	3	4	5	6	7	8	9	10	11	12	13	14	15
JUL	12	25	37	49	61	72	83	94	105	116	127	138	150	161	173

DAY	16	17	18	19	20	21	22	23	24	25	26	27	28	29	30	31
JUL	185	198	210	223	236	249	263	276	289	303	316	329	342	354	7	19

DAY	1	2	3	4	5	6	7	8	9	10	11	12	13	14	15
AUG	30	42	53	64	75	86	97	108	120	131	143	155	167	180	193

DAY	16	17	18	19	20	21	22	23	24	25	26	27	28	29	30	31
AUG	206	220	233	247	260	273	286	299	312	324	336	349	0	12	23	35

DAY	1	2	3	4	5	6	7	8	9	10	11	12	13	14	15
SEP	46	57	67	78	89	100	112	124	136	148	161	175	188	202	216

DAY	16	17	18	19	20	21	22	23	24	25	26	27	28	29	30	31
SEP	230	244	257	270	283	295	307	319	331	342	354	5	16	27	38	

DAY	1	2	3	4	5	6	7	8	9	10	11	12	13	14	15
OCT	48	59	70	81	93	104	116	129	142	155	169	184	198	212	226

DAY	16	17	18	19	20	21	22	23	24	25	26	27	28	29	30	31
OCT	239	252	265	277	289	301	312	324	335	346	357	8	19	29	40	51

DAY	1	2	3	4	5	6	7	8	9	10	11	12	13	14	15
NOV	62	74	85	97	109	122	136	150	164	178	192	206	220	233	246

DAY	16	17	18	19	20	21	22	23	24	25	26	27	28	29	30	31
NOV	259	271	282	294	305	316	327	338	348	359	10	21	32	43	55	

DAY	1	2	3	4	5	6	7	8	9	10	11	12	13	14	15
DEC	66	78	91	103	116	130	144	158	172	186	200	213	226	239	251

DAY	16	17	18	19	20	21	22	23	24	25	26	27	28	29	30	31
DEC	263	274	285	296	307	318	329	339	350	2	13	24	36	48	60	72

188

SUN*MOON ANGLES FOR 1955

DAY	1	2	3	4	5	6	7	8	9	10	11	12	13	14	15
JAN	85	98	111	125	138	152	166	179	192	205	218	230	242	254	265

DAY	16	17	18	19	20	21	22	23	24	25	26	27	28	29	30	31
JAN	276	287	297	308	319	330	342	353	5	17	29	42	54	67	80	93

DAY	1	2	3	4	5	6	7	8	9	10	11	12	13	14	15
FEB	106	120	133	146	159	172	185	197	210	221	233	244	255	266	277

DAY	16	17	18	19	20	21	22	23	24	25	26	27	28	29	30	31
FEB	288	299	310	321	333	345	357	10	23	36	50	63	76			

DAY	1	2	3	4	5	6	7	8	9	10	11	12	13	14	15
MAR	89	102	115	128	141	153	165	178	190	201	213	224	235	246	257

DAY	16	17	18	19	20	21	22	23	24	25	26	27	28	29	30	31
MAR	267	278	290	301	313	325	338	351	4	18	31	45	59	72	85	98

DAY	1	2	3	4	5	6	7	8	9	10	11	12	13	14	15
APR	111	123	135	147	159	171	182	193	204	215	226	237	248	259	270

DAY	16	17	18	19	20	21	22	23	24	25	26	27	28	29	30	31
APR	281	293	305	318	331	345	359	13	27	41	55	68	81	93	106	

DAY	1	2	3	4	5	6	7	8	9	10	11	12	13	14	15
MAY	118	130	141	153	164	175	186	197	207	218	229	240	251	263	275

DAY	16	17	18	19	20	21	22	23	24	25	26	27	28	29	30	31
MAY	287	299	313	326	340	354	8	23	37	50	63	76	88	100	112	124

DAY	1	2	3	4	5	6	7	8	9	10	11	12	13	14	15
JUN	135	146	157	168	179	189	200	211	222	234	245	257	269	282	295

DAY	16	17	18	19	20	21	22	23	24	25	26	27	28	29	30	31
JUN	308	322	336	350	4	18	32	45	58	71	83	94	106	117	128	

DAY	1	2	3	4	5	6	7	8	9	10	11	12	13	14	15
JUL	139	150	161	171	182	194	205	216	228	240	252	265	278	291	304

DAY	16	17	18	19	20	21	22	23	24	25	26	27	28	29	30	31
JUL	318	332	346	0	13	27	40	52	64	76	88	99	110	121	131	142

DAY	1	2	3	4	5	6	7	8	9	10	11	12	13	14	15
AUG	153	165	176	187	199	211	224	236	249	262	275	288	301	315	328

DAY	16	17	18	19	20	21	22	23	24	25	26	27	28	29	30	31
AUG	342	355	8	21	34	46	57	69	80	91	102	113	124	135	146	158

DAY	1	2	3	4	5	6	7	8	9	10	11	12	13	14	15
SEP	169	182	194	207	219	232	245	259	272	285	298	311	324	337	350

DAY	16	17	18	19	20	21	22	23	24	25	26	27	28	29	30	31
SEP	2	15	27	38	50	61	72	82	93	104	115	127	138	150	163	

DAY	1	2	3	4	5	6	7	8	9	10	11	12	13	14	15
OCT	176	189	202	215	229	242	255	268	281	294	307	319	332	344	356

DAY	16	17	18	19	20	21	22	23	24	25	26	27	28	29	30	31
OCT	7	19	30	41	52	63	74	84	95	107	118	131	143	156	169	183

DAY	1	2	3	4	5	6	7	8	9	10	11	12	13	14	15
NOV	197	210	224	238	251	264	277	289	302	314	325	337	348	359	11

DAY	16	17	18	19	20	21	22	23	24	25	26	27	28	29	30	31
NOV	21	32	43	54	65	76	87	98	110	123	136	149	163	177	191	

DAY	1	2	3	4	5	6	7	8	9	10	11	12	13	14	15
DEC	205	219	233	246	259	271	283	295	307	318	329	340	351	2	12

DAY	16	17	18	19	20	21	22	23	24	25	26	27	28	29	30	31
DEC	23	34	45	56	67	79	91	103	116	129	142	156	170	184	199	213

```
DAY   1   2   3   4   5   6   7   8   9  10  11  12  13  14  15
JAN 226 239 252 264 276 287 299 310 320 331 342 353   4  15  26

DAY  16  17  18  19  20  21  22  23  24  25  26  27  28  29  30  31
JAN  37  48  60  72  84  96 109 122 136 150 164 178 192 206 219 232

DAY   1   2   3   4   5   6   7   8   9  10  11  12  13  14  15
FEB 244 256 268 279 290 301 311 322 333 344 355   6  18  29  41

DAY  16  17  18  19  20  21  22  23  24  25  26  27  28  29  30  31
FEB  53  66  78  91 104 117 131 144 158 172 185 199 211 224

DAY   1   2   3   4   5   6   7   8   9  10  11  12  13  14  15
MAR 236 248 259 270 281 292 303 313 325 336 347 359  11  24  36

DAY  16  17  18  19  20  21  22  23  24  25  26  27  28  29  30  31
MAR  49  61  74  87 100 114 127 140 153 167 179 192 204 216 228 239

DAY   1   2   3   4   5   6   7   8   9  10  11  12  13  14  15
APR 250 261 272 283 294 305 316 328 340 352   5  18  31  44  57

DAY  16  17  18  19  20  21  22  23  24  25  26  27  28  29  30  31
APR  71  84  97 110 123 136 149 161 173 185 197 208 220 231 241

DAY   1   2   3   4   5   6   7   8   9  10  11  12  13  14  15
MAY 252 263 274 285 297 309 321 333 346 359  13  27  40  54  67

DAY  16  17  18  19  20  21  22  23  24  25  26  27  28  29  30  31
MAY  81  94 107 119 131 144 155 167 178 190 201 212 223 234 244 255

DAY   1   2   3   4   5   6   7   8   9  10  11  12  13  14  15
JUN 267 278 290 302 314 327 341 355   9  23  37  50  64  77  90

DAY  16  17  18  19  20  21  22  23  24  25  26  27  28  29  30  31
JUN 103 115 127 138 149 161 172 183 194 204 215 226 237 249 260

DAY   1   2   3   4   5   6   7   8   9  10  11  12  13  14  15
JUL 272 284 296 309 322 336 350   4  19  33  47  60  73  86  98

DAY  16  17  18  19  20  21  22  23  24  25  26  27  28  29  30  31
JUL 109 121 132 143 154 165 176 187 198 209 220 231 243 254 266

DAY   1   2   3   4   5   6   7   8   9  10  11  12  13  14  15
AUG 291 304 318 332 346   0  15  29  42  55  68  80  92 103 114

DAY  16  17  18  19  20  21  22  23  24  25  26  27  28  29  30  31
AUG 125 136 147 158 169 180 191 202 214 225 237 249 262 274 287 300

DAY   1   2   3   4   5   6   7   8   9  10  11  12  13  14  15
SEP 314 328 342 356  10  23  36  49  61  73  84  95 106 117 128

DAY  16  17  18  19  20  21  22  23  24  25  26  27  28  29  30  31
SEP 139 150 161 173 184 196 208 220 232 245 257 270 283 297 310

DAY   1   2   3   4   5   6   7   8   9  10  11  12  13  14  15
OCT 324 338 351   4  17  30  42  53  65  76  87  98 109 120 131

DAY  16  17  18  19  20  21  22  23  24  25  26  27  28  29  30  31
OCT 142 154 165 177 190 202 215 228 241 254 267 280 293 306 319 332

DAY   1   2   3   4   5   6   7   8   9  10  11  12  13  14  15
NOV 345 358  10  22  33  45  56  67  78  89 100 111 122 133 145

DAY  16  17  18  19  20  21  22  23  24  25  26  27  28  29  30  31
NOV 157 170 183 196 209 223 236 250 263 276 289 302 314 326 338

DAY   1   2   3   4   5   6   7   8   9  10  11  12  13  14  15
DEC 350   2  13  25  36  47  57  68  79  90 101 113 125 137 149

DAY  16  17  18  19  20  21  22  23  24  25  26  27  28  29  30  31
DEC 163 176 190 204 218 231 245 258 271 284 296 308 319 331 342 353
```

190

SUN*MOON ANGLES FOR 1957

```
DAY    1    2    3    4    5    6    7    8    9   10   11   12   13   14   15
JAN    4   15   26   37   47   58   69   80   92  104  116  128  141  155  169

DAY   16   17   18   19   20   21   22   23   24   25   26   27   28   29   30   31
JAN  183  197  211  225  239  252  264  277  288  300  311  322  333  344  355    6

DAY    1    2    3    4    5    6    7    8    9   10   11   12   13   14   15
FEB   17   28   39   50   61   72   84   96  108  121  134  148  162  177  191

DAY   16   17   18   19   20   21   22   23   24   25   26   27   28   29   30   31
FEB  205  219  232  245  257  269  281  292  303  314  325  336  347

DAY    1    2    3    4    5    6    7    8    9   10   11   12   13   14   15
MAR  358    9   20   31   42   54   65   77   90  102  115  129  143  157  171

DAY   16   17   18   19   20   21   22   23   24   25   26   27   28   29   30   31
MAR  185  199  212  225  238  250  261  273  284  295  306  317  327  338  349    1

DAY    1    2    3    4    5    6    7    8    9   10   11   12   13   14   15
APR   12   24   35   47   60   72   85   98  111  125  138  152  166  179  193

DAY   16   17   18   19   20   21   22   23   24   25   26   27   28   29   30   31
APR  206  218  230  242  253  264  275  286  297  308  319  331  342  354    6

DAY    1    2    3    4    5    6    7    8    9   10   11   12   13   14   15
MAY   18   30   43   55   68   82   95  108  121  135  148  161  174  187  199

DAY   16   17   18   19   20   21   22   23   24   25   26   27   28   29   30   31
MAY  211  223  234  245  256  267  278  289  300  312  323  335  347    0   12   26

DAY    1    2    3    4    5    6    7    8    9   10   11   12   13   14   15
JUN   39   52   66   79   92  105  118  131  144  156  168  180  192  204  215

DAY   16   17   18   19   20   21   22   23   24   25   26   27   28   29   30   31
JUN  226  237  248  259  270  281  293  304  316  329  341  355    8   22   35

DAY    1    2    3    4    5    6    7    8    9   10   11   12   13   14   15
JUL   49   63   76   89  102  115  127  139  151  163  174  186  197  208  219

DAY   16   17   18   19   20   21   22   23   24   25   26   27   28   29   30   31
JUL  230  241  252  263  274  286  298  310  323  336  350    4   18   32   46   60

DAY    1    2    3    4    5    6    7    8    9   10   11   12   13   14   15
AUG   73   86   98  110  122  134  145  157  168  179  190  201  212  223  234

DAY   16   17   18   19   20   21   22   23   24   25   26   27   28   29   30   31
AUG  245  256  267  279  292  304  318  331  345    0   14   28   42   56   69   81

DAY    1    2    3    4    5    6    7    8    9   10   11   12   13   14   15
SEP   93  105  116  128  139  150  161  172  183  194  205  216  227  238  250

DAY   16   17   18   19   20   21   22   23   24   25   26   27   28   29   30   31
SEP  261  274  286  299  313  327  341  355    9   23   37   50   63   75   87

DAY    1    2    3    4    5    6    7    8    9   10   11   12   13   14   15
OCT   98  109  120  131  142  153  164  175  186  197  209  220  232  244  256

DAY   16   17   18   19   20   21   22   23   24   25   26   27   28   29   30   31
OCT  269  281  295  308  322  336  350    4   17   30   43   55   67   79   90  101

DAY    1    2    3    4    5    6    7    8    9   10   11   12   13   14   15
NOV  112  123  134  145  156  167  178  190  202  214  226  238  251  264  277

DAY   16   17   18   19   20   21   22   23   24   25   26   27   28   29   30   31
NOV  290  304  317  331  344  357   10   23   35   47   58   70   81   92  103

DAY    1    2    3    4    5    6    7    8    9   10   11   12   13   14   15
DEC  113  124  135  147  158  170  182  195  208  221  234  247  260  273  286

DAY   16   17   18   19   20   21   22   23   24   25   26   27   28   29   30   31
DEC  299  312  325  338  350    2   15   26   38   49   60   71   82   93  104  115
```

191

SUN*MOON ANGLES FOR 1958

```
DAY    1    2    3    4    5    6    7    8    9   10   11   12   13   14   15
JAN  126  138  150  162  175  188  202  215  229  242  255  268  281  294  306

DAY   16   17   18   19   20   21   22   23   24   25   26   27   28   29   30   31
JAN  319  331  343  355    6   17   29   40   51   61   72   83   94  105  117  129

DAY    1    2    3    4    5    6    7    8    9   10   11   12   13   14   15
FEB  142  155  168  182  196  210  224  237  250  263  276  288  300  312  324

DAY   16   17   18   19   20   21   22   23   24   25   26   27   28   29   30   31
FEB  335  347  358    9   20   31   41   52   63   74   85   97  109

DAY    1    2    3    4    5    6    7    8    9   10   11   12   13   14   15
MAR  121  134  148  162  176  190  204  218  232  245  258  270  282  294  305

DAY   16   17   18   19   20   21   22   23   24   25   26   27   28   29   30   31
MAR  317  328  339  350    0   11   22   33   44   55   66   78   90  102  115  128

DAY    1    2    3    4    5    6    7    8    9   10   11   12   13   14   15
APR  142  156  170  184  199  212  226  239  251  264  275  287  298  309  320

DAY   16   17   18   19   20   21   22   23   24   25   26   27   28   29   30   31
APR  331  342  352    3   14   26   37   48   60   72   84   97  110  124  137

DAY    1    2    3    4    5    6    7    8    9   10   11   12   13   14   15
MAY  151  165  179  193  207  220  233  245  257  268  279  291  301  312  323

DAY   16   17   18   19   20   21   22   23   24   25   26   27   28   29   30   31
MAY  334  345  356    8   19   31   43   55   68   81   94  107  120  134  147  161

DAY    1    2    3    4    5    6    7    8    9   10   11   12   13   14   15
JUN  175  188  201  214  226  238  249  261  272  283  294  304  315  327  338

DAY   16   17   18   19   20   21   22   23   24   25   26   27   28   29   30   31
JUN  350    1   14   26   39   52   65   78   91  104  117  130  144  157  170

DAY    1    2    3    4    5    6    7    8    9   10   11   12   13   14   15
JUL  183  195  207  219  231  242  253  264  275  286  297  308  319  331  343

DAY   16   17   18   19   20   21   22   23   24   25   26   27   28   29   30   31
JUL  356    9   22   35   48   62   75   88  101  114  127  140  153  165  177  189

DAY    1    2    3    4    5    6    7    8    9   10   11   12   13   14   15
AUG  201  212  223  234  245  256  267  278  289  301  313  325  338  351    4

DAY   16   17   18   19   20   21   22   23   24   25   26   27   28   29   30   31
AUG   18   32   45   59   72   85   98  111  123  136  148  159  171  182  194  205

DAY    1    2    3    4    5    6    7    8    9   10   11   12   13   14   15
SEP  216  226  237  248  259  270  282  294  306  319  332  346  359   13   28

DAY   16   17   18   19   20   21   22   23   24   25   26   27   28   29   30   31
SEP   41   55   68   81   94  106  118  130  142  153  164  175  186  197  208

DAY    1    2    3    4    5    6    7    8    9   10   11   12   13   14   15
OCT  218  229  240  252  263  275  287  300  313  326  340  354    8   23   37

DAY   16   17   18   19   20   21   22   23   24   25   26   27   28   29   30   31
OCT   50   63   76   88  100  112  123  134  145  156  167  178  189  200  211  222

DAY    1    2    3    4    5    6    7    8    9   10   11   12   13   14   15
NOV  233  244  256  268  281  294  307  320  334  349    3   17   30   44   57

DAY   16   17   18   19   20   21   22   23   24   25   26   27   28   29   30   31
NOV   69   81   93  104  115  126  137  148  158  169  180  191  203  214  226

DAY    1    2    3    4    5    6    7    8    9   10   11   12   13   14   15
DEC  238  250  262  275  288  301  315  329  343  356   10   23   36   49   61

DAY   16   17   18   19   20   21   22   23   24   25   26   27   28   29   30   31
DEC   73   84   95  106  117  127  138  149  160  172  183  195  207  220  232  245
```

SUN*MOON ANGLES FOR 1959

DAY	1	2	3	4	5	6	7	8	9	10	11	12	13	14	15
JAN	257	270	283	296	310	323	337	350	3	16	28	40	52	63	74

DAY	16	17	18	19	20	21	22	23	24	25	26	27	28	29	30	31
JAN	85	96	107	118	129	140	152	163	176	188	201	214	226	239	253	266

DAY	1	2	3	4	5	6	7	8	9	10	11	12	13	14	15
FEB	279	292	305	318	331	343	356	8	20	31	43	54	65	75	86

DAY	16	17	18	19	20	21	22	23	24	25	26	27	28	29	30	31
FEB	97	108	119	131	143	155	168	181	194	208	221	235	248			

DAY	1	2	3	4	5	6	7	8	9	10	11	12	13	14	15
MAR	261	274	287	300	312	325	337	348	0	11	23	34	44	55	66

DAY	16	17	18	19	20	21	22	23	24	25	26	27	28	29	30	31
MAR	77	88	99	111	123	135	148	161	175	189	203	217	230	244	257	270

DAY	1	2	3	4	5	6	7	8	9	10	11	12	13	14	15
APR	283	295	307	318	330	341	352	3	14	25	36	47	58	69	80

DAY	16	17	18	19	20	21	22	23	24	25	26	27	28	29	30	31
APR	92	104	116	129	142	155	169	184	198	212	226	239	252	265	277	

DAY	1	2	3	4	5	6	7	8	9	10	11	12	13	14	15
MAY	289	301	312	323	334	345	356	7	17	28	39	51	62	74	85

DAY	16	17	18	19	20	21	22	23	24	25	26	27	28	29	30	31
MAY	98	110	123	137	151	165	179	193	207	221	234	247	259	271	283	294

DAY	1	2	3	4	5	6	7	8	9	10	11	12	13	14	15
JUN	305	316	327	338	349	0	11	22	33	45	56	68	80	93	106

DAY	16	17	18	19	20	21	22	23	24	25	26	27	28	29	30	31
JUN	119	133	147	161	175	189	203	216	229	241	253	265	276	287	298	

DAY	1	2	3	4	5	6	7	8	9	10	11	12	13	14	15
JUL	309	320	331	342	353	4	16	28	40	52	64	77	89	103	116

DAY	16	17	18	19	20	21	22	23	24	25	26	27	28	29	30	31
JUL	130	143	157	171	184	197	210	223	234	246	257	268	279	290	301	312

DAY	1	2	3	4	5	6	7	8	9	10	11	12	13	14	15
AUG	323	335	346	358	10	23	35	48	61	74	87	100	113	127	140

DAY	16	17	18	19	20	21	22	23	24	25	26	27	28	29	30	31
AUG	153	166	179	192	204	216	227	238	249	260	271	282	293	304	316	328

DAY	1	2	3	4	5	6	7	8	9	10	11	12	13	14	15
SEP	340	352	5	18	31	44	57	71	84	97	110	123	136	149	161

DAY	16	17	18	19	20	21	22	23	24	25	26	27	28	29	30	31
SEP	173	185	197	208	219	230	241	252	263	274	285	297	308	321	333	

DAY	1	2	3	4	5	6	7	8	9	10	11	12	13	14	15
OCT	346	359	13	26	40	54	67	81	94	106	119	131	143	155	166

DAY	16	17	18	19	20	21	22	23	24	25	26	27	28	29	30	31
OCT	178	189	200	211	222	233	243	254	266	277	289	301	313	326	340	353

DAY	1	2	3	4	5	6	7	8	9	10	11	12	13	14	15
NOV	7	21	35	49	63	76	89	101	113	125	136	147	159	170	181

DAY	16	17	18	19	20	21	22	23	24	25	26	27	28	29	30	31
NOV	191	202	213	224	235	246	257	269	281	293	306	319	333	347	1	

DAY	1	2	3	4	5	6	7	8	9	10	11	12	13	14	15
DEC	16	30	44	57	70	82	94	106	117	128	139	150	161	172	183

DAY	16	17	18	19	20	21	22	23	24	25	26	27	28	29	30	31
DEC	194	205	216	227	238	250	262	274	286	299	313	327	341	355	9	23

SUN*MOON ANGLES FOR 1960

DAY	1	2	3	4	5	6	7	8	9	10	11	12	13	14	15
JAN	37	50	62	75	86	98	109	120	130	141	152	163	174	185	196

DAY	16	17	18	19	20	21	22	23	24	25	26	27	28	29	30	31
JAN	208	219	231	243	255	268	281	294	307	321	335	349	3	16	29	42

DAY	1	2	3	4	5	6	7	8	9	10	11	12	13	14	15
FEB	54	66	77	88	99	110	121	132	143	154	165	177	189	201	213

DAY	16	17	18	19	20	21	22	23	24	25	26	27	28	29	30	31
FEB	225	237	250	263	276	289	303	316	330	343	356	9	21	34		

DAY	1	2	3	4	5	6	7	8	9	10	11	12	13	14	15
MAR	46	57	69	80	90	101	112	123	134	146	158	170	182	194	207

DAY	16	17	18	19	20	21	22	23	24	25	26	27	28	29	30	31
MAR	220	233	247	260	273	286	299	312	325	338	350	2	14	26	37	48

DAY	1	2	3	4	5	6	7	8	9	10	11	12	13	14	15
APR	60	70	81	92	103	115	126	138	150	163	175	189	202	216	229

DAY	16	17	18	19	20	21	22	23	24	25	26	27	28	29	30	31
APR	243	256	270	282	295	308	320	332	344	355	7	18	29	40	51	

DAY	1	2	3	4	5	6	7	8	9	10	11	12	13	14	15
MAY	62	73	84	95	107	118	131	143	156	170	184	198	212	226	239

DAY	16	17	18	19	20	21	22	23	24	25	26	27	28	29	30	31
MAY	253	266	278	291	303	315	326	337	349	360	11	22	33	44	55	66

DAY	1	2	3	4	5	6	7	8	9	10	11	12	13	14	15
JUN	77	88	100	112	125	138	151	165	179	194	208	222	236	249	261

DAY	16	17	18	19	20	21	22	23	24	25	26	27	28	29	30	31
JUN	274	286	297	309	320	331	342	353	4	15	26	37	48	59	70	

DAY	1	2	3	4	5	6	7	8	9	10	11	12	13	14	15
JUL	82	94	107	120	133	147	161	175	190	204	218	231	244	256	268

DAY	16	17	18	19	20	21	22	23	24	25	26	27	28	29	30	31
JUL	280	291	302	313	324	335	346	357	8	19	30	42	53	65	77	90

DAY	1	2	3	4	5	6	7	8	9	10	11	12	13	14	15
AUG	103	116	129	143	157	171	185	199	213	225	238	250	262	273	284

DAY	16	17	18	19	20	21	22	23	24	25	26	27	28	29	30	31
AUG	295	306	317	328	339	350	1	13	24	36	48	61	73	86	99	112

DAY	1	2	3	4	5	6	7	8	9	10	11	12	13	14	15
SEP	126	140	153	167	180	194	206	219	231	243	254	265	276	287	298

DAY	16	17	18	19	20	21	22	23	24	25	26	27	28	29	30	31
SEP	309	320	331	343	355	6	19	31	44	57	70	83	96	109	122	

DAY	1	2	3	4	5	6	7	8	9	10	11	12	13	14	15
OCT	136	149	162	175	187	199	211	223	235	246	257	268	278	289	300

DAY	16	17	18	19	20	21	22	23	24	25	26	27	28	29	30	31
OCT	312	323	335	347	360	13	26	39	53	66	79	92	105	118	131	144

DAY	1	2	3	4	5	6	7	8	9	10	11	12	13	14	15
NOV	156	168	180	192	203	215	226	237	248	258	269	280	291	303	315

DAY	16	17	18	19	20	21	22	23	24	25	26	27	28	29	30	31
NOV	327	340	353	7	21	35	48	62	75	88	101	113	125	137	149	

DAY	1	2	3	4	5	6	7	8	9	10	11	12	13	14	15
DEC	161	172	184	195	206	217	227	238	249	260	271	283	295	307	320

DAY	16	17	18	19	20	21	22	23	24	25	26	27	28	29	30	31
DEC	333	347	1	15	29	43	57	70	83	95	107	119	130	142	153	164

SUN*MOON ANGLES FOR 1961

```
DAY    1    2    3    4    5    6    7    8    9   10   11   12   13   14   15
JAN  174  185  196  207  218  229  240  251  262  274  286  299  312  326  340

DAY   16   17   18   19   20   21   22   23   24   25   26   27   28   29   30   31
JAN  354    8   22   36   50   63   75   87   99  111  122  133  144  155  166  176

DAY    1    2    3    4    5    6    7    8    9   10   11   12   13   14   15
FEB  187  198  209  220  232  243  255  267  280  292  306  320  334  348    2

DAY   16   17   18   19   20   21   22   23   24   25   26   27   28   29   30   31
FEB   16   29   43   55   68   80   91  102  113  124  135  146  157

DAY    1    2    3    4    5    6    7    8    9   10   11   12   13   14   15
MAR  168  179  190  201  213  225  237  249  262  274  287  301  314  328  342

DAY   16   17   18   19   20   21   22   23   24   25   26   27   28   29   30   31
MAR  356    9   22   35   48   60   71   83   94  105  115  126  137  148  159  171

DAY    1    2    3    4    5    6    7    8    9   10   11   12   13   14   15
APR  183  194  207  219  232  244  257  270  284  297  310  324  337  350    3

DAY   16   17   18   19   20   21   22   23   24   25   26   27   28   29   30   31
APR   16   28   40   52   63   74   85   96  107  118  129  140  152  164  176

DAY    1    2    3    4    5    6    7    8    9   10   11   12   13   14   15
MAY  189  201  215  228  241  254  267  280  293  306  319  332  345  357    9

DAY   16   17   18   19   20   21   22   23   24   25   26   27   28   29   30   31
MAY   21   32   44   55   66   77   88   99  110  121  133  145  157  170  184  197

DAY    1    2    3    4    5    6    7    8    9   10   11   12   13   14   15
JUN  211  224  238  251  264  277  290  303  315  327  339  351    3   14   25

DAY   16   17   18   19   20   21   22   23   24   25   26   27   28   29   30   31
JUN   36   47   58   69   80   91  102  114  126  139  152  165  179  193  207

DAY    1    2    3    4    5    6    7    8    9   10   11   12   13   14   15
JUL  221  235  248  261  274  286  299  311  322  334  345  356    7   18   29

DAY   16   17   18   19   20   21   22   23   24   25   26   27   28   29   30   31
JUL   40   51   62   73   84   96  108  120  133  147  161  175  189  203  217  231

DAY    1    2    3    4    5    6    7    8    9   10   11   12   13   14   15
AUG  244  257  270  282  293  305  316  327  338  349    0   11   22   33   44

DAY   16   17   18   19   20   21   22   23   24   25   26   27   28   29   30   31
AUG   55   66   78   90  103  115  129  142  156  170  185  199  213  226  239  252

DAY    1    2    3    4    5    6    7    8    9   10   11   12   13   14   15
SEP  264  276  287  298  309  320  331  342  353    4   15   26   37   49   61

DAY   16   17   18   19   20   21   22   23   24   25   26   27   28   29   30   31
SEP   73   85   98  111  124  138  152  166  180  194  207  220  233  245  257

DAY    1    2    3    4    5    6    7    8    9   10   11   12   13   14   15
OCT  268  280  291  301  312  323  334  345  356    8   19   31   43   56   68

DAY   16   17   18   19   20   21   22   23   24   25   26   27   28   29   30   31
OCT   81   94  107  120  133  147  161  174  187  201  213  225  237  249  260  271

DAY    1    2    3    4    5    6    7    8    9   10   11   12   13   14   15
NOV  282  292  303  314  325  337  349    1   13   25   38   51   63   76   89

DAY   16   17   18   19   20   21   22   23   24   25   26   27   28   29   30   31
NOV  102  116  129  142  155  168  181  193  205  217  228  239  250  261  272

DAY    1    2    3    4    5    6    7    8    9   10   11   12   13   14   15
DEC  283  294  305  317  328  341  353    6   19   32   46   59   72   85   98

DAY   16   17   18   19   20   21   22   23   24   25   26   27   28   29   30   31
DEC  111  124  136  149  161  173  185  197  208  219  230  241  251  262  273  284
```

DAY	1	2	3	4	5	6	7	8	9	10	11	12	13	14	15
JAN	296	308	320	333	346	359	13	26	40	54	67	80	93	106	118

DAY	16	17	18	19	20	21	22	23	24	25	26	27	28	29	30	31
JAN	130	142	154	165	177	188	199	209	220	231	242	253	264	275	287	299

DAY	1	2	3	4	5	6	7	8	9	10	11	12	13	14	15
FEB	312	325	339	352	6	21	35	48	62	75	88	100	112	123	135

DAY	16	17	18	19	20	21	22	23	24	25	26	27	28	29	30	31
FEB	146	157	168	179	190	201	211	222	233	244	256	268	280			

DAY	1	2	3	4	5	6	7	8	9	10	11	12	13	14	15
MAR	292	305	318	332	346	0	15	29	42	56	69	81	93	105	116

DAY	16	17	18	19	20	21	22	23	24	25	26	27	28	29	30	31
MAR	127	138	149	160	170	181	192	203	215	226	237	249	261	274	286	299

DAY	1	2	3	4	5	6	7	8	9	10	11	12	13	14	15
APR	313	327	341	355	9	23	36	49	62	74	86	97	108	119	130

DAY	16	17	18	19	20	21	22	23	24	25	26	27	28	29	30	31
APR	141	152	163	174	185	196	208	220	232	244	256	269	282	295	309	

DAY	1	2	3	4	5	6	7	8	9	10	11	12	13	14	15
MAY	322	336	350	4	17	30	43	55	67	78	89	100	111	122	133

DAY	16	17	18	19	20	21	22	23	24	25	26	27	28	29	30	31
MAY	144	155	167	178	190	202	215	227	240	253	266	279	292	305	319	332

DAY	1	2	3	4	5	6	7	8	9	10	11	12	13	14	15
JUN	346	359	11	24	36	48	59	70	81	92	103	114	125	136	148

DAY	16	17	18	19	20	21	22	23	24	25	26	27	28	29	30	31
JUN	160	172	185	197	210	223	237	250	263	276	289	303	316	328	341	

DAY	1	2	3	4	5	6	7	8	9	10	11	12	13	14	15
JUL	353	6	17	29	40	51	62	73	84	95	106	118	129	141	154

DAY	16	17	18	19	20	21	22	23	24	25	26	27	28	29	30	31
JUL	167	180	193	206	220	234	247	261	274	287	299	312	324	336	348	359

DAY	1	2	3	4	5	6	7	8	9	10	11	12	13	14	15
AUG	11	22	33	44	55	66	77	88	99	111	123	135	148	161	175

DAY	16	17	18	19	20	21	22	23	24	25	26	27	28	29	30	31
AUG	189	203	217	230	244	257	270	283	295	307	319	330	341	353	4	14

DAY	1	2	3	4	5	6	7	8	9	10	11	12	13	14	15
SEP	25	36	47	58	69	80	92	104	116	129	142	156	170	184	198

DAY	16	17	18	19	20	21	22	23	24	25	26	27	28	29	30	31
SEP	213	226	240	253	266	278	290	301	312	323	334	345	356	7	18	

DAY	1	2	3	4	5	6	7	8	9	10	11	12	13	14	15
OCT	29	40	51	62	74	86	98	110	123	137	151	165	179	193	207

DAY	16	17	18	19	20	21	22	23	24	25	26	27	28	29	30	31
OCT	221	234	247	259	271	282	294	305	315	326	337	348	359	10	21	33

DAY	1	2	3	4	5	6	7	8	9	10	11	12	13	14	15
NOV	44	56	67	80	92	105	118	132	145	160	174	188	201	214	227

DAY	16	17	18	19	20	21	22	23	24	25	26	27	28	29	30	31
NOV	240	251	263	274	285	296	307	318	329	340	351	2	14	25	37	

DAY	1	2	3	4	5	6	7	8	9	10	11	12	13	14	15
DEC	49	62	74	87	100	113	127	140	154	168	181	194	207	219	231

DAY	16	17	18	19	20	21	22	23	24	25	26	27	28	29	30	31
DEC	242	254	265	276	286	297	308	319	331	342	354	6	18	31	44	56

SUN*MOON ANGLES FOR 1963

DAY	1	2	3	4	5	6	7	8	9	10	11	12	13	14	15
JAN	69	82	96	109	122	135	148	161	174	186	198	210	222	233	244

DAY	16	17	18	19	20	21	22	23	24	25	26	27	28	29	30	31
JAN	255	266	277	287	299	310	322	334	346	359	12	25	38	51	65	78

DAY	1	2	3	4	5	6	7	8	9	10	11	12	13	14	15
FEB	91	104	117	130	142	154	166	178	190	201	212	223	234	245	256

DAY	16	17	18	19	20	21	22	23	24	25	26	27	28	29	30	31
FEB	267	278	289	301	313	325	338	352	5	19	33	47	60			

DAY	1	2	3	4	5	6	7	8	9	10	11	12	13	14	15
MAR	74	87	99	112	124	136	147	159	170	181	193	203	214	225	236

DAY	16	17	18	19	20	21	22	23	24	25	26	27	28	29	30	31
MAR	247	258	269	281	293	305	318	332	345	359	14	28	42	56	69	82

DAY	1	2	3	4	5	6	7	8	9	10	11	12	13	14	15
APR	94	106	118	129	140	152	163	174	185	195	206	217	228	239	251

DAY	16	17	18	19	20	21	22	23	24	25	26	27	28	29	30	31
APR	262	274	286	299	312	326	340	354	9	23	37	50	63	76	88	

DAY	1	2	3	4	5	6	7	8	9	10	11	12	13	14	15
MAY	100	111	122	133	144	155	166	177	188	199	210	221	233	244	256

DAY	16	17	18	19	20	21	22	23	24	25	26	27	28	29	30	31
MAY	269	281	294	308	322	336	350	4	18	32	45	57	70	81	93	104

DAY	1	2	3	4	5	6	7	8	9	10	11	12	13	14	15
JUN	115	126	137	148	159	170	181	192	204	216	227	240	252	265	278

DAY	16	17	18	19	20	21	22	23	24	25	26	27	28	29	30	31
JUN	291	305	318	332	346	0	13	26	39	51	63	74	86	97	108	

DAY	1	2	3	4	5	6	7	8	9	10	11	12	13	14	15
JUL	119	130	141	152	163	175	186	198	211	223	236	249	262	275	288

DAY	16	17	18	19	20	21	22	23	24	25	26	27	28	29	30	31
JUL	302	315	329	342	355	8	20	32	44	56	67	78	89	100	111	122

DAY	1	2	3	4	5	6	7	8	9	10	11	12	13	14	15
AUG	133	145	156	168	181	193	206	219	233	246	259	273	286	299	312

DAY	16	17	18	19	20	21	22	23	24	25	26	27	28	29	30	31
AUG	325	337	350	2	14	25	37	48	59	70	81	92	103	114	126	137

DAY	1	2	3	4	5	6	7	8	9	10	11	12	13	14	15
SEP	150	162	175	189	202	216	230	243	257	270	283	295	308	320	332

DAY	16	17	18	19	20	21	22	23	24	25	26	27	28	29	30	31
SEP	344	355	7	18	29	40	51	62	73	84	95	106	118	130	143	

DAY	1	2	3	4	5	6	7	8	9	10	11	12	13	14	15
OCT	156	170	184	198	212	226	239	253	266	278	290	302	314	326	337

DAY	16	17	18	19	20	21	22	23	24	25	26	27	28	29	30	31
OCT	348	359	10	21	32	43	54	64	76	87	99	111	123	136	150	164

DAY	1	2	3	4	5	6	7	8	9	10	11	12	13	14	15
NOV	178	193	207	221	234	247	260	272	284	296	307	318	329	340	351

DAY	16	17	18	19	20	21	22	23	24	25	26	27	28	29	30	31
NOV	2	13	23	34	45	56	68	80	92	104	117	130	144	158	172	

DAY	1	2	3	4	5	6	7	8	9	10	11	12	13	14	15
DEC	187	201	214	228	241	253	265	276	288	299	310	321	331	342	353

DAY	16	17	18	19	20	21	22	23	24	25	26	27	28	29	30	31
DEC	4	15	26	38	49	61	73	85	98	111	125	138	152	166	180	194

197

DAY	1	2	3	4	5	6	7	8	9	10	11	12	13	14	15
JAN	208	220	233	245	256	268	279	290	301	311	322	333	344	355	7

DAY	16	17	18	19	20	21	22	23	24	25	26	27	28	29	30	31
JAN	18	30	42	55	67	80	93	106	120	133	146	160	173	186	199	212

DAY	1	2	3	4	5	6	7	8	9	10	11	12	13	14	15
FEB	224	236	247	258	269	280	291	302	313	324	335	347	359	11	24

DAY	16	17	18	19	20	21	22	23	24	25	26	27	28	29	30	31
FEB	37	49	63	76	89	102	115	128	141	154	167	179	191	204		

DAY	1	2	3	4	5	6	7	8	9	10	11	12	13	14	15
MAR	216	227	238	249	260	271	282	293	304	316	327	340	352	5	19

DAY	16	17	18	19	20	21	22	23	24	25	26	27	28	29	30	31
MAR	32	45	59	72	85	98	111	124	136	149	161	173	185	196	207	218

DAY	1	2	3	4	5	6	7	8	9	10	11	12	13	14	15
APR	229	240	251	262	273	284	296	308	320	333	346	360	13	27	41

DAY	16	17	18	19	20	21	22	23	24	25	26	27	28	29	30	31
APR	55	68	81	94	107	119	131	143	155	166	177	188	199	210	221	

DAY	1	2	3	4	5	6	7	8	9	10	11	12	13	14	15
MAY	232	243	254	265	277	289	301	314	327	341	355	9	23	37	51

DAY	16	17	18	19	20	21	22	23	24	25	26	27	28	29	30	31
MAY	64	77	90	102	114	126	137	148	159	170	181	192	203	214	225	236

DAY	1	2	3	4	5	6	7	8	9	10	11	12	13	14	15
JUN	247	259	270	283	295	309	322	336	350	5	19	33	46	59	72

DAY	16	17	18	19	20	21	22	23	24	25	26	27	28	29	30	31
JUN	85	96	108	119	131	142	152	163	174	185	196	207	218	230	241	

DAY	1	2	3	4	5	6	7	8	9	10	11	12	13	14	15
JUL	253	266	278	291	305	318	332	346	0	14	28	41	54	67	79

DAY	16	17	18	19	20	21	22	23	24	25	26	27	28	29	30	31
JUL	90	101	113	123	134	145	156	167	178	189	201	213	225	237	249	262

DAY	1	2	3	4	5	6	7	8	9	10	11	12	13	14	15
AUG	275	288	301	315	328	342	356	9	23	36	48	60	72	83	94

DAY	16	17	18	19	20	21	22	23	24	25	26	27	28	29	30	31
AUG	105	116	127	138	149	160	172	183	195	208	220	233	246	258	272	285

DAY	1	2	3	4	5	6	7	8	9	10	11	12	13	14	15
SEP	298	311	325	338	351	4	17	29	41	53	64	75	86	97	107

DAY	16	17	18	19	20	21	22	23	24	25	26	27	28	29	30	31
SEP	118	130	141	153	165	177	190	203	216	229	242	255	268	281	295	

DAY	1	2	3	4	5	6	7	8	9	10	11	12	13	14	15
OCT	307	320	333	346	358	10	22	33	44	55	66	77	88	99	110

DAY	16	17	18	19	20	21	22	23	24	25	26	27	28	29	30	31
OCT	121	133	145	158	171	184	198	211	225	238	251	265	278	290	303	315

DAY	1	2	3	4	5	6	7	8	9	10	11	12	13	14	15
NOV	327	339	351	2	14	25	36	46	57	68	79	90	101	113	125

DAY	16	17	18	19	20	21	22	23	24	25	26	27	28	29	30	31
NOV	138	151	164	178	192	206	220	233	247	260	273	285	297	309	320	

DAY	1	2	3	4	5	6	7	8	9	10	11	12	13	14	15
DEC	332	343	354	5	16	26	37	48	59	70	81	93	105	117	130

DAY	16	17	18	19	20	21	22	23	24	25	26	27	28	29	30	31
DEC	144	157	171	186	200	214	228	241	254	266	278	290	301	313	324	334

DAY	1	2	3	4	5	6	7	8	9	10	11	12	13	14	15
JAN	345	355	6	17	28	39	50	61	73	85	97	110	123	136	150

DAY	16	17	18	19	20	21	22	23	24	25	26	27	28	29	30	31
JAN	164	179	193	207	220	233	246	258	270	281	292	303	314	325	336	346

DAY	1	2	3	4	5	6	7	8	9	10	11	12	13	14	15
FEB	357	8	20	31	43	54	66	79	91	104	117	131	144	158	172

DAY	16	17	18	19	20	21	22	23	24	25	26	27	28	29	30	31
FEB	186	200	213	226	238	250	261	272	283	294	305	316	327			

DAY	1	2	3	4	5	6	7	8	9	10	11	12	13	14	15
MAR	338	349	0	12	24	36	48	61	73	86	99	113	126	139	153

DAY	16	17	18	19	20	21	22	23	24	25	26	27	28	29	30	31
MAR	167	180	193	206	218	230	241	252	263	274	285	296	307	318	330	341

DAY	1	2	3	4	5	6	7	8	9	10	11	12	13	14	15
APR	353	5	18	31	43	56	69	83	96	109	122	135	148	161	174

DAY	16	17	18	19	20	21	22	23	24	25	26	27	28	29	30	31
APR	186	198	210	221	233	244	255	265	276	287	299	310	322	334	347	

DAY	1	2	3	4	5	6	7	8	9	10	11	12	13	14	15
MAY	0	13	26	39	53	66	79	93	106	118	131	144	156	168	180

DAY	16	17	18	19	20	21	22	23	24	25	26	27	28	29	30	31
MAY	191	202	214	225	235	246	257	268	280	291	303	315	328	341	354	8

DAY	1	2	3	4	5	6	7	8	9	10	11	12	13	14	15
JUN	22	36	49	63	76	89	102	115	127	139	150	162	173	184	195

DAY	16	17	18	19	20	21	22	23	24	25	26	27	28	29	30	31
JUN	206	217	228	239	250	261	273	284	297	309	322	336	350	4	18	

DAY	1	2	3	4	5	6	7	8	9	10	11	12	13	14	15
JUL	32	46	60	73	86	98	110	122	133	144	155	166	177	188	199

DAY	16	17	18	19	20	21	22	23	24	25	26	27	28	29	30	31
JUL	210	221	232	243	255	267	279	291	304	317	331	345	0	14	28	42

DAY	1	2	3	4	5	6	7	8	9	10	11	12	13	14	15
AUG	55	68	81	93	104	115	127	138	148	159	170	181	192	203	215

DAY	16	17	18	19	20	21	22	23	24	25	26	27	28	29	30	31
AUG	226	238	249	261	274	287	300	313	327	341	355	10	23	37	50	62

DAY	1	2	3	4	5	6	7	8	9	10	11	12	13	14	15
SEP	74	86	97	108	119	130	141	152	163	174	185	197	208	220	232

DAY	16	17	18	19	20	21	22	23	24	25	26	27	28	29	30	31
SEP	244	257	270	283	296	309	323	337	351	4	18	31	43	55	67	

DAY	1	2	3	4	5	6	7	8	9	10	11	12	13	14	15
OCT	78	89	100	111	122	133	144	155	167	178	190	202	215	227	240

DAY	16	17	18	19	20	21	22	23	24	25	26	27	28	29	30	31
OCT	253	266	279	292	305	319	332	345	358	11	23	35	47	58	69	80

DAY	1	2	3	4	5	6	7	8	9	10	11	12	13	14	15
NOV	91	102	113	124	135	147	159	171	184	196	209	222	235	249	262

DAY	16	17	18	19	20	21	22	23	24	25	26	27	28	29	30	31
NOV	275	288	301	314	327	339	351	3	15	27	38	49	60	71	82	

DAY	1	2	3	4	5	6	7	8	9	10	11	12	13	14	15
DEC	92	104	115	126	138	151	163	177	190	203	217	231	244	258	271

DAY	16	17	18	19	20	21	22	23	24	25	26	27	28	29	30	31
DEC	283	296	308	320	332	344	355	6	18	29	39	50	61	72	83	94

SUN*MOON ANGLES FOR 1966

DAY	1	2	3	4	5	6	7	8	9	10	11	12	13	14	15
JAN	106	118	130	143	156	170	183	198	212	226	239	252	265	278	290

DAY	16	17	18	19	20	21	22	23	24	25	26	27	28	29	30	31
JAN	302	313	325	336	347	358	9	20	30	41	52	63	74	86	97	110

DAY	1	2	3	4	5	6	7	8	9	10	11	12	13	14	15
FEB	122	135	149	163	177	191	206	220	233	246	259	271	283	294	305

DAY	16	17	18	19	20	21	22	23	24	25	26	27	28	29	30	31
FEB	316	327	338	349	0	11	22	33	44	55	67	78	90			

DAY	1	2	3	4	5	6	7	8	9	10	11	12	13	14	15
MAR	103	116	129	143	157	171	186	200	213	227	239	252	264	275	286

DAY	16	17	18	19	20	21	22	23	24	25	26	27	28	29	30	31
MAR	297	308	319	330	341	352	3	14	25	37	48	60	72	85	98	111

DAY	1	2	3	4	5	6	7	8	9	10	11	12	13	14	15
APR	124	138	152	166	180	194	207	220	232	244	256	267	278	289	300

DAY	16	17	18	19	20	21	22	23	24	25	26	27	28	29	30	31
APR	311	322	333	344	355	7	19	31	43	55	68	81	94	107	121	

DAY	1	2	3	4	5	6	7	8	9	10	11	12	13	14	15
MAY	134	148	161	175	188	200	213	225	236	248	259	270	281	292	303

DAY	16	17	18	19	20	21	22	23	24	25	26	27	28	29	30	31
MAY	314	325	337	349	1	13	26	39	52	65	78	91	105	118	131	144

DAY	1	2	3	4	5	6	7	8	9	10	11	12	13	14	15
JUN	157	169	182	194	206	217	229	240	251	262	273	284	295	306	318

DAY	16	17	18	19	20	21	22	23	24	25	26	27	28	29	30	31
JUN	330	342	355	8	21	35	49	62	75	89	102	115	127	140	152	

DAY	1	2	3	4	5	6	7	8	9	10	11	12	13	14	15
JUL	164	176	187	199	210	221	232	243	254	265	276	288	299	311	324

DAY	16	17	18	19	20	21	22	23	24	25	26	27	28	29	30	31
JUL	337	350	4	18	32	46	59	73	86	98	111	123	135	147	158	170

DAY	1	2	3	4	5	6	7	8	9	10	11	12	13	14	15
AUG	181	192	203	214	225	236	247	258	269	281	293	305	318	332	345

DAY	16	17	18	19	20	21	22	23	24	25	26	27	28	29	30	31
AUG	0	14	28	42	56	69	82	94	106	118	129	141	152	163	174	185

DAY	1	2	3	4	5	6	7	8	9	10	11	12	13	14	15
SEP	196	207	218	229	240	251	263	274	287	300	313	327	341	355	9

DAY	16	17	18	19	20	21	22	23	24	25	26	27	28	29	30	31
SEP	24	37	51	64	76	88	100	111	123	134	145	156	166	177	188	

DAY	1	2	3	4	5	6	7	8	9	10	11	12	13	14	15
OCT	199	210	222	233	245	257	269	282	295	308	322	336	350	4	18

DAY	16	17	18	19	20	21	22	23	24	25	26	27	28	29	30	31
OCT	32	45	57	69	81	93	104	115	126	136	147	158	169	180	192	203

DAY	1	2	3	4	5	6	7	8	9	10	11	12	13	14	15
NOV	215	227	239	251	264	277	290	304	317	331	345	358	11	24	37

DAY	16	17	18	19	20	21	22	23	24	25	26	27	28	29	30	31
NOV	49	61	73	84	95	106	117	127	138	149	161	172	184	196	208	

DAY	1	2	3	4	5	6	7	8	9	10	11	12	13	14	15
DEC	221	234	246	259	273	286	299	312	325	338	351	4	17	29	40

DAY	16	17	18	19	20	21	22	23	24	25	26	27	28	29	30	31
DEC	52	63	74	85	96	107	118	129	140	152	164	177	189	202	215	229

DAY	1	2	3	4	5	6	7	8	9	10	11	12	13	14	15
JAN	242	255	268	281	294	307	320	332	344	356	8	20	31	43	54

DAY	16	17	18	19	20	21	22	23	24	25	26	27	28	29	30	31
JAN	64	75	86	97	108	119	131	143	156	169	183	196	210	224	237	250

DAY	1	2	3	4	5	6	7	8	9	10	11	12	13	14	15
FEB	264	276	289	301	313	325	337	349	0	11	22	33	44	55	66

DAY	16	17	18	19	20	21	22	23	24	25	26	27	28	29	30	31
FEB	77	88	99	111	123	136	149	162	176	190	204	218	232			

DAY	1	2	3	4	5	6	7	8	9	10	11	12	13	14	15
MAR	245	258	271	283	295	307	318	330	341	352	3	14	25	35	46

DAY	16	17	18	19	20	21	22	23	24	25	26	27	28	29	30	31
MAR	57	68	80	91	103	116	129	142	156	170	185	199	213	227	240	253

DAY	1	2	3	4	5	6	7	8	9	10	11	12	13	14	15
APR	265	277	289	300	311	322	333	344	355	6	16	27	38	50	61

DAY	16	17	18	19	20	21	22	23	24	25	26	27	28	29	30	31
APR	73	85	97	110	124	137	151	165	179	194	207	221	234	246	258	

DAY	1	2	3	4	5	6	7	8	9	10	11	12	13	14	15
MAY	270	282	293	304	315	325	336	347	358	9	21	32	44	56	68

DAY	16	17	18	19	20	21	22	23	24	25	26	27	28	29	30	31
MAY	80	93	106	120	133	147	161	175	188	202	215	227	240	252	263	274

DAY	1	2	3	4	5	6	7	8	9	10	11	12	13	14	15
JUN	285	296	307	318	329	340	351	3	15	27	39	51	64	77	90

DAY	16	17	18	19	20	21	22	23	24	25	26	27	28	29	30	31
JUN	103	116	130	143	157	170	183	196	209	221	233	244	255	266	277	

DAY	1	2	3	4	5	6	7	8	9	10	11	12	13	14	15
JUL	288	299	310	321	333	345	357	9	22	35	48	61	74	87	101

DAY	16	17	18	19	20	21	22	23	24	25	26	27	28	29	30	31
JUL	114	127	140	153	166	178	190	202	214	226	237	248	259	269	280	291

DAY	1	2	3	4	5	6	7	8	9	10	11	12	13	14	15
AUG	303	314	326	339	351	5	18	31	45	58	72	85	98	111	123

DAY	16	17	18	19	20	21	22	23	24	25	26	27	28	29	30	31
AUG	136	148	160	172	184	196	207	218	229	240	251	261	272	284	295	307

DAY	1	2	3	4	5	6	7	8	9	10	11	12	13	14	15
SEP	320	333	346	0	14	27	41	55	68	81	94	107	119	131	143

DAY	16	17	18	19	20	21	22	23	24	25	26	27	28	29	30	31
SEP	155	166	177	188	199	210	221	232	243	254	265	276	288	301	314	

DAY	1	2	3	4	5	6	7	8	9	10	11	12	13	14	15
OCT	327	341	355	9	23	37	51	64	77	89	102	113	125	136	148

DAY	16	17	18	19	20	21	22	23	24	25	26	27	28	29	30	31
OCT	159	169	180	191	202	213	224	235	246	258	269	282	294	307	321	335

DAY	1	2	3	4	5	6	7	8	9	10	11	12	13	14	15
NOV	349	3	17	31	45	58	71	83	95	106	118	129	139	150	161

DAY	16	17	18	19	20	21	22	23	24	25	26	27	28	29	30	31
NOV	172	183	194	205	216	227	239	251	263	276	288	302	315	329	343	

DAY	1	2	3	4	5	6	7	8	9	10	11	12	13	14	15
DEC	357	11	25	38	51	63	75	87	98	109	120	130	141	152	163

DAY	16	17	18	19	20	21	22	23	24	25	26	27	28	29	30	31
DEC	174	185	197	209	221	233	245	257	270	283	296	310	323	337	351	4

SUN*MOON ANGLES FOR 1968

DAY	1	2	3	4	5	6	7	8	9	10	11	12	13	14	15
JAN	17	30	43	55	66	77	88	99	110	121	132	143	154	166	177

DAY	16	17	18	19	20	21	22	23	24	25	26	27	28	29	30	31
JAN	189	202	214	227	240	252	265	278	292	305	318	331	344	357	10	22

DAY	1	2	3	4	5	6	7	8	9	10	11	12	13	14	15
FEB	34	45	57	68	79	89	100	111	122	134	145	157	170	182	195

DAY	16	17	18	19	20	21	22	23	24	25	26	27	28	29	30	31
FEB	208	221	235	248	261	274	287	300	313	325	338	350	2	14		

DAY	1	2	3	4	5	6	7	8	9	10	11	12	13	14	15
MAR	26	37	48	59	69	80	91	102	114	125	138	150	163	176	190

DAY	16	17	18	19	20	21	22	23	24	25	26	27	28	29	30	31
MAR	203	217	231	244	257	270	283	296	308	320	332	344	355	6	17	28

DAY	1	2	3	4	5	6	7	8	9	10	11	12	13	14	15
APR	39	50	61	72	83	94	106	118	130	143	157	170	184	198	212

DAY	16	17	18	19	20	21	22	23	24	25	26	27	28	29	30	31
APR	226	240	253	266	279	291	302	314	325	337	348	358	9	20	31	

DAY	1	2	3	4	5	6	7	8	9	10	11	12	13	14	15
MAY	42	53	64	75	87	99	111	124	137	151	165	179	194	208	222

DAY	16	17	18	19	20	21	22	23	24	25	26	27	28	29	30	31
MAY	235	248	261	273	285	296	308	319	329	340	351	2	13	24	35	46

DAY	1	2	3	4	5	6	7	8	9	10	11	12	13	14	15
JUN	58	69	81	94	106	119	133	147	161	175	189	203	217	230	243

DAY	16	17	18	19	20	21	22	23	24	25	26	27	28	29	30	31
JUN	255	267	278	290	301	311	322	333	344	355	6	18	29	41	53	

DAY	1	2	3	4	5	6	7	8	9	10	11	12	13	14	15
JUL	65	77	90	103	116	129	143	157	171	185	199	212	224	237	249

DAY	16	17	18	19	20	21	22	23	24	25	26	27	28	29	30	31
JUL	260	271	282	293	304	315	326	337	349	0	12	24	36	48	61	74

DAY	1	2	3	4	5	6	7	8	9	10	11	12	13	14	15
AUG	86	100	113	126	140	154	167	180	193	206	218	230	241	252	263

DAY	16	17	18	19	20	21	22	23	24	25	26	27	28	29	30	31
AUG	274	285	296	307	319	330	342	354	6	19	31	44	57	70	84	97

DAY	1	2	3	4	5	6	7	8	9	10	11	12	13	14	15
SEP	110	123	136	149	162	175	187	199	211	222	233	244	255	266	277

DAY	16	17	18	19	20	21	22	23	24	25	26	27	28	29	30	31
SEP	288	299	311	323	335	348	0	14	27	40	54	67	81	94	107	

DAY	1	2	3	4	5	6	7	8	9	10	11	12	13	14	15
OCT	120	132	144	157	168	180	192	203	214	225	236	247	258	269	280

DAY	16	17	18	19	20	21	22	23	24	25	26	27	28	29	30	31
OCT	291	303	315	328	341	354	8	22	36	50	63	77	90	102	115	127

DAY	1	2	3	4	5	6	7	8	9	10	11	12	13	14	15
NOV	138	150	161	172	183	194	205	216	227	238	249	260	272	283	295

DAY	16	17	18	19	20	21	22	23	24	25	26	27	28	29	30	31
NOV	308	321	334	348	2	17	31	45	58	71	84	96	108	120	131	

DAY	1	2	3	4	5	6	7	8	9	10	11	12	13	14	15
DEC	142	153	164	175	186	197	208	219	230	241	252	264	276	288	301

DAY	16	17	18	19	20	21	22	23	24	25	26	27	28	29	30	31
DEC	314	328	342	356	11	25	38	52	65	77	89	100	112	123	134	144

SUN*MOON ANGLES FOR 1969

DAY	1	2	3	4	5	6	7	8	9	10	11	12	13	14	15
JAN	155	166	177	188	199	210	221	233	244	256	268	281	294	308	321

DAY	16	17	18	19	20	21	22	23	24	25	26	27	28	29	30	31
JAN	335	350	4	17	31	44	56	68	80	91	102	113	124	135	146	157

DAY	1	2	3	4	5	6	7	8	9	10	11	12	13	14	15
FEB	168	179	190	202	214	226	238	250	263	276	289	303	316	330	344

DAY	16	17	18	19	20	21	22	23	24	25	26	27	28	29	30	31
FEB	357	10	23	36	48	59	71	82	93	104	115	126	137			

DAY	1	2	3	4	5	6	7	8	9	10	11	12	13	14	15
MAR	148	159	171	183	195	207	220	233	246	259	272	285	298	312	325

DAY	16	17	18	19	20	21	22	23	24	25	26	27	28	29	30	31
MAR	338	351	3	15	27	39	51	62	73	84	95	106	117	128	139	151

DAY	1	2	3	4	5	6	7	8	9	10	11	12	13	14	15
APR	163	176	189	202	215	228	242	255	268	282	294	307	320	332	344

DAY	16	17	18	19	20	21	22	23	24	25	26	27	28	29	30	31
APR	356	8	20	31	42	53	64	75	86	97	108	120	132	144	157	

DAY	1	2	3	4	5	6	7	8	9	10	11	12	13	14	15
MAY	170	183	197	211	225	238	252	265	278	290	303	315	327	338	350

DAY	16	17	18	19	20	21	22	23	24	25	26	27	28	29	30	31
MAY	1	12	23	34	45	56	67	78	89	101	113	125	138	151	165	179

DAY	1	2	3	4	5	6	7	8	9	10	11	12	13	14	15
JUN	193	207	221	235	248	261	274	286	298	309	321	332	343	354	5

DAY	16	17	18	19	20	21	22	23	24	25	26	27	28	29	30	31
JUN	16	27	38	49	60	71	83	95	107	119	133	146	160	175	189	

DAY	1	2	3	4	5	6	7	8	9	10	11	12	13	14	15
JUL	203	217	231	244	257	269	281	292	304	315	326	337	348	358	9

DAY	16	17	18	19	20	21	22	23	24	25	26	27	28	29	30	31
JUL	20	31	43	54	65	77	89	102	115	129	142	156	171	185	199	213

DAY	1	2	3	4	5	6	7	8	9	10	11	12	13	14	15
AUG	226	239	251	263	274	286	297	308	319	330	341	352	3	14	25

DAY	16	17	18	19	20	21	22	23	24	25	26	27	28	29	30	31
AUG	37	48	60	73	85	98	111	125	139	153	167	180	194	207	220	232

DAY	1	2	3	4	5	6	7	8	9	10	11	12	13	14	15
SEP	244	256	267	278	289	300	311	322	333	344	356	7	19	31	43

DAY	16	17	18	19	20	21	22	23	24	25	26	27	28	29	30	31
SEP	56	69	82	95	108	121	135	148	162	175	188	201	213	225	236	

DAY	1	2	3	4	5	6	7	8	9	10	11	12	13	14	15
OCT	248	259	270	281	292	303	314	325	337	349	1	13	26	39	52

DAY	16	17	18	19	20	21	22	23	24	25	26	27	28	29	30	31
OCT	65	78	91	105	118	131	144	156	169	181	193	205	217	228	239	250

DAY	1	2	3	4	5	6	7	8	9	10	11	12	13	14	15
NOV	261	272	283	294	305	317	329	341	354	7	20	34	48	61	74

DAY	16	17	18	19	20	21	22	23	24	25	26	27	28	29	30	31
NOV	87	100	113	126	138	150	162	174	185	197	208	219	230	241	251	

DAY	1	2	3	4	5	6	7	8	9	10	11	12	13	14	15
DEC	262	273	285	296	308	321	334	347	1	15	29	43	56	70	83

DAY	16	17	18	19	20	21	22	23	24	25	26	27	28	29	30	31
DEC	95	107	120	131	143	154	166	177	188	199	210	220	231	242	253	264

SUN*MOON ANGLES FOR 1970

DAY	1	2	3	4	5	6	7	8	9	10	11	12	13	14	15
JAN	276	288	300	313	326	340	354	9	23	37	50	64	76	89	101

DAY	16	17	18	19	20	21	22	23	24	25	26	27	28	29	30	31
JAN	113	124	135	146	157	168	179	190	201	212	222	234	245	256	268	280

DAY	1	2	3	4	5	6	7	8	9	10	11	12	13	14	15
FEB	293	306	320	334	348	2	16	30	44	57	69	82	93	105	116

DAY	16	17	18	19	20	21	22	23	24	25	26	27	28	29	30	31
FEB	127	138	149	159	170	181	192	203	215	226	238	250	262			

DAY	1	2	3	4	5	6	7	8	9	10	11	12	13	14	15
MAR	274	287	301	314	328	342	356	10	24	37	49	62	74	85	96

DAY	16	17	18	19	20	21	22	23	24	25	26	27	28	29	30	31
MAR	107	118	129	140	151	162	173	184	196	208	220	232	244	257	270	283

DAY	1	2	3	4	5	6	7	8	9	10	11	12	13	14	15
APR	296	310	323	337	350	4	17	30	42	54	65	77	88	99	110

DAY	16	17	18	19	20	21	22	23	24	25	26	27	28	29	30	31
APR	120	131	142	154	165	177	189	202	215	227	240	253	267	280	293	

DAY	1	2	3	4	5	6	7	8	9	10	11	12	13	14	15
MAY	306	319	332	345	358	10	23	35	46	57	68	79	90	101	112

DAY	16	17	18	19	20	21	22	23	24	25	26	27	28	29	30	31
MAY	123	135	146	159	171	184	197	210	224	237	250	264	277	290	303	315

DAY	1	2	3	4	5	6	7	8	9	10	11	12	13	14	15
JUN	328	340	352	4	16	27	39	50	60	71	82	93	104	116	128

DAY	16	17	18	19	20	21	22	23	24	25	26	27	28	29	30	31
JUN	140	153	166	179	193	207	220	234	248	261	274	286	299	311	323	

DAY	1	2	3	4	5	6	7	8	9	10	11	12	13	14	15
JUL	335	347	358	9	20	31	42	53	64	75	86	97	109	121	134

DAY	16	17	18	19	20	21	22	23	24	25	26	27	28	29	30	31
JUL	147	161	175	189	203	217	231	244	257	270	282	294	306	318	329	340

DAY	1	2	3	4	5	6	7	8	9	10	11	12	13	14	15
AUG	351	2	13	24	35	46	57	68	79	91	103	116	129	142	156

DAY	16	17	18	19	20	21	22	23	24	25	26	27	28	29	30	31
AUG	170	185	199	213	227	240	253	265	277	289	300	311	322	333	344	355

DAY	1	2	3	4	5	6	7	8	9	10	11	12	13	14	15
SEP	6	17	28	39	50	62	73	86	98	111	124	138	152	166	180

DAY	16	17	18	19	20	21	22	23	24	25	26	27	28	29	30	31
SEP	194	208	221	234	247	259	271	282	293	304	315	326	336	347	358	

DAY	1	2	3	4	5	6	7	8	9	10	11	12	13	14	15
OCT	10	21	32	44	56	68	81	93	106	120	133	147	161	175	188

DAY	16	17	18	19	20	21	22	23	24	25	26	27	28	29	30	31
OCT	202	215	227	240	251	263	274	285	295	306	317	328	339	351	2	14

DAY	1	2	3	4	5	6	7	8	9	10	11	12	13	14	15
NOV	26	38	51	63	76	89	102	115	129	142	156	169	182	195	207

DAY	16	17	18	19	20	21	22	23	24	25	26	27	28	29	30	31
NOV	219	231	242	254	264	275	286	297	308	319	331	343	355	7	20	

DAY	1	2	3	4	5	6	7	8	9	10	11	12	13	14	15
DEC	33	46	59	72	85	98	111	124	137	150	162	175	187	199	211

DAY	16	17	18	19	20	21	22	23	24	25	26	27	28	29	30	31
DEC	222	233	244	255	265	276	287	299	310	322	334	347	0	13	27	40

SUN*MOON ANGLES FOR 1971

DAY	1	2	3	4	5	6	7	8	9	10	11	12	13	14	15
JAN	54	67	80	93	106	119	131	143	155	167	179	190	201	212	223

DAY	16	17	18	19	20	21	22	23	24	25	26	27	28	29	30	31
JAN	234	245	256	267	278	289	301	314	327	340	353	7	21	35	49	62

DAY	1	2	3	4	5	6	7	8	9	10	11	12	13	14	15
FEB	75	88	101	113	125	137	148	159	170	181	192	203	214	225	236

DAY	16	17	18	19	20	21	22	23	24	25	26	27	28	29	30	31
FEB	247	258	269	281	293	306	319	333	347	1	15	29	43			

DAY	1	2	3	4	5	6	7	8	9	10	11	12	13	14	15
MAR	57	70	82	95	106	118	129	140	151	162	173	184	195	205	216

DAY	16	17	18	19	20	21	22	23	24	25	26	27	28	29	30	31
MAR	228	239	250	262	274	287	300	313	327	341	355	9	23	37	51	63

DAY	1	2	3	4	5	6	7	8	9	10	11	12	13	14	15
APR	76	88	99	110	121	132	143	154	165	176	187	198	209	221	232

DAY	16	17	18	19	20	21	22	23	24	25	26	27	28	29	30	31
APR	244	257	269	282	295	308	322	336	350	4	18	31	44	57	69	

DAY	1	2	3	4	5	6	7	8	9	10	11	12	13	14	15
MAY	80	92	103	113	124	135	146	157	168	180	191	203	215	227	240

DAY	16	17	18	19	20	21	22	23	24	25	26	27	28	29	30	31
MAY	252	265	278	291	305	318	332	346	359	12	25	38	50	61	73	84

DAY	1	2	3	4	5	6	7	8	9	10	11	12	13	14	15
JUN	95	105	116	127	139	150	162	173	186	198	210	223	236	249	262

DAY	16	17	18	19	20	21	22	23	24	25	26	27	28	29	30	31
JUN	275	289	302	315	328	341	354	7	19	31	42	54	65	76	87	

DAY	1	2	3	4	5	6	7	8	9	10	11	12	13	14	15
JUL	98	109	120	131	143	155	168	180	193	206	220	233	246	260	273

DAY	16	17	18	19	20	21	22	23	24	25	26	27	28	29	30	31
JUL	286	299	312	324	337	349	1	13	24	35	46	57	68	79	90	101

DAY	1	2	3	4	5	6	7	8	9	10	11	12	13	14	15
AUG	113	124	136	149	162	175	189	202	216	230	244	257	270	283	295

DAY	16	17	18	19	20	21	22	23	24	25	26	27	28	29	30	31
AUG	308	320	331	343	354	6	17	28	39	49	60	71	82	94	106	118

DAY	1	2	3	4	5	6	7	8	9	10	11	12	13	14	15
SEP	130	143	156	170	184	198	212	226	240	253	266	279	291	302	314

DAY	16	17	18	19	20	21	22	23	24	25	26	27	28	29	30	31
SEP	325	336	347	358	9	20	31	42	53	64	75	87	99	111	124	

DAY	1	2	3	4	5	6	7	8	9	10	11	12	13	14	15
OCT	137	151	165	179	194	208	222	235	248	261	273	284	296	307	318

DAY	16	17	18	19	20	21	22	23	24	25	26	27	28	29	30	31
OCT	329	340	350	1	12	23	34	46	57	69	80	93	105	118	132	146

DAY	1	2	3	4	5	6	7	8	9	10	11	12	13	14	15
NOV	160	174	188	202	216	229	241	254	265	277	288	299	310	320	331

DAY	16	17	18	19	20	21	22	23	24	25	26	27	28	29	30	31
NOV	342	353	4	16	27	39	50	62	75	87	100	113	127	140	154	

DAY	1	2	3	4	5	6	7	8	9	10	11	12	13	14	15
DEC	168	182	195	208	221	233	245	256	268	279	289	300	311	322	333

DAY	16	17	18	19	20	21	22	23	24	25	26	27	28	29	30	31
DEC	345	356	8	20	32	44	57	69	82	95	108	122	135	149	162	175

SUN*MOON ANGLES FOR 1972

DAY	1	2	3	4	5	6	7	8	9	10	11	12	13	14	15
JAN	188	200	212	224	236	247	258	269	280	291	302	313	324	336	348

DAY	16	17	18	19	20	21	22	23	24	25	26	27	28	29	30	31
JAN	0	13	25	38	51	65	78	91	104	117	130	143	155	168	180	192

DAY	1	2	3	4	5	6	7	8	9	10	11	12	13	14	15
FEB	204	215	226	237	248	259	270	281	292	303	315	327	340	353	6

DAY	16	17	18	19	20	21	22	23	24	25	26	27	28	29	30	31
FEB	19	33	46	60	73	87	100	112	125	137	149	161	172	184		

DAY	1	2	3	4	5	6	7	8	9	10	11	12	13	14	15
MAR	195	206	217	228	239	250	261	272	283	295	307	320	333	346	0

DAY	16	17	18	19	20	21	22	23	24	25	26	27	28	29	30	31
MAR	14	28	42	56	69	82	95	107	119	131	142	153	165	176	187	198

DAY	1	2	3	4	5	6	7	8	9	10	11	12	13	14	15
APR	209	220	230	241	253	264	275	287	300	313	326	340	354	9	23

DAY	16	17	18	19	20	21	22	23	24	25	26	27	28	29	30	31
APR	37	51	64	77	89	101	113	124	135	146	157	168	179	190	201	

DAY	1	2	3	4	5	6	7	8	9	10	11	12	13	14	15
MAY	212	223	234	246	257	269	282	294	308	322	336	350	4	18	32

DAY	16	17	18	19	20	21	22	23	24	25	26	27	28	29	30	31
MAY	46	59	71	83	95	106	117	128	139	150	161	172	183	194	205	217

DAY	1	2	3	4	5	6	7	8	9	10	11	12	13	14	15
JUN	228	240	252	265	277	290	304	318	332	346	0	14	27	40	52

DAY	16	17	18	19	20	21	22	23	24	25	26	27	28	29	30	31
JUN	65	76	88	99	110	121	132	143	154	165	176	188	199	211	223	

DAY	1	2	3	4	5	6	7	8	9	10	11	12	13	14	15
JUL	236	248	261	274	288	301	315	328	342	355	8	21	34	46	58

DAY	16	17	18	19	20	21	22	23	24	25	26	27	28	29	30	31
JUL	69	80	91	102	113	124	135	147	158	170	182	194	207	219	232	245

DAY	1	2	3	4	5	6	7	8	9	10	11	12	13	14	15
AUG	258	272	285	298	311	325	338	350	3	15	27	39	50	62	73

DAY	16	17	18	19	20	21	22	23	24	25	26	27	28	29	30	31
AUG	84	94	105	116	128	139	151	163	176	189	202	216	229	242	256	269

DAY	1	2	3	4	5	6	7	8	9	10	11	12	13	14	15
SEP	282	295	308	320	333	345	357	9	20	31	43	54	64	75	86

DAY	16	17	18	19	20	21	22	23	24	25	26	27	28	29	30	31
SEP	97	108	120	132	144	157	170	184	198	212	225	239	253	266	278	

DAY	1	2	3	4	5	6	7	8	9	10	11	12	13	14	15
OCT	291	303	315	327	339	350	1	12	23	34	45	56	67	78	89

DAY	16	17	18	19	20	21	22	23	24	25	26	27	28	29	30	31
OCT	101	112	125	138	151	165	179	193	207	221	235	248	261	273	285	297

DAY	1	2	3	4	5	6	7	8	9	10	11	12	13	14	15
NOV	309	320	331	342	353	4	15	26	37	48	59	70	81	93	105

DAY	16	17	18	19	20	21	22	23	24	25	26	27	28	29	30	31
NOV	118	131	145	159	173	187	201	215	229	242	254	267	278	290	301	

DAY	1	2	3	4	5	6	7	8	9	10	11	12	13	14	15
DEC	312	323	334	345	356	7	17	28	39	51	62	74	86	99	112

DAY	16	17	18	19	20	21	22	23	24	25	26	27	28	29	30	31
DEC	125	139	153	167	181	195	208	222	234	247	259	270	282	293	303	314

DAY	1	2	3	4	5	6	7	8	9	10	11	12	13	14	15
JAN	325	336	347	358	9	20	32	44	55	68	80	93	106	119	133

DAY	16	17	18	19	20	21	22	23	24	25	26	27	28	29	30	31
JAN	147	160	174	188	201	214	226	238	250	261	272	283	294	305	316	327

DAY	1	2	3	4	5	6	7	8	9	10	11	12	13	14	15
FEB	338	349	1	13	25	37	50	62	75	88	101	115	128	141	154

DAY	16	17	18	19	20	21	22	23	24	25	26	27	28	29	30	31
FEB	168	180	193	206	218	229	241	252	263	273	284	295	306			

DAY	1	2	3	4	5	6	7	8	9	10	11	12	13	14	15
MAR	318	329	341	353	6	19	32	45	58	71	84	97	110	123	136

DAY	16	17	18	19	20	21	22	23	24	25	26	27	28	29	30	31
MAR	149	161	174	186	198	209	220	232	243	253	264	275	286	297	309	321

DAY	1	2	3	4	5	6	7	8	9	10	11	12	13	14	15
APR	334	346	0	13	27	40	54	67	81	94	106	119	131	143	155

DAY	16	17	18	19	20	21	22	23	24	25	26	27	28	29	30	31
APR	167	179	190	201	212	223	234	245	256	267	278	290	302	314	327	

DAY	1	2	3	4	5	6	7	8	9	10	11	12	13	14	15
MAY	341	354	8	22	36	50	64	77	89	102	114	126	138	149	161

DAY	16	17	18	19	20	21	22	23	24	25	26	27	28	29	30	31
MAY	172	183	194	205	215	226	237	248	260	271	283	296	308	322	336	350

DAY	1	2	3	4	5	6	7	8	9	10	11	12	13	14	15
JUN	4	18	32	46	59	72	85	97	109	120	132	143	154	165	176

DAY	16	17	18	19	20	21	22	23	24	25	26	27	28	29	30	31
JUN	186	197	208	219	230	242	254	266	278	291	304	317	331	346	0	

DAY	1	2	3	4	5	6	7	8	9	10	11	12	13	14	15
JUL	14	28	41	54	67	79	91	103	114	125	136	147	158	169	180

DAY	16	17	18	19	20	21	22	23	24	25	26	27	28	29	30	31
JUL	191	202	213	225	237	249	261	274	287	300	314	328	342	355	9	23

DAY	1	2	3	4	5	6	7	8	9	10	11	12	13	14	15
AUG	36	49	61	73	85	96	107	118	129	139	150	161	173	184	196

DAY	16	17	18	19	20	21	22	23	24	25	26	27	28	29	30	31
AUG	208	220	232	245	257	270	284	297	310	324	337	351	4	17	30	42

DAY	1	2	3	4	5	6	7	8	9	10	11	12	13	14	15
SEP	54	66	77	88	99	110	121	132	143	154	166	178	190	203	215

DAY	16	17	18	19	20	21	22	23	24	25	26	27	28	29	30	31
SEP	228	241	254	267	280	294	307	320	333	346	359	11	23	35	46	

DAY	1	2	3	4	5	6	7	8	9	10	11	12	13	14	15
OCT	57	68	79	90	101	112	123	135	147	159	171	184	197	211	224

DAY	16	17	18	19	20	21	22	23	24	25	26	27	28	29	30	31
OCT	237	251	264	277	290	303	315	328	340	352	4	15	27	38	49	59

DAY	1	2	3	4	5	6	7	8	9	10	11	12	13	14	15
NOV	70	81	92	103	115	127	139	152	165	178	192	206	219	233	246

DAY	16	17	18	19	20	21	22	23	24	25	26	27	28	29	30	31
NOV	259	272	285	297	310	321	333	345	356	7	18	29	39	50	61	

DAY	1	2	3	4	5	6	7	8	9	10	11	12	13	14	15
DEC	72	83	95	106	118	131	144	158	172	186	200	214	228	241	254

DAY	16	17	18	19	20	21	22	23	24	25	26	27	28	29	30	31
DEC	267	279	291	303	314	325	336	347	358	9	20	30	41	52	63	75

SUN*MOON ANGLES FOR 1974

DAY	1	2	3	4	5	6	7	8	9	10	11	12	13	14	15
JAN	86	98	111	124	137	151	165	179	193	207	221	235	248	260	272

DAY	16	17	18	19	20	21	22	23	24	25	26	27	28	29	30	31
JAN	284	295	306	317	328	338	349	0	11	22	33	44	56	67	79	92

DAY	1	2	3	4	5	6	7	8	9	10	11	12	13	14	15
FEB	104	117	131	145	159	173	187	201	214	227	240	252	264	275	286

DAY	16	17	18	19	20	21	22	23	24	25	26	27	28	29	30	31
FEB	297	308	319	329	340	351	2	14	25	37	49	61	74			

DAY	1	2	3	4	5	6	7	8	9	10	11	12	13	14	15
MAR	86	99	112	126	139	153	167	181	194	207	220	232	244	255	266

DAY	16	17	18	19	20	21	22	23	24	25	26	27	28	29	30	31
MAR	277	288	299	310	321	332	343	355	7	19	31	44	56	69	82	95

DAY	1	2	3	4	5	6	7	8	9	10	11	12	13	14	15
APR	108	122	135	148	162	175	187	200	212	224	235	246	257	268	279

DAY	16	17	18	19	20	21	22	23	24	25	26	27	28	29	30	31
APR	290	301	312	324	336	348	0	13	26	39	52	65	79	92	105	

DAY	1	2	3	4	5	6	7	8	9	10	11	12	13	14	15
MAY	118	131	144	157	169	181	193	204	216	227	238	249	260	271	282

DAY	16	17	18	19	20	21	22	23	24	25	26	27	28	29	30	31
MAY	293	305	317	329	342	355	8	22	35	49	62	76	89	102	115	127

DAY	1	2	3	4	5	6	7	8	9	10	11	12	13	14	15
JUN	139	151	163	175	186	197	208	219	230	241	252	263	274	286	298

DAY	16	17	18	19	20	21	22	23	24	25	26	27	28	29	30	31
JUN	310	323	336	350	4	18	32	46	59	73	86	98	111	123	134	

DAY	1	2	3	4	5	6	7	8	9	10	11	12	13	14	15
JUL	146	157	168	179	190	201	212	223	234	245	256	268	280	292	305

DAY	16	17	18	19	20	21	22	23	24	25	26	27	28	29	30	31
JUL	318	331	345	359	14	28	42	55	69	81	94	105	117	128	139	150

DAY	1	2	3	4	5	6	7	8	9	10	11	12	13	14	15
AUG	161	172	183	194	205	216	227	239	250	262	274	287	300	313	327

DAY	16	17	18	19	20	21	22	23	24	25	26	27	28	29	30	31
AUG	341	355	10	24	37	51	64	76	88	99	110	121	132	143	154	165

DAY	1	2	3	4	5	6	7	8	9	10	11	12	13	14	15
SEP	176	187	198	210	221	233	245	257	269	282	295	309	323	337	351

DAY	16	17	18	19	20	21	22	23	24	25	26	27	28	29	30	31
SEP	5	19	32	45	57	69	80	92	103	114	125	135	146	157	169	

DAY	1	2	3	4	5	6	7	8	9	10	11	12	13	14	15
OCT	180	192	204	215	228	240	253	265	278	292	305	319	332	346	359

DAY	16	17	18	19	20	21	22	23	24	25	26	27	28	29	30	31
OCT	12	25	37	49	61	72	83	94	105	116	127	138	149	161	173	185

DAY	1	2	3	4	5	6	7	8	9	10	11	12	13	14	15
NOV	197	210	222	235	248	261	275	288	301	314	327	340	353	5	17

DAY	16	17	18	19	20	21	22	23	24	25	26	27	28	29	30	31
NOV	29	41	52	63	74	85	96	106	118	129	141	153	165	178	191	

DAY	1	2	3	4	5	6	7	8	9	10	11	12	13	14	15
DEC	204	217	231	244	257	270	284	296	309	321	334	346	357	9	20

DAY	16	17	18	19	20	21	22	23	24	25	26	27	28	29	30	31
DEC	31	42	53	64	75	86	97	108	120	132	144	157	171	184	198	212

DAY	1	2	3	4	5	6	7	8	9	10	11	12	13	14	15
JAN	226	239	253	266	278	291	303	315	326	338	349	0	11	22	33

DAY	16	17	18	19	20	21	22	23	24	25	26	27	28	29	30	31
JAN	44	55	66	77	88	99	111	124	137	150	164	178	192	206	220	234

DAY	1	2	3	4	5	6	7	8	9	10	11	12	13	14	15
FEB	247	260	272	284	296	307	319	330	341	352	3	13	24	35	46

DAY	16	17	18	19	20	21	22	23	24	25	26	27	28	29	30	31
FEB	57	68	80	92	104	116	130	143	157	172	186	200	214			

DAY	1	2	3	4	5	6	7	8	9	10	11	12	13	14	15
MAR	228	241	253	265	277	288	300	311	322	332	343	354	5	16	27

DAY	16	17	18	19	20	21	22	23	24	25	26	27	28	29	30	31
MAR	38	50	61	73	85	98	111	124	138	152	166	180	194	208	221	234

DAY	1	2	3	4	5	6	7	8	9	10	11	12	13	14	15
APR	246	258	269	281	292	302	313	324	335	346	357	9	20	32	44

DAY	16	17	18	19	20	21	22	23	24	25	26	27	28	29	30	31
APR	56	68	81	93	107	120	134	148	161	175	188	202	214	227	238	

DAY	1	2	3	4	5	6	7	8	9	10	11	12	13	14	15
MAY	250	261	272	283	294	305	316	327	339	350	2	14	26	39	51

DAY	16	17	18	19	20	21	22	23	24	25	26	27	28	29	30	31
MAY	64	77	90	104	117	130	144	157	170	183	195	207	219	231	242	253

DAY	1	2	3	4	5	6	7	8	9	10	11	12	13	14	15
JUN	264	275	286	297	308	320	332	344	356	9	21	35	48	61	75

DAY	16	17	18	19	20	21	22	23	24	25	26	27	28	29	30	31
JUN	88	101	114	127	140	152	165	177	189	201	212	223	235	246	256	

DAY	1	2	3	4	5	6	7	8	9	10	11	12	13	14	15
JUL	267	278	290	301	313	325	338	351	4	17	31	45	59	72	85

DAY	16	17	18	19	20	21	22	23	24	25	26	27	28	29	30	31
JUL	98	111	123	136	148	159	171	183	194	205	216	227	238	249	260	271

DAY	1	2	3	4	5	6	7	8	9	10	11	12	13	14	15
AUG	282	294	306	319	332	346	0	14	28	42	55	69	82	95	107

DAY	16	17	18	19	20	21	22	23	24	25	26	27	28	29	30	31
AUG	119	131	142	154	165	176	187	198	209	220	231	242	253	264	276	288

DAY	1	2	3	4	5	6	7	8	9	10	11	12	13	14	15
SEP	300	313	327	341	355	9	24	38	51	64	77	90	101	113	124

DAY	16	17	18	19	20	21	22	23	24	25	26	27	28	29	30	31
SEP	136	147	158	169	180	190	201	212	223	235	246	258	270	282	295	

DAY	1	2	3	4	5	6	7	8	9	10	11	12	13	14	15
OCT	308	322	336	350	5	19	32	46	59	71	83	95	106	117	128

DAY	16	17	18	19	20	21	22	23	24	25	26	27	28	29	30	31
OCT	139	150	161	172	183	194	205	216	228	240	252	264	277	290	303	317

DAY	1	2	3	4	5	6	7	8	9	10	11	12	13	14	15
NOV	331	345	359	13	26	39	51	63	75	87	98	109	119	130	141

DAY	16	17	18	19	20	21	22	23	24	25	26	27	28	29	30	31
NOV	152	163	175	186	198	210	222	234	247	259	272	285	299	312	326	

DAY	1	2	3	4	5	6	7	8	9	10	11	12	13	14	15
DEC	339	352	6	18	31	43	55	66	77	88	99	110	121	132	143

DAY	16	17	18	19	20	21	22	23	24	25	26	27	28	29	30	31
DEC	154	166	178	190	203	216	229	242	255	268	281	294	307	320	333	346

209

SUN*MOON ANGLES FOR 1976

DAY	1	2	3	4	5	6	7	8	9	10	11	12	13	14	15	
JAN	358	10	22	34	45	57	68	78	89	100	111	122	134	146	158	

DAY	16	17	18	19	20	21	22	23	24	25	26	27	28	29	30	31
JAN	170	183	197	210	224	237	250	263	276	289	302	314	327	339	351	2

DAY	1	2	3	4	5	6	7	8	9	10	11	12	13	14	15	
FEB	14	25	36	47	58	69	79	90	102	113	125	137	150	163	177	

DAY	16	17	18	19	20	21	22	23	24	25	26	27	28	29	30	31
FEB	191	205	218	232	246	259	271	284	296	308	320	332	343	354		

DAY	1	2	3	4	5	6	7	8	9	10	11	12	13	14	15	
MAR	5	16	27	38	49	60	70	72	93	105	117	130	143	157	171	

DAY	16	17	18	19	20	21	22	23	24	25	26	27	28	29	30	31
MAR	185	199	213	227	240	253	266	278	290	302	313	324	335	346	357	8

DAY	1	2	3	4	5	6	7	8	9	10	11	12	13	14	15	
APR	19	30	41	52	63	74	86	98	111	124	137	151	165	180	194	

DAY	16	17	18	19	20	21	22	23	24	25	26	27	28	29	30	31
APR	208	221	235	248	260	272	283	295	306	317	328	339	349	0	11	

DAY	1	2	3	4	5	6	7	8	9	10	11	12	13	14	15	
MAY	22	33	45	56	68	80	93	106	119	133	147	161	175	189	202	

DAY	16	17	18	19	20	21	22	23	24	25	26	27	28	29	30	31
MAY	216	229	241	253	265	276	287	298	309	320	331	342	353	4	16	27

DAY	1	2	3	4	5	6	7	8	9	10	11	12	13	14	15	
JUN	39	51	64	76	89	102	116	129	143	157	170	184	197	210	223	

DAY	16	17	18	19	20	21	22	23	24	25	26	27	28	29	30	31
JUN	235	246	258	269	280	291	302	313	324	335	346	358	10	22	35	

DAY	1	2	3	4	5	6	7	8	9	10	11	12	13	14	15	
JUL	48	60	73	87	100	113	126	140	153	166	179	192	204	216	228	

DAY	16	17	18	19	20	21	22	23	24	25	26	27	28	29	30	31
JUL	239	250	261	272	283	294	305	316	328	340	352	5	18	31	44	57

DAY	1	2	3	4	5	6	7	8	9	10	11	12	13	14	15	
AUG	71	84	97	110	123	136	149	161	174	186	197	209	220	231	242	

DAY	16	17	18	19	20	21	22	23	24	25	26	27	28	29	30	31
AUG	253	264	275	286	297	309	321	334	347	0	14	27	41	54	68	81

DAY	1	2	3	4	5	6	7	8	9	10	11	12	13	14	15	
SEP	94	107	119	132	144	156	168	179	190	202	212	223	234	245	256	

DAY	16	17	18	19	20	21	22	23	24	25	26	27	28	29	30	31
SEP	267	278	290	302	315	328	341	355	9	23	37	51	64	77	90	

DAY	1	2	3	4	5	6	7	8	9	10	11	12	13	14	15	
OCT	102	115	126	138	149	161	172	183	194	204	215	226	237	248	259	

DAY	16	17	18	19	20	21	22	23	24	25	26	27	28	29	30	31
OCT	271	283	295	308	322	335	349	4	18	32	46	59	72	84	96	108

DAY	1	2	3	4	5	6	7	8	9	10	11	12	13	14	15	
NOV	120	131	142	153	164	174	185	196	207	218	229	241	252	264	276	

DAY	16	17	18	19	20	21	22	23	24	25	26	27	28	29	30	31
NOV	289	302	316	329	343	358	12	26	39	52	65	77	89	100	112	

DAY	1	2	3	4	5	6	7	8	9	10	11	12	13	14	15	
DEC	122	133	144	155	166	177	188	199	210	222	234	246	258	270	283	

DAY	16	17	18	19	20	21	22	23	24	25	26	27	28	29	30	31
DEC	296	310	324	337	351	5	19	32	45	57	69	80	91	102	113	124

DAY	1	2	3	4	5	6	7	8	9	10	11	12	13	14	15
JAN	135	146	157	168	179	191	203	215	227	240	252	265	278	291	305

DAY	16	17	18	19	20	21	22	23	24	25	26	27	28	29	30	31
JAN	318	332	345	358	11	24	36	48	60	71	82	93	103	114	125	136

DAY	1	2	3	4	5	6	7	8	9	10	11	12	13	14	15
FEB	148	159	171	184	196	209	222	235	248	261	274	287	300	313	326

DAY	16	17	18	19	20	21	22	23	24	25	26	27	28	29	30	31
FEB	339	351	4	16	28	39	50	61	72	83	94	105	116			

DAY	1	2	3	4	5	6	7	8	9	10	11	12	13	14	15
MAR	127	139	151	164	177	190	203	217	230	243	257	270	283	295	308

DAY	16	17	18	19	20	21	22	23	24	25	26	27	28	29	30	31
MAR	320	333	345	356	8	19	30	41	52	63	74	85	96	107	119	131

DAY	1	2	3	4	5	6	7	8	9	10	11	12	13	14	15
APR	144	157	170	184	198	212	226	239	253	266	278	291	303	315	326

DAY	16	17	18	19	20	21	22	23	24	25	26	27	28	29	30	31
APR	338	349	0	11	22	33	44	55	66	77	89	100	112	125	138	

DAY	1	2	3	4	5	6	7	8	9	10	11	12	13	14	15
MAY	151	165	179	193	207	221	235	248	261	274	286	297	309	320	331

DAY	16	17	18	19	20	21	22	23	24	25	26	27	28	29	30	31
MAY	342	353	4	14	25	36	47	59	70	82	94	106	119	132	146	160

DAY	1	2	3	4	5	6	7	8	9	10	11	12	13	14	15
JUN	174	189	203	217	230	243	256	268	280	291	302	313	324	335	346

DAY	16	17	18	19	20	21	22	23	24	25	26	27	28	29	30	31
JUN	357	8	19	30	41	53	65	77	89	102	115	128	142	156	170	

DAY	1	2	3	4	5	6	7	8	9	10	11	12	13	14	15
JUL	185	198	212	225	238	250	262	273	284	295	306	317	328	339	350

DAY	16	17	18	19	20	21	22	23	24	25	26	27	28	29	30	31
JUL	1	13	24	36	48	60	73	85	98	112	125	139	153	166	180	194

DAY	1	2	3	4	5	6	7	8	9	10	11	12	13	14	15
AUG	206	219	231	243	254	265	276	287	298	309	320	332	343	355	7

DAY	16	17	18	19	20	21	22	23	24	25	26	27	28	29	30	31
AUG	19	31	44	56	69	82	96	109	122	136	149	162	175	188	200	212

DAY	1	2	3	4	5	6	7	8	9	10	11	12	13	14	15
SEP	224	235	246	257	268	279	290	301	313	324	336	348	1	14	27

DAY	16	17	18	19	20	21	22	23	24	25	26	27	28	29	30	31
SEP	40	53	66	79	93	106	119	132	145	157	169	181	193	205	216	

DAY	1	2	3	4	5	6	7	8	9	10	11	12	13	14	15
OCT	227	238	249	260	271	282	293	305	317	329	342	355	8	22	35

DAY	16	17	18	19	20	21	22	23	24	25	26	27	28	29	30	31
OCT	49	63	76	89	102	115	127	139	151	163	174	185	196	207	218	229

DAY	1	2	3	4	5	6	7	8	9	10	11	12	13	14	15
NOV	240	251	262	273	285	297	309	322	335	348	2	16	30	44	58

DAY	16	17	18	19	20	21	22	23	24	25	26	27	28	29	30	31
NOV	71	84	97	109	121	132	144	155	166	177	188	199	210	220	231	

DAY	1	2	3	4	5	6	7	8	9	10	11	12	13	14	15
DEC	242	254	265	277	289	301	314	328	342	356	10	25	39	52	65

DAY	16	17	18	19	20	21	22	23	24	25	26	27	28	29	30	31
DEC	78	90	102	113	125	136	147	157	168	179	190	201	212	223	234	246

211

SUN*MOON ANGLES FOR 1978

DAY	1	2	3	4	5	6	7	8	9	10	11	12	13	14	15
JAN	257	269	282	295	308	322	336	350	4	18	32	45	58	70	82

DAY	16	17	18	19	20	21	22	23	24	25	26	27	28	29	30	31
JAN	94	105	116	127	138	148	159	170	181	193	204	215	227	239	251	263

DAY	1	2	3	4	5	6	7	8	9	10	11	12	13	14	15
FEB	276	289	302	316	330	344	358	11	25	38	50	62	74	85	96

DAY	16	17	18	19	20	21	22	23	24	25	26	27	28	29	30	31
FEB	107	118	128	139	150	162	173	185	196	208	221	233	246			

DAY	1	2	3	4	5	6	7	8	9	10	11	12	13	14	15
MAR	258	271	285	298	311	325	338	352	5	17	30	42	53	65	76

DAY	16	17	18	19	20	21	22	23	24	25	26	27	28	29	30	31
MAR	87	98	108	119	130	142	153	165	177	190	202	215	228	241	254	268

DAY	1	2	3	4	5	6	7	8	9	10	11	12	13	14	15
APR	281	294	307	320	333	345	358	10	22	33	45	56	67	78	89

DAY	16	17	18	19	20	21	22	23	24	25	26	27	28	29	30	31
APR	100	111	122	134	146	158	171	184	197	211	224	238	251	265	278	

DAY	1	2	3	4	5	6	7	8	9	10	11	12	13	14	15
MAY	290	303	315	328	340	351	3	14	26	37	48	59	69	80	92

DAY	16	17	18	19	20	21	22	23	24	25	26	27	28	29	30	31
MAY	103	114	126	139	152	165	179	193	207	221	234	248	261	274	286	299

DAY	1	2	3	4	5	6	7	8	9	10	11	12	13	14	15
JUN	310	322	334	345	356	7	18	29	40	51	62	73	84	96	108

DAY	16	17	18	19	20	21	22	23	24	25	26	27	28	29	30	31
JUN	120	133	146	160	174	189	203	217	231	244	257	270	282	293	305	

DAY	1	2	3	4	5	6	7	8	9	10	11	12	13	14	15
JUL	316	328	339	350	0	11	22	33	44	55	67	78	90	102	115

DAY	16	17	18	19	20	21	22	23	24	25	26	27	28	29	30	31
JUL	128	142	156	170	185	199	213	226	240	252	264	276	288	299	310	321

DAY	1	2	3	4	5	6	7	8	9	10	11	12	13	14	15
AUG	332	343	354	5	16	27	38	49	61	73	85	98	111	124	138

DAY	16	17	18	19	20	21	22	23	24	25	26	27	28	29	30	31
AUG	152	166	181	194	208	221	234	246	258	269	281	292	303	313	324	335

DAY	1	2	3	4	5	6	7	8	9	10	11	12	13	14	15
SEP	346	358	9	20	32	44	56	69	81	94	107	121	135	148	162

DAY	16	17	18	19	20	21	22	23	24	25	26	27	28	29	30	31
SEP	176	189	202	215	227	239	250	262	273	284	294	305	316	327	339	

DAY	1	2	3	4	5	6	7	8	9	10	11	12	13	14	15
OCT	350	2	14	26	39	52	65	78	91	104	117	131	144	157	170

DAY	16	17	18	19	20	21	22	23	24	25	26	27	28	29	30	31
OCT	183	195	207	219	231	242	253	264	275	286	297	308	319	331	343	355

DAY	1	2	3	4	5	6	7	8	9	10	11	12	13	14	15
NOV	8	21	34	47	61	74	87	100	113	126	139	151	163	175	187

DAY	16	17	18	19	20	21	22	23	24	25	26	27	28	29	30	31
NOV	199	210	222	233	244	254	265	276	287	299	310	323	335	348	2	

DAY	1	2	3	4	5	6	7	8	9	10	11	12	13	14	15
DEC	15	29	43	56	70	83	96	108	120	133	145	156	168	179	190

DAY	16	17	18	19	20	21	22	23	24	25	26	27	28	29	30	31
DEC	202	212	223	234	245	256	267	278	290	302	315	328	341	355	9	23

DAY	1	2	3	4	5	6	7	8	9	10	11	12	13	14	15
JAN	37	51	64	77	90	102	114	126	137	149	160	171	182	193	203

DAY	16	17	18	19	20	21	22	23	24	25	26	27	28	29	30	31
JAN	214	225	236	247	258	270	282	294	307	321	334	349	3	17	31	45

DAY	1	2	3	4	5	6	7	8	9	10	11	12	13	14	15
FEB	58	71	83	95	107	118	129	140	151	162	173	184	195	205	216

DAY	16	17	18	19	20	21	22	23	24	25	26	27	28	29	30	31
FEB	228	239	251	263	275	288	301	315	328	343	357	11	25			

DAY	1	2	3	4	5	6	7	8	9	10	11	12	13	14	15
MAR	38	51	64	76	87	99	110	121	132	143	153	164	175	186	198

DAY	16	17	18	19	20	21	22	23	24	25	26	27	28	29	30	31
MAR	209	221	233	245	257	270	283	296	310	323	337	351	5	18	31	44

DAY	1	2	3	4	5	6	7	8	9	10	11	12	13	14	15
APR	56	68	79	90	101	112	123	134	145	156	167	179	191	203	215

DAY	16	17	18	19	20	21	22	23	24	25	26	27	28	29	30	31
APR	227	240	253	266	279	292	306	319	332	346	359	12	24	36	48	

DAY	1	2	3	4	5	6	7	8	9	10	11	12	13	14	15
MAY	60	71	82	93	104	115	126	137	148	160	172	185	197	210	223

DAY	16	17	18	19	20	21	22	23	24	25	26	27	28	29	30	31
MAY	237	250	263	276	289	302	315	328	341	353	6	18	29	41	52	63

DAY	1	2	3	4	5	6	7	8	9	10	11	12	13	14	15
JUN	74	85	96	107	118	129	141	154	166	180	193	206	220	233	247

DAY	16	17	18	19	20	21	22	23	24	25	26	27	28	29	30	31
JUN	260	273	286	299	311	324	336	348	0	11	22	33	44	55	66	

DAY	1	2	3	4	5	6	7	8	9	10	11	12	13	14	15
JUL	77	88	99	111	123	135	148	161	175	189	203	217	230	244	257

DAY	16	17	18	19	20	21	22	23	24	25	26	27	28	29	30	31
JUL	270	283	295	307	319	330	342	353	4	15	26	37	48	59	70	81

DAY	1	2	3	4	5	6	7	8	9	10	11	12	13	14	15
AUG	92	104	117	129	143	156	170	185	199	213	227	240	253	266	278

DAY	16	17	18	19	20	21	22	23	24	25	26	27	28	29	30	31
AUG	290	302	313	324	335	346	357	8	19	30	41	52	63	75	86	99

DAY	1	2	3	4	5	6	7	8	9	10	11	12	13	14	15
SEP	111	124	138	152	166	180	194	208	222	235	248	260	272	284	295

DAY	16	17	18	19	20	21	22	23	24	25	26	27	28	29	30	31
SEP	306	317	328	339	350	1	11	23	34	45	57	69	81	94	106	

DAY	1	2	3	4	5	6	7	8	9	10	11	12	13	14	15
OCT	120	133	147	161	175	189	203	216	229	241	253	265	276	287	298

DAY	16	17	18	19	20	21	22	23	24	25	26	27	28	29	30	31
OCT	309	320	331	342	353	4	16	27	39	51	64	76	89	102	115	129

DAY	1	2	3	4	5	6	7	8	9	10	11	12	13	14	15
NOV	142	156	169	183	196	209	221	234	245	256	267	278	289	300	311

DAY	16	17	18	19	20	21	22	23	24	25	26	27	28	29	30	31
NOV	322	333	345	356	9	21	33	46	59	72	85	98	111	124	137	

DAY	1	2	3	4	5	6	7	8	9	10	11	12	13	14	15
DEC	150	163	176	189	201	213	225	236	247	258	269	279	290	301	313

DAY	16	17	18	19	20	21	22	23	24	25	26	27	28	29	30	31
DEC	324	336	349	1	14	27	41	54	67	80	93	106	119	132	144	157

DAY	1	2	3	4	5	6	7	8	9	10	11	12	13	14	15
JAN	169	181	193	204	215	226	237	248	259	270	281	292	304	316	328

DAY	16	17	18	19	20	21	22	23	24	25	26	27	28	29	30	31
JAN	341	354	8	21	35	49	62	75	88	101	114	126	138	150	161	173

DAY	1	2	3	4	5	6	7	8	9	10	11	12	13	14	15
FEB	184	195	206	217	228	238	249	260	272	283	295	308	320	334	347

DAY	16	17	18	19	20	21	22	23	24	25	26	27	28	29	30	31
FEB	1	15	29	43	57	70	83	96	108	120	131	142	154	165		

DAY	1	2	3	4	5	6	7	8	9	10	11	12	13	14	15
MAR	176	187	198	208	219	230	241	253	264	276	288	301	314	328	342

DAY	16	17	18	19	20	21	22	23	24	25	26	27	28	29	30	31
MAR	356	10	24	38	52	65	78	90	102	113	124	135	146	157	168	179

DAY	1	2	3	4	5	6	7	8	9	10	11	12	13	14	15
APR	189	200	212	223	234	246	258	270	282	295	309	323	337	351	5

DAY	16	17	18	19	20	21	22	23	24	25	26	27	28	29	30	31
APR	19	33	46	59	71	83	94	105	116	127	138	149	160	171	182	

DAY	1	2	3	4	5	6	7	8	9	10	11	12	13	14	15
MAY	193	205	217	228	240	253	265	278	291	305	318	332	346	360	14

DAY	16	17	18	19	20	21	22	23	24	25	26	27	28	29	30	31
MAY	27	40	52	64	75	87	98	109	119	130	141	152	164	175	187	199

DAY	1	2	3	4	5	6	7	8	9	10	11	12	13	14	15
JUN	211	224	236	249	262	275	288	302	315	329	342	355	8	21	33

DAY	16	17	18	19	20	21	22	23	24	25	26	27	28	29	30	31
JUN	45	56	68	79	90	101	112	123	134	145	157	169	181	194	207	

DAY	1	2	3	4	5	6	7	8	9	10	11	12	13	14	15
JUL	220	233	246	259	272	286	299	312	325	338	350	3	15	26	38

DAY	16	17	18	19	20	21	22	23	24	25	26	27	28	29	30	31
JUL	49	60	71	82	93	104	115	127	139	151	163	176	189	203	216	230

DAY	1	2	3	4	5	6	7	8	9	10	11	12	13	14	15
AUG	243	257	270	283	296	308	321	333	345	357	8	19	30	41	52

DAY	16	17	18	19	20	21	22	23	24	25	26	27	28	29	30	31
AUG	63	74	85	96	108	120	132	145	158	171	185	199	213	227	240	254

DAY	1	2	3	4	5	6	7	8	9	10	11	12	13	14	15
SEP	267	279	292	304	316	327	339	350	1	12	23	34	45	55	66

DAY	16	17	18	19	20	21	22	23	24	25	26	27	28	29	30	31
SEP	78	89	101	113	125	138	152	166	180	194	208	222	236	249	262	

DAY	1	2	3	4	5	6	7	8	9	10	11	12	13	14	15
OCT	274	286	298	309	320	331	342	353	4	15	26	37	48	59	71

DAY	16	17	18	19	20	21	22	23	24	25	26	27	28	29	30	31
OCT	82	94	106	119	133	146	160	175	189	203	217	230	243	256	268	279

DAY	1	2	3	4	5	6	7	8	9	10	11	12	13	14	15
NOV	291	302	313	323	334	345	356	7	18	29	41	52	64	76	88

DAY	16	17	18	19	20	21	22	23	24	25	26	27	28	29	30	31
NOV	101	114	127	141	155	169	183	197	210	223	236	248	260	271	282	

DAY	1	2	3	4	5	6	7	8	9	10	11	12	13	14	15
DEC	293	304	315	325	336	348	359	10	22	34	45	58	70	83	96

DAY	16	17	18	19	20	21	22	23	24	25	26	27	28	29	30	31
DEC	109	122	136	149	163	177	190	203	215	227	239	250	261	272	283	294

DAY	1	2	3	4	5	6	7	8	9	10	11	12	13	14	15
JAN	305	316	327	338	350	2	14	26	39	52	64	77	90	104	117

DAY	16	17	18	19	20	21	22	23	24	25	26	27	28	29	30	31
JAN	130	143	156	169	182	194	206	218	229	240	251	262	273	284	295	306

DAY	1	2	3	4	5	6	7	8	9	10	11	12	13	14	15
FEB	318	329	342	354	7	20	33	46	60	73	86	99	112	125	138

DAY	16	17	18	19	20	21	22	23	24	25	26	27	28	29	30	31
FEB	150	162	174	186	197	209	220	231	242	253	263	274	286			

DAY	1	2	3	4	5	6	7	8	9	10	11	12	13	14	15
MAR	297	309	321	334	347	0	14	28	42	55	69	82	95	107	120

DAY	16	17	18	19	20	21	22	23	24	25	26	27	28	29	30	31
MAR	132	144	155	167	178	189	200	211	222	233	244	255	266	277	289	301

DAY	1	2	3	4	5	6	7	8	9	10	11	12	13	14	15
APR	314	327	341	355	9	23	37	51	64	77	90	102	114	126	137

DAY	16	17	18	19	20	21	22	23	24	25	26	27	28	29	30	31
APR	148	159	170	181	192	203	214	225	236	247	259	270	282	295	308	

DAY	1	2	3	4	5	6	7	8	9	10	11	12	13	14	15
MAY	322	336	350	4	18	32	46	59	72	84	96	108	119	130	141

DAY	16	17	18	19	20	21	22	23	24	25	26	27	28	29	30	31
MAY	152	163	174	185	196	207	218	229	241	253	265	277	290	304	317	331

DAY	1	2	3	4	5	6	7	8	9	10	11	12	13	14	15
JUN	346	0	14	28	41	54	66	78	90	101	112	123	134	145	156

DAY	16	17	18	19	20	21	22	23	24	25	26	27	28	29	30	31
JUN	167	178	189	201	212	224	236	248	261	274	287	300	314	328	342	

DAY	1	2	3	4	5	6	7	8	9	10	11	12	13	14	15
JUL	355	9	22	35	48	60	71	83	94	105	116	127	138	149	160

DAY	16	17	18	19	20	21	22	23	24	25	26	27	28	29	30	31
JUL	171	183	195	207	219	232	245	258	271	284	297	311	324	338	351	4

DAY	1	2	3	4	5	6	7	8	9	10	11	12	13	14	15
AUG	17	29	41	53	64	75	86	97	108	119	130	141	153	165	177

DAY	16	17	18	19	20	21	22	23	24	25	26	27	28	29	30	31
AUG	190	202	215	228	242	255	268	281	295	308	321	333	346	358	10	22

DAY	1	2	3	4	5	6	7	8	9	10	11	12	13	14	15
SEP	34	45	56	67	78	89	100	111	122	134	146	158	171	184	198

DAY	16	17	18	19	20	21	22	23	24	25	26	27	28	29	30	31
SEP	211	225	239	252	265	278	291	304	316	328	340	352	3	15	26	

DAY	1	2	3	4	5	6	7	8	9	10	11	12	13	14	15
OCT	37	48	59	69	80	91	103	114	126	139	152	165	179	193	207

DAY	16	17	18	19	20	21	22	23	24	25	26	27	28	29	30	31
OCT	221	235	248	261	274	286	298	310	322	333	345	356	7	18	29	39

DAY	1	2	3	4	5	6	7	8	9	10	11	12	13	14	15
NOV	50	61	72	83	95	107	119	132	145	159	173	188	202	216	230

DAY	16	17	18	19	20	21	22	23	24	25	26	27	28	29	30	31
NOV	243	256	268	280	292	303	314	326	337	347	358	9	20	31	42	

DAY	1	2	3	4	5	6	7	8	9	10	11	12	13	14	15
DEC	53	64	75	87	100	112	125	139	153	167	181	196	209	223	236

DAY	16	17	18	19	20	21	22	23	24	25	26	27	28	29	30	31
DEC	249	261	273	284	295	306	317	328	339	349	0	11	22	34	45	57

215

SUN*MOON ANGLES FOR 1982

```
DAY    1    2    3    4    5    6    7    8    9   10   11   12   13   14   15
JAN   69   81   93  106  120  133  147  161  175  189  202  215  228  240  252

DAY   16   17   18   19   20   21   22   23   24   25   26   27   28   29   30   31
JAN  264  275  286  297  308  319  329  340  352    3   14   26   38   50   63   75

DAY    1    2    3    4    5    6    7    8    9   10   11   12   13   14   15
FEB   88  101  114  128  141  155  168  182  195  207  220  232  243  255  266

DAY   16   17   18   19   20   21   22   23   24   25   26   27   28   29   30   31
FEB  277  287  298  309  320  331  343  355    7   19   32   45   58

DAY    1    2    3    4    5    6    7    8    9   10   11   12   13   14   15
MAR   71   84   97  110  123  136  149  162  175  187  200  211  223  234  245

DAY   16   17   18   19   20   21   22   23   24   25   26   27   28   29   30   31
MAR  256  267  278  289  300  311  323  335  348    0   13   27   40   54   67   80

DAY    1    2    3    4    5    6    7    8    9   10   11   12   13   14   15
APR   93  106  119  132  144  156  168  180  192  203  215  226  237  247  258

DAY   16   17   18   19   20   21   22   23   24   25   26   27   28   29   30   31
APR  269  280  292  303  316  328  341  355    8   22   36   50   63   76   89

DAY    1    2    3    4    5    6    7    8    9   10   11   12   13   14   15
MAY  102  115  127  139  150  162  174  185  196  207  218  228  239  250  261

DAY   16   17   18   19   20   21   22   23   24   25   26   27   28   29   30   31
MAY  273  284  297  309  322  336  350    4   18   32   46   59   72   85   98  110

DAY    1    2    3    4    5    6    7    8    9   10   11   12   13   14   15
JUN  122  133  144  156  167  178  189  199  210  221  232  243  255  266  279

DAY   16   17   18   19   20   21   22   23   24   25   26   27   28   29   30   31
JUN  291  304  317  331  345    0   14   28   42   55   68   80   92  104  116

DAY    1    2    3    4    5    6    7    8    9   10   11   12   13   14   15
JUL  127  138  149  160  171  182  192  203  215  226  237  249  261  274  287

DAY   16   17   18   19   20   21   22   23   24   25   26   27   28   29   30   31
JUL  300  313  327  341  355    9   23   37   50   62   75   86   98  109  120  131

DAY    1    2    3    4    5    6    7    8    9   10   11   12   13   14   15
AUG  142  153  164  175  186  197  209  220  232  245  257  270  283  296  310

DAY   16   17   18   19   20   21   22   23   24   25   26   27   28   29   30   31
AUG  323  337  351    5   18   31   44   56   68   79   90  101  112  123  134  145

DAY    1    2    3    4    5    6    7    8    9   10   11   12   13   14   15
SEP  156  168  179  191  203  216  228  241  254  267  280  293  306  320  333

DAY   16   17   18   19   20   21   22   23   24   25   26   27   28   29   30   31
SEP  346  359   12   25   37   49   60   71   82   93  104  115  126  137  149

DAY    1    2    3    4    5    6    7    8    9   10   11   12   13   14   15
OCT  161  173  185  198  211  224  237  250  263  276  289  302  315  328  341

DAY   16   17   18   19   20   21   22   23   24   25   26   27   28   29   30   31
OCT  353    6   17   29   40   51   62   73   84   95  106  117  129  141  153  166

DAY    1    2    3    4    5    6    7    8    9   10   11   12   13   14   15
NOV  179  192  206  219  233  246  259  272  285  298  310  323  335  346  358

DAY   16   17   18   19   20   21   22   23   24   25   26   27   28   29   30   31
NOV    9   21   31   42   53   64   75   86   97  108  120  133  146  159  172

DAY    1    2    3    4    5    6    7    8    9   10   11   12   13   14   15
DEC  186  200  214  228  241  255  267  280  292  304  316  327  339  350    1

DAY   16   17   18   19   20   21   22   23   24   25   26   27   28   29   30   31
DEC   12   22   33   44   55   66   77   88  100  112  125  138  152  166  180  194
```

216

DAY	1	2	3	4	5	6	7	8	9	10	11	12	13	14	15
JAN	208	222	236	249	261	274	285	297	308	319	330	341	352	3	13

DAY	16	17	18	19	20	21	22	23	24	25	26	27	28	29	30	31
JAN	24	35	46	57	69	81	93	105	118	131	145	159	173	188	202	215

DAY	1	2	3	4	5	6	7	8	9	10	11	12	13	14	15
FEB	229	242	254	266	278	289	300	311	321	332	343	354	5	16	27

DAY	16	17	18	19	20	21	22	23	24	25	26	27	28	29	30	31
FEB	39	50	62	74	87	99	112	126	139	153	167	181	195			

DAY	1	2	3	4	5	6	7	8	9	10	11	12	13	14	15
MAR	208	221	234	246	258	269	280	291	302	312	323	334	345	357	8

DAY	16	17	18	19	20	21	22	23	24	25	26	27	28	29	30	31
MAR	20	32	44	56	69	82	95	108	121	135	148	162	175	189	201	214

DAY	1	2	3	4	5	6	7	8	9	10	11	12	13	14	15
APR	226	238	249	260	271	282	293	304	315	326	338	349	2	14	26

DAY	16	17	18	19	20	21	22	23	24	25	26	27	28	29	30	31
APR	39	52	65	78	91	104	118	131	144	157	170	182	195	206	218	

DAY	1	2	3	4	5	6	7	8	9	10	11	12	13	14	15
MAY	229	241	252	262	273	284	295	307	318	330	343	355	8	22	35

DAY	16	17	18	19	20	21	22	23	24	25	26	27	28	29	30	31
MAY	48	62	75	88	101	114	127	140	152	164	176	188	199	210	222	233

DAY	1	2	3	4	5	6	7	8	9	10	11	12	13	14	15
JUN	243	254	265	276	288	300	312	324	337	350	4	17	31	45	59

DAY	16	17	18	19	20	21	22	23	24	25	26	27	28	29	30	31
JUN	72	85	98	111	123	135	147	159	170	181	192	203	214	225	236	

DAY	1	2	3	4	5	6	7	8	9	10	11	12	13	14	15
JUL	247	258	269	281	293	305	318	332	345	359	13	28	42	55	69

DAY	16	17	18	19	20	21	22	23	24	25	26	27	28	29	30	31
JUL	82	94	106	118	130	141	152	163	174	185	196	207	218	229	240	252

DAY	1	2	3	4	5	6	7	8	9	10	11	12	13	14	15
AUG	263	275	287	300	313	327	341	355	9	24	38	51	64	77	89

DAY	16	17	18	19	20	21	22	23	24	25	26	27	28	29	30	31
AUG	101	112	123	135	145	156	167	178	189	200	211	223	234	246	258	270

DAY	1	2	3	4	5	6	7	8	9	10	11	12	13	14	15
SEP	282	295	309	323	337	351	5	19	33	46	59	71	83	94	105

DAY	16	17	18	19	20	21	22	23	24	25	26	27	28	29	30	31
SEP	116	127	138	149	160	171	182	193	205	217	228	240	253	265	278	

DAY	1	2	3	4	5	6	7	8	9	10	11	12	13	14	15
OCT	291	305	318	332	346	0	13	27	39	51	63	75	86	97	108

DAY	16	17	18	19	20	21	22	23	24	25	26	27	28	29	30	31
OCT	119	130	141	152	163	175	186	198	211	223	235	248	261	274	287	301

DAY	1	2	3	4	5	6	7	8	9	10	11	12	13	14	15
NOV	314	327	341	354	7	19	31	43	55	66	77	88	99	109	121

DAY	16	17	18	19	20	21	22	23	24	25	26	27	28	29	30	31
NOV	132	143	155	167	179	192	205	218	231	244	257	270	283	296	309	

DAY	1	2	3	4	5	6	7	8	9	10	11	12	13	14	15
DEC	322	335	347	359	11	23	34	45	56	67	78	89	100	111	123

DAY	16	17	18	19	20	21	22	23	24	25	26	27	28	29	30	31
DEC	134	146	159	172	185	198	212	226	239	253	266	279	291	304	316	328

SUN*MOON ANGLES FOR 1984

DAY	1	2	3	4	5	6	7	8	9	10	11	12	13	14	15
JAN	340	351	3	14	25	36	47	58	68	79	90	102	114	126	138

DAY	16	17	18	19	20	21	22	23	24	25	26	27	28	29	30	31
JAN	151	165	178	192	206	220	234	248	261	273	286	297	309	321	332	343

DAY	1	2	3	4	5	6	7	8	9	10	11	12	13	14	15
FEB	354	5	16	27	38	48	59	71	82	93	105	118	131	144	158

DAY	16	17	18	19	20	21	22	23	24	25	26	27	28	29	30	31
FEB	172	186	201	215	228	242	255	267	279	290	302	313	324	335		

DAY	1	2	3	4	5	6	7	8	9	10	11	12	13	14	15
MAR	346	357	7	18	29	40	51	63	74	86	98	111	124	138	152

DAY	16	17	18	19	20	21	22	23	24	25	26	27	28	29	30	31
MAR	166	181	195	209	222	235	248	260	271	283	294	305	316	327	337	348

DAY	1	2	3	4	5	6	7	8	9	10	11	12	13	14	15
APR	359	10	22	33	45	56	68	81	93	106	120	133	147	161	175

DAY	16	17	18	19	20	21	22	23	24	25	26	27	28	29	30	31
APR	189	203	216	228	240	252	264	275	286	297	308	319	330	341	352	

DAY	1	2	3	4	5	6	7	8	9	10	11	12	13	14	15
MAY	3	15	27	39	51	64	77	90	103	116	130	143	157	170	184

DAY	16	17	18	19	20	21	22	23	24	25	26	27	28	29	30	31
MAY	196	209	221	233	245	256	267	278	289	300	311	322	333	345	357	9

DAY	1	2	3	4	5	6	7	8	9	10	11	12	13	14	15
JUN	22	34	47	60	74	87	100	113	127	140	153	166	178	190	202

DAY	16	17	18	19	20	21	22	23	24	25	26	27	28	29	30	31
JUN	214	226	237	248	259	270	281	292	303	315	327	339	351	4	17	

DAY	1	2	3	4	5	6	7	8	9	10	11	12	13	14	15
JUL	31	44	58	71	84	98	111	123	136	148	160	172	184	196	207

DAY	16	17	18	19	20	21	22	23	24	25	26	27	28	29	30	31
JUL	218	229	240	251	262	273	284	296	308	320	333	346	0	13	27	41

DAY	1	2	3	4	5	6	7	8	9	10	11	12	13	14	15
AUG	55	68	82	95	107	119	131	143	155	166	178	189	200	211	222

DAY	16	17	18	19	20	21	22	23	24	25	26	27	28	29	30	31
AUG	233	244	255	266	277	289	301	314	327	341	355	9	24	38	51	65

DAY	1	2	3	4	5	6	7	8	9	10	11	12	13	14	15
SEP	78	90	102	114	126	137	149	160	171	182	193	204	214	225	236

DAY	16	17	18	19	20	21	22	23	24	25	26	27	28	29	30	31
SEP	248	259	271	283	295	309	322	336	350	5	19	33	47	60	72	

DAY	1	2	3	4	5	6	7	8	9	10	11	12	13	14	15
OCT	85	96	108	119	130	141	152	163	174	185	196	207	218	229	241

DAY	16	17	18	19	20	21	22	23	24	25	26	27	28	29	30	31
OCT	253	265	277	290	303	317	331	345	359	13	27	40	53	65	77	89

DAY	1	2	3	4	5	6	7	8	9	10	11	12	13	14	15
NOV	100	111	122	133	144	155	166	177	188	199	211	223	235	247	259

DAY	16	17	18	19	20	21	22	23	24	25	26	27	28	29	30	31
NOV	272	285	299	312	326	340	353	7	20	33	45	57	69	80	91	

DAY	1	2	3	4	5	6	7	8	9	10	11	12	13	14	15
DEC	102	113	124	135	146	157	168	180	192	204	216	229	242	255	268

DAY	16	17	18	19	20	21	22	23	24	25	26	27	28	29	30	31
DEC	281	294	307	320	334	347	0	12	25	37	48	60	71	82	92	103

SUN*MOON ANGLES FOR 1985

```
DAY    1    2    3    4    5    6    7    8    9   10   11   12   13   14   15
JAN  114  125  136  148  160  172  185  197  210  224  237  250  263  276  289

DAY   16   17   18   19   20   21   22   23   24   25   26   27   28   29   30   31
JAN  302  315  327  340  352    4   16   28   39   50   61   72   82   93  104  116

DAY    1    2    3    4    5    6    7    8    9   10   11   12   13   14   15
FEB  127  139  152  164  178  191  205  218  232  246  259  272  284  297  309

DAY   16   17   18   19   20   21   22   23   24   25   26   27   28   29   30   31
FEB  321  333  345  356    8   19   30   41   51   62   73   84   95

DAY    1    2    3    4    5    6    7    8    9   10   11   12   13   14   15
MAR  107  119  131  144  157  171  185  199  213  227  241  254  267  279  291

DAY   16   17   18   19   20   21   22   23   24   25   26   27   28   29   30   31
MAR  303  315  326  337  348  359   10   21   32   43   54   65   76   87   99  112

DAY    1    2    3    4    5    6    7    8    9   10   11   12   13   14   15
APR  124  138  151  166  180  194  208  222  235  248  261  273  285  297  308

DAY   16   17   18   19   20   21   22   23   24   25   26   27   28   29   30   31
APR  319  330  341  352    2   13   24   35   46   58   69   81   93  106  119

DAY    1    2    3    4    5    6    7    8    9   10   11   12   13   14   15
MAY  133  147  161  175  189  203  217  230  243  255  267  278  290  301  312

DAY   16   17   18   19   20   21   22   23   24   25   26   27   28   29   30   31
MAY  322  333  344  355    6   17   29   40   52   64   76   89  102  115  129  143

DAY    1    2    3    4    5    6    7    8    9   10   11   12   13   14   15
JUN  156  170  184  198  211  224  236  248  260  271  282  293  304  315  326

DAY   16   17   18   19   20   21   22   23   24   25   26   27   28   29   30   31
JUN  337  348  359   11   23   35   48   60   73   86   99  112  126  139  153

DAY    1    2    3    4    5    6    7    8    9   10   11   12   13   14   15
JUL  166  179  192  205  218  230  241  253  264  275  285  296  307  318  330

DAY   16   17   18   19   20   21   22   23   24   25   26   27   28   29   30   31
JUL  341  353    6   18   31   44   57   70.  83   96  109  123  136  149  162  174

DAY    1    2    3    4    5    6    7    8    9   10   11   12   13   14   15
AUG  187  199  211  222  234  245  256  267  277  288  300  311  323  335  348

DAY   16   17   18   19   20   21   22   23   24   25   26   27   28   29   30   31
AUG    1   14   27   40   54   67   80   94  106  119  132  144  157  169  181  192

DAY    1    2    3    4    5    6    7    8    9   10   11   12   13   14   15
SEP  204  215  226  237  248  258  269  281  292  304  316  329  342  355    9

DAY   16   17   18   19   20   21   22   23   24   25   26   27   28   29   30   31
SEP   23   37   50   64   77   90  103  115  127  139  151  163  174  185  196

DAY    1    2    3    4    5    6    7    8    9   10   11   12   13   14   15
OCT  207  218  228  239  250  261  273  285  297  309  322  336  350    4   18

DAY   16   17   18   19   20   21   22   23   24   25   26   27   28   29   30   31
OCT   32   46   59   72   85   98  110  121  133  144  155  166  177  188  199  209

DAY    1    2    3    4    5    6    7    8    9   10   11   12   13   14   15
NOV  220  231  242  254  265  277  290  303  316  330  344  358   12   26   40

DAY   16   17   18   19   20   21   22   23   24   25   26   27   28   29   30   31
NOV   54   66   79   91  103  114  125  136  147  158  168  179  190  201  212

DAY    1    2    3    4    5    6    7    8    9   10   11   12   13   14   15
DEC  224  235  247  259  271  284  297  310  324  338  352    6   20   33   46

DAY   16   17   18   19   20   21   22   23   24   25   26   27   28   29   30   31
DEC   59   71   83   94  105  116  127  138  148  159  170  182  193  205  216  228
```

219

SUN*MOON ANGLES FOR 1986

```
DAY   1   2   3   4   5   6   7   8   9  10  11  12  13  14  15
JAN 240 253 265 278 291 305 318 332 346 359  13  26  38  51  62

DAY  16  17  18  19  20  21  22  23  24  25  26  27  28  29  30  31
JAN  74  85  96 107 117 128 139 150 162 173 185 197 210 222 235 248

DAY   1   2   3   4   5   6   7   8   9  10  11  12  13  14  15
FEB 260 273 287 300 313 326 340 353   5  18  30  42  53  64  75

DAY  16  17  18  19  20  21  22  23  24  25  26  27  28  29  30  31
FEB  86  97 108 119 130 141 153 165 178 191 204 217 230

DAY   1   2   3   4   5   6   7   8   9  10  11  12  13  14  15
MAR 243 256 269 282 295 308 321 334 346 358  10  21  33  44  55

DAY  16  17  18  19  20  21  22  23  24  25  26  27  28  29  30  31
MAR  66  76  87  98 110 121 133 145 158 171 185 198 212 225 239 252

DAY   1   2   3   4   5   6   7   8   9  10  11  12  13  14  15
APR 265 278 291 303 316 328 339 351   2  13  24  35  46  57  68

DAY  16  17  18  19  20  21  22  23  24  25  26  27  28  29  30  31
APR  79  90 102 114 126 139 152 165 179 193 207 221 235 248 261

DAY   1   2   3   4   5   6   7   8   9  10  11  12  13  14  15
MAY 274 286 298 310 321 333 344 355   6  17  27  38  49  60  72

DAY  16  17  18  19  20  21  22  23  24  25  26  27  28  29  30  31
MAY  83  95 107 120 133 146 160 174 189 203 217 231 244 257 269 281

DAY   1   2   3   4   5   6   7   8   9  10  11  12  13  14  15
JUN 293 304 315 326 337 348 359   9  20  31  43  54  66  77  90

DAY  16  17  18  19  20  21  22  23  24  25  26  27  28  29  30  31
JUN 102 115 128 142 156 170 184 199 212 226 239 251 263 275 286

DAY   1   2   3   4   5   6   7   8   9  10  11  12  13  14  15
JUL 297 308 319 330 341 352   3  14  25  37  49  61  73  85  98

DAY  16  17  18  19  20  21  22  23  24  25  26  27  28  29  30  31
JUL 111 125 138 152 166 180 194 207 220 233 245 256 268 279 290 301

DAY   1   2   3   4   5   6   7   8   9  10  11  12  13  14  15
AUG 312 323 334 345 356   8  20  32  44  56  69  82  95 108 121

DAY  16  17  18  19  20  21  22  23  24  25  26  27  28  29  30  31
AUG 135 149 162 176 189 202 214 226 238 249 260 271 282 293 304 315

DAY   1   2   3   4   5   6   7   8   9  10  11  12  13  14  15
SEP 326 338 350   2  14  27  40  53  66  79  92 105 118 132 145

DAY  16  17  18  19  20  21  22  23  24  25  26  27  28  29  30  31
SEP 158 170 183 195 207 218 230 241 252 263 273 284 296 307 319

DAY   1   2   3   4   5   6   7   8   9  10  11  12  13  14  15
OCT 331 343 356   9  22  35  49  62  75  89 102 115 127 140 152

DAY  16  17  18  19  20  21  22  23  24  25  26  27  28  29  30  31
OCT 164 176 187 199 210 221 232 243 254 265 276 287 299 311 323 336

DAY   1   2   3   4   5   6   7   8   9  10  11  12  13  14  15
NOV 349   3  17  31  44  58  71  85  97 110 122 134 145 157 168

DAY  16  17  18  19  20  21  22  23  24  25  26  27  28  29  30  31
NOV 179 190 201 212 223 234 245 256 267 279 291 303 316 329 343

DAY   1   2   3   4   5   6   7   8   9  10  11  12  13  14  15
DEC 357  11  25  39  53  66  79  92 104 115 127 138 149 160 171

DAY  16  17  18  19  20  21  22  23  24  25  26  27  28  29  30  31
DEC 182 193 203 214 225 236 248 259 271 283 296 309 322 336 350   5
```

SUN*MOON ANGLES FOR 1987

```
DAY    1    2    3    4    5    6    7    8    9   10   11   12   13   14   15
JAN   19   33   47   60   72   84   96  107  118  129  140  151  162  173  184

DAY   16   17   18   19   20   21   22   23   24   25   26   27   28   29   30   31
JAN  195  206  217  228  240  252  264  276  289  303  316  330  344  358   12   26

DAY    1    2    3    4    5    6    7    8    9   10   11   12   13   14   15
FEB   39   52   64   76   87   99  110  120  131  142  153  164  175  187  198

DAY   16   17   18   19   20   21   22   23   24   25   26   27   28   29   30   31
FEB  210  222  234  246  258  271  284  298  311  325  339  352    6

DAY    1    2    3    4    5    6    7    8    9   10   11   12   13   14   15
MAR   19   31   44   56   67   78   90  100  111  122  133  144  156  167  179

DAY   16   17   18   19   20   21   22   23   24   25   26   27   28   29   30   31
MAR  191  203  216  226  241  254  267  280  294  307  320  333  346  359   12   24

DAY    1    2    3    4    5    6    7    8    9   10   11   12   13   14   15
APR   36   47   58   70   81   91  102  113  125  136  148  160  172  185  197

DAY   16   17   18   19   20   21   22   23   24   25   26   27   28   29   30   31
APR  211  224  237  251  264  277  290  303  316  328  341  353    5   16   28

DAY    1    2    3    4    5    6    7    8    9   10   11   12   13   14   15
MAY   39   50   61   72   83   94  105  116  128  140  153  166  179  193  206

DAY   16   17   18   19   20   21   22   23   24   25   26   27   28   29   30   31
MAY  220  234  247  261  274  286  299  311  323  335  347  358    9   20   31   42

DAY    1    2    3    4    5    6    7    8    9   10   11   12   13   14   15
JUN   53   64   75   86   98  109  121  134  147  160  174  188  203  217  231

DAY   16   17   18   19   20   21   22   23   24   25   26   27   28   29   30   31
JUN  244  257  270  282  294  306  318  329  340  351    2   13   24   35   46

DAY    1    2    3    4    5    6    7    8    9   10   11   12   13   14   15
JUL   57   68   80   91  103  116  129  142  156  170  185  199  213  227  240

DAY   16   17   18   19   20   21   22   23   24   25   26   27   28   29   30   31
JUL  253  265  277  289  300  312  323  334  345  356    6   17   28   39   51   62

DAY    1    2    3    4    5    6    7    8    9   10   11   12   13   14   15
AUG   74   86   98  111  124  138  152  166  180  195  208  222  235  247  259

DAY   16   17   18   19   20   21   22   23   24   25   26   27   28   29   30   31
AUG  271  283  294  305  316  327  338  348  360   11   22   33   45   57   69   81

DAY    1    2    3    4    5    6    7    8    9   10   11   12   13   14   15
SEP   94  107  120  134  148  162  176  190  203  216  229  241  253  264  275

DAY   16 ° 17   18   19   20   21   22   23   24   25   26   27   28   29   30   31
SEP  286  297  308  319  330  341  352    4   15   27   39   52   64   77   90

DAY    1    2    3    4    5    6    7    8    9   10   11   12   13   14   15
OCT  103  117  130  144  157  171  184  197  209  221  233  244  256  267  278

DAY   16   17   18   19   20   21   22   23   24   25   26   27   28   29   30   31
OCT  288  299  310  322  333  345  357    9   22   34   47   60   74   87  100  113

DAY    1    2    3    4    5    6    7    8    9   10   11   12   13   14   15
NOV  126  139  152  165  177  189  201  213  224  236  247  257  268  279  290

DAY   16   17   18   19   20   21   22   23   24   25   26   27   28   29   30   31
NOV  301  313  325  337  350    2   16   29   43   56   69   83   96  108  121

DAY    1    2    3    4    5    6    7    8    9   10   11   12   13   14   15
DEC  133  146  158  170  181  193  204  215  226  237  248  259  270  281  292

DAY   16   17   18   19   20   21   22   23   24   25   26   27   28   29   30   31
DEC  304  316  329  342  356   10   24   37   51   65   78   91  103  115  127  139
```

221

SUN*MOON ANGLES FOR   1988

DAY	1	2	3	4	5	6	7	8	9	10	11	12	13	14	15	
JAN	150	162	173	184	195	206	217	228	238	249	260	272	284	296	308	

DAY	16	17	18	19	20	21	22	23	24	25	26	27	28	29	30	31
JAN	322	335	349	3	18	32	45	59	72	84	97	108	120	131	143	154

DAY	1	2	3	4	5	6	7	8	9	10	11	12	13	14	15	
FEB	165	175	186	197	208	219	230	241	252	264	276	289	302	315	329	

DAY	16	17	18	19	20	21	22	23	24	25	26	27	28	29	30	31
FEB	343	357	11	25	39	52	65	77	89	101	112	123	134	145		

DAY	1	2	3	4	5	6	7	8	9	10	11	12	13	14	15	
MAR	156	167	178	189	200	211	222	234	245	258	270	283	296	310	323	

DAY	16	17	18	19	20	21	22	23	24	25	26	27	28	29	30	31
MAR	337	351	5	19	32	45	58	70	82	93	104	115	126	137	147	158

DAY	1	2	3	4	5	6	7	8	9	10	11	12	13	14	15	
APR	169	181	192	204	216	228	240	253	266	279	292	305	319	332	346	

DAY	16	17	18	19	20	21	22	23	24	25	26	27	28	29	30	31
APR	359	13	26	38	50	62	73	85	96	106	117	128	139	150	162	

DAY	1	2	3	4	5	6	7	8	9	10	11	12	13	14	15	
MAY	174	186	198	210	223	236	249	262	275	288	302	315	328	341	354	

DAY	16	17	18	19	20	21	22	23	24	25	26	27	28	29	30	31
MAY	7	19	31	43	54	65	76	87	98	109	120	132	143	155	167	180

DAY	1	2	3	4	5	6	7	8	9	10	11	12	13	14	15	
JUN	193	206	219	233	246	259	273	286	299	311	324	337	349	1	13	

DAY	16	17	18	19	20	21	22	23	24	25	26	27	28	29	30	31
JUN	24	36	47	58	68	79	90	101	113	124	136	149	162	175	189	

DAY	1	2	3	4	5	6	7	8	9	10	11	12	13	14	15	
JUL	202	216	230	243	257	270	283	295	307	320	332	343	355	6	17	

DAY	16	17	18	19	20	21	22	23	24	25	26	27	28	29	30	31
JUL	28	39	50	61	72	83	94	106	118	130	143	157	171	184	199	213

DAY	1	2	3	4	5	6	7	8	9	10	11	12	13	14	15	
AUG	226	240	253	266	279	291	303	314	326	337	348	359	10	21	32	

DAY	16	17	18	19	20	21	22	23	24	25	26	27	28	29	30	31
AUG	43	54	65	76	88	100	112	125	138	152	166	180	194	208	222	236

DAY	1	2	3	4	5	6	7	8	9	10	11	12	13	14	15	
SEP	249	261	274	285	297	308	319	330	341	352	3	14	25	36	47	

DAY	16	17	18	19	20	21	22	23	24	25	26	27	28	29	30	31
SEP	58	70	82	94	107	120	133	147	161	175	189	203	217	230	243	

DAY	1	2	3	4	5	6	7	8	9	10	11	12	13	14	15	
OCT	255	267	279	290	301	312	322	333	344	355	6	17	29	40	52	

DAY	16	17	18	19	20	21	22	23	24	25	26	27	28	29	30	31
OCT	64	76	89	102	115	128	142	156	170	184	197	211	223	236	248	259

DAY	1	2	3	4	5	6	7	8	9	10	11	12	13	14	15	
NOV	270	281	292	303	314	325	336	347	358	10	22	34	46	59	72	

DAY	16	17	18	19	20	21	22	23	24	25	26	27	28	29	30	31
NOV	84	97	110	124	137	151	164	177	190	203	215	227	239	250	261	

DAY	1	2	3	4	5	6	7	8	9	10	11	12	13	14	15	
DEC	272	283	293	304	315	327	339	351	3	15	28	41	54	67	80	

DAY	16	17	18	19	20	21	22	23	24	25	26	27	28	29	30	31
DEC	93	106	119	132	145	158	170	183	195	207	218	229	240	251	262	273

SUN*MOON ANGLES FOR 1989

```
DAY   1   2   3   4   5   6   7   8   9  10  11  12  13  14  15
JAN 284 295 306 318 330 343 356   9  22  35  49  62  75  88 101

DAY  16  17  18  19  20  21  22  23  24  25  26  27  28  29  30  31
JAN 114 127 139 151 163 175 186 198 209 220 230 241 252 263 274 286

DAY   1   2   3   4   5   6   7   8   9  10  11  12  13  14  15
FEB 297 309 322 335 348   2  16  30  44  57  70  83  96 109 121

DAY  16  17  18  19  20  21  22  23  24  25  26  27  28  29  30  31
FEB 133 144 156 167 178 189 200 210 221 232 243 254 266

DAY   1   2   3   4   5   6   7   8   9  10  11  12  13  14  15
MAR 277 289 302 315 328 342 356  10  24  38  52  65  78  90 102

DAY  16  17  18  19  20  21  22  23  24  25  26  27  28  29  30  31
MAR 114 126 137 148 159 170 180 191 202 213 224 235 247 258 270 283

DAY   1   2   3   4   5   6   7   8   9  10  11  12  13  14  15
APR 295 309 322 336 350   5  19  33  46  59  72  84  96 107 118

DAY  16  17  18  19  20  21  22  23  24  25  26  27  28  29  30  31
APR 129 140 151 162 173 183 195 206 217 229 241 253 265 278 290

DAY   1   2   3   4   5   6   7   8   9  10  11  12  13  14  15
MAY 304 318 331 346   0  14  27  40  53  65  77  88 100 110 121

DAY  16  17  18  19  20  21  22  23  24  25  26  27  28  29  30  31
MAY 132 143 154 165 176 188 200 211 224 236 248 261 274 287 300 314

DAY   1   2   3   4   5   6   7   8   9  10  11  12  13  14  15
JUN 328 341 355   8  21  34  46  58  70  81  92 103 114 124 136

DAY  16  17  18  19  20  21  22  23  24  25  26  27  28  29  30  31
JUN 147 158 170 182 194 207 219 232 245 258 271 284 298 311 324

DAY   1   2   3   4   5   6   7   8   9  10  11  12  13  14  15
JUL 337 350   3  16  28  39  51  62  73  84  95 106 117 128 140

DAY  16  17  18  19  20  21  22  23  24  25  26  27  28  29  30  31
JUL 152 164 176 189 202 215 229 242 255 269 282 295 308 321 333 345

DAY   1   2   3   4   5   6   7   8   9  10  11  12  13  14  15
AUG 357   9  21  32  43  54  65  76  87  98 109 121 133 145 158

DAY  16  17  18  19  20  21  22  23  24  25  26  27  28  29  30  31
AUG 171 184 198 212 226 239 253 266 279 292 304 316 328 340 351   2

DAY   1   2   3   4   5   6   7   8   9  10  11  12  13  14  15
SEP  14  25  36  46  57  68  79  91 102 114 126 139 152 166 180

DAY  16  17  18  19  20  21  22  23  24  25  26  27  28  29  30  31
SEP 194 208 222 236 249 262 275 287 299 310 322 333 344 355   6

DAY   1   2   3   4   5   6   7   8   9  10  11  12  13  14  15
OCT  17  28  39  50  61  72  83  95 107 120 133 146 160 174 189

DAY  16  17  18  19  20  21  22  23  24  25  26  27  28  29  30  31
OCT 203 217 231 244 257 269 281 292 303 314 325 336 347 358   9  20

DAY   1   2   3   4   5   6   7   8   9  10  11  12  13  14  15
NOV  31  42  53  65  76  88 101 114 127 141 155 169 183 197 211

DAY  16  17  18  19  20  21  22  23  24  25  26  27  28  29  30  31
NOV 224 237 250 261 273 284 295 306 317 328 339 350   1  12  23

DAY   1   2   3   4   5   6   7   8   9  10  11  12  13  14  15
DEC  35  46  58  70  82  95 108 122 135 149 163 177 191 204 217

DAY  16  17  18  19  20  21  22  23  24  25  26  27  28  29  30  31
DEC 229 241 253 264 275 286 297 308 319 330 341 352   4  15  27  40
```

223

SUN*MOON ANGLES FOR 1990

DAY	1	2	3	4	5	6	7	8	9	10	11	12	13	14	15
JAN	52	64	77	90	103	117	130	144	157	170	183	196	208	220	232

DAY	16	17	18	19	20	21	22	23	24	25	26	27	28	29	30	31
JAN	243	254	265	276	287	298	309	320	332	344	356	8	21	34	46	60

DAY	1	2	3	4	5	6	7	8	9	10	11	12	13	14	15
FEB	73	86	99	112	125	138	151	163	176	188	200	211	223	234	245

DAY	16	17	18	19	20	21	22	23	24	25	26	27	28	29	30	31
FEB	256	266	277	288	300	311	323	336	348	1	14	28	42			

DAY	1	2	3	4	5	6	7	8	9	10	11	12	13	14	15
MAR	55	69	82	95	108	120	133	145	157	168	180	191	203	214	225

DAY	16	17	18	19	20	21	22	23	24	25	26	27	28	29	30	31
MAR	236	246	257	268	280	291	303	315	328	341	355	9	23	37	51	64

DAY	1	2	3	4	5	6	7	8	9	10	11	12	13	14	15
APR	78	90	103	115	127	138	150	161	172	183	194	205	216	227	238

DAY	16	17	18	19	20	21	22	23	24	25	26	27	28	29	30	31
APR	249	260	272	284	296	309	322	336	350	4	18	32	46	60	73	

DAY	1	2	3	4	5	6	7	8	9	10	11	12	13	14	15
MAY	85	97	109	121	132	143	154	165	176	187	198	209	220	231	242

DAY	16	17	18	19	20	21	22	23	24	25	26	27	28	29	30	31
MAY	254	266	278	290	304	317	331	345	0	14	28	41	55	67	80	91

DAY	1	2	3	4	5	6	7	8	9	10	11	12	13	14	15
JUN	103	114	125	136	147	158	169	180	191	202	213	225	237	248	261

DAY	16	17	18	19	20	21	22	23	24	25	26	27	28	29	30	31
JUN	273	286	300	313	327	341	355	9	23	36	49	61	73	85	96	

DAY	1	2	3	4	5	6	7	8	9	10	11	12	13	14	15
JUL	107	118	129	140	151	162	173	185	196	208	220	232	244	257	270

DAY	16	17	18	19	20	21	22	23	24	25	26	27	28	29	30	31
JUL	283	297	310	324	338	351	5	18	30	43	54	66	77	89	100	110

DAY	1	2	3	4	5	6	7	8	9	10	11	12	13	14	15
AUG	121	132	144	155	166	178	190	203	215	228	241	254	267	281	294

DAY	16	17	18	19	20	21	22	23	24	25	26	27	28	29	30	31
AUG	307	320	334	346	359	12	24	36	47	59	70	81	91	102	113	125

DAY	1	2	3	4	5	6	7	8	9	10	11	12	13	14	15
SEP	136	148	160	172	185	198	211	225	238	251	265	278	291	304	316

DAY	16	17	18	19	20	21	22	23	24	25	26	27	28	29	30	31
SEP	329	341	353	5	17	28	39	50	61	72	83	94	105	117	128	

DAY	1	2	3	4	5	6	7	8	9	10	11	12	13	14	15
OCT	140	153	166	179	193	207	221	234	248	261	274	287	299	311	323

DAY	16	17	18	19	20	21	22	23	24	25	26	27	28	29	30	31
OCT	335	346	358	9	20	31	42	53	64	74	86	97	109	121	133	146

DAY	1	2	3	4	5	6	7	8	9	10	11	12	13	14	15
NOV	160	174	188	202	216	230	243	256	269	281	293	305	316	328	339

DAY	16	17	18	19	20	21	22	23	24	25	26	27	28	29	30	31
NOV	350	1	12	22	33	44	55	66	77	89	101	113	126	140	153	

DAY	1	2	3	4	5	6	7	8	9	10	11	12	13	14	15
DEC	168	182	196	210	224	237	250	262	274	286	297	309	320	330	341

DAY	16	17	18	19	20	21	22	23	24	25	26	27	28	29	30	31
DEC	352	3	14	25	36	47	58	70	82	94	107	120	133	147	161	176

SUN*MOON ANGLES FOR 1991

DAY	1	2	3	4	5	6	7	8	9	10	11	12	13	14	15
JAN	190	203	217	230	243	255	266	278	289	300	311	321	332	343	354

DAY	16	17	18	19	20	21	22	23	24	25	26	27	28	29	30	31
JAN	5	16	28	39	51	63	76	88	101	114	128	142	155	169	183	196

DAY	1	2	3	4	5	6	7	8	9	10	11	12	13	14	15
FEB	209	222	234	246	257	269	280	290	301	312	323	334	345	357	9

DAY	16	17	18	19	20	21	22	23	24	25	26	27	28	29	30	31
FEB	21	33	45	58	71	84	97	110	123	136	150	163	176			

DAY	1	2	3	4	5	6	7	8	9	10	11	12	13	14	15
MAR	189	201	214	225	237	248	259	270	281	292	303	314	325	337	349

DAY	16	17	18	19	20	21	22	23	24	25	26	27	28	29	30	31
MAR	1	14	27	40	53	66	80	93	106	119	132	144	157	170	182	194

DAY	1	2	3	4	5	6	7	8	9	10	11	12	13	14	15
APR	206	217	228	239	250	261	272	283	294	306	317	330	342	355	9

DAY	16	17	18	19	20	21	22	23	24	25	26	27	28	29	30	31
APR	22	36	49	63	76	89	102	115	127	139	152	163	175	187	198	

DAY	1	2	3	4	5	6	7	8	9	10	11	12	13	14	15
MAY	209	220	231	242	253	264	275	286	298	310	323	336	350	4	18

DAY	16	17	18	19	20	21	22	23	24	25	26	27	28	29	30	31
MAY	32	46	59	72	85	98	110	122	134	146	157	169	180	191	202	212

DAY	1	2	3	4	5	6	7	8	9	10	11	12	13	14	15
JUN	223	234	245	256	268	280	292	305	318	331	345	359	14	28	42

DAY	16	17	18	19	20	21	22	23	24	25	26	27	28	29	30	31
JUN	55	68	81	93	105	117	129	140	151	162	173	184	194	205	216	

DAY	1	2	3	4	5	6	7	8	9	10	11	12	13	14	15
JUL	227	239	250	262	274	287	300	313	327	341	355	9	23	37	51

DAY	16	17	18	19	20	21	22	23	24	25	26	27	28	29	30	31
JUL	63	76	88	100	111	122	133	144	155	166	177	188	199	210	221	233

DAY	1	2	3	4	5	6	7	8	9	10	11	12	13	14	15
AUG	245	257	270	283	296	309	323	337	351	5	19	32	45	58	70

DAY	16	17	18	19	20	21	22	23	24	25	26	27	28	29	30	31
AUG	81	93	104	115	126	136	147	158	170	181	192	204	216	228	241	253

DAY	1	2	3	4	5	6	7	8	9	10	11	12	13	14	15
SEP	266	279	292	306	319	333	347	0	13	26	39	51	62	74	85

DAY	16	17	18	19	20	21	22	23	24	25	26	27	28	29	30	31
SEP	96	107	117	128	139	151	162	174	186	199	211	224	237	250	263	

DAY	1	2	3	4	5	6	7	8	9	10	11	12	13	14	15
OCT	276	289	302	315	328	342	354	7	19	31	43	54	65	76	87

DAY	16	17	18	19	20	21	22	23	24	25	26	27	28	29	30	31
OCT	98	109	120	131	143	155	167	180	193	206	219	233	246	259	272	285

DAY	1	2	3	4	5	6	7	8	9	10	11	12	13	14	15
NOV	298	311	323	336	348	0	12	23	34	45	56	67	78	89	100

DAY	16	17	18	19	20	21	22	23	24	25	26	27	28	29	30	31
NOV	111	123	135	147	160	173	187	201	214	228	241	255	268	280	293	

DAY	1	2	3	4	5	6	7	8	9	10	11	12	13	14	15
DEC	305	317	329	341	352	3	14	25	36	47	57	68	79	91	102

DAY	16	17	18	19	20	21	22	23	24	25	26	27	28	29	30	31
DEC	114	127	139	153	166	180	194	209	222	236	249	262	275	287	299	310

SUN*MOON ANGLES FOR 1992

DAY	1	2	3	4	5	6	7	8	9	10	11	12	13	14	15	
JAN	321	333	344	354	5	16	27	38	49	60	71	82	94	106	119	

DAY	16	17	18	19	20	21	22	23	24	25	26	27	28	29	30	31
JAN	132	146	160	174	188	202	216	230	243	256	268	280	291	302	313	324

DAY	1	2	3	4	5	6	7	8	9	10	11	12	13	14	15	
FEB	335	346	356	7	18	29	40	52	63	75	87	100	113	126	140	

DAY	16	17	18	19	20	21	22	23	24	25	26	27	28	29	30	31
FEB	154	168	182	196	210	223	236	248	260	271	283	294	304	315		

DAY	1	2	3	4	5	6	7	8	9	10	11	12	13	14	15	
MAR	326	337	348	359	10	22	33	45	57	69	82	94	108	121	134	

DAY	16	17	18	19	20	21	22	23	24	25	26	27	28	29	30	31
MAR	148	162	176	190	203	216	228	240	252	263	274	285	296	306	317	328

DAY	1	2	3	4	5	6	7	8	9	10	11	12	13	14	15	
APR	340	351	3	15	27	39	52	65	78	91	104	117	130	144	157	

DAY	16	17	18	19	20	21	22	23	24	25	26	27	28	29	30	31
APR	170	183	196	208	220	232	243	254	265	276	287	298	309	320	332	

DAY	1	2	3	4	5	6	7	8	9	10	11	12	13	14	15	
MAY	344	356	9	22	35	48	61	74	87	101	114	127	140	153	165	

DAY	16	17	18	19	20	21	22	23	24	25	26	27	28	29	30	31
MAY	177	189	201	213	224	235	246	257	268	279	290	301	313	325	338	351

DAY	1	2	3	4	5	6	7	8	9	10	11	12	13	14	15	
JUN	4	17	31	44	58	71	85	98	111	123	136	148	160	171	183	

DAY	16	17	18	19	20	21	22	23	24	25	26	27	28	29	30	31
JUN	194	205	216	227	238	249	260	271	283	295	307	319	332	346	359	

DAY	1	2	3	4	5	6	7	8	9	10	11	12	13	14	15	
JUL	13	27	41	55	68	82	94	107	119	131	142	154	165	176	187	

DAY	16	17	18	19	20	21	22	23	24	25	26	27	28	29	30	31
JUL	198	209	220	231	242	253	265	276	288	301	314	327	341	355	9	23

DAY	1	2	3	4	5	6	7	8	9	10	11	12	13	14	15	
AUG	38	51	65	78	90	102	114	125	136	147	158	169	180	191	202	

DAY	16	17	18	19	20	21	22	23	24	25	26	27	28	29	30	31
AUG	213	224	235	247	259	270	283	296	309	322	336	351	5	19	33	47

DAY	1	2	3	4	5	6	7	8	9	10	11	12	13	14	15	
SEP	60	72	84	96	107	118	129	140	151	162	173	184	195	206	218	

DAY	16	17	18	19	20	21	22	23	24	25	26	27	28	29	30	31
SEP	229	241	253	265	278	291	304	318	332	346	0	14	28	41	53	

DAY	1	2	3	4	5	6	7	8	9	10	11	12	13	14	15	
OCT	65	77	88	100	110	121	132	143	154	165	177	188	200	212	224	

DAY	16	17	18	19	20	21	22	23	24	25	26	27	28	29	30	31
OCT	236	248	261	274	287	300	314	328	341	355	8	21	33	46	57	69

DAY	1	2	3	4	5	6	7	8	9	10	11	12	13	14	15	
NOV	80	91	102	112	123	134	146	157	169	181	193	205	218	231	244	

DAY	16	17	18	19	20	21	22	23	24	25	26	27	28	29	30	31
NOV	257	270	283	296	309	323	336	348	1	13	25	37	48	59	70	

DAY	1	2	3	4	5	6	7	8	9	10	11	12	13	14	15	
DEC	81	92	103	114	125	137	149	161	173	186	199	212	226	239	252	

DAY	16	17	18	19	20	21	22	23	24	25	26	27	28	29	30	31
DEC	266	279	292	304	317	329	341	353	5	16	28	39	50	61	72	83

SUN*MOON ANGLES FOR 1993

```
DAY   1    2    3    4    5    6    7    8    9   10   11   12   13   14   15
JAN  93  105  116  128  140  153  166  179  193  207  220  234  248  261  274

DAY  16   17   18   19   20   21   22   23   24   25   26   27   28   29   30   31
JAN 286  299  311  322  334  345  356    8   19   29   40   51   62   73   84   96

DAY   1    2    3    4    5    6    7    8    9   10   11   12   13   14   15
FEB 107  119  132  145  159  173  187  201  215  229  242  255  268  280  292

DAY  16   17   18   19   20   21   22   23   24   25   26   27   28   29   30   31
FEB 304  315  326  337  348  359   10   21   32   42   53   65   76

DAY   1    2    3    4    5    6    7    8    9   10   11   12   13   14   15
MAR  88  100  112  125  138  152  167  181  195  209  223  236  249  261  273

DAY  16   17   18   19   20   21   22   23   24   25   26   27   28   29   30   31
MAR 285  296  307  318  329  340  351    2   13   24   35   46   57   69   81   94

DAY   1    2    3    4    5    6    7    8    9   10   11   12   13   14   15
APR 106  120  133  147  161  176  190  203  217  230  242  254  266  277  288

DAY  16   17   18   19   20   21   22   23   24   25   26   27   28   29   30   31
APR 299  310  321  332  343  354    5   17   28   40   52   64   76   89  102

DAY   1    2    3    4    5    6    7    8    9   10   11   12   13   14   15
MAY 116  129  143  157  171  184  198  210  223  235  247  258  269  280  291

DAY  16   17   18   19   20   21   22   23   24   25   26   27   28   29   30   31
MAY 302  313  324  335  347  358   10   22   35   47   60   73   86   99  113  126

DAY   1    2    3    4    5    6    7    8    9   10   11   12   13   14   15
JUN 139  153  166  179  192  204  216  228  239  250  261  272  283  294  305

DAY  16   17   18   19   20   21   22   23   24   25   26   27   28   29   30   31
JUN 317  328  340  352    5   18   30   44   57   70   84   97  110  123  136

DAY   1    2    3    4    5    6    7    8    9   10   11   12   13   14   15
JUL 149  161  174  186  198  209  220  232  243  254  265  276  287  298  310

DAY  16   17   18   19   20   21   22   23   24   25   26   27   28   29   30   31
JUL 322  334  347    0   13   27   41   54   68   81   94  107  120  132  144  156

DAY   1    2    3    4    5    6    7    8    9   10   11   12   13   14   15
AUG 168  179  191  202  213  224  235  246  257  268  279  291  303  315  328

DAY  16   17   18   19   20   21   22   23   24   25   26   27   28   29   30   31
AUG 341  355    9   23   37   51   65   78   91  103  115  127  139  150  162  173

DAY   1    2    3    4    5    6    7    8    9   10   11   12   13   14   15
SEP 184  195  206  217  227  238  249  261  272  284  296  309  323  336  350

DAY  16   17   18   19   20   21   22   23   24   25   26   27   28   29   30   31
SEP   5   19   33   47   60   73   86   98  110  121  132  143  155  165  176

DAY   1    2    3    4    5    6    7    8    9   10   11   12   13   14   15
OCT 187  198  209  220  231  242  254  266  278  291  304  317  331  345    0

DAY  16   17   18   19   20   21   22   23   24   25   26   27   28   29   30   31
OCT  14   28   41   54   67   79   91  102  114  125  136  147  157  168  179  190

DAY   1    2    3    4    5    6    7    8    9   10   11   12   13   14   15
NOV 201  213  224  236  248  260  272  285  299  312  326  340  354    8   21

DAY  16   17   18   19   20   21   22   23   24   25   26   27   28   29   30   31
NOV  34   47   59   71   83   94  105  116  127  138  149  160  171  182  194

DAY   1    2    3    4    5    6    7    8    9   10   11   12   13   14   15
DEC 205  217  230  242  255  267  281  294  307  321  334  348    1   14   27

DAY  16   17   18   19   20   21   22   23   24   25   26   27   28   29   30   31
DEC  39   51   62   74   85   96  106  117  128  139  151  162  174  186  198  211
```

227

SUN*MOON ANGLES FOR 1994

```
DAY    1    2    3    4    5    6    7    8    9   10   11   12   13   14   15
JAN  224  237  250  263  276  289  302  315  328  341  354    6   18   30   42

DAY   16   17   18   19   20   21   22   23   24   25   26   27   28   29   30   31
JAN   53   64   75   86   96  107  118  130  142  154  166  179  192  205  219  232

DAY    1    2    3    4    5    6    7    8    9   10   11   12   13   14   15
FEB  245  259  272  284  297  310  322  334  346  358   10   21   32   43   54

DAY   16   17   18   19   20   21   22   23   24   25   26   27   28   29   30   31
FEB   65   76   87   98  109  121  133  146  159  172  186  200  213

DAY    1    2    3    4    5    6    7    8    9   10   11   12   13   14   15
MAR  227  241  254  267  280  292  304  316  328  339  351    2   13   24   35

DAY   16   17   18   19   20   21   22   23   24   25   26   27   28   29   30   31
MAR   45   56   67   78   89  101  113  126  139  152  166  180  194  208  222  236

DAY    1    2    3    4    5    6    7    8    9   10   11   12   13   14   15
APR  249  262  274  286  298  309  321  332  343  354    5   16   26   37   48

DAY   16   17   18   19   20   21   22   23   24   25   26   27   28   29   30   31
APR   59   71   82   94  107  120  133  147  161  175  189  203  217  231  244

DAY    1    2    3    4    5    6    7    8    9   10   11   12   13   14   15
MAY  256  268  280  291  303  314  325  336  346  357    8   19   30   41   53

DAY   16   17   18   19   20   21   22   23   24   25   26   27   28   29   30   31
MAY   65   77   89  102  115  128  142  156  170  184  198  212  225  238  250  262

DAY    1    2    3    4    5    6    7    8    9   10   11   12   13   14   15
JUN  273  284  295  306  317  328  339  350    1   12   24   36   48   60   72

DAY   16   17   18   19   20   21   22   23   24   25   26   27   28   29   30   31
JUN   85   98  111  125  139  152  166  180  193  206  219  231  243  255  266

DAY    1    2    3    4    5    6    7    8    9   10   11   12   13   14   15
JUL  277  288  299  310  321  332  343  355    7   19   31   44   56   69   82

DAY   16   17   18   19   20   21   22   23   24   25   26   27   28   29   30   31
JUL   95  109  122  135  149  162  175  188  200  213  225  236  247  258  269  280

DAY    1    2    3    4    5    6    7    8    9   10   11   12   13   14   15
AUG  291  302  313  325  337  349    1   14   27   40   53   66   80   93  106

DAY   16   17   18   19   20   21   22   23   24   25   26   27   28   29   30   31
AUG  119  132  145  157  170  182  194  206  217  228  239  250  261  272  283  294

DAY    1    2    3    4    5    6    7    8    9   10   11   12   13   14   15
SEP  306  318  330  343  356    9   23   36   50   63   77   90  103  115  128

DAY   16   17   18   19   20   21   22   23   24   25   26   27   28   29   30   31
SEP  140  152  164  176  187  198  209  220  231  242  253  264  275  286  298

DAY    1    2    3    4    5    6    7    8    9   10   11   12   13   14   15
OCT  311  324  337  350    4   18   32   46   59   73   86   98  111  123  134

DAY   16   17   18   19   20   21   22   23   24   25   26   27   28   29   30   31
OCT  146  157  168  179  190  201  212  223  234  245  256  267  279  291  304  317

DAY    1    2    3    4    5    6    7    8    9   10   11   12   13   14   15
NOV  331  344  359   13   27   41   54   67   80   92  104  116  127  138  149

DAY   16   17   18   19   20   21   22   23   24   25   26   27   28   29   30   31
NOV  160  171  182  193  203  214  225  237  248  260  272  284  297  311  324

DAY    1    2    3    4    5    6    7    8    9   10   11   12   13   14   15
DEC  338  352    7   21   34   48   61   73   85   97  108  119  130  141  151

DAY   16   17   18   19   20   21   22   23   24   25   26   27   28   29   30   31
DEC  162  173  184  195  206  218  229  241  253  266  278  291  305  318  332  346
```

SUN*MOON ANGLES FOR 1995

```
DAY   1    2    3    4    5    6    7    8    9   10   11   12   13   14   15
JAN   0   14   27   40   53   65   76   88   99  110  120  131  142  153  164

DAY  16   17   18   19   20   21   22   23   24   25   26   27   28   29   30   31
JAN 175  187  199  211  223  235  248  260  273  286  300  313  327  340  354    7

DAY   1    2    3    4    5    6    7    8    9   10   11   12   13   14   15
FEB  20   32   44   56   67   78   89  100  111  122  133  144  155  167  179

DAY  16   17   18   19   20   21   22   23   24   25   26   27   28   29   30   31
FEB 192  204  217  230  243  256  269  282  295  308  321  334  347

DAY   1    2    3    4    5    6    7    8    9   10   11   12   13   14   15
MAR   0   12   24   35   47   58   69   79   90  101  112  124  135  147  160

DAY  16   17   18   19   20   21   22   23   24   25   26   27   28   29   30   31
MAR 172  185  198  212  225  239  252  265  278  291  304  316  329  341  353    4

DAY   1    2    3    4    5    6    7    8    9   10   11   12   13   14   15
APR  16   27   38   49   60   70   81   92  104  115  127  140  153  166  179

DAY  16   17   18   19   20   21   22   23   24   25   26   27   28   29   30   31
APR 193  207  221  235  248  261  274  287  299  311  323  334  346  357    8

DAY   1    2    3    4    5    6    7    8    9   10   11   12   13   14   15
MAY  19   30   41   51   62   74   85   96  108  121  133  147  160  174  188

DAY  16   17   18   19   20   21   22   23   24   25   26   27   28   29   30   31
MAY 203  217  231  244  257  270  282  294  305  317  328  339  350    1   11   22

DAY   1    2    3    4    5    6    7    8    9   10   11   12   13   14   15
JUN  33   44   56   67   78   90  103  115  128  142  156  170  184  198  213

DAY  16   17   18   19   20   21   22   23   24   25   26   27   28   29   30   31
JUN 226  239  252  264  276  288  299  310  321  332  343  354    5   16   27

DAY   1    2    3    4    5    6    7    8    9   10   11   12   13   14   15
JUL  38   50   61   73   85   98  111  124  138  152  166  180  194  208  221

DAY  16   17   18   19   20   21   22   23   24   25   26   27   28   29   30   31
JUL 234  246  258  270  281  292  303  314  325  336  347  358    9   21   33   44

DAY   1    2    3    4    5    6    7    8    9   10   11   12   13   14   15
AUG  57   69   81   94  107  121  134  148  162  176  189  203  215  228  240

DAY  16   17   18   19   20   21   22   23   24   25   26   27   28   29   30   31
AUG 251  263  274  284  295  306  317  328  340  351    3   15   27   40   52   65

DAY   1    2    3    4    5    6    7    8    9   10   11   12   13   14   15
SEP  78   91  104  118  131  145  158  171  184  197  209  221  232  243  254

DAY  16   17   18   19   20   21   22   23   24   25   26   27   28   29   30   31
SEP 265  276  287  298  309  321  333  345  357   10   22   35   48   62   75

DAY   1    2    3    4    5    6    7    8    9   10   11   12   13   14   15
OCT  88  101  114  127  140  153  165  178  189  201  213  224  235  246  257

DAY  16   17   18   19   20   21   22   23   24   25   26   27   28   29   30   31
OCT 267  278  290  301  313  325  338  350    4   17   31   44   58   71   84   97

DAY   1    2    3    4    5    6    7    8    9   10   11   12   13   14   15
NOV 110  123  135  147  159  170  182  193  204  215  226  237  248  259  270

DAY  16   17   18   19   20   21   22   23   24   25   26   27   28   29   30   31
NOV 281  293  305  317  330  344  357   11   25   39   53   67   80   92  105

DAY   1    2    3    4    5    6    7    8    9   10   11   12   13   14   15
DEC 117  128  140  151  162  173  184  195  206  217  228  239  250  261  273

DAY  16   17   18   19   20   21   22   23   24   25   26   27   28   29   30   31
DEC 285  297  310  323  337  351    5   20   34   47   61   74   86   98  109  121
```

SUN*MOON ANGLES FOR 1996

DAY	1	2	3	4	5	6	7	8	9	10	11	12	13	14	15
JAN	132	143	154	165	175	186	197	208	219	230	242	253	265	277	290

DAY	16	17	18	19	20	21	22	23	24	25	26	27	28	29	30	31
JAN	303	317	331	345	359	13	27	41	54	66	78	90	101	112	123	134

DAY	1	2	3	4	5	6	7	8	9	10	11	12	13	14	15
FEB	145	156	167	178	189	200	211	223	235	246	259	271	284	297	311

DAY	16	17	18	19	20	21	22	23	24	25	26	27	28	29	30	31
FEB	325	339	353	7	20	33	46	58	70	81	92	103	114	125		

DAY	1	2	3	4	5	6	7	8	9	10	11	12	13	14	15
MAR	136	147	158	169	181	192	204	216	229	241	254	267	280	293	307

DAY	16	17	18	19	20	21	22	23	24	25	26	27	28	29	30	31
MAR	320	334	347	0	13	26	38	50	61	72	83	94	105	116	127	138

DAY	1	2	3	4	5	6	7	8	9	10	11	12	13	14	15
APR	150	161	173	186	198	211	224	237	250	263	276	290	303	316	329

DAY	16	17	18	19	20	21	22	23	24	25	26	27	28	29	30	31
APR	341	354	6	18	30	41	53	64	75	86	96	108	119	130	142	

DAY	1	2	3	4	5	6	7	8	9	10	11	12	13	14	15
MAY	154	167	180	193	206	220	233	247	260	273	286	299	312	324	336

DAY	16	17	18	19	20	21	22	23	24	25	26	27	28	29	30	31
MAY	348	0	11	22	34	45	56	67	77	88	100	111	123	135	148	161

DAY	1	2	3	4	5	6	7	8	9	10	11	12	13	14	15
JUN	174	188	202	216	230	244	257	270	283	295	307	319	330	342	353

DAY	16	17	18	19	20	21	22	23	24	25	26	27	28	29	30	31
JUN	4	15	26	37	48	59	70	81	93	104	117	129	142	156	170	

DAY	1	2	3	4	5	6	7	8	9	10	11	12	13	14	15
JUL	184	199	213	227	240	253	266	278	290	302	313	324	336	347	358

DAY	16	17	18	19	20	21	22	23	24	25	26	27	28	29	30	31
JUL	8	19	30	41	52	63	75	87	99	111	124	138	152	166	180	195

DAY	1	2	3	4	5	6	7	8	9	10	11	12	13	14	15
AUG	209	222	236	248	261	273	284	296	307	318	329	340	351	2	12

DAY	16	17	18	19	20	21	22	23	24	25	26	27	28	29	30	31
AUG	24	35	46	58	69	81	94	107	120	134	148	162	176	190	204	217

DAY	1	2	3	4	5	6	7	8	9	10	11	12	13	14	15
SEP	230	242	254	266	277	289	300	310	321	332	343	354	6	17	28

DAY	16	17	18	19	20	21	22	23	24	25	26	27	28	29	30	31
SEP	40	52	64	77	90	103	116	130	144	157	171	185	198	211	223	

DAY	1	2	3	4	5	6	7	8	9	10	11	12	13	14	15
OCT	235	247	258	269	280	291	302	313	324	335	347	358	10	22	35

DAY	16	17	18	19	20	21	22	23	24	25	26	27	28	29	30	31
OCT	47	60	73	86	99	113	126	139	152	165	178	191	203	215	227	238

DAY	1	2	3	4	5	6	7	8	9	10	11	12	13	14	15
NOV	250	260	271	282	293	304	315	327	339	351	4	16	29	43	56

DAY	16	17	18	19	20	21	22	23	24	25	26	27	28	29	30	31
NOV	69	82	95	108	121	134	147	159	171	183	195	207	218	229	240	

DAY	1	2	3	4	5	6	7	8	9	10	11	12	13	14	15
DEC	251	262	273	284	295	306	318	331	344	357	10	24	38	51	65

DAY	16	17	18	19	20	21	22	23	24	25	26	27	28	29	30	31
DEC	78	91	104	116	128	140	152	164	175	187	198	209	220	231	241	253

230

SUN*MOON ANGLES FOR 1997

DAY	1	2	3	4	5	6	7	8	9	10	11	12	13	14	15
JAN	263	274	286	298	310	323	336	350	4	18	32	46	59	73	85

DAY	16	17	18	19	20	21	22	23	24	25	26	27	28	29	30	31
JAN	98	110	122	133	145	156	167	178	189	200	211	221	232	243	254	266

DAY	1	2	3	4	5	6	7	8	9	10	11	12	13	14	15
FEB	278	290	303	316	329	343	358	12	26	40	53	66	79	91	103

DAY	16	17	18	19	20	21	22	23	24	25	26	27	28	29	30	31
FEB	114	126	137	148	159	169	180	191	202	213	224	235	247			

DAY	1	2	3	4	5	6	7	8	9	10	11	12	13	14	15
MAR	259	271	283	296	310	323	338	352	6	20	33	47	59	72	84

DAY	16	17	18	19	20	21	22	23	24	25	26	27	28	29	30	31
MAR	95	106	118	128	139	150	161	172	183	194	205	217	229	241	253	265

DAY	1	2	3	4	5	6	7	8	9	10	11	12	13	14	15
APR	278	291	305	319	332	346	0	14	27	40	52	64	76	87	98

DAY	16	17	18	19	20	21	22	23	24	25	26	27	28	29	30	31
APR	109	120	131	142	153	164	175	187	199	211	223	236	249	262	275	

DAY	1	2	3	4	5	6	7	8	9	10	11	12	13	14	15
MAY	288	301	315	328	341	355	8	20	33	45	57	68	79	90	101

DAY	16	17	18	19	20	21	22	23	24	25	26	27	28	29	30	31
MAY	112	123	134	145	157	169	181	193	206	219	232	245	259	272	285	298

DAY	1	2	3	4	5	6	7	8	9	10	11	12	13	14	15
JUN	311	324	337	350	2	14	26	38	49	60	71	82	93	104	115

DAY	16	17	18	19	20	21	22	23	24	25	26	27	28	29	30	31
JUN	126	138	150	163	176	189	202	216	229	243	256	269	282	295	308	

DAY	1	2	3	4	5	6	7	8	9	10	11	12	13	14	15
JUL	320	332	344	356	8	19	30	41	52	63	74	85	96	108	119

DAY	16	17	18	19	20	21	22	23	24	25	26	27	28	29	30	31
JUL	132	144	157	171	184	198	212	226	240	253	266	279	291	303	315	327

DAY	1	2	3	4	5	6	7	8	9	10	11	12	13	14	15
AUG	339	350	1	12	23	34	45	56	67	78	89	101	113	126	139

DAY	16	17	18	19	20	21	22	23	24	25	26	27	28	29	30	31
AUG	152	166	180	194	208	222	236	249	262	274	287	298	310	321	332	343

DAY	1	2	3	4	5	6	7	8	9	10	11	12	13	14	15
SEP	354	5	16	27	37	48	60	71	83	95	107	120	133	147	161

DAY	16	17	18	19	20	21	22	23	24	25	26	27	28	29	30	31
SEP	175	190	204	218	231	244	257	269	280	292	303	314	325	336	346	

DAY	1	2	3	4	5	6	7	8	9	10	11	12	13	14	15
OCT	357	8	19	30	42	53	65	77	89	102	115	128	142	156	170

DAY	16	17	18	19	20	21	22	23	24	25	26	27	28	29	30	31
OCT	184	198	212	225	237	250	261	273	284	295	306	317	327	338	349	0

DAY	1	2	3	4	5	6	7	8	9	10	11	12	13	14	15
NOV	12	23	35	47	59	72	84	97	110	124	137	151	165	178	192

DAY	16	17	18	19	20	21	22	23	24	25	26	27	28	29	30	31
NOV	205	217	230	241	253	264	275	286	297	307	318	329	341	352	4	

DAY	1	2	3	4	5	6	7	8	9	10	11	12	13	14	15
DEC	17	29	41	54	67	80	93	106	119	132	145	159	172	184	197

DAY	16	17	18	19	20	21	22	23	24	25	26	27	28	29	30	31
DEC	209	221	232	243	254	265	276	287	298	309	320	332	344	357	10	23

SUN*MOON ANGLES FOR 1998

DAY	1	2	3	4	5	6	7	8	9	10	11	12	13	14	15	
JAN	36	49	62	75	88	101	114	127	140	152	165	177	189	200	212	

DAY	16	17	18	19	20	21	22	23	24	25	26	27	28	29	30	31
JAN	223	234	244	255	266	277	288	300	312	324	336	350	3	16	30	44

DAY	1	2	3	4	5	6	7	8	9	10	11	12	13	14	15	
FEB	57	70	84	96	109	122	134	146	157	169	180	191	202	213	224	

DAY	16	17	18	19	20	21	22	23	24	25	26	27	28	29	30	31
FEB	235	246	257	268	279	291	303	316	329	343	356	10	24			

DAY	1	2	3	4	5	6	7	8	9	10	11	12	13	14	15	
MAR	38	52	65	79	91	104	116	127	139	150	161	172	183	194	205	

DAY	16	17	18	19	20	21	22	23	24	25	26	27	28	29	30	31
MAR	215	226	237	248	260	272	284	296	309	323	336	350	5	19	33	47

DAY	1	2	3	4	5	6	7	8	9	10	11	12	13	14	15	
APR	60	73	85	97	109	120	131	142	153	164	175	186	197	208	219	

DAY	16	17	18	19	20	21	22	23	24	25	26	27	28	29	30	31
APR	230	242	253	265	278	291	304	317	331	345	0	14	28	41	54	

DAY	1	2	3	4	5	6	7	8	9	10	11	12	13	14	15	
MAY	67	79	90	102	113	124	135	145	156	167	178	190	201	212	224	

DAY	16	17	18	19	20	21	22	23	24	25	26	27	28	29	30	31
MAY	236	248	261	273	286	300	313	327	341	355	9	22	35	48	60	72

DAY	1	2	3	4	5	6	7	8	9	10	11	12	13	14	15	
JUN	83	94	105	116	127	138	149	160	172	183	195	207	219	232	244	

DAY	16	17	18	19	20	21	22	23	24	25	26	27	28	29	30	31
JUN	257	270	283	297	310	324	337	351	4	17	29	41	53	64	75	

DAY	1	2	3	4	5	6	7	8	9	10	11	12	13	14	15	
JUL	86	97	108	119	130	142	153	165	177	190	202	215	228	241	254	

DAY	16	17	18	19	20	21	22	23	24	25	26	27	28	29	30	31
JUL	268	281	294	307	320	333	346	359	11	23	34	46	57	68	79	89

DAY	1	2	3	4	5	6	7	8	9	10	11	12	13	14	15	
AUG	100	112	123	135	147	159	172	185	198	211	225	238	252	265	278	

DAY	16	17	18	19	20	21	22	23	24	25	26	27	28	29	30	31
AUG	291	304	317	329	341	353	4	16	27	38	49	60	71	82	93	104

DAY	1	2	3	4	5	6	7	8	9	10	11	12	13	14	15	
SEP	116	128	140	153	166	180	194	208	221	235	249	262	275	287	300	

DAY	16	17	18	19	20	21	22	23	24	25	26	27	28	29	30	31
SEP	312	323	335	346	357	8	19	30	41	52	63	74	85	97	109	

DAY	1	2	3	4	5	6	7	8	9	10	11	12	13	14	15	
OCT	121	134	147	161	175	189	203	217	231	244	257	270	282	294	305	

DAY	16	17	18	19	20	21	22	23	24	25	26	27	28	29	30	31
OCT	316	328	339	349	0	11	22	33	44	55	66	78	90	102	114	127

DAY	1	2	3	4	5	6	7	8	9	10	11	12	13	14	15	
NOV	141	155	169	183	198	212	225	239	251	263	275	286	298	309	319	

DAY	16	17	18	19	20	21	22	23	24	25	26	27	28	29	30	31
NOV	330	341	352	3	14	25	36	48	59	71	83	96	108	122	135	

DAY	1	2	3	4	5	6	7	8	9	10	11	12	13	14	15	
DEC	149	163	178	191	205	218	231	243	255	267	278	289	300	311	321	

DAY	16	17	18	19	20	21	22	23	24	25	26	27	28	29	30	31
DEC	332	343	354	6	17	29	41	53	65	77	90	103	117	130	144	157

SUN*MOON ANGLES FOR 1999

```
DAY    1    2    3    4    5    6    7    8    9   10   11   12   13   14   15
JAN  171  185  198  210  223  235  246  257  268  279  290  301  312  323  334

DAY   16   17   18   19   20   21   22   23   24   25   26   27   28   29   30   31
JAN  346  358   10   22   34   47   60   72   86   99  112  125  138  152  165  177

DAY    1    2    3    4    5    6    7    8    9   10   11   12   13   14   15
FEB  190  202  214  225  237  248  259  270  280  291  303  314  326  337  350

DAY   16   17   18   19   20   21   22   23   24   25   26   27   28   29   30   31
FEB    2   15   28   42   55   68   81   95  108  120  133  146  158

DAY    1    2    3    4    5    6    7    8    9   10   11   12   13   14   15
MAR  170  182  194  205  216  227  238  249  260  271  282  293  305  317  330

DAY   16   17   18   19   20   21   22   23   24   25   26   27   28   29   30   31
MAR  342  356    9   23   37   50   64   77   90  103  116  128  140  151  163  174

DAY    1    2    3    4    5    6    7    8    9   10   11   12   13   14   15
APR  186  197  208  219  230  241  251  263  274  285  297  310  323  336  350

DAY   16   17   18   19   20   21   22   23   24   25   26   27   28   29   30   31
APR    4   18   32   46   60   73   86   98  110  122  133  145  156  167  178

DAY    1    2    3    4    5    6    7    8    9   10   11   12   13   14   15
MAY  189  200  211  222  233  244  255  267  279  291  304  317  331  345  359

DAY   16   17   18   19   20   21   22   23   24   25   26   27   28   29   30   31
MAY   14   28   42   55   68   81   93  104  116  127  138  149  160  171  182  193

DAY    1    2    3    4    5    6    7    8    9   10   11   12   13   14   15
JUN  204  215  226  238  249  261  273  286  299  313  327  341  355    9   23

DAY   16   17   18   19   20   21   22   23   24   25   26   27   28   29   30   31
JUN   37   50   63   75   86   98  109  120  131  142  153  164  175  186  197

DAY    1    2    3    4    5    6    7    8    9   10   11   12   13   14   15
JUL  209  220  232  244  257  270  283  296  310  323  337  351    5   18   31

DAY   16   17   18   19   20   21   22   23   24   25   26   27   28   29   30   31
JUL   44   56   68   80   91  102  113  124  135  146  157  168  180  191  203  216

DAY    1    2    3    4    5    6    7    8    9   10   11   12   13   14   15
AUG  228  241  253  267  280  293  307  320  334  347    0   13   25   37   49

DAY   16   17   18   19   20   21   22   23   24   25   26   27   28   29   30   31
AUG   61   72   83   94  105  116  127  138  150  161  173  186  198  211  224  237

DAY    1    2    3    4    5    6    7    8    9   10   11   12   13   14   15
SEP  251  264  277  290  303  316  329  342  354    7   19   30   42   53   64

DAY   16   17   18   19   20   21   22   23   24   25   26   27   28   29   30   31
SEP   75   86   97  108  119  130  142  155  167  180  193  207  220  234  247

DAY    1    2    3    4    5    6    7    8    9   10   11   12   13   14   15
OCT  261  274  287  299  312  324  336  348    0   11   23   34   45   55   66

DAY   16   17   18   19   20   21   22   23   24   25   26   27   28   29   30   31
OCT   77   88   99  111  123  135  148  161  174  188  202  216  230  243  257  269

DAY    1    2    3    4    5    6    7    8    9   10   11   12   13   14   15
NOV  282  294  306  318  329  341  352    3   14   25   36   47   58   68   80

DAY   16   17   18   19   20   21   22   23   24   25   26   27   28   29   30   31
NOV   91  103  115  127  141  154  168  182  197  211  225  238  251  264  276

DAY    1    2    3    4    5    6    7    8    9   10   11   12   13   14   15
DEC  288  299  311  322  333  344  355    6   16   27   38   49   60   71   83

DAY   16   17   18   19   20   21   22   23   24   25   26   27   28   29   30   31
DEC   95  108  121  134  148  162  176  190  204  218  231  244  257  268  280  291
```

233

SUN*MOON ANGLES FOR 2000

DAY	1	2	3	4	5	6	7	8	9	10	11	12	13	14	15	
JAN	302	313	324	335	346	357	8	19	30	41	52	64	76	89	101	

DAY	16	17	18	19	20	21	22	23	24	25	26	27	28	29	30	31
JAN	115	128	142	156	170	184	197	211	224	236	248	260	271	283	293	304

DAY	1	2	3	4	5	6	7	8	9	10	11	12	13	14	15	
FEB	315	326	337	348	359	10	22	34	46	58	71	83	96	110	123	

DAY	16	17	18	19	20	21	22	23	24	25	26	27	28	29	30	31
FEB	136	150	164	177	190	203	216	228	240	251	262	273	284	295		

DAY	1	2	3	4	5	6	7	8	9	10	11	12	13	14	15	
MAR	306	317	328	339	351	3	15	28	40	53	66	79	92	105	119	

DAY	16	17	18	19	20	21	22	23	24	25	26	27	28	29	30	31
MAR	132	145	148	171	183	196	208	219	231	242	253	264	275	286	297	308

DAY	1	2	3	4	5	6	7	8	9	10	11	12	13	14	15	
APR	319	331	344	356	9	22	36	49	62	76	89	102	115	127	140	

DAY	16	17	18	19	20	21	22	23	24	25	26	27	28	29	30	31
APR	152	165	177	188	200	211	223	234	244	255	266	277	288	300	312	

DAY	1	2	3	4	5	6	7	8	9	10	11	12	13	14	15	
MAY	324	337	350	4	18	31	45	59	72	85	98	111	123	135	147	

DAY	16	17	18	19	20	21	22	23	24	25	26	27	28	29	30	31
MAY	159	170	182	193	204	215	226	236	247	258	270	281	293	305	318	332

DAY	1	2	3	4	5	6	7	8	9	10	11	12	13	14	15	
JUN	345	359	13	28	41	55	68	81	94	106	118	130	141	153	164	

DAY	16	17	18	19	20	21	22	23	24	25	26	27	28	29	30	31
JUN	175	186	196	207	218	229	240	252	263	275	287	300	313	327	341	

DAY	1	2	3	4	5	6	7	8	9	10	11	12	13	14	15	
JUL	355	9	23	37	51	64	77	89	101	113	124	135	146	157	168	

DAY	16	17	18	19	20	21	22	23	24	25	26	27	28	29	30	31
JUL	179	189	200	211	223	234	246	258	270	283	296	309	323	337	351	5

DAY	1	2	3	4	5	6	7	8	9	10	11	12	13	14	15	
AUG	19	33	46	59	71	83	95	106	117	128	139	150	161	172	183	

DAY	16	17	18	19	20	21	22	23	24	25	26	27	28	29	30	31
AUG	194	205	217	229	241	253	266	279	292	305	319	333	347	0	14	27

DAY	1	2	3	4	5	6	7	8	9	10	11	12	13	14	15	
SEP	40	53	65	76	87	98	109	120	131	142	153	164	176	188	199	

DAY	16	17	18	19	20	21	22	23	24	25	26	27	28	29	30	31
SEP	212	224	237	249	262	275	288	302	315	329	342	355	8	21	33	

DAY	1	2	3	4	5	6	7	8	9	10	11	12	13	14	15	
OCT	45	57	68	79	90	101	112	123	134	145	157	169	181	194	206	

DAY	16	17	18	19	20	21	22	23	24	25	26	27	28	29	30	31
OCT	219	232	245	259	272	285	298	311	324	337	349	2	14	25	37	48

DAY	1	2	3	4	5	6	7	8	9	10	11	12	13	14	15	
NOV	59	70	81	92	102	114	125	137	149	162	174	188	201	214	228	

DAY	16	17	18	19	20	21	22	23	24	25	26	27	28	29	30	31
NOV	241	255	268	281	293	306	318	330	342	354	6	17	28	39	50	

DAY	1	2	3	4	5	6	7	8	9	10	11	12	13	14	15	
DEC	60	71	82	93	105	116	128	141	154	167	181	195	209	223	236	

DAY	16	17	18	19	20	21	22	23	24	25	26	27	28	29	30	31
DEC	250	263	275	288	300	312	323	335	346	357	8	19	30	40	51	62

Bibliography

Billings, M.D., John J. The Ovulation Method — Natural Family Planning. Collegeville, Minnesota: The Liturgical Press, 1972.

Bills, Rex E. The Rulership Book. Richmond, Virginia: Macoy Publishing & Masonic Supply Co., 1971.

Carter, C.E.O. An Encyclopaedia of Psychological Astrology. London: The Theosophical Publishing House, 1963.

Cornell, M.D., H.L. Encyclopaedia of Medical Astrology. St. Paul, Minnesota and New York, N.Y.: Llewellyn Publications and Samuel Weiser, Inc., 1972.

Crawford, Christina. Mommie Dearest. New York, N.Y.: William Morrow and Company, Inc., 1978.

David, Lester. Ethel. New York, N.Y.: The World Publishing Company, 1971.

DiDonato, Pietro. Immigrant Saint. New York, N.Y.: McGraw-Hill Company, Inc., 1960.

Doig, Desmond. Mother Teresa. Her People and Her Work. New York: Harper & Row.

Gandhi, Mohandas K. An Autobiography. The Story of my Experiments with Truth. Boston: Beacon Press, 1957.

Garrison, Omar V. Medical Astrology. New York: University Books, Inc., 1971.

Grell, Paul R. Keywords. Tempe, Arizona: The American Federation of Astrologers, 1970.

Haich, Elisabeth. Initiation. London: George Allen & Unwin Ltd., 1965.

Hickey, Isabel M. Astrology A Cosmic Science. Water Town, Mass.: Isabel M. Hickey, 1970.

Higham, Charles. Kate. New York, N.Y.: W.W. Norton & Co., Inc., 1976.

Hotchner, A.E. Sophia. New York, N.Y.: William Morrow and Company, Inc., 1979.

Kelley, Kitty. Elizabeth Taylor, The Last Star. New York, N.Y.: Simon & Schuster, 1981.

Kippley, John and Sheila. The Art of Natural Family Planning. P.O. Box 11084, Cincinnati, Ohio 45211: Couple to Couple League, International, Inc., 1979.

Lauersen, M.D., Niels and Whitney, Steven. It's Your Body. New York: Grosset & Dunlap, 1977.

Ostrander, Sheila & Schroeder, Lynn. Astrological Birth Control. Englewood Cliffs, N.J.: Prentice-Hall, Inc., 1972.

Perry, Inez Eudora. The Zodiac and the Salts of Salvation. New York: Samuel Weiser, Inc., 1971.

Richards, Ralph and Chapman, David F. Anatomy and Physiology — A SELF INSTRUCTIONAL COURSE. Edinburgh London and New York: Churchill Livingstone, 1977.

Rodden, Lois M. Profiles of Women. Tempe, Arizona: The American Federation of Astrologers, Inc., 1979.

Rudhyar, Dane. The Lunation Cycle. St. Paul, Minnesota: Llewellyn Publications, 1967.

Sakoian, Frances and Acker, Louis S. The Astrology of Human Relationships. New York, Hagerstown, San Francisco, London: Harper & Row, 1976.

Sheen, Fulton J. Way to Happiness. New York: Doubleday & Company, Inc., 1954.

Silber, M.D., Sherman J. How to Get Pregnant. New York: Charles Scribner's Sons, 1980.

Sills, Beverly. Bubbles. New York: Grosset & Dunlap, 1981.

Wickenburg, Joanne. Astrological Correspondence Courses. Seattle, Washington: "Search," 1977.

Windeler, Robert. The Films of Shirley Temple. Secaucus, New Jersey: Citadel Press, 1978.